Playing by Ear and the Tip of the Tongue

Linguistic Approaches to Literature (LAL)

Linguistic Approaches to Literature (LAL) provides an international forum for researchers who believe that the application of linguistic methods leads to a deeper and more far-reaching understanding of many aspects of literature. The emphasis will be on pragmatic approaches intersecting with areas such as experimental psychology, psycholinguistics, computational linguistics, cognitive linguistics, stylistics, discourse analysis, sociolinguistics, rhetoric, and philosophy.

For an overview of all books published in this series, please see
http://benjamins.com/catalog/lal

Editors

Volume 14

Playing by Ear and the Tip of the Tongue. Precategorial information in poetry
by Reuven Tsur

Playing by Ear and the Tip of the Tongue

Precategorial information in poetry

Reuven Tsur

Tel Aviv University

John Benjamins Publishing Company

Amsterdam / Philadelphia

The paper used in this publication meets the minimum requirements of the American National Standard for Information Sciences – Permanence of Paper for Printed Library Materials, ANSI z39.48-1984.

The research for this book was partly supported by Grant No. 228/11 from the Israel Science Foundation.

Library of Congress Cataloging-in-Publication Data

Tsur, Reuven.
    Playing by ear and the tip of the tongue : precategorial information in poetry /
        Reuven Tsur.
    p. cm. (Linguistic Approaches to Literature, ISSN 1569-3112 ; v. 14)
    Includes bibliographical references and index.
    1. Poetics--Psychological aspects. 2. Sound symbolism. 3. Versification. 4. Cognition.
        5. Psycholinguistics. I. Title.
    P311.T725   2012
    808.1--dc23   2012026171
    ISBN 978 90 272 3349 3   (Hb ; alk. paper)
    ISBN 978 90 272 7325 3   (Eb)

John Benjamins Publishing Co. · P.O. Box 36224 · 1020 ME Amsterdam · The Netherlands
John Benjamins North America · P.O. Box 27519 · Philadelphia PA 19118-0519 · USA

The sound files for this book are available online:
http://dx.doi.org/10.1075/lal.14.media

The research for this book was partly supported by Grant No. 228/11 from the
Israel Science Foundation

Table of contents

Media files for this volume can be found online at
http://dx.doi.org/10.1075/lal.14.media

⌒ This logo marks the availability of an audio file.

Preface

This book explores a paradox inherent in poetic language. Language consists of words, that is, semantic categories labelled by clusters of phonetic categories. With such highly "categorial" tools, poetic language is supposed to convey experiences a substantial part of which is precategorial and nonconceptual. The book explores how poetic language attempts to escape the tyranny of conceptual and phonetic categories. It is an attempt to integrate (with some innovations) what I have said during the years about the rich precategorial auditory information reverberating in the background while we read poetry, and the literary structures that tend to diffuse semantic information, resulting in some thick, undifferentiated, perceptual qualities. Though at my age I can hardly say anything without relying on my work during the past decades, I feel I have quite a few new insights too. And, I also feel it's time to bring together most of that material into one volume. Initially, I intended to give only a concise summary of certain issues from my book *What Makes Sound Patterns Expressive? – The Poetic Mode of Speech Perception.* However, as it happened, reviewers asked for elucidations precisely at the points where I tried to be most concise. So, I had to expand to some extent my discussion of those issues.

CHAPTER 1

Introduction

1.1 Precategorial information and critical communication

This book is about the processing and "loosening" of phonetic and semantic categories in poetry. It explores how manipulations in a poetic text may render precategorial information available to the reader's perception, what reasons can be given for the effects of such manipulations, and how can one direct the attention of one's interlocutor to such precategorial information. It proposes hypotheses based on nonaesthetic experiments by others; but, in itself, is mainly speculative. There is one notable exception: in several chapters I submit certain vocal aspects of poetic language to an instrumental analysis, for which I elaborated a theoretical framework in my books on poetic rhythm and expressive sound patterns. The object of this book is, then, twofold: to explore the problematic relationship between precategorial information and the semantic or phonetic categories in poetry; and to inquire into critical communication: the almost impossible task of communicating one's precategorial perceptions, for which there is not even a proper metalanguage. The latter point is explicitly discussed, and at great length, in Chapter 13; but in all the chapters an effort is made to create an efficient metalanguage to handle the issue. To put it differently, in order to contrive an experimental study, one must first know what are the qualities and perceptions to be explored in it.

The dictum "*panta rei*" (everything flows) has been attributed to the Greek philosopher Heraclitus. You cannot put your leg twice into the same river, because by the second time it is not the same river anymore. One of his disciples improved on this, claiming that you cannot put your leg into the same river even once, because in the meantime the river changes. The same disciple is reported to have also said that you cannot refer to the same thing twice by the same word, because the thing changes. This disciple pursued this conception to its logical end: he stopped talking. We, of course, categorize the stream of information into relatively clear-cut and stable categories, and name not the changing stream of information, but the relatively stable categories.

We are flooded by a "*pandemonium*" of preategorial sensory information, day by day, moment by moment, which we categorize into a relatively small number of more easily-handled categories for efficient use, which constitute "ordinary consciousness". Much depends on one's categorization strategy. Rapid categorization has the obvious advantage of allowing fast response to rapidly-changing situations, but at the expense of ignoring much vital precategorial information. Delay in categorization has the advantage of affording access to vital precategorial sensory information, but has the obvious disadvantage of slowing down response.

I propose to introduce my subject through what Hartvig Dahl called the "natural experiment" of Helen Keller, who was deaf and blind. She began to acquire the basic skills of communication as late as at the age of six plus. Before that age, she tells us in a less known book of hers, *The World I Live In* (p. 117), she had no word for, e.g. ice cream.

> When I wanted anything I liked – ice cream, for instance, of which I was very fond – I had a delicious taste on my tongue (which, by the way, I never have now), and in my hand I felt the turning of the freezer. I made the sign, and my mother knew I wanted ice cream. I "thought" and desired in my fingers.
>
> (Dahl 1965: 537)

Later, after having acquired the word *ice cream*, the peculiar sensation on her tongue and fingertips disappeared: "the blind impetus, which had before driven me hither and thither *at the dictates of my sensations*, vanished forever" (Dahl 1965: 542).[1]

Most normal adults delay categorization for fractions of seconds, so as to gather information required for making adequate judgments about reality. This is a requirement for satisfactory adaptation. In Helen Keller's case, categorization was delayed for over six years; and the story can demonstrate the advantages and disadvantages of rapid and delayed categorization. A category with a verbal label constitutes a relatively small load on one's cognitive system, and is easily manipulable; on the other hand, it entails the loss of important sensory information that might be crucial for the process of accurate adaptation. Delayed categorization, by contrast, may burden the human memory system with too much sensory load; this may be available for adaptive purposes and afford great flexibility, but may be time-and-energy consuming, and occupy too much mental processing space. Furthermore, delayed categorization may involve a period of uncertainty that may be quite unpleasant, or even intolerable for some individuals. Rapid categorization, by contrast, may involve the loss of vital information, and lead to maladaptive strategies in life. In Helen Keller's case, we see an opposition between a precategoric sensation on her tongue and fingertips, and a word. The former constitutes delayed, the latter relatively rapid categorization.

---

1.   I am indebted to Professor Pinchas Noy for the Helen Keller story.

The diffuse sensations are recoded into a compact, focussed concept, and tagged with a verbal label.

The mental economy involved in such a process has been described by George Miller as follows:

> The input is given in a code that contains many chunks with few bits per chunk. The operator recodes the input into another code that contains fewer chunks with more bits per chunk. There are many ways to do this recoding, but probably the simplest is to group the input events, apply a new name to the group, and then remember the new name rather than the original input events.
>
> (Miller 1970: 44)

This would explain why Helen Keller lost the sensations on her tongue and fingertips. She remembered the new name "ice cream" rather than the original input events. Delayed categorization makes possible to perceive some of the precategorial information before it is replaced by the name (cf. below, Chapter 14).

A more sophisticated case of recoding information into a more parsimonious code may be observed on the phonetic level, where speech is transmitted in an acoustic stream of information, then recoded into a stream of phonetic categories. "The difference in information rate between the two levels of speech code is staggering" say Liberman et al. (1972). "To transmit the signal in acoustic form and in high fidelity costs about 70.000 bits per second; for reasonable intelligibility we need about 40.000 bits per second. [...] We should suppose that a great deal of nervous tissue would have to be devoted to the storage of even relatively short stretches". To prevent flooding of the system, recoding (phonetic categorization) is necessary. "By recoding into a phonetic representation, we reduce the cost to less than 40 bits per second, thus effecting a saving of 1,000 times".

Both language and speech consist, then, of highly categorized entities. Words refer to concepts, not to unique experiences. The categories of speech are unitary events; the auditory information that transmits them is typically excluded from consciousness. A similar process one may observe in semantic categories. When we say "love", "green", "table" or "ecstasy" we are not referring to nonconceptual qualities or events, but to the *concepts* of "love", "greenness", "table", or "ecstasy". Thus, language is particularly ill-suited to convey unique emotional experiences, unique sensations, mystic insights and the like. As I said, speech too focuses on speech categories and typically excludes the rich precategorial sensory information. For the past forty years or so I have been exploring how poets attempt to overcome this limitation of language and speech. On the whole, they try to express the unspeakable by having recourse to rich precategorial information, sensory and semantic. The present book explores techniques by which the relationship of categories to precategorial information can be loosened both in the phonetic and the semantic dimension. In the semantic dimension, this may be accomplished by having recourse to metaphor, ambiguity, or by activating the right hemisphere of the brain in processing the message, via the orientation or space perception mechanism (see below, Chapters 5 and 14).

1.2 "Speech mode", "Nonspeech mode", "Poetic mode"

As to the auditory dimension, Liberman and his colleagues distinguish between a speech mode and a nonspeech mode of aural perception, with separate pathways in the brain. In the latter, the perceived sound has a shape similar to that of the sound wave that carries it (music, sonar, natural noises). In the former there is no similarity between the perceived sound and that of the acoustic information. The precategorial sound information that transmits speech is immediately recoded into phonetic categories and excluded from awareness.

I claim that there is a third, "poetic mode of speech perception", in which we listen to a stream of abstract phonetic categories. There is much experimental evidence of the existence of lingering auditory information. In Chapters 2 and 11 I will present some such evidence. At the same time, at a lower level and subliminally, we may attend to the rich precategorial information which may affect the perceived quality of poetic language in a variety of ways. Due to the subliminal perception of such precategorial information we perceive, e.g. [u] as "lower", "larger" and "darker" than [i].

As to references on experimental evidence for the existence of separate neural pathways for the speech mode and the nonspeech mode, research has shown that speech stimuli presented to the right ear (hence *mainly* to the left cerebral hemisphere) are better identified than those presented to the left ear (hence, *mainly* to the right cerebral hemisphere), and the reverse is true for melodies and sonar signals (see Liberman et al. 1967:444; my italics; additional evidence can be found in Chapter 11). It is important for our purpose to emphasize "mainly". Much crippling scepticism has sprung from an all-or-nothing conception of lateralization; and there are considerable differences, *on various linguistic levels*, between linguistic categories that cannot, and that can, be processed, less efficiently though, by the right hemisphere. On the grammatic level, for instance, function words can be understood only by the left hemisphere; content words can be understood in some circumstances by the right hemisphere too. Jakobson (1980) tells about a patient with a damaged left hemisphere who could understand the noun "inn", but not the preposition "in". A few years ago, in a lecture at a Porter Institute conference, Tel Aviv University, Eran Zeidel told about a patient who could read the noun "bee", but not the auxiliary verb "be". A similar story can be told about phonetic categories.

> A significantly greater right-ear advantage was found for the encoded stops than for the unencoded steady-state vowels. The fact that the steady-state vowels are less strongly lateralized in the dominant (speech) hemisphere may be taken to mean that these sounds, being unencoded, can be, and presumably sometimes are, processed as if they were nonspeech.
>
> (ibid, cf. Jakobson & Waugh 1979: 30–35, Jakobson 1980)

In Chapters 2 and 12 I point out two rare cases of Symbolist poems, in which isolated periodic speech sounds (vowels and liquids) can be construed as speech and nonspeech at the same time.

If right-ear (left hemisphere) advantage is characteristic of the speech mode, and left-ear (right hemisphere) advantage of the nonspeech mode, one might reasonably speculate that the poetic mode of speech perception is characterized by some way of overcoming this channel separation or specialization. Certain perceptual qualities that are characteristic of a certain acoustic signal when processed in the nonspeech mode (that is, mainly by the right hemisphere) are eliminated from consciousness when the same signal is processed in the speech mode (that is, mainly by the left hemisphere). In the poetic mode, some "cross talk" may occur between the two circuits: some nonspeech qualities of the signal seem to become accessible, however faintly, to consciousness. The poetic mode exploits these cross talks for poetic effects.

1.3   Thing destruction and thing-free qualities

The dichotomy of categories vs precategorial information may be related to two additional dichotomies, suggested by Anton Ehrenzweig (1965, *passim*) as part of his aesthetic conception: Gestalts vs Gestalt-free qualities, and things vs thing-free qualities. During the years, I wrote two papers on "Oceanic dedifferentiation" in relation to poetry. The earlier one (1988), published in *Journal of Pragmatics*, is included in this book as Chapter 4. A later one was written for my 2003 book *On the Shore of Nothingness*. The later paper begins with the following paragraph.

> Ordinary consciousness organises percepts into objects that have stable shapes with clear-cut boundaries between them. It is intimately associated with voluntary control. Altered states of consciousness consist in some kind of withdrawal from the achievements of ordinary consciousness. This withdrawal may turn out to be a difficult achievement, because it involves the voluntary abandonment of voluntary control. Religion, meditation and mystic experience involve such altered states of consciousness, in this mounting order of difficulty. Hypnosis, dream and the hypnagogic state (drowsiness preceding sleep) too are altered states of consciousness. They involve regression, to some degree or other, to

some lowly-differentiated state of mind, the relinquishing of conscious control. These states of consciousness are not easily accessible to the arts, and least of all to poetry, the medium of which is conceptual language. In relation to music and the visual arts, Anton Ehrenzweig speaks of "thing-destruction" "suspension of boundaries", "thing-free" and "Gestalt-free" qualities, and of a "secondary elaboration", or "superimposition", of some organizing pattern on the resulting diffuse qualities. These critical terms seem to have considerable descriptive contents to allow the critic to point out the source of those "unspeakable" effects. Ehrenzweig relates these notions to Freud's notion of "Oceanic Dedifferentiation" (or "Undifferentiation"), and to Bergson's "Metaphysical Intuition".

(Tsur 2003: 231)

In Chapter 4 I explore instances of metaphors of the structure IMMERSION in an ABSTRACTION suggesting such "Oceanic Dedifferentiation". Ehrenzweig (1965) explores the various relationships between well-defined shapes ("prägnant Gestalts") and Gestalt-free, inarticulate "mannerisms" in painting and music. Taking a close look at a good wallpaper, he says, we may see a series of similar, well-designed shapes, one beside the other. Looking at it from a distance, we will find the wall paper Gestalt-free, ambiguous; we may project on it any shape. A good wall paper passes unnoticed; nevertheless, it makes all the difference whether it is there or not. Similarly, in a painting, or even an etching, while we direct our attention to the shapes of the picture, we subliminally perceive such Gestalt-free elements as *chiaroscuro* effects, shades and lights, irregular brush-strokes and scribblings. It is these elements that give the picture its peculiar depth, its plastic quality. It is not impossible to imitate the shapes drawn by a great master – imitating them will only prove that what gives them their peculiar character is precisely the barely noticed irregular strokes which the disciples find so difficult or even impossible to imitate. Gestalt-free elements are frequently created by superimposition of well-defined shapes, which sometimes "blend" so successfully that it takes a great conscious effort to tell them apart and contemplate them in isolation. In this way, says Ehrenzweig, the artist dissects "the shapes around him … into arbitrary fragments and rejoins them into arbitrary form phantasies" (143). It is this process which Ehrenzweig calls *thing-destruction*, that results in *thing-free qualities*.

In music, the tones and melodies are the things and Gestalts. The quality of the tone is created by subliminally perceived irregular sounds like *vibratos*, and *glissandos* "sandwiched" between two sounds, or repressed overtones. Both in painting and music, an increase of "depth", "thickness", "plastic quality", reinforcement of Gestalts may be noticed with the amplification of the Gestalt-free elements, and of their irregularity – up to the point of greatest "saturation"; this passed, the Gestalt-free elements begin to draw conscious attention and give way to completely different qualities. According to Ehrenzweig, what distinguishes great masters of the violin is precisely this large unnoticeable amount of irregular *vibratos* and *glissandos*; with salon musicians and some second-rate singers the *vibratos* and *glissandos* become consciously audible – that is why some people feel them to be "cheap", sentimental. In true polyphony, the superimposition of various melodies creates sustained passages of inarticulate (Gestalt-free) structures; polyphony as thing-free hearing is comparable with the painter's thing-free vision. Another quality of the tone, its colour, is determined by its **overtones**:

> But instead of this chord which should often sound quite agreeable, we usually hear a single tone, the fundamental. The others are "repressed" and replaced by the experience of tone colour which is projected onto the audible fundamental […]. Without tone colour fusion we would have to analyze the complex and often confusingly similar composition of overtone chords, in order to infer the substance of the sounding things and so identify them. Hence a conscious overtone perception, if it were possible, would be biologically less serviceable.
>
> (Ehrenzweig 1965: 154)

Harmonious fusion of sounds consists in the mingling of overtones of various tones, thus creating a *thing-free quality*, that is, a "mixture" of overtones, which no tone corresponds to. Ehrenzweig quotes Arnold Schönberg, who claims in his book on harmony that many composers are in a continuous chase after the still unheard overtone. Several aspects of overtone fusion in music and speech will be discussed in Chapter 2; in poetry reading, in Chapter 7.

As I have suggested, in verbal arts the most obvious "things" are words; the most obvious way to evoke a "thing-free vision" is to divert attention away from denotations to connotations, diffuse semantic features and minute, divergent phonetic details. When the neoclassic poet offers the reader "what oft was thought but ne'er so well express'd" (Pope, *Essay on Criticism*), the share of thing-free qualities is quite negligible. When, on the other hand, romantic and impressionist poets offer us elusive atmospheres, transient moods, the intuition of some transcendental truth, thing-free qualities may play an overwhelming part in the total effect of the poem.

Ehrenzweig's general aesthetic framework has the merit of offering terms that are applicable across sensory modes, such as *Gestalt, Gestalt-free, things, thing-free, thing-destruction*. In fact, human art is typically created in the visual and the auditory modes, in which these distinctions are fairly obvious. On the other hand, these terms can be applied to the specific arts only *via* terms that have well-articulated descriptive contents in the criticisms of their respective arts. We have found, indeed, that Ehrenzweig uses such terms as *chiaroscuro effects, vibrato, glissando, true polyphony*. In the next section I will offer one possible example of such a mediating system: Christine Brooke-Rose's (1958: 209) discussion of noun-metaphors, according to which certain qualities are *abstracted* from *concrete nouns*.

In my work on metaphor I conceive of words and of objects as of bundles of features. Likewise, in my work on the sound patterns of poetry I conceive of speech sounds as of bundles of features. In my work both on metaphor and the sound patterns of poetry I explore how the perception of such features may be rendered more compact or more diffuse by poetic manipulation. In Chapter 3 (on the Tip-of-the-tongue phenomenon) we will have an opportunity to observe at considerable length the underlying cognitive mechanism, where the various semantic and phonetic features fail to integrate into one compact entity. This pre-occupation has two obvious merits: the Tip-of-the-tongue phenomenon (TOT phenomenon) has, most conspicuously, considerable psychological reality; and it clearly demonstrates a relationship between the diffuse structure and the percep-tion of an intensive, lowly-differentiated quality. Such a quality, as we shall see, still has a definite character determined by the particular features involved.

1.4   "The *Roses* of her Cheeks"

Let us consider, then, a fairly trivial metaphor and Christine Brooke-Rose's minia-ture theory of metaphor focussed on it.

> When we use a noun metaphorically, we make abstractions of certain attributes which it possesses, leaving out others which would not fit; for instance, in "the *roses* of her cheeks", we think only of pinkness and softness, not of thorns, leaves, yellowness or dark red. The metaphoric term, though a noun, becomes the bearer of one or more attributes.   (1958: 209)

Here I wish to make a few points. First, the concrete noun *roses* is conceived of as of a bundle of attributes or *features*. Secondly, the majority of these attributes are denoted by abstract nouns; the reason for this can be illuminated by the etymologies of the words "concrete" and "abstract". The former is derived from a word meaning "grown together", the latter from a word meaning "to take away". Concrete nouns denote objects in which several attributes are "grown together", abstract nouns denote attributes in isolation, taken away from the concrete object, e.g. *fragrance, pinkness, softness, yellowness, dark red*. In this sense, "features" and "attributes" are precategorial elements. Thirdly, in every speech activity Jespersen (1960: 19) dis-tinguished **ex**pression, **sup**pression and **im**pression. *Expression* is what the speaker actually said; *suppression* is what might be but has not been said; *impression* is the perceived quality of the discourse, resulting from the interaction of *expression* and *suppression*. In Christine Brooke-Rose's example, the words *The roses of her cheeks* constitute the expression; the abstractions *fragrance, pinkness, softness*, which have not been explicitly mentioned, constitute the suppression; the shortest way to point at the resulting impression is to point to the perceived difference of effects between

The roses of her cheeks and *The fragrance, pinkness and softness of her cheeks*. The impression here is also affected by the fact that the list of attributes is open-ended, and one might add further items to it, such as *beauty, freshness*, or may further specify e.g. *softness*, by the particular silky or velvety texture of the roses. The decomposition of a concrete noun into an indefinite number of attributes that are compatible with the headword of the expression may be experienced in some cases as *insight*. Eventually, the unique impression of the metaphoric expression seems to be due to the very number of these attributes caught – so to speak – in a glimpse, so that any one of them is prevented, in Bergson's phrase, from "usurping" the others' place in our attention (quoted by Ehrenzweig 1965:34–35).

The relationship between the concept denoted by *roses* and its features is considerably loosened. The various features become semantically active in their own right, whereas some others, no less essential to the concept "roses", are left out as irrelevant. In light of our foregoing discussion, we could put this in a slightly different way. When we use the word *roses*, we refer to a concept. Having a concept enables us to generalize across situations and instances. The more features of the unique instance or situation we leave out, the easier it is to generalize across situations. When we name a concept, instead of bringing out the complexity of the experience, we reduce experience to a single item which falls under acknowledged categories. In the above metaphorical use, we decompose, so to speak, the single item into its component features. There is no escape from denoting concepts in verbal communication; but an awareness of the concept and, at the same time, of its features, brings us nearer to the unique, individual experience, with all the disquieting elements implied. It has something of the unpredictability, of the feeling of trembling on the brink of chaos.

Here an additional distinction must be made. As will be pointed out time and again in this book, sharp outlines increase the interaction of such thing-free qualities *within* the boundaries; the dimmer the outlines, the stronger their interaction *across* the boundaries (see, e.g. Chapter 2). Objects with characteristic visual shapes (as roses or cheeks) tend to inhibit the interaction of thing-free qualities across their boundaries; thus, those thing-free qualities are felt to be active, but kept in control. The next section will illuminate the mechanism underlying such inhibition. As will be seen in Chapters 2, 4–6, the full effect of thing-free qualities can be experienced where visual shapes are sufficiently weak. In Chapters 2 and 7 we will find a similar principle with reference to precategorial auditory information too.

1.5   Perceptual boundaries and fusion

The phenomenon known as "illusory boundaries" may illuminate two issues relevant to our inquiry. First, as recent brain research suggests, even in the processing of highly "intellectual" geometric shapes, in certain conditions information pro-cessing is based on incoming data from the environment to form a perception, and no higher brain image is necessarily involved. Second, it may serve as additional evidence for the phenomenon just mentioned, and discussed at some length in Chapter 2. There I invoke the Gestalt rule that some perceptual processes are inhibited across the boundaries of strong Gestalts; they increase to the degree that the Gestalt boundaries are weakened or impaired. I also quote Ehrenzweig, who adduces evidence for this regarding colour induction in visual perception and overtone fusion in polyphonic music. Then I suggest that this principle may apply to overtone interaction in speech perception as well, and thus account for some conspicuous but elusive phenomena in poetry, for which we don't even have a metalanguage to describe it. For instance, some repetitive sound patterns are perceived as compact, and some as relatively diffuse (compare, for instance, Pope's and Milton's alliterations). In the strong Gestalts of Pope's poetry the interacting overtones of speech sounds are contained within the verse line boundaries, and reinforce each other; in Milton's weak Gestalts overtones may be fused across verse boundaries and diffused over relatively large areas, generating a dense thing-free texture.

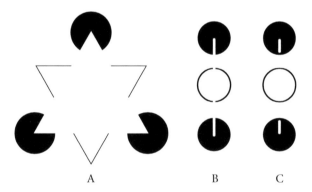

A   B   C

Figure 1. Closed Gestalt boundaries inhibit the generation of illusory objects across them (C); their disruption may facilitate it (A and B)

Figures 1A–1B show instances of illusory boundaries (or contours). Michael Gazzaniga defines illusory contours as "an illusion where contours are perceived, even though there is no line, luminance or color change" (Kindle eBook). In Figure 1A we see the famous "Kanizsa triangle": a triangle with white contour and white fill is superimposed upon a triangle with black contour and white fill. At the edges of the white triangle there are three small black disks; these edges conceal parts of the disks as well. In an important sense both triangles are equally real, we see them out there on the paper, irrespective of how they were generated, the superimposed triangle concealing parts of the other triangle from vision. In another sense, however, they substantially differ. The black triangle was generated by drawing its lines in black ink (or some equivalent); the outlines of the white triangle have not been traced by drawing in any way: it is a "virtual image", so to speak. Note that we clearly see the white object with its sharp outlines even where the background too is white. The small black disks are disrupted by small wedge-shaped white patches; likewise, the continuity of the outlines of the black triangle too is disrupted at three points. Such disruptions of contours seem to be an essential (though not sufficient) condition for the "illusory boundaries" to arise (it also requires carefully-controlled directions). Such a conclusion may be suggested by Figures 1B and 1C. In both figures we see two small black disks enclosing a small white disk with a black contour. In the black disks there is a small white vertical strip. In Figure 1B, the white strip is continuously drawn out from the upper black disk through the middle white disk, to the lower black disk, generating illusory boundaries of an elongate object; in Figure C, it is not. Again, the difference seems to be that in Figure B, in all three disks the contours are disrupted in carefully-controlled directions, whereas in Figure C they are intact.

Recent brain research suggests that this is not an *inference* by analogy with what we know is the case with physical boundaries, but rather an *immediate response* of the brain's visual cells. "Orientation selective cells are capable of responding to virtual lines. [...] There are many variants of this Kanizsa figure and their characteristic is that they are all open to only one plausible interpretation. The interpretation is probably dictated by the physiology of orientation selective cells in the cortex" (Zeki 2004: 181).

> It has been supposed that the interpretation that the brain gives to the configuration shown in Figure 1A is imposed top-down (Gregory 1972). If so, then higher areas of the brain should become engaged when subjects view such figures. But imaging experiments show that, when human subjects view and interpret such incomplete figures as triangles, activity in the brain does not involve the frontal lobes.   (Zeki 2004: 182)

The same holds true, says Zeki, of colour perception and ambiguous figures.

> To account for colour constancy, for example, both Helmholtz and Hering invoked higher (cerebral) factors such as judgment, learning, and memory. Similar higher factors have been invoked to account for ambiguous figures such as the Rubin vase (see Chapter 10, Figure 1a). But the mandatory involvement of higher centres in colour vision or in the perception of illusory figures is doubtful, since all imaging studies of colour vision and illusory figures are united in showing that there is no involvement of frontal or prefrontal cortex.
> (Zeki 2004: 175)

For our purpose, the bottom line is this: not only physical boundaries may block the interaction of physical forces across them, but perceptual boundaries too may disrupt the interaction of perceptual phenomena across them, whereas the weakening or disruption of perceptual boundaries may boost such interaction. For our purpose, however, there is a substantial difference between "illusory boundaries" or ambiguous figures on the one hand, and "colour induction" in visual perception or "overtone fusion" in music on the other: whereas colour induction and overtone fusion induce interaction of thing-free and Gestalt-free qualities, illusory boundaries generate stable Gestalts. The phenomenon we are dealing with, namely overtone fusion in speech perception, is more like colour induction and overtone fusion in music than like illusory boundaries.

1.6 "Precategorial" – predecessors and successors

I have taken the notion of "precategorial auditory information" from Al Liberman and his colleagues (see, e.g. Liberman et al. 1972) at the Haskins Laboratories (they use "categorical" and "precategorical"; I omitted the *c*, to distinguish my terms from Kant's). In speech research this notion is well-established, though usually it is difficult directly to observe it by introspection. It can be accessed, mainly, in laboratory conditions. In Chapter 11 I present an instance of such artificial conditions, with sound files available online. I found that this is part of a much wider issue: the construction of "ordinary consciousness", and the notion "precategorial information" can be applied to semantic categories as well. The present book offers a wide range of aspects of language and literature to which the term can fruitfully be applied. Following my work, the term is increasingly adopted in the cognitive study of literature. I will briefly present here the work of three researchers.

The researcher whose conception of precategorial information is nearest to mine is Margaret Freeman. In her article "The Aesthetics of Human Experience: Minding, Metaphor, and Icon in Poetic Expression" she bases her approach to literature, she says, on Vico's, Susanne K. Langer's (1953, 1967), and Maurice Merleau-Ponty's (1962 [1945], 1968) theories (Freeman 2011:717), but from my work, too, she adopts the notion of "precategorial". "In my analysis of Matthew Arnold's poem 'Dover Beach,' I apply Vico's arguments in his new science that relate to aesthetics by revising the way we metaphorically construct "mind" as object and by understanding the role of the imagination in creating meaning. This goes to show how poets create an aesthetic language to break through the conventional uses of discursive language, which conceal our underlying, precategorial responses to the world we experience" (Freeman 2011:720). In Chapter 14 I will also discuss the differences between our approaches.

As I said, my work is essentially speculative; frequently I adopt experimental results of others, and apply them in my work as hypotheses. In an attempt to obtain more direct empirical support for my work, I googled the web for "precategorical". Some items that turned up refer to the work of the speech researchers from whom I took the notion of "precategorical information"; but most of them refer to my own work. It is David Miall's neuropsychological evidence, and Sarah Jackson's think-aloud experiment that come nearest to an empirical support of my work.

David S. Miall has reviewed brain-scanning (evoked response potentials, or ERP) and imaging (fMRI) studies that focus on response to various aspects of language during the first 500 milliseconds of response.

> The neuropsychological evidence points to a temporal gap between the immediate onset of feeling and its cognitive consequents that unfold several hundred milliseconds later; thus we can also regard the gap as occurring between the precategorical and cognitive phases of response, to adopt Tsur's term (1992, p. viii). The mirror neuron system, it will be recalled, invokes our capacities at the precategorical level.   (Miall 2011a: 295)

Miall uses the term in additional places, among others, in an article that has just appeared in *Poetics Today*:

> The mirror neuron system invokes capacities at the precategorical, prereflective level, that is, responses that are temporally prior to, or at the borders of consciousness. This capacity we have to enact the entities, objects, and events we perceive, re-engages the body, through, in Shusterman's words, the "primordial perception or experience of the world that lies below the level of reflective or thematized consciousness and beneath all language and concepts"; the level that Merleau-Ponty terms "primary subjectivity" (Shusterman 2008: 57).
> (Miall 2011b: 701–702)

In his earlier work, Miall utilized the notion with an eye on textual analysis. "Following Tsur, Miall and Kuiken see the literary disturbance and delaying of text processing as making 'precategorical' and 'lowly categorized' information – including what we call 'gut' feelings – available to readers" (Alan Richardson 2006) *Literary Theory and Criticism: An Oxford Guide*. Oxford University Press (p. 548).

Likewise, in a pilot think-aloud experiment presented at PALA 2009, Sarah Jackson extensively applied my theoretical battery (including "sensory precategorial information") to a short passage from T.S. Eliot's "Ash Wednesday" and four readings thereof. She found that in some places reader's reactions were triggered by textual features that worked against each other, producing cognitive overload and blurring perceptual organisation. She concluded that in some readers this led to a regression of the perceiving consciousness and a perception of what could be termed an altered state of consciousness.

1.7   Guide through this book

Phenomenologically, the intense co-presence of phonetic and semantic precategorial information can be observed in the Tip-of-the-Tongue phenomenon, when one has on the tip of one's tongue a word that will not come into mind. In such states, people report the experiencing of some intense but lowly-differentiated mass of something, an "intense absence" which can be satisfied only with that one particular word. Such a quality is not unlike the dense atmosphere experienced in much romantic and symbolist poetry. In Chapter 3, I discuss Roger Brown and David McNeill's experiment, which offers a model for the underlying cognitive mechanism, and demonstrates that all the precategorial semantic and phonetic information is, indeed, present in the TOT state, but will not integrate into a compact word (Brown 1970). The TOT state is widely recognized as associated with Freudian psychopathology of everyday life. Roger Brown and David McNeill demonstrated that this is a cognitive phenomenon that may well occur without the unconscious Freudian conflicts. I came to the conclusion that a more adequate description might be as follows: There is a mechanism of retrieving words from long-term memory, which usually works smoothly, unnoticed. Sometimes this smooth working is disrupted so that we have a word on the tip of our tongue and become aware of the process. Such disruption may be exploited by psychodynamic processes for psychopathological purposes, or by poetic language for aesthetic purposes. This would hold true of Freudian slips of the tongue as well, and of misquoting a memorized passage (see, e.g. Tsur 1992b: 149–152; 2003: 2004–206; 2004: 65–67).

Intuitively, some alliterations "click", some "clink"; that is, in certain circumstances some rich precategorial auditory information is perceived reverberating in the background while we read poetry; and in some circumstances the sound patterns are perceived as "opaque". Chapter 2 explores those circumstances with reference to Gestalt theory, speech research and research on perception and personality. This phenomenon can be conveyed only through an "ostensive definition", that is, by pointing to an example. Such "ostensive definition" assumes an intuitive understanding, that is to say, that participants have sufficiently grasped the phenomenon to recognize the type of information being given. Figure 1 above may be regarded as a conspicuous instance of ostensive definition of illusory boundaries; or even of the wider principle of perceptual interaction across perceptual boundaries: strong perceptual boundaries may inhibit perceptual interaction across them; their weakening or disruption may boost it. Pointing at alliterations of Pope and Milton as instances of opaque and reverberating sound patterns, respectively, may be a much less clear-cut case of the same. However, a discussion of Pope's strong and Milton's weak versification boundaries (which most readers of poetry have sufficiently grasped) may guide participants to attend to the phenomenon in question.

Chapter 5 explores two linguistic devices that typically are felt to diffuse semantic information and generate, in certain circumstances, dense thing-free qualities in poetry: a combination of deixis with abstract nouns; and constructions of the ABSTRACT of the CONCRETE form. They are at their most effective when they occur together. It has been found that these devices and the underlying mental processes are most relevant to seventeenth-century Jesuit meditation, for instance (Tsur 2003:95; Tsur & Benari 2002), and may account for some crucial issues in romantic and symbolist poetry, and in Whitman's "meditative catalogues" (Tsur 2008:456–468).

Chapter 6 points out that the preceding chapter offers convenient tools for distinguishing between symbol and allegory. It demonstrates this by close readings of poems by Keats, Spenser, and Baudelaire.

Chapter 7 examines Hopkins' "The Windhover" and its notorious linguistic devices (such as "dapple-dawn-drawn falcon"), explores their relation to precategorial information, and shows in great detail how they may contribute to an ecstatic quality in a poem. In the second part of this chapter I submit a reading of this poem to instrumental analysis, exploring through electronic manipulations, how the weakening of intonation contours may boost the interaction of precategorial information.

In Chapters 2 through 7 I make a crucial distinction between categorial and precategorial information, or between Gestalts and Gestalt-free qualities, involving, I would say, a qualitative leap. In Chapters 8 and 9 I deal with what could be described as differences in degree. I explore the well-known stylistic device "defamiliarization", which treats highly-categorized phenomena not in terms of precategorial information, but of lower categories. This device is frequently exploited in fiction for ironic, witty, satirical, or even absurd effects. But in Yeats's sonnet "Leda and the Swan", for instance, it suggests an overwhelming, staggering emotional experience. Chapter 9 argues that such emotional terms as "sad' may refer to the mental processes of a flesh-and-blood person, or to some aesthetic qualities of a piece of music or poetry, suggesting some structural resemblance between the music and an emotion, such as low energy level, slow movement, and a withdrawn, unassertive attitude suggested by the minor key. It examines the convergent/divergent dichotomic spectrum, where the nearer a poetic structure to the divergent extreme, the more it is prone to suggest emotional qualities or subtle irony. This chapter also expounds another nonconceptual phenomenon, called by Gestalt theorists "perceptual forces". Such perceptual forces are generated when there is an intruding event between the middle and the boundaries of some perceptual unit, upsetting its balance. The effects of such intrusion are explored on a macro scale with reference to verse line boundaries and, on a micro scale, with those of phonemes.

Chapter 10 explores another central Gestalt notion: figure–ground relationship in visual designs, music and poetry. The Gestalt notion "figure–ground phenomenon" refers to the characteristic organisation of perception into a figure that 'stands out' against an undifferentiated background. What is figural at any one moment depends on patterns of sensory stimulation and on the momentary interests of the perceiver. Figure–ground relationship is an important element of the way we organise reality in our awareness, including works of art. Poets may rely on our habitual figure–ground organisations in extra-linguistic reality to exploit our flexibility in shifting attention from one aspect to another so as to achieve certain poetic effects by inducing us to reverse the habitual figure–ground relationships. This flexibility has precedent in music and the visual arts. Works by Escher, Bach, Mozart, Beethoven, Dickinson, Shakespeare, Sidney, Shelley, Beckett and Alterman are examined.

Chapter 11 explores additional aspects of the poetic mode of speech perception, the effect of precategorial auditory information on size–sound symbolism. I compare three approaches to cases when, e.g. a voice is said to be "thick": the mediated-association approach, the assumption that the voice shares some inter-sensory quality with the visual or tactile apprehension of thickness, and an evolutionary approach. There seems to be an intercultural intuition that high front vowels like [i] are perceived as smaller than low back vowels like [u]. By examining a total of 136 languages, Ultan (1978) demonstrated this on a large scale in a wide variety of the world's languages. Diffloth (1994) provides an alleged counterexample to this generalization from a Vietnamese dialect. In a thought experiment I point out a hidden conflict in his argument, suggesting that it becomes a counterexample only if you change, midway, the rules of the game. Chapter 12 presents an integrated and condensed account of my arguments concerning Literary Synaesthesia in three of my earlier books (Tsur 1987, Chapter 12; 1992b, Chapter 4; 1992a, Chapters 9 & 19 [=2008, Chapters 10 & 20]), throwing it into the perspective of more recent neuropsychological research by Ramachandran and Hubbard (2001), Newberg et al. (2001), and Cytowic (2003); a closer look at this book reveals that its informant didn't "taste shapes" as the title "The Man who Tastes Shapes" suggests, but sensed tastes in the haptic mode; such an understanding would render this case too congruous with Ullmann's (1957) "Panchronistic Tendencies in Synaesthesia". This chapter distinguishes between synaesthesia as a neuropsychological and a literary phenomenon and, within the latter, between a variety of possible poetic effects. Among other things, it is a powerful tool to suggest some lowly-differentiated precategorial quality. Toward its end, the chapter brings together the gist of my discussions of two French sonnets notorious for their extreme synaesthetic imagery, Baudelaire's "Correspondances" and Rimbaud's "Voyelles" (discussed at great length in Tsur 1992a, Chapter 19 [=2008, Chapter 20], and Tsur 1992b, Chapter 4, respectively). They explore in the verbal mode extreme instances of what in the visual mode, Ehrenzweig describes as follows: the artist dissects "the shapes around him [...] into arbitrary fragments and rejoins them into arbitrary form phantasies" (1965:143), upon which the poets superimpose a pattern of "emotive crescendo", by "retro-relating" the last line that suggests some ecstatic transport.

In Chapter 13 I explore the issue of precategorial information in a wider cultural perspective: the place of nonconceptual information in university education. I argue that our Western academic education gives conspicuous priority to conceptual instruction and neglects, to a considerable extent, sensuous information, intuitions and tacit knowledge. However, even in the exact sciences, let alone the humanities, our explicit knowledge is insufficient for applying definitions or equations; they are governed by intuitive and tacit knowledge. In literary studies, the tutor's task is to make students aware of certain elusive aspects of the text, and that in some instances certain kinds of response *are possible* (and not that one *must* respond in a certain way). In perspective of the present book, a crucial question arises: how do you communicate responses to precategorial information for which there is no name in language; and when you give it a name it ceases to be precategorial information, as in Helen Keller's case?

In Chapter 14 I discuss theoretical and practical issues that arose in course of the present book. It is called "Points and Counterpoints" because each section confronts at least two possible points of view on one issue.

CHAPTER 2

The poetic mode of speech perception revisited

What our ear tells our mind

2.1 Stating the problem

This chapter is an attempt to integrate (with some innovations) what I have said during the years about the rich precategorial auditory information reverberating in the background while we read poetry. My work on this topic draws upon two different sources. One is Anton Ehrenzweig's seminal work on Gestalt-free and thing-free qualities in the visual arts and music, and the interaction of such qualities within and across the boundaries of Gestalts. When boundaries are clear-cut, colour interaction is increased *within* them and inhibited *across* them; the more blurred the boundaries, the stronger the interaction *across* them. Ehrenzweig discusses this via colour induction in the visual domain, and overtone fusion in polyphonic music. Overtone fusion in music may generate hitherto unheard tone colours, and enhance the Gestalt-free *texture*. In speech, vowels are uniquely determined by concentrations of overtones called "formants". I claim that in certain circumstances the musical effects of poetry are crucially affected by similar overtone fusion. My other source is, obviously, speech research, which explores the transmission of speech through a stream of precategorial sound information, subsequently recoded into a sequence of speech categories.

Traditional literary scholarship has explored the versification devices which render poetry more musical than prose: metre, rhyme, alliteration, etc. In this chapter I propose to go two steps beyond that. What I propose to explore is quite elusive, and traditional scholarship doesn't even have a vocabulary to refer to it. And even when I propose one, it will be impossible to define the conditions in which the terms apply. But, I hope, they will enable us to discuss elusive intuitions in a meaningful way. Thus, the present chapter is about precategorial information and, at the same time, about the exigencies of critical communication.

As a first approximation, let us make the following distinction: Sometimes we experience the sound patterns of poetry as relatively opaque speech categories;

and sometimes as abounding in rich resonance, in lingering precategorial auditory information reverberating in the back of our mind – in other words, alliterations may "click" or "clink". The reverberating background texture sometimes acts in a way that is similar to the Gestalt-free shadings, scribblings and slight variations of color in the background of visual designs. They foreground the speech categories and sound patterns, round them out, as it were, making them more plastic and plump. Let me clarify what I mean by "resonance", "lingering auditory information" and "reverberating overtones", through an example adapted from Leonard Bernstein: "Depress middle C very carefully so as not to let it sound; then sharply strike and quickly release the C an octave below. As soon as the lower C is released what will you hear? The *upper* C! It seems like magic, because you have really not "struck" this higher C, but the lower one" (Bernstein 2004: 198), exciting the upper C-string to vibrate sympathetically as the first overtone of the C an octave below. Such activation of overtones is called resonance.

As a kind of "ostensive definition" of what I mean with reference to verbal structures, let me give three brief examples. First, a most elementary, nonpoetic example. Consider the name of the German philosopher *Kant*, and the word *can't* (contraction of *cannot*), in British English. In the former, the [n] is a full consonant; in the latter it is attenuated into the [+NASAL] feature of the nasal vowel [ã]. In the former it is perceived as relatively opaque; in the latter as more resonant than either a nasal consonant, or an oral vowel (e.g. [a]). Second, consider the following stanza from FitzGerald's "The Rubáiyát" of Omar Khayyám:

> Some for the Glories of this World; and some
> Sigh for the Prophet's Paradise to come;
>   Ah, take the Cash and let the Credit go,
> Nor heed the rumble of a distant Drum!

Consider the three rhyme words, *some–come–Drum*. Some readers report that they are aware of a rich body of reverberating auditory information in *Drum*, but are not aware of a similar richness in the preceding rhyme-fellows. To be sure, traditional criticism has an excellent explanation for this, as far as it goes. There is an exceptionally rich alliteration pattern in *rumble–distant–Drum*. The phrase refers to reverberating sound; the consonants [r] and [m], in turn, are perceived as *somehow* imitating sounds in nature. The present chapter purports to go two steps further, and invoke the rich precategorial auditory information on the one hand, and the fusion of such auditory information on the other. The point is that in certain circumstances such resonance is enhanced, and in some inhibited. In this stanza of the "Rubáiyát" there are additional alliterations, though less resonating: *Prophet's Paradise* and *Cash–Credit*. Intuitively, they are perceived as less reverberating, more "opaque", and having a "leaner body".

Third, let us consider another classical example, Tennyson's notorious verse line "And murmuring of innumerable bees". It contains the sound cluster *mər* three times: twice in *murmuring*, and once in *innumerable*. Now, consider John Crowe Ransom's transcription of this line: "And murdering of innumerable beeves" – the reverberating background texture disappears. Ransom's transcription contains the sound cluster *mər* only twice; the rich precategorial information associated with it still could reverberate in acoustic memory (just as in *can't*), but it doesn't. Obviously, the onomatopoeia disappeared too. I will return to these examples. At the present stage of my argument I only want to point out one more thing. The [b] of *innumerable* and *bees* (or *beeves*) is part of another alliteration pattern, but not of the onomatopoeia. But even the [b] seems to have a fuller, richer, more resonant body in Tennyson's line than in Ransom's rewriting. In course of this paper we shall encounter a wide range of conditions that may enhance or inhibit the reverberating sound information.

Such "ostensive definition" assumes an intuitive understanding, that is to say, that participants have sufficiently grasped the phenomenon to recognize the type of information being given. Alternatively, the vocabulary and theoretical framework to be expounded here may be useful in directing attention to certain elusive aspects of the sound dimension of a poem. Paraphrasing Morris Weitz (1962: 59), it can be used as a crucial recommendation what to look for and how to look at it in a given sound pattern.

The catch is that if someone cannot hear what I attribute to those examples, I cannot argue with him, nor bring him any proofs. Some people may raise an eyebrow at such an ostensive definition of my elusive topic. According to Frank Sibley (1962: 77), however, that is precisely how aesthetic concepts are and should be handled. "If we are not following rules and there are no conditions to appeal to" Sibley says, "how are we to know when they are applicable? One very natural way to counter this question is to point out that some other sorts of concepts also are not condition-governed. We do not apply simple color-words by following rules or in accordance with principles. We see that the book is red by looking, just as we tell that the tea is sweet by tasting it. So too, it might be said, we just see (or fail to see) that things are delicate, balanced, and the like"; or, "reverberating" at that. Or, as Manfred Bierwisch (1970: 108) says, poetics must accept effects as given.

Another vantage point to approach this phenomenon is from the Jakobsonian model of language functions. From the reader's point of view, there is a hierarchy of *arbitrary* signs: graphemes→ phonemes→ meaning→ extralinguistic referent (each later item being the signified of the preceding one). Man, as a sign-using animal, is programmed to reach the extralinguistic referent as fast as possible. According to Jakobson, what differentiates the referential function is focusing on the extralinguistic context; the poetic function focuses on the message. Figurative language directs attention to the semantic component of language, whereas the patterning of speech categories (versification) to the phonetic component. I have elsewhere discussed picture poetry, that forces the reader to attend back to the patterning of graphemes – hence perceived as so "artificial".

From the listener's point of view, speech sounds are transmitted by a stream of rich precategorial auditory information, which is immediately recoded into phonetic categories, and excluded from awareness. We only perceive a unitary, discrete phonetic category as [i] or [u]. Some of the precategorial auditory information, however, lingers on subliminally in active memory, and is available for certain cognitive tasks and aesthetic effects. Such lingering auditory information normally serves to preserve verbal material in active memory for efficient processing. It is active, usually, in the background, unnoticed. The present suggestion is twofold: first, that in poetic language, some or many listeners attend back not only to the patterning of speech categoies explored by traditional rhetoric and criticism, but also to the lingering precategorial auditory information, turning it to aesthetic end in that it is perceived as musicality, onomatopoeia, or expressive sound patterns; and second, that in some circumstances more of the reverberating precategorial auditory information is perceived, and in some – less.

2.2   Some experimental evidence

There is plenty of experimental evidence for the reverberation and interaction of lingering auditory information. I will briefly mention only three sets of experiments. First, evidence for reverberation. Liberman et al. (1972) describe a series of experiments by Crowder and Morton (1969), who found that in auditory (but not visual) presentation, vowels produce a recency effect in certain cognitive tasks, but stops do not. Part of the explanation seems to be as follows:

> The special process that decodes the stops strips away all auditory information and presents to immediate perception a categorical linguistic event the listener can be aware of only as /b, d, g, p, t, or k/. Thus, there is for these segments no auditory, precategorical form that is available to consciousness for a time long enough to produce a recency effect. The relatively unencoded vowels, on the other hand, are capable of being perceived in a different way […]. The listener can make relatively fine discriminations within phonetic classes because the auditory characteristics of the signal can be preserved for a while. […] In the experiment by Crowder, we may suppose that these same auditory characteristics of the vowel, held for several seconds in an echoic sensory register, provide the subjects with rich, precategorical information that enables him to recall the most recently presented items with relative ease.

Second, let us turn to a set of experiments conducted for a different purpose. Researchers at the Haskins Laboratories (e.g. Liberman and Mann 1981: 128–129; Brady et al. 1983: 349–355; Mann 1984: 1–10), investigated the possible causes of some children's difficulty to learn to read, and revealed a deficiency in the use of phonetic coding by poor readers; good readers, by contrast, seem to make an excellent use of it. In one experimental task, poor readers had greater difficulty than good readers in tapping once or three times in response to the number of syllables in such spoken words as *pig* or *elephant*, or once, twice or three times in response to the number of phonemes in such words as *eye, pie* or *spy*. This has been interpreted as a deficiency in the use of phonetic coding. In another task, they had to memorize groups of words – either rhymed or unrhymed, as in the following ones:

chain	train	brain	rain	pain
cat	fly	score	meat	scale

Good readers did consistently better with both kinds of groups than poor readers. However, with the rhymed groups, their performance seriously deteriorated. While their reliance on phonetic representation increased their overall performance, the similar sounds of the rhyming words reverberating in their acoustic memory seem to have caused confusion. Good readers made efficient use of phonetic coding, whereas the poor readers made inefficient use of the acoustic information in short-term memory, and so were not penalized by the similar sounds of the rhyming words.

The sound patterns of poetry in general, and rhyme in particular, typically exploit the precategorial acoustic information and, actually, enhance its memory traces. In nonaesthetic memory experiments, this reliance on phonetic representation reveals two typical effects. It enables verbal material to linger for some time in short-term memory for more efficient processing, but also may cause acoustic confusion in certain circumstances.

The disadvantage of efficient readers with rhymed words seems to contradict our commonsense observation that versification facilitates the memorization of texts. But the contradiction is only apparent. In the experiment, the effect depends on the distance between the rhyming words. As Crowder (1983: 255) suggested in the set of experiments quoted below, "if the two units are too close together, they will integrate rather than inhibit. If they integrate, the subject will lose valuable information". In poetry, by contrast, the rhyme words are further away from one another, and break up a longer text into easily-remembered chunks. At the same time, the reverberating similar sounds unify the segmented text, and also enlist auditory memory in the service of remembering (in Chapter 7 we will see how such closely-packed strings work in Hopkins' poetry). When in the experiment the rhyme words come in close succession in a meaningless list, there is no intervening text to organize, nor is there a meaningful context that would impose semantic or grammatical constraints: it makes no difference which word comes first, which comes next. It is this context-governed process with which rhyme interacts in memory: it eliminates certain possibilities allowed by syntax and context.[1]

So, the fusion of formants becomes mere confusion. What in the nonaesthetic memory experiments is called acoustic *confusion*, in an aesthetic context co-occurs with a coherent text, and may be perceived in the background as "harmonious *fusion*", "musicality".

Third, experimental literature suggests three possibilities in the perception of successive speech stimuli. If a subsequent stimulus is very similar to the preceding stimulus, it may generate an enhanced response, because of integration with the lingering auditory information; if it is moderately similar, it will be reduced, inhibiting the lingering auditory information ("lateral inhibition"); if there is no similarity, it will be unaffected. In ordinary verbal communication usually one of the latter two possibilities is the case (Crowder 1982, a–b). As to rhyme or FitzGerald's "rumble–Drum" alliteration, obviously the "very similar" option is the case. Robert G. Crowder suggests (personal communication) that there would be precedent for the assumption that the total effect would be the larger for having had a repeated sound. This depends on his assumption that both inhibitory and

---

1.   Likewise, metre breaks up the text into segments, enhances the unity of the segments, enlists auditory memory in the service of remembering, and eliminates alternative possibilities of word combination. To be sure, semantic, syntactic, and versification constraints are no foolproof guarantee for, only increase the likelihood of, correct remembering. Thus, for instance, in his *Psychopathology of Everyday Life*, Freud mentions a young woman who, for good psychopathological reasons, misquoted four lines from Keats's "Ode to Apollo" as

> In thy Western house of gold
>   Where thou livest in thy state,
> Bards, that once sublimely told
>   Prosaic truths that came too late.

The correct lines read as follows (the words replaced by others being italicized):

> In thy western *halls* of gold
>   *When* thou *sittest* in thy state,
> Bards, that *erst* sublimely told
>   *Heroic deeds and sang of fate.*

The misquoted passage conforms with the syntactic and versification constraints; and misquoted words are overdetermined by the semantic constraints of the original and the memorizer's assumed psychopathological motives. (I have elsewhere discussed at greater length the cognitive processes underlying this misquote; Tsur, 1992: 148–153).

enhancing interaction takes place within the formant energy of the words, even though they may be spoken at different pitches (formants are concentrations of overtones that uniquely determine vowels). Thus, such sound patterns as rhyme and alliteration not only "exploit" the working of the auditory short-term memory, but actually enhance it.

A chapter in one of my books is called "Musicality in Verse, and Phonological Universals" (Tsur 1992: 52–88). I took the first part of this phrase from Kenneth Burke, the second from Roman Jakobson, and combined them. It took months before I discovered that I had created a most powerful alliteration: the word "verse" recurs entirely in the word "uni*vers*als". The sound sequence [ju] too is repeated in "Musicality … Universals". It would appear that in prose discourse our pronunciation of the same sound sequence in two words tends to be moderately similar, so as to reduce the lingering auditory information, directing attention away from the sounds to the referents. One may attend back to the alliteration by lengthening the sequence [vɜrs] of "uni*vers*als" and slightly raising its pitch, so as to render it more similar to "*verse*". Likewise, the following sentence occurs in Ehrenzweig's account of Chevreuil's colour-induction experiment quoted below: "On a *green gr*ound the *gr*ey square would turn a distinct pink". I have quoted the passage numberless times during the past four decades or so, but only now, when writing the present paper I noticed the exceptionally powerful alliteration.

Crowder raises the question what the lateral inhibitory process is good for. "In vision, a system of recurrent lateral inhibition […] has the obvious adaptive consequence of edge-sharpening. Something quite similar may go on in speech perception. For example, in rapid fluent speech, people rarely achieve the 'target values' of vowels, in terms of formant frequency. A system that could enhance the discriminability of adjacent vowels with high spectral overlap would be handy, especially if it operated at a very early, sensory, level of processing" (Crowder 1983: 256). For our purpose, probably another function of lateral inhibition in speech perception would be to prevent the sound stratum from distracting attention from the extralinguistic referent in the referential function. And conversely, we must carefully articulate the 'target values' of formant frequencies, if we want them to enhance rather than inhibit the lingering auditory information. This may illuminate the phonetic mechanism underlying the "poetic function".

2.3   Speech mode, nonspeech mode and poetic mode

Liberman and his colleagues at the Haskins Laboratories distinguish between a speech mode and a nonspeech mode of auditory perception, which follow different paths in the neural system (see Chapter 1). In the speech mode there is typically a lack of correspondence between acoustic cue and perceived phoneme: we hear a unitary phoneme that is very different from the stream of auditory information that conveys it. In the nonspeech mode (natural noises, music, sonar etc.), by contrast, the shape of the perceived sound is similar to the shape of the sound wave. We seem to be tuned, normally, to the nonspeech mode; but as soon as the incoming stream of sounds gives the lightest indication that it may be carrying linguistic information, we automatically switch to the speech mode. In certain laboratory conditions we may hear the phoneme in one ear, and the inarticulate noise in the other (for a different instance of artificial conditions see Chapter 11, below). We may also *see* it by converting speech into colour patches in images called sonograms or spectrograms.

I have suggested that there is a third, "poetic mode", in which you hear the phonetic categories as in the speech mode, but some of the lingering precategorial auditory information becomes available too. Pronounce [ʃ] and [s] and try to determine which one is higher. Most people find that [s] is higher. Or pronounce [i] and [u] on the same pitch; you will probably find that [u] is lower and darker than [i]. As Figures 1 and 2 show, the second formant of [s] and [i] is higher than that of [ʃ] and [u]. The first two formants of [u] are nearer together than those of [i] and, as Delattre et al. (1952) demonstrated, the human ear can even be fooled into hearing an [u] carried by two formants, when, in fact, generating one formant at an intermediate pitch. This indistinctness of [u] is perceived as darkness, as it were. Likewise, most people judge [ʃ] as darker than [s]; indeed, as Figure 1 shows, its first and second formants are nearer together than those of [s].

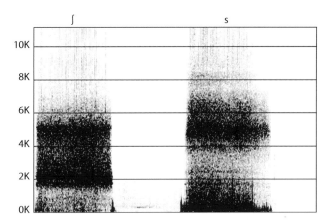

Figure 1. Sonograms of [ʃ] and [s], representing the first and second formant, and indicating why [s] is somehow "higher"

We must consider yet another distinction, that of relative "encodedness". Ask someone to pronounce [ba], [da] and [ga] on the same pitch and tell which one is higher. Not as with [s] and [ʃ] or [i] and [u], most (but not all) people will have difficulty to tell this. The only difference between [ba], [da], and [ga] is the onset frequency of the so called second formant transition, in this ascending order (see Chapter 11, below). But stop consonants are highly encoded, that is, little or no lingering auditory information reaches awareness.

One may make two successive distinctions in the acoustic structure of speech sounds. Some speech sounds (as [p, t, k]) are abrupt; some are continuous. Continuous speech sounds may be periodic (as [l, m, n, j]; or aperiodic (as [ʃ, s, f]). [r] is continuous, periodic, and multiply interrupted. Abrupt sounds are usually highly encoded; continuous aperiodic sounds somewhat less encoded, and periodic sounds relatively unencoded. Even among vowels, as we have seen, nasal vowels are less encoded than oral vowels. Voiced stops are an interesting case in point: stops are abrupt, whereas voicing is periodic. I have used above the pair of onomatopoetic verbs *click* and *clink*. The word-final [k] in *click* is exceptionally sharp and abrupt; the nasal vowel in *clink* is periodic and reverberating and, according to Liberman and his colleagues at the Haskins Laboratories, quite readily available to awareness.

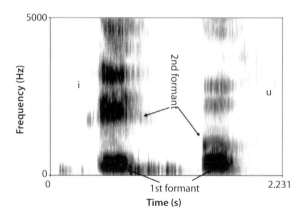

Figure 2. Spectrograms of [i] and [u]. The second formant is higher and the distance between the first two formants greater in [i] than in [u]

Coarticulation increases the encodedness of speech sounds. There is experimental evidence that in isolated vowels and continuants more precategorial information reaches awareness than when pronounced with another speech sound (Rakerd 1984; Repp 1984). In [ʃ, s] it is easier to discern which one is higher than in [ʃa, sa]. Symbolist poets sometimes capitalize on this fact, enhancing the reverberation of speech sounds. In Rimbaud's "*Voyelles*" the vowels [a, e, i, ü, o] are directly named, with no consonantal context, yielding a stream of acoustic energy (see Chapter 12). The Hungarian poet Kosztolányi wrote a poem inspired by his wife's name, *Ilona*, all continuous periodic sounds. In one of the stanzas he enumerates the isolated sounds of her name: "*Csupa l,/csupa i,/csupa o, csupa a*" – all continuous streams of periodic sounds.

We have been exploring the question, why in some poetic contexts one may discern reverberating auditory information in the background, bestowing on the speech sounds plasticity and a "fuller body", whereas in other contexts speech sounds are perceived as relatively "lean" and sharply defined. Lingering precategorial auditory information is the clue. One distinction we have made concerns "encodedness". In some speech sounds the precategorial auditory information is more readily available than in others.

This by itself, however, would be a quite rigid phenomenon, insufficient to account for the experience we set out to explain. But, in certain circumstances, readers and poets may switch attention from one aspect of the speech sounds to another. Consider our example "And murmuring of innumerable bees" as opposed to "And murdering of innumerable beeves". I have suggested that the [b] of *innumerable* is no part of the onomatopoeia, but even the [b] seems to have a fuller, richer, more resonant body in Tennyson's line than in Ransom's rewriting. In *murmuring* and *innumerable* the meaning directs attention to the rich precategorial auditory information available in the continuous periodic consonants [m], [n], [r], and [l]. The voiced stop [b] is perceived in the *murdering* context as a unitary speech sound that typically blocks, so to speak, the passage of reverberating acoustic energy. The *murmuring* context, by contrast, separates the periodic "voiced" feature in [b] and activates it, blending its voiced, periodic element with that of [l]. Such an "aspect-switching" will appear less incredible if we note that one of the most effective cues for voiced consonants is an articulatory gesture plus voice onset time: that is, how much time passes between the articulatory gesture and the beginning of voicing. In the present distinction there need be no difference in voice onset time, but in attention: whether we focus on the successive articulatory gesture + voicing, or on the minute pause between them.

There are indications that this is not a mere freak of an artificial rewrite exercise. Thus, for instance, Iván Fónagy (1961), in his study of the expressiveness of speech sounds compared the relative frequency of phonemes in six especially angry poems and six especially tender poems by a variety of poets in French, German and Hungarian. Such voiceless stops as [p, t, k] are "angry" for most poets. I interpreted this fact as having to do with their abrupt and highly encoded nature. Tender moods are more open to uncategorized sensory information than aggressive moods. Now consider the relative frequency of /g/ and /d/ in Victor Hugo's and Paul Verlaine's poems. /g/ occurs over one and a half times more frequently in Verlaine's tender poems than in his angry ones (1.63: 1.07), whereas we find almost the reverse proportion in Hugo's poems: 0.96% in his tender poems, and 1.35% in his angry ones. As to /d/, again, the same sound has opposite emotional tendencies for the two poets, but with reverse effects. For Verlaine it has a basically aggressive quality (10.11: 7.93), whereas for Hugo it has a basically tender quality (7.09: 5.76) – again, in almost the same reverse proportion. The reason seems to be similar to the one we have offered for the shift of perceived qualities of [b] in the *murmuring* and *murdering* contexts: "aspect-switching". If you attend to the [g] or [d] as a unitary abrupt stop consonant, it may have a strong aggressive potential; if you attend to the periodic voiced ingredient, it may contribute to a tender quality. Obviously, Hugo and Verlaine applied the same cognitive mechanism to these voiced stops, but with a reverse focus.

2.4   Colour and overtone interaction

As I mentioned above, in this paper I make an attempt to apply to poetry Anton Ehrenzweig's work on colour and overtone interaction in the visual arts and music. According to the Gestalt psychologists, "colour interaction increases within the boundaries of a good Gestalt while it is inhibited across its borders" (Ehrenzweig 1970: 172). In the visual domain, the process was demonstrated experimentally, in a most dramatic way, back in the early nineteenth century. Ehrenzweig (1970: 170–171) describes a demonstration of colour induction by Chevreuil (which I attempted to replicate in Plates 1 and 2). "The experiment which demonstrated interaction most clearly was to place a small grey square on a large ground of colour. On a green ground the grey square would turn a distinct pink". I have found that it takes the square a few seconds to turn pink.

"A few years later a most paradoxical phenomenon was observed; when a sheet of semi-transparent tissue paper was placed over the whole area the saturation of the green ground was of course severely diminished. One would have expected that the colour induction in the grey would be reduced to the same extent, that is to say that the induced pink of the grey square would also become much paler. But the opposite happened: the pinkness of the grey square became more pronounced". It was Helmholz who found an explanation for this paradox: the tissue paper made the outline of the grey square fuzzier and this weakening of its form increased colour interaction across its boundaries. "A comparatively crude weakening of the line was sufficient to compensate – indeed more than compensate – for the enormous loss in the saturation of the colours," says Ehrenzweig. "As in all relationships between form and colour the reverse effect can also happen. Strong colour interaction tends to make sharp outlines seem much softer than they are".

Ehrenzweig argues that the same relationships hold in music between melodic shapes and overtone interaction (overtones being the physical correlates of "sound colour") (Ehrenzweig 1965: 172–173). This is more immediately relevant than colour induction to poetry reading, where we are dealing with intonation shapes and overtone interaction (where overtones are the physical correlates of vowels). "To the extent to which a musical note is fitted into a clean melodic 'line' it is prevented from fusing into harmonic tone 'colour'; conversely a strong chord will temporarily fuse the loose strands of polyphony into solid tone colour so that the separate melodic lines disappear altogether. I have mentioned that the ear constantly oscillates between the harmonic fusion and polyphonic separation of the melodic lines; this conflict between 'form' and 'colour' belongs to the very life of music" (1970: 173). There are good reasons to suppose that a similar dynamics, with the necessary changes, may occur in poetic language, in respect of the lingering rich precategorial auditory information on the one hand, and, on the other, clear-cut speech categories and good syntactic and prosodic Gestalts.

Thus, one of the several ways to manipulate the precategorial auditory information in poetry concerns Gestalts and boundaries. Stronger boundaries would inhibit interaction across them, the weakening of boundaries may boost it. That may be one difference between the perceived quality of Pope's (or Spenser's) and Milton's alliterations.

At this point we may try to account for some of the sound effects in FitzGerald's stanza quoted above. Consider the phrase "*rumble* of a *distant Drum*". The repeated sound cluster [rʌm] + [l] are lowly-encoded speech sounds, that is, much of the rich precategorial auditory information may reach awareness. In light of Crowder's experiments with lateral inhibition, in such repeated sound clusters, the similar formants may be integrated in certain circumstances, and enhance each other. Furthermore, *rumble* is defined by the *Merriam-Webster Collegiate Dictionary* as "a low heavy continuous reverberating […] sound", and may direct attention to the reverberating periodic background texture of these phonemes. According to the foregoing discussion, it may also direct attention to the periodic ingredient in the voiced stops [b] and repeated [d]. That is why this phrase tends to be perceived as reverberating, as having a "full body".

Or, consider the [r] in *rumble*, *drum*, *Prophet*, *Paradise* and *Credit*. The [r], as I said, is periodic and multiply interrupted, and lowly-encoded. Thus, the reader/listener has the option to switch between three aspects of the sound, according to the context: the unitary speech sound; its interrupted (that is, abrupt) nature, sometimes suggesting threat, aggression or frightening noises; and its periodic nature, suggesting a soft resonant quality (as in *murmuring*).

In *Prophet, Paradise* and *Credit* [r] is associated with the unvoiced stops ([p] and [k]), which are likely to direct attention away from its resonance to the unitary speech sound.

As we have seen, reverberating precategorial auditory information is inhibited across strong Gestalt boundaries. If the Gestalt is weakened, reverberation increases; if it is improved, reverberation decreases. This applies to music; and, I suggest, to phonetics too. Consider the alliteration in the line "Ah, take the Cash and let the Credit go". Here the unvoiced [k] sound is repeated, which is highly encoded, that is, little or no precategorial information reaches awareness. The alliterating syllables *Cash* and *Credit* are stressed, foreground the strong positions and enforce the symmetrical structure, strengthening the overall Gestalt. Even if *some* precategorial sound information could be perceived, reverberation would be contained. Indeed, the alliteration sounds relatively dull, hard and compact. Compare now this alliteration with another repeated [k], in No 3 of the *Rubáiyát*:

> And, as the **Cock crew**, those who stood before
>   The Tavern shouted – »Open then the Door!
>   «You know how little while we have to stay,
>   «And, once departed, may return no more.»
>
> Fitzgerald: Omar Khayyam 3

Here two consecutive stressed syllables blur the metric pattern. We are on slippery ground. But it would appear that the alliteration in *Cock crew* sounds less compact than in *Cash* and *Credit*. To be sure, the word *crew* (but not *Cash* and *Credit*) refers to a sound, and thus could activate whatever inarticulate sound information is available in the highly-encoded [k] and the lowly-encoded, multiply interrupted [r]. But notice this. Manipulating the second alliterating stressed syllable into a strong position strongly enhances metre and the alliteration may be perceived as somewhat more tightly packed, less resonant.

> And, as the Cock that crew – who stood before

Now suppose all these differences reflect a mere whimsey, my idiosyncratic impression, and doesn't conform with your intuition. The present apparatus enables me at least to communicate what I mean; and allows you to know what it is you are expected to but don't hear. We *hear* (or fail to hear) that *Cock that crew* is less resonant than *Cock crew*. But the present apparatus renders the topic *discussible*, and in some instances, at least, my argument may even help to direct your attention to what I hear.

Or take the phrase *Prophet's Paradise*. Among the unvoiced stops, [p] is phonetically softer, less compact than [k]. But the proximity and syntactic connection between the two words enhances their popping noise, and the intervening unstressed syllable in a weak position renders the *pr* alliteration relatively nonresonant.

We have been discussing the version of the third and fourth edition of the *Rubáiyát*. In the second edition FitzGerald had:

> Some for the Glories of This World; and some
> Sigh for the Prophet's Paradise to come;
>   Ah, take the Cash, and let the **Promise** go,
> Nor heed the **music** of a distant Drum!

Credit and *Promise* are interchangeable in the sense that both refer to an expectation of future fulfillment. By substituting *Credit* for *Promise*, FitzGerald improved by one masterstroke both the parallelism of figurative language and the alliteration pattern. In the earlier version, *Promise* joins the *Prophet's Paradise* alliteration pattern as a third member. *Promise* belongs to the *Prophet's* semantic field, just as *Credit* belongs to the same semantic field as *Cash*. Thus, *Prophet's Paradise* plus *Promise* constitute a unit that runs on from one line to the next one, both in the semantics and alliteration respect, weakening the line-as-a-unit. The substitution of *Credit* for *Promise* enhances the symmetry and closed character of the lines; briefly – strengthen their Gestalt. It would appear that *Promise* is less obtrusive than the other two members; the intervening line and clause boundary seems to weaken acoustic interaction across it. "Music of a distant Drum" too directs attention to the auditory element in meaning. But notice this: *music* shares with *rumble* the stress pattern, and the meaning component [+SOUND]. But the focus of the alliteration shifts from *rumble–Drum*, to *distant Drum*, foregrounding the abrupt [d] rather than the reverberating [rʌm]. Consequently, the repeated [d] changes its character: one tends to attend to the harder unitary phoneme rather than to the reverberating, periodic voicing. Thus, it is perceived more as a sound imitation of "beating drumsticks" than of "reverberating membrane".

Alliterations like "Ah, take the Cash and let the Credit go" or *Prophet's Paradise* would be typical of Pope, while alliterations like *Cock crew* would be typical of Milton or Shelley, and quite untypical of Fitzgerald or Pope.

This may also explain why Milton and Shelley, two of the most deviant poets in English (see Tsur, 1998), are thought to be two of the most musical poets too. Their frequent strings of stressed syllables in weak positions and other deviations blur the metric Gestalt; their frequent enjambments blur the Gestalt of the verse lines. This may background the sound patterns, but increase their overtone interaction over considerable stretches of text.

According to Jakobson (1960), rhyme and alliteration focus attention on the sound stratum of a text; the present conception further distinguishes between two layers within the sound stratum: the string of phonetic categories and stream of precategorial auditory information. Traditional criticism typically deals with the string of phonetic categories. The present work assumes that by moving from the phonetic categories to the precategorial sound information one does not merely restate the issues once in "phonetics language" and once in "acoustics language", but crucial distinctions can be made on the precategorial level that are not automatically implied by the phonetic categories. It propounds a vocabulary and theoretical framework that enable us to handle the precategorial auditory information in a principled manner. In the present case, for instance, in onomatopoeia it may point out and account for the more fine-grained interaction of sound and meaning. Moreover, it may offer *several* interacting reasons why in "rumble of a distant Drum" the precategorial auditory information is more obtrusive, more resonating, than in its rhyme fellows or some other alliteration patterns in the stanza.

2.5   Individual differences

The experiments with efficient and poor readers may suggest that there are individual differences in the handling of precategorial auditory information. I will point out two kinds of reasons for such individual differences: the ones related to phonetic coding, and those related to personality style. From the afore-mentioned experiments (Liberman and Mann 1981; Brady et al. 1983; Mann 1984) we know that some persons have a deficit in phonetic coding; but it doesn't say what coding they are using instead. Crowder and Wagner (1992: 228–230) summarize an experiment by Byrne and Shea which strongly suggests that they are using a semantic code. In this experiment, subjects had to take a "reading test", reading out lists of words and then, unexpectedly, were given a memory test. They were presented with the words read earlier, interspersed with a number of additional words, to which they had to respond "old" or "new". The "new" words were either phonetically or semantically related to the "old" words. "Assume the prior items were *home* and *carpet: house* and *rug* would be the semantically similar foils and *comb* and *market* would be the phonetically similar foils". Good readers tended to confuse both phonetically and semantically related words, poor readers semantically related words. This would suggest that good readers use both phonetic and semantic coding, poor readers mainly semantic coding. Crowder and Wagner insist: "The fact that poor readers seem to be using 'too much' meaningful processing does not imply that they are *better at* top-down processing than good readers. It is just that they may be so deficient in bottom-up processing they have no other recourse".

There are personality styles that are intolerant of unique, unclassifiable sensations, which too may penalize some persons in responding to precategorial auditory information. Such intolerance is intimately related to the intolerance of the uncertainty typically associated with delayed closure (see above, Chapter 1). Consider the following description: "The leveler is more anxious to categorize sensations and less willing to give up a category once he has established it. Red is red, and there's an end on't. He levels (suppresses) differences and emphasizes similarities in the interest of perceptual stability. For him the unique, unclassifiable sensation is particularly offensive, while the sharpener at least tolerates such anomalies, and may actually seek out ambiguity and variability of classification" (Ohmann 1970: 231).

The foregoing line of investigation may have tapped a kind of individual differences in verbal strategies that may characterize very advanced readers too; I mean students and professors of literature. Such measures as the ones applied to first graders would be insufficient to measure a literature student's relative reliance on phonetic coding. However, we may find in prosody classes students of literature who are incapable of telling which syllable of a bisyllabic word in their mother tongue is stressed, even though they can pronounce it correctly. This suggests that they can spontaneously retrieve the word from long-term memory together with its sound pattern and stress pattern, as a compact package (cf. the TOT phenomenon, Chapter 3). But it does not reverberate in their processing space to enable them to inspect it from a higher standpoint.[2] Some professors, in their published work, consistently prefer to rely on the meanings rather than the sounds of poetry. The plain fact seems to be that even at this level of students and professors of literature there are individual differences in this respect, and there are persons who do not seem to feel at ease with phonetic representation, and seek to fall back as frequently as possible on semantic coding. This is most conspicuous in the response of various readers to what Snyder (1930) called "hypnotic poetry". In

---

2.   While proofreading this book I came across Stephen Nadeau's (2012) study, that may illuminate the neural mechanism underlying the two kinds of coding, as well as the word retrieval mechanism discussed in Chapter 3. It presents a neuropsychological model that predicts two pathways enabling the naming of concepts. "A model in which the only link from the concept representations domain to the articulatory motor domain is the direct one cannot account for observations that normal subjects exhibit phonologic slips of the tongue". "Further evidence of two pathways supporting naming of concepts has been provided by a subject who, depending upon type of verbal cue provided, could be induced to use either the whole word (direct) naming route or the phonologic (indirect) naming route" (Kindle eBook) – producing, however, only clusters of similar-meaning words or similar-sound gibberish. Normal subjects can, of course, freely switch from one route to the other. Yet, some persons may be more at ease with the direct naming than with the phonologic route (this seems to be the case with poor readers too). The above-mentioned students may have a smoother access to the direct naming than the phonologic route. Just now I am involved in a controversy with an anonymous referee of one of my papers, who claims he cannot hear that a nasal vowel is more reverberant than its oral counterpart.

a number of poems by Poe, Coleridge, and certain other poets, many readers are inclined to "attend away" from the meaning of the words, and to become "spell-bound" by their sound. The reader feels as if he were entangled by the sounds of these poems, and tends to perceive their meaning relatively dimly. However, some other readers respond quite differently: they may find the sound effects of the same poems rather boring and unemotional. Such differences may be due to a person's being high or low on the personality variable "absorption" (Glicksohn, Tsur & Goodblatt 1991; Tsur 2006: 130–137). Still other readers may ignore all in all the sound effects of the same poems and seek to account for their significance solely in terms of their meaning. More often than not, such interpretations will also ignore the possible hypnotic effect of these poems. Such an inclination to account for the significance of poems solely in terms of their meaning may also be an indication of a basic preference for semantic rather than phonetic coding.

Let me adduce an illuminating piece of direct evidence for this tendency, on the professor level. In my research on the rhythmical performance of poetry I explored two recordings by John Gielgud of the last line of Shakespeare's Sonnet 129. I made Gielgud's readings available on my webpage and sent a request to the PSYART and Coglit lists to respond to them. I received all in all five fairly detailed responses. An outstanding psychoanalytic critic who had extensively written on this poem commented at the end of his response: "My attention was called to the rhythm of the second reading and it was somehow distracting and thereby detracting".

In Chapter 7, on Hopkins's "The Windhover", I apply many of the distinctions propounded in the present chapter, in an attempt to explore the contribution of semantic and auditory precategorial information to the mystic effect of the poem. As to the rich precategorial auditory information, I am experimenting with weakening intonation boundaries to find out whether it tends to increase what is perceived as overtone interaction across them.

2.6   Summary and conclusions

In this chapter I made an attempt to explore what our ear tells our mind when reading poetry. Researchers in instrumental phonetics distinguish a speech mode and a nonspeech mode of listening. I suggest that there is a third, poetic mode of speech perception too, where people attend to the clear-cut phonetic categories, but some of the inarticulate, precategorial auditory information does reach awareness. This auditory information has a mysterious effect on the perceptual and expressive qualities of the speech sounds. The business of this chapter has been to explore an elusive aspect of this mysterious effect and the underlying cognitive mechanisms, epitomized as "some alliteration patterns we hear as 'click', some as 'clink'". The basic fact in such an endeavour is that there is a string of phonetic categories underlain by a stream of precategorial auditory information. In such a hierarchic structure there always lurks the danger of reductionism. The critic is prone to merely restate in acoustics-language (or brain-language) what could be said in phonetics-language. Cognitive Poetics is particularly susceptible to this danger. I claim that in this case there is no automatic one-to-one corre- spondence between the two levels of information. The precategorial information may affect, or fail to affect, awareness in a variety of ways. First, there are two context-independent ways. Some speech sounds are highly-encoded, some lowly- encoded; that is to say, in some speech sounds little or no precategorial informa- tion reaches awareness, in some – relatively much. Likewise, some personality styles are more, some less tolerant of unique uncategorized sensations. The most elementary context concerns co-articulation: Vowels in consonantal context are perceived as more encoded than isolated vowels; the same is true of continuants in vocalic context. As to the effect of the contents, the same lowly-encoded speech sounds may be heard with their precategorial auditory information reverberat- ing in the background when referring to some sound or noise, or, in a neutral context may be perceived as a unitary phonetic category. There are techniques by which overtone interaction can be enhanced or inhibited, most notably by simi- larity, proximity, and Gestalt boundaries. If a subsequent stimulus is very similar to the preceding stimulus, it may generate an enhanced response; if it is moder- ately similar, lateral inhibition sets in. If the similar stimuli are too close together, in nonaesthetic memory experiments it may cause confusion; they will integrate rather than inhibit, and the subject will lose valuable information. Such confusion may become exceptionally effective musical fusion in an aesthetic context. Over- tone interaction, just like colour interaction, increases within the boundaries of a good Gestalt while it is inhibited across its borders. Both poets and vocal perform- ers have their own techniques to weaken or strengthen the boundaries, so as to increase or decrease the interaction. If an alliteration pattern is under the control of a strong Gestalt, it may keep down the resonance; the weaker the Gestalts, the less restrained the reverberation of the precategorial sound information. Such voiced stops as [b, d, g] consist of an abrupt articulatory gesture and a stream of periodic voicing. Consequently, the reader or the poet has an option to switch between three aspects, as the context may demand: they may attend to a unitary voiced stop, or to the abrupt articulatory gesture, or to the periodic stream of voicing. [b] is perceived as more reverberating in a "murmuring" context than in a "murdering" context; Verlaine and Hugo attend to opposite aspects in [d] and [g], for opposite emotive effects. Consequently, speech sounds and repetitive patterns may be per- ceived as opaque and tightly packed together in certain circumstances; in other circumstances as plastic and freely reverberating. This chapter has explored what reasons can be given to support one impression rather than another.

CHAPTER 3

The TOT phenomenon

A psycholinguistic model of poetry

3.1 The TOT phenomenon

One aesthetically significant aspect of precategorial information is that it can be perceived as some intense, lowly-differentiated thing-free presence. This is particularly important in certain kinds of mystic or symbolist poetry. I found that the most convenient way to make students aware of this fact is to ask them to recall an instance when they had a word on the tip of their tongue and couldn't recall it. When I ask them what it feels like, most of them have a vivid recollection of being engulfed by an intensely felt lowly-differentiated presence which couldn't be related to any one of the senses – perhaps to the tactile sense, felt all over the surface of their body. And, not quite surprisingly, some of them reported a sense of frustration. When the forgotten word comes to mind, that peculiar feeling disappears. A similar process was reported in the introduction by Helen Keller whose peculiar sensations on her tongue and fingertips disappeared when she mastered, e.g. the word *ice cream*, at the age of six. Language is all categories – semantic and phonetic. The Tip of the Tongue phenomenon is the quintessence of exposure to precategorial information in the verbal mode. This phenomenon occurs when the semantic and phonetic features fail to "grow together" into a clear-cut word, that is, the combination of clear-cut semantic and phonetic categories. Here we are exposed to a phenomenon which is all diffuse precategorial information, and is associated with an intense, lowly-differentiated perceptual quality.

The TIP-OF-THE-TONGUE phenomenon is associated, in the mind of the general public, with Freud's *Psychopathology of Everyday Life*. But already William James had some illuminating comments on it. Freud (1916) explored those "slips" of consciousness when one has got a word on "the tip of the tongue", but it would not come into mind. He has got the word somewhere in the preconscious mind, but he cannot bring it to the surface. This particular missing word kindles in him a particular feeling. I would say it has a particular flavour, which cannot be rivaled by any other word; no synonym may satisfy that particular feeling of want, except that one, particular, awaited word. The greater charge of mental energy the suppressed word has, the clearer may be the special feeling. Once the suppressed word or meaning reaches full consciousness, the feeling or flavour disappears. A point similar to Freud's was already made by William James: "And the gap of one word does not feel like the gap of another, all empty of content as both might seem necessarily to be when described as gaps [...]". And again, "But the feeling of an absence is *toto coelo* other than the absence of a feeling [...]. The rhythm of a lost word may be there without a sound to clothe it [...]" (quoted by Ehrenzweig 1965: 10). The great Hungarian poet Miklós Radnóti suggests a similar process as part of the creative moment in poetry. In the afterword to his collection of brilliant poetry translations, *In the Footsteps of Orpheus*, he quotes a verse line from Vergilius in his own translation, to indicate that creative moment:

> Its tune already fumbles in my ear, I'm still searching for the words.[1]

In discussing poetic and figurative language, linguists sometimes use such terms as "suppressed" or "secondary" meanings. It is suggested here that "suppressed" or "secondary" meanings may rely on the same underlying cognitive mechanism, and have similar perceived effects as the TOT phenomenon, with one all-important difference though: the TOT experience may contain an element of frustration that is absent in "mere" suppressed meanings characteristic of the language of poetry. "It is a gap that is intensely active", says James of TOT. In order to indicate the underlying mechanism, I shall extensively quote from Roger Brown's paper on TOT.

Brown (1970) in collaboration with David McNeill carried out an ingenious experiment. "The idea of the experiment is that when examining the words that come to mind when searching for one that does not come we should be able to discover the principles governing the classification system utilized in our memory" (274). It will be recalled that Freud claimed to discover by essentially the same technique the unconscious psychodynamic motives of *his* informants. How can one possibly "neutralize" the personal elements in such an experiment? This is, perhaps, the simplest and most ingenious part of Brown's and McNeill's experiment. They compiled a list of words that occurred at least once in four million, but no more frequently than once in a million. In order to induce a TOT state in potential subjects, they read out the definitions of these words to groups of Harvard and Radcliff undergraduates, and requested those who entered in such

---

1. There is considerable discrepancy between this translation and Vergilius' original: "*numeros memini, si verba tenerem*" (I remember the notes, had I the words sure – translated by J.W. MacKail). Thus, the verse line describes only Radnóti's, not necessarily Vergilius' creative experience. Note, however, that MacKail's is a plain prose translation, whereas Radnóti's renders in Hungarian the quantitative dactylic hexameter of the Latin verse.

a state to record certain data concerning their responses. The subjects produced words of SIMILAR MEANING (SM) as well as of SIMILAR SOUND (SS). To explain the data they collected, Brown and McNeill propose a model of a dictionary in which words are entered on keysort cards instead of pages and the cards are punched for various features of the words entered. "With real cards, paper ones, it is possible to retrieve from the total deck any subset punched for a common feature by putting a metal rod through the proper hole. We will suppose that there is in the mind some speedier equivalent of this retrieval technique" (292). For the word *sextant*, e.g., the following definition was read: "A navigational instrument used in measuring angular distances, especially the altitude of sun, moon and stars at sea". The SM words included: *astrolabe, compass, dividers* and *protractor*. The SS words included: *secant, sextet* and *sexton*. "The problem begins with a definition rather than a word and so the subject must enter his dictionary backward". One may imagine that it is somehow possible to extract from the definition a set of semantic features such as 'navigation, instrument, having to do with geometry'. "Metal rods thrust into the holes for each of these features might fish up such collection of entries as *astrolabe, compass, dividers* and *protractor*. This first retrieval, which is in response to the definition, must be semantically based and will not, therefore, account for the appearance of such SS words as *sextet* and *sexton*" (*idem*, 293).

> In the TOT case the first retrieval must include a card with the definition of *sextant* entered on it but with the word itself incompletely entered. The card might, for instance, have the following information about the word: two-syllables, initial s, final t. The entry would be a punchcard equivalent of s_ _т. Perhaps an incomplete entry of this sort is James's "singularly definite gap" and the basis of generic recall.

The subject with a correct definition, matching the input, and an incomplete word entry will know that he knows the word, will feel that he almost has it, that it is on the tip of his tongue. If he is asked to guess the number of syllables and the initial letter he should, in the case we have imagined, be able to do so. He should also be able to produce SS words. "The features that appear in the incomplete entry (two-syllables, initial s, final t) can be used as the basis for a second retrieval. The subset of cards defined by the interaction of all three features would include cards for *secant* and *sextet*. If one feature not used then *sexton* would be added to the set".

> Which of the facts about TOT states can now be accounted for? We know that subjects were able, when they had not recalled the target, to distinguish between words resembling the target in sound (SS words) and words resembling the target in meaning only (SM words). The basis for this distinction in the model would seem to be the distinction between the first and second retrievals. Membership in the first subset retrieved defined SM words and membership in the second subset defined SS words.

Brown reports that when a subject produced several ss words but had not recalled the target he could sometimes accurately rank-order the ss words for similarity to the target. The model offers an account of this ranking performance. "If the incomplete entry *sextant* includes three features of the word then ss words having only one or two of these features (e.g. *sexton*) should be judged less similar to the target than ss words having all three of them (e.g. *secant*)."

> When the ss word has all of the features of the incomplete entry (as do *secant* and *sextet* in our example) what prevents its being mistaken for the target? why didn't the subject who produced *sextet* think that the word was "right"? Because of the definitions. The forms meet all the requirements of the incomplete entry but the definitions do not match.

The TOT state often ended in recognitions; i.e. the subject failed to recall the word but when the experimenter read out *sextant* the subject recognized it as the word he had been seeking. The model accounts for this outcome as follows.

> Suppose that there is only s_ _T in memory, plus the definition. The experimenter now says (in effect) that there exists a word *sextant* which has the definition in question. The word *sextant* then satisfies all the data points available to the subject; it has the right number of syllables, the right initial letter, the right final letter, and it is said to have the right definition. The result is recognition [...]

Subjects in a TOT state sometimes recalled the target word without any prompting. The incomplete entry theory does not admit of such a possibility.

> If we suppose that the entry is not s_ _T but something more like *Sextan*T with the italicized lower-case letters representing the faint-entry section) we must still explain how it happens that the faintly entered, and at first inaccessible, middle letters are accessible in the case of recall.

> Perhaps it works something like this. The features that are first recalled operate as we have suggested, to retrieve a set of ss words. Whenever an ss word (such as *secant*) includes middle letters that are matched in the faintly entered section of the target then those faintly entered letters become accessible. The match brings out the missing parts the way the heat brings out anything written in lemon juice. In other words, when *secant* is retrieved the target entry grows from *sextan*T to SEX*t*ANT. The retrieval of *sextet* brings out the remaining letters and the subject recalls the complete word – SEXTANT.

There is one more outcome of the TOT experiment that has not yet been explained: Subjects whose state ended in recall had, before they found the target, more correct information about it than did subjects whose state ended in recognition. Brown explains this as follows.

> More correct information means fewer features to be brought out by duplication in ss words and so should mean a greater likelihood that all essential features will be brought out in a short period of time.   (ibid., 293–296)

The foregoing experiment and model strongly support certain contemporary linguistic theories that conceive of words as of bundles of semantic and phonological features. That is, it strongly suggests that not only a theory based on Christine Brooke-Rose's discussion of noun metaphors (mentioned in Chapter 1), but also the theory of metaphors based on a "componential" or "semantic feature" analysis may have psychological reality.[2] All the evidence produced strongly suggests that some of these features are stored in long-term memory in such a way that they are available separately. Likewise, additional information appears to be stored separately, as e.g. information about abstract structures as stress-pattern, number of syllables, the order of phonemes (or letters). "Partial recall is necessarily also *generic* since the class of words defined by possession of any *part* of the target word will include words other than the target. [...] The whole word is represented in *abstract form recall* but not at the letter-by-letter level that constitutes its identity. The recall of an abstract form is also necessarily *generic*, since any such form defines a class of words extending beyond the target" (p. 277).

When the retrieval of a word is smooth and undisturbed, all the separately stored pieces of information emerge "grown together", as a single, complete and unique word. The speaker is unaware of its various features. The TOT state occurs when the "entry" is incomplete and/or the merger of features is impeded. Then there is an intense but undifferentiated, diffuse feeling: perception is directed toward many of the features and abstract forms, but is focussed on none of them. The greater the number of retrieved semantic and phonological features, the more intense the feeling; that is, as long as they are kept apart, and do not reach full consciousness. I wish to propose this state of impeded merger as a model for the intense yet undifferentiated feeling that attends with suppressed and/or divergent meanings reinforced by divergent sound textures. The completely retrieved *concrete* word has a distinct sound pattern and distinctly defined meaning. In this sense, it has a strong shape, "*prägnant gestalt*". The divergent meanings and sounds of the diffuse word are abstract, generic, have weak gestalt.

---

2. Victoria Fromkin (1973), based on another "psychopathology" of everyday life on the *slips of the tongue*, has found further evidence for the psychological reality of both of words as bundles of semantic features, and of words as bundles of phonological features. I have elsewhere discussed at some length the poetic issues implied by her findings (Tsur 1992b: 69–70; 2004).

I have suggested, then, that the intense yet undifferentiated feeling experienced while reading a highly divergent poem in which we perceive an intense emotional or mystical quality might be, psycholinguistically, a corollary of some dense texture of semantic and phonological features which, for some reason, are prevented from "growing together" into a distinct word that denotes some clear-cut notion. The greater the number of "retrieved" but diffuse features, the more "saturated" their texture is.

Now how can one possibly prevent the large number of semantic and phonological features from converging in a single word? Just as composers, according to Schönberg, create the "still unheard" overtone to which no fundamental corresponds, through mingling the overtones of dissimilar tones; in some (exceedingly divergent) poems all the retrieval phenomena of the TOT state may be present, and with so ample information that in ordinary TOT state it ought to end, beyond doubt, in recall. And as long as no "recall" takes place, an unusually intense, "saturated" feeling may be experienced. In our case, however, "recall" is impossible for a very simple reason: there exists no word that would match all the data, and the diffuse features *must* remain in an unintegrated state. English romantic poetry, and French Impressionistic poetry even more so, frequently took advantage of this mechanism. They could "saturate" the "thick texture" of diffuse features with no risk of "successful recall" of the non-existent word.

The most obvious technique to "destroy" things and generate "thing-free" qualities in verbal arts is the use of metaphor. Some theories of metaphor conceive of poems as of sequences of words and images from which certain common qualities may be *abstracted*. The mere fact that certain images occur side by side may induce the cooperating reader to abstract from them certain qualities; an abstract category is brought to mind, just as in the TOT state, through the mentioning of its members. But, by contrast with the TOT phenomenon, the conjuring up of the abstract category may be the main purpose, and there may be, sometimes, no additional, "suppressed" member at all, to be recalled. Wimsatt's theory of the "Concrete Universal" may be quoted as a case in point.

> For behind a metaphor lies a resemblance between two classes, and hence a more general third class. This class is unnamed and most likely remains unnamed and is apprehended only through metaphor. It is a new conception for which there is no other expression. Keats' discovering Homer is like a traveler in the realms of gold, like an astronomer who discovers a planet, like Cortez gazing at the pacific. The title of the sonnet, "On First Looking into Chapman's Homer" seems to furnish not so much the subject of the poem but the fourth member of

> a central metaphor, the real subject of the poem being an abstraction, a certain
> kind of thrill in discovering, for which there is no name and no other description,
> only the four members of the metaphor pointing, as to the center of their pattern.
>
> (Wimsatt, 1964:79–80)

Insofar as that particular abstraction ("the thrill") is abstracted from things or words or situations which, on a more concrete level, are perceived as belonging to fundamentally different categories (unlike "chairness", for instance, that is abstracted from chairs only), it is perceived as a thing-free quality. Underlying the phenomenon discussed by Wimsatt it is easy to recognize the mechanism by which the common features are extracted from SIMILAR MEANING words in the TOT state.

The psycholinguistic mechanism underlying this phenomenon can be illuminated by experiments related to the Stroop effect as well. There is convincing experimental evidence that the superordinate categories of parallel entities is present, simultaneously though subliminally, in active memory. This can be demonstrated with the help of the Stroop test, which has revealed an involuntary and subliminal cognitive mechanism of some interest for our present inquiry. In this test, colour names (e.g. "yellow") are written in different-coloured ink (e.g. "blue"). If the subject is required to read the word, he has little interference from the ink colour, but if he is required to name the ink colour, he has great difficulty because of interference from the colour name (Posner 1973:26). The findings of this experiment suggested a further study, concerning the automatic activation of superordinates. In this study, subjects were presented with lists of three words which they were to remember. The three words came from the same category (e.g. "maple", "oak", "elm"). The subjects were then shown one of the words in the list (e.g. "oak"), the name of the category (e.g. "tree"), or a neutral word unrelated to the list. These visually presented words were written in coloured ink. The subjects were asked to name the colour of the ink as rapidly as possible. Based on the Stroop effect, it was expected that if the word shown to the subject was in activated memory, the subjects would have greater trouble inhibiting a tendency to vocalise the word name. Such a tendency would slow their response to naming the ink colour. The experimental data showed that words from the list ("maple", "oak", "elm") and the category name ("tree") produced greater interference with colour naming than control words. This study suggests that the category name is activated when a list word is presented, without any requirement to do so (Posner 1973:86). Such abstractions extracted from parallel entities are highly functional from the cognitive point of view: they facilitate the preservation of parallel entities in active memory. One might perhaps cautiously suggest that the same principle may be extended to *ad hoc* categories too. Such an assumption, however, requires further experimental testing.

Now notice that not only the SM aspects of the TOT phenomenon are relevant to the reading of poetry. The experiment provides ample evidence of subliminal sound-matching during the TOT state.

> When complete recall of a word has not occurred but is felt to be imminent there is likely to be accurate generic recall. Generic recall of the *abstract form* variety is evidenced by the subject's knowledge of the number of syllables in the target and the location of the primary stress. Generic recall of the *partial* variety is evidenced by the subject's knowledge of letters in the target word. This knowledge shows a bowed serial-position effect for it is better for the ends of a word than for the middle and somewhat better for the beginning positions than for the final positions.   (Brown 1970: 291)

The mechanisms underlying generic recall seem to be at work in poetry too, but quite differently. In partial generic recall sounds, or strings of consecutive sounds, are matched with similar strings in suppressed "target words". In poetry too, sound-matching takes place simultaneously with the matching of semantic features, but their targets typically diverge, to varying degrees. In the following notorious line by Milton, there are a number of semantic features common to *all* the various items; in addition, *pairs* of nouns are matched through similar strings of sounds:

Rocks, caves, lakes, fens, bogs, dens, and shades of death.

In the case of *sextant, sexton, secant, sextet* the matching of the sounds of the ss words helped to enhance the sounds of the target word. Here too, where there is no target word, pairs of words may be matched, enhancing their sounds. Consider such pairs as *fens-dens, dens-death, rocks-lakes, rocks-bogs* (notice that /k/ and /g/ are contrasted only by the feature [±VOICED]), *lakes-caves (shades)*. The matching of sounds, however consistent, manifests no patent purpose here; it does not point in the direction of any *target*-word. There is here ample sound material for the "retrieval" of a forgotten word, had there *been* any. However, here they result in a thick texture of divergent sound patterns rather than the recall of a single "convergent" word. Items in this list also share such semantic features as unfavorable, and perhaps unwholesome, topographic conditions. Thus, a saturated feeling of imminence, of an immensely active "on-the-brink" state is made to endure beyond its natural momentary existence. Notice that the divergent, "emotional" texture of this line is amplified by the suspension of opposition between metrical prominence and non-prominence for a stretch of six syllables, even though some performers may accentuate syllables 1–4–6 or 2–4–6, so as to preserve the iambic lilt. In terms of our discussion in Chapter 2, such blurring of the rhythmic gestalt may boost the interaction of shared phonetic and semantic features.

One of the possible effects of the TOT experiment (not demonstrated at a significant level) is analogous to the repetition of sound clusters in changing orders, quite frequent in poetry.

> A subject trying to find the word *ambergris* thinks of *Seagram*. The usual sorts of resemblance that constitute the main effects of the experiment (short strings of identical letters at the beginning and ends of the words) are absent. Still there is a resemblance that can hardly be accidental. All the letters of *Seagram* are contained in *ambergris*. The word found seems to utilize the same letter-stock or sound as the word sought without regard for order. This is a fascinating outcome because it corresponds with one kind of rather common reading mistake and, together with the reading mistakes, it suggests that order may be a feature of a word that is stored independently of letters.   (Brown 1970: 275)

Sound clusters repeated in poetry without regard for order is, then, a further step along the convergence/divergence spectrum, either because it amplifies the diffusion of perception, or because the independently stored "order-feature" of words remains independent and abstract.

To be sure, occasionally it *may* happen in poetry, however divergent, that both semantic and phonological features point in the same direction of a "convergent", distinct word. Consider the last line of Baudelaire's "*Recueillement*":[3]

Entends, ma chère, entends, la douce Nuit qui marche.

As I have elsewhere suggested (Tsur, online) in a reading of this poem, the appearance of the "sweet Night" has a refreshing effect. The consonant cluster repeated in a changed order, "*ma chère-marche*", has two consonants in common with the "suppressed" word "*fraîche*", while the remaining consonant pair [m/f] are matched by virtue of their shared phonological features [+LABIAL +CONTINUOUS]. In the rich divergent texture of the poem, the reader is likely to persist in his divergent perception rather than reduce these features to the "recall" of a single convergent word, thus condensing rather than focussing the features perceived.[4]

It would appear at first sight that generic recall mechanisms of the *abstract form* variety have little relevance to our inquiry. Since there exists no uniquely identifiable word to be retrieved, one may, evidently, have no knowledge of the number of its syllables, or of the location of its primary stress. On second thoughts, however, it is precisely these features of language that are systematized into syllabo-tonic

---

3.   This poem is discussed at considerable length in a different perspective in Chapter 7.

4.   I hope my use of the terms *convergent/divergent* is self-explanatory here. I have explained them in Chapter 9 and elsewhere (Tsur 1978; 1977: 175–189, 232–238) as a pair of technical terms designating poetic structures correlated with witty and emotional qualities, respectively.

metre. Moreover, the number of syllables and the location of main stress – though dissociated from any unique word – may reach awareness *near* the line terminal. In a paper on requiredness in iambic verse (Tsur 1972), I argued that in an iambic pentameter or tetrameter line, least tension arises when syntactic break occurs at the end or the middle of the line. Otherwise, the nearer the break to the end, the greater the demand of the line upon its remaining chunk. The underlying mechanism – I claimed – is that of perceptual leveling-and-sharpening. The present analogy with the TOT state highlights another aspect of the phenomenon. Suppose there is a syntactic juncture after the fourth or fifth position of a pentameter line. The reader or listener will not have "at the tip of his tongue" the number of syllables and the location of the main stress of the next word or phrase. The possible variations of word-boundary and main stress in the next 5–6 syllables are too numerous, and the "generic recall" of the abstract forms too vague. Now suppose there occurs a syntactic juncture, or the performer fortuitously stops, after the eighth or ninth position of a pentameter line. The listener experiences something very similar to generic recall of the *abstract form* variety. He "knows" the number of syllables and the exact location in the next "word" (between quotes, because the word may turn out, eventually, to be a phrase; and there may be no main stress there at all: a poet like Donne may surprise his reader with two unstressed function-words in the last two positions, as in "Batter my heart, three person'd God; for, you").

Now, suppose the verse under consideration is *rhymed*; say, heroic couplets. In every second line there will be intense "generic recall" of the *partial* variety too, in the final position of the word. Such a conception highlights an important aspect of "antigrammatic" rhyming as expounded by Wimsatt (1964: 153 ff.; cf. also Tsur 2008: 277–281 and elsewhere). Word pairs of the same category (part of speech) and the same syntactic function constitute "tame" rhymes. The greater the number of dissimilar semantic and syntactic features in the rhyme-fellows, the more powerful the rhyme. "Tame" rhymes strike us as less "poetical", more "prosaic". Our model may account for this as follows: in poetic language (and especially in highly divergent poetry), most effects of the TOT phenomenon occur, sometimes with an amplitude that exceeds what would be sufficient to evoke successful retrieval of a word. Typically, the dissociated features of words are effectively kept apart in poetry, without possibility of surface realization in an actual word. Where rhyming is involved, the mechanisms of generic recall tend to converge in a single word, and "successful recall" is nearer than ever (this is, of course, a feeling, not a possibility). The greater the number of semantic and syntactic features that do not match in the two rhyme-fellows, the better the safeguards against the surface realization of all the features in a single word; the quasi-retrieved features persist in trembling "on the brink", as if "recall" were imminent, but might never occur. A "tame rhyme" has an ambiguous, indistinct nature, analogous to the "recall" of, say, *secant* instead of *sextant*. It is imperfect both as retrieval and as poetry. A concrete, distinct word is substituted for the intense yet vague feeling of imminence; the diffuse, "abstract" features have "grown together"; but the relief in perfect "recovery" is absent too.

3.2   Referentiality, serial position, and the "God-gifted organ-voice of England"

In his poem "Milton", Tennyson refers to him as the "God-gifted organ-voice of England". There seems to be general consensus through the ages regarding this evaluation. For over four decades I have been chasing the verbal correlates of the quality described by this phrase. In my books on poetic rhythm (Tsur 1977; 1998 [2012²]) I showed at length that in his versification Milton is one of the most deviant poets in English, both statistically and qualitatively. In Chapter 8, below, I compare the structure of Milton's and Poe's alliteration and their contribution to their respective emotional and witty qualities. In Chapter 2 I point out the possible contribution of the resulting weak gestalts to overtone fusion in Milton's alliterations. Back in 1972 I had a strong intuition that Milton's consonant clusters had something to do with this "organ-voice"; but a simple consonant count found no significant differences between his and Spenser's poetry. In what follows I will suggest a possible explanation supported by Brown's and Brady et al.'s empirical findings.

Now, let us return to Brown's suggestion that "Generic recall of the *partial* variety is evidenced by the subject's knowledge of letters in the target word. This knowledge shows a bowed serial-position effect since it is better for the ends of a word than for the middle and somewhat better for beginning positions than for final positions" (Brown 1970: 291). The accuracy of the recall of letters were tested for the following positions: first, second, third, third-last, second-last, and last. "The ss curve is at all points above the sm curve [...]. The values for the last three positions of the ss curve quite closely match the values for the first three positions. The values for the last three positions of the sm curve, on the other hand, are well above the values of the first three positions. Consequently, the *relative* superiority of the ss curve is greater in the first three positions" (Brown 1970: 286–287). One should not be surprised that words deliberately provided for their similar sounds are more similar to the target word than words provided for their similar meanings. It seems, however, to be significant that accuracy is *relatively* better at the beginning for ss words, and relatively better at the end for sm words.

A later, unrelated, experiment with listening to, and recalling monosyllabic words in a noise-masked condition shows that there is a smaller number of errors in the final position than in the initial position (Brady et al. 1983: 359). The uneven distribution of errors across the positions seems to correspond with the relative acoustic saliency of the segments. The results of research on the speech cues suggest that the consonant in final position is more clearly represented in the acoustic signal than is the initial consonant. "Syllable final formants have been observed to have transitions of greater duration [..] and greater frequency change than have initial transitions. [...] Thus final consonants may be easier to perceive because a greater amount of information specifies their identity" (ibid, 359). If further data confirm this tendency, it may have some explanatory power for certain observed facts and qualities in poetry. Thus, for instance, one prominent feature of what Tennyson described in Milton as "God-gifted organ-voice of England," is an obtrusive effect of "powerful" consonants in some passages of the strongest musical impact. The consonant clusters, not necessarily repetitive, impinge on one's perception more powerfully than e.g. in Spenser. A consonant count in these passages reveals a slightly greater number of consonants in Milton's iambic pentameter lines than in that of some other poets. This numerical difference is too small to account for the compelling perceptual difference. Oras (1957), however, found a significant difference between the position of consonant strings in stressed syllables in Milton and Spenser. Milton typically resorts to monosyllabics like *earth, arms, Heav'ns, world, rowld, hunt.* Spenser's strings of consonants typically occur at the onset of stressed syllables, as in *prey, stray, bray, speed, steed, smoke, stroke* (12). If it is true that when attention is focussed on the meaning of words more information is allocated to the final phonemes, then Milton's consonant strings are bound to be found more obtrusive upon one's attention. This effect may be amplified by the heightened interaction of gestalt-free elements in divergent poetry as Milton's, where the number of run-on lines and "thing-free qualities" is much greater than in Spenser's convergent poetry.

3.3   Summary and conclusions

It appears that we have hit here upon a more general principle underlying cognitive poetics, concerning the relationship between the nature of poetic language, cognitive processes, and psychopathological disturbances. We have discussed at considerable length a psycholinguistic mechanism which, when it functions smoothly, allows us to retrieve from long-term memory compact configurations of phonological and semantic features called *words*. When, however, the smooth functioning of this mechanism is disturbed for some reason, when, for instance, we have a word on the tip of our tongue, we have an intense diffuse feeling that seems to contain as ingredients many, or most, or all of the phonological and semantic features that were somehow prevented from growing together into the one specific word. Only the diffuse presence of these features can explain the fact that people in the TOT state are capable of producing SIMILAR-SOUND words and SIMILAR-MEANING words, as well as much other information. All this information may lead, eventually, to the recall – or, at least, to the recognition – of the word. That is why the absence of this word is experienced as a *unique* gap. I have elsewhere characterized attitudes, feelings, and affects (including feelings so conspicuously associated with the TOT state) as a highly versatile device of information-holding, integration, orientation and retrieval (Tsur 1983a: 19–24; 1992a [2008²], Chapter 1). One of the crucial uses of this mechanism is its use as a word retrieval device.

> We have access to a huge reservoir of words in our long-term memory, from which we retrieve with amazing ease and speed the words we are looking for. [...] It is the mechanism just described that underlies this high-efficiency retrieval device. This is indicated by the TIP-OF-THE-TONGUE phenomenon. Here we can see the working of the word-retrieval device in slow motion. When we have a word at the tip of our tongue, we feel an "intensely active gap" in our consciousness, which is vague and formless but, at the same time, has a uniquely definite conscious character. Any delay between the anticipation and the picking out of words from semantic memory creates a state of unfulfilled readiness, and the inner aspect of that active schema is an affect. (Tsur 1983a: 22–23; 1992a [2008²], Chapter 1).

Thus far we have described the TOT phenomenon (and the mechanism from the disturbance of which it results) as a cognitive phenomenon *par excellence*. Since Freud's brilliant *Psychopathology of Everyday Life*, the TOT phenomenon has widely been associated with Freudian depth-psychology. However, since the more recent experiments of Roger Brown and David MacNeill (Brown 1970), we have to recognize that TOT *per se* is a cognitive phenomenon. We have got here a typical cognitive process (the retrieval of words from semantic memory), which may be disrupted; this disruption is accompanied by a characteristic feeling (as mentioned above). My claim is that the disruption can be effected in the service of poetic language on the one hand, or of psychopathology on the other. One efficient way of poetic language to arouse feelings and affects is to keep semantic and phonological information in a diffuse state, that is, to prevent semantic and phonological elements from growing together into compact linguistic units. In poetic language, the experienced feeling or affect is a significant regional quality of the expressed and suppressed semantic and phonetic information, whereas in the psychopathology of everyday life, the peculiar feeling is rather a corollary of the suppression of the forgotten word, that reflects some conflict of wishes.

Freud's by now famous young man who forgot the word *aliquis* in Vergilius' line "deplored the fact that the present generation of his people was being deprived of its rights, and like Dido he presaged that a new generation would take upon itself revenge against the oppressors. He therefore expressed the wish for posterity. In this moment he was interrupted by the contrary thought": "Do you really wish so much for posterity? That is not true. Just think in what predicament you would be if you should now receive information that you must expect posterity from the quarter you have in mind. No, you want no posterity – as much as you need it for your vengeance" (Freud, 1916).

The upshot of the foregoing discussion is as follows: both poetic language and Freudian psychopathology of everyday life exploit the smooth functioning of cognitive processes as well as their disruption, each for its own purposes. Here I can't do better than repeat what I have already suggested elsewhere (Tsur 1983a: 8–9; 1992a [2008^2]: 5). When we epitomize the response to poetry as organized violence against cognitive processes, we must understand, in the first place, those cognitive phenomena that are being violated, or modified, as well as the *kinds* of violation we might expect to encounter in relation to poetry. In the second place, it is not enough to know that it is an "organized violence"; we must understand the principles of organization. Furthermore, there may also be "organized violence" against cognitive processes according to different, non-aesthetic principles. The same cognitive processes are violated in the use of poetic language and in the TIP-OF-THE-TONGUE phenomenon. However, the violence against this process is organized according to aesthetic principles in the case of poetic language, whereas it is organized (and highly organized at that) according to psychopathological principles in the case of the TOT phenomenon.

CHAPTER 4

"Oceanic" dedifferentiation and poetic metaphor

This chapter is an exercise in handling one kind of dedifferentiated thing-free qualities, as encountered in neighbouring domains: cognitive poetics and psychoanalytic aesthetics of music. Accordingly, my terms will be derived from semantics, cognitive psychology and psychoanalytic theory. Great care will be taken to emphasize the descriptive content of these terms, and to de-emphasize what the phenomena described may **mean**. It is claimed that this shift of emphasis facilitates a more adequate handling of certain sensuous elements in music and metaphor, that are usually neglected; and, by the same token, it focuses attention on what can be more readily accepted without being committed to any particular theory in the afore-mentioned domains.

Both psychotherapists and literary critics find it hard, or even confusing, to handle the qualities discussed here. An early section of this chapter will be devoted to meta-criticism: it will attempt to explain the theoreticians' cognitive processes underlying this difficulty, but no reference will be made to unconscious processes that may or may not exploit these cognitive difficulties in the service of certain quite obvious defense-mechanisms. It will be noticed, nevertheless, that the cognitive notion of "rapid" and "delayed conceptualization" expounded below have their origins in the psychoanalytic notion of "rapid" and "delayed closure". Such a conception conforms with a wider conception of cognitive poetics which I have expounded elsewhere (Tsur 1983:3–8; see now Tsur 1992a [2008[2]]:4–10 and *passim*), that there are certain mental processes, describable in cognitive terms that may be exploited or disturbed in the service of either some aesthetic or some psychopathological organization (see Chapter 3). Apropos the last pair of my examples I shall try to draw the subtle demarcation line between cognitive poetics and psychoanalytic criticism.

4.1 Rapid vs. delayed conceptualization

The Jerusalem psychiatrist Pinchas Noy has suggested what appears to be a quite unorthodox Freudian view: if someone chooses to play the flute out of all possible instruments, it does not necessarily indicate his phallic interests aroused by the shape of the instrument; it may be, as well, that he simply likes the sound of the flute (Noy, personal communication). This, in turn, does not necessarily imply that one's liking for the sound of the flute is completely meaningless from the psychoanalytic point of view; only that the interpreter must perform a much more delicate, or even elusive, task on the descriptive level before he can proceed to offer an interpretation. It is all too easy (but quite frequently counterintuitive) to isolate the characteristic shape of the flute and abstract a similar shape from the human phallus and then transfer to the flute-player's alleged motives certain concepts related to the male's generative power. It is like looking for one's keys under the street-lamp rather than in the darkness where they have been lost. It is quite possible that a person chooses to play the flute because he likes its sound. But it is more difficult to isolate the perceptual attributes of the flute-sound (as opposed to the sounds of e.g. the violin or the oboe) and indicate their possible relationships with human motives than to do the same with the "phallic shape" of the instrument.

Suppose, for instance, that a lover of classical music devotes much time and energy to the improvement of his stereo-system, drags around his speakers in his room, and keeps toying with the potentiometers of his amplifier, in search of a full sound-quality in which the bass is "thick" and has "plenty of punch", the mid-range is "smooth" and the highs are very clear. When he does not achieve this sound-quality, he has an uneasy feeling that may perhaps be described as frustration; when he achieves it, he feels some kind of intense pleasure, or even fulfillment.

An orthodox Freudian may be tempted to explain such an activity by pointing out a possible symbolic relationship between the increase of volume and power associated with amplifiers and a wish to increase one's sexual power or "potency"; he may even refer to the etymology of "potentiometer" shared with (sexual) "potency". The objection that such an interpretation does not conform with the unique conscious quality of the experience of the person concerned can be dismissed by saying that it is an unconscious wish which is, by definition, not accessible to consciousness. Such an interpretation would be akin to regarding the flute as a phallic symbol rather than considering its sound-quality as relevant to one's motives. Alternatively, Noy (personal communication) would assume that the person in question has a legitimate aesthetic interest in the sound-quality he is searching for (remember, "aesthetic" is derived from a Greek word meaning "sense perception"). The "thick" bass that has "plenty of punch" is felt to be pressing against his whole being, as if he were "plunged" or "immersed" in it.

It is not quite clear to what extent we have here actual tactile sensation arising from the sound-pressure of the "punching" bass, or some kind of synaesthetic transfer from aural to the tactile mode. The main point is that the listener may have here the sensation of an undifferentiated thing-free quality pressing against the whole outer surface of the body, or enveloping one's whole being, arousing a smooth but intense flow resulting in a heightened awareness of the close relatedness of the limbs with all the other parts of the body, having, so to speak, a heightened flow of free communication between them, (as if some barriers were removed from within one's personality), or even an heightened experience of unity in diversity of one's own personality, a feeling that may perhaps be described as totality of experience, or rather as the experience of totality.

There is a good chance that the person concerned would accept such a description and interpretation as conforming with the unique conscious quality of his experience. At the same time, the Freudian analyst could proceed and relate this experience with other experiences and personality variables, or theoretical constructs, as required by his practice. Thus, for instance, he could relate this experience with Ehrenzweig's concept (1970:135) of "a creative ego rhythm that swings between focussed Gestalt and an oceanic undifferentiation". The London psychoanalysts D.W. Winnicott and Marion Milner have stressed the importance for a creative ego to be able to suspend the boundaries between self and not-self in order to become more at home in the world of reality where the objects and self are clearly held apart (ibid).

> Seen in this way, the oceanic experience of fusion, of a "return to the womb", represents the minimum content of all art; Freud saw in it only the basic religious experience. But it seems now that it belongs to all creativity (ibid).

It should be noted that the varieties of thing-free qualities to be discussed in this chapter, whether related to the response to metaphors or to other mental experiences, may not be regarded as "oceanic experience" proper but, at best, as various degrees of approximation to that state. Moreover, the term "oceanic experience" will be used in such a way that one need not commit oneself to the entire Freudian theory in order to benefit from its use. A certain descriptive content of this term will be emphasized, whereas its combinational potentials to other aspects of Freudian theory will only be briefly indicated. The descriptive content of this term refers to an experience of fusion and dedifferentiation with which many persons may be familiar through introspection, namely, the intense experiencing of one's own self, or of relationship to one's environment, resulting from a suspension of boundaries. According to Ehrenzweig's description (1970:304), "at an extreme limit it may remove the boundaries of individual existence and so produce a mystic oceanic feeling" (for a neuro-psychological explanation see Chapter 5).

I have dwelled at considerable length on these examples not in order to say something on psychotherapy but to say something on description and interpretation, when the issues under discussion are highly elusive aspects of sensuous qualities. At first glance one might say that the difference between the "phallic" and the "sound-quality" interpretation of playing the flute is that between a conceptual and a perceptual interpretation. On second thoughts, however, it emerges that the characteristic shape too is one of the perceptual qualities of a flute; so the contrast is to be sought elsewhere. As a matter of fact, the visual shape and the sound-texture of a flute may be contrasted in several meaningful respects. First, the visual mode (through which the shape of the flute is perceived) is more highly differentiated than the aural mode (through which the sound of the flute is perceived). Second, as both Gestalt theory and the practice of the Rorschach ink-blot test would assure us, stable "good" shapes are highly differentiated, and as such may be characterized as relatively rational, whereas Gestalt-free **textures** (whether visual or aural) are lowly differentiated, and as such, may be characterized as relatively emotional. Third, the shape of a flute is "carried" by a stable object, whereas the texture of a flute's sound is what Ehrenzweig (1965) called a "thing-free" quality. Thus, stable characteristic visual shapes (especially, "good, clear-cut" shapes) are readily conceptualized (and labelled as e.g. "cylindrical"); whereas sound-textures, at their extreme at least, always remain unique unclassifiable sensations. The "phallic" interpretations of flute-playing is further facilitated by the fact that within the Freudian system there is an outstanding category with which cylindrical shapes are all too easily matched. On the other hand, it is rather difficult to isolate (and natural languages offer no labels for) perceptual features characterizing sound-textures which can readily be used across situations. Consequently, we ought to characterize the over-all contrast between the two kinds of categorization as **rapid** and **delayed conceptualization**. In the present context we ought to add a fourth contrast between the shape and sound of a flute: the latter is more closely relevant than the former to the purpose for which musical instruments are typically constructed and played. So, the phallic interpretation of playing the flute can be described in O.J. Harvey's words (1970:316) as the result of "a greater insensitivity to subtle and minimal cues and hence a greater susceptibility to false but obtrusive cues". So we should not be surprised, nor attribute it to unconscious wishes inaccessible to introspection, if we found that the interpretations of a person's behaviour resulting from delayed conceptualization are frequently more acceptable to him than those resulting from rapid conceptualization.

4.2   Poetic metaphors

The foregoing discussion bears on the explication of poetic metaphors in more than one respect. In poetic metaphor, too, the explicator is quite frequently confronted with some elusive sensuous quality. In this sensuous quality, too, it is rather difficult to isolate perceptual features that can be meaningfully related to other aspects of the text. When confronted with such a problem, the explicators of metaphors too would quite frequently have recourse to more easily accessible concepts, that are more easily related to other conceptual elements of the text. Literary critics frequently pay lip service to the sensuous element in metaphor; but when they have to cope with particular metaphors, they typically have recourse to the non-sensuous, conceptual components in them. As will be seen, in the ensuing examples critics tend to avoid discussion of the sensuous elements. Most discussions of the sensuous elements in metaphor by literary critics seem to act in accordance with the principle pointed out by Max Black (1962: 225): "when in doubt about some peculiarity of language, attribute its existence to the pleasure it gives a reader. A principle that has the merit of working well in default of any evidence".

Now it should be noticed that I have placed the foregoing discussion of sound-qualities in a psychotherapeutic context. In psychotherapy one may get confirmation or disconfirmation of one's interpretation by the person concerned, either by direct comment, or in some indirect way, as e.g. by responding or not responding to treatment, whereas the poetic text will neither make direct comments, nor yield to treatment in a literal sense of the expression. This is, in fact, my justification for beginning my argument with a rather long discussion of techniques of psychotherapeutic interpretation: to suggest that certain techniques may be more adequate in principle than others, and to illustrate this in a domain where adequacy can independently be assessed.

Whether one accepts my comments on psychotherapy or not, one thing I claim to have proposed, though not proved: that there may be certain differences between rapid and delayed conceptualization in dealing with sensory information, and that the latter is likely to be more adequate as the basis of interpretation.

Let us turn now to specific examples and consider the following two metaphors:

1.   But ye loveres, that bathen in gladnesse

(Chaucer: *Troilus & Cresseyde*, I.).

2.   Steep'd me in poverty to the very lips

(Shakespeare: *Othello*, IV. ii.).

In her brilliant paper on understanding poetic metaphors, Reinhart (1976: 396) quotes Leech's comment on Excerpt 1:

> The lovers' attitude to gladness is that they whole-heartedly commit themselves to it. Gladness is their element – they see nothing beyond it. Their delight is simple, uncomplicated, untarnished by worry, like that of a person enjoying the water – the natural gift of God.   (Leech 1969: 155)

On Excerpt 2 Reinhart (1976: 397) quotes Richards:

> For poverty, the tenor is a state of deprivation, of dessication, but the vehicle – the sea or vat in which Othello is to be steeped gives us an instance of superfluity.
> (Richards 1939: 105)

Reinhart quotes these and other instances in the interest of her meta-critical preoccupation with their use of or failure to use what she calls "focus-interpretation" and "vehicle-interpretation". But it also appears to serve well my own meta-critical preoccupations in the present chapter. Leech's explication contains components that may be felt alien to Chaucer's metaphor. Words like "attitude", "whole-heartedly", "commit" contain and emphasize the feature [+INTENTIONAL] or even [+PURPOSEFUL], whereas Chaucer's "bathen in" appears to suggest a more passive, or receptive, or even dedifferentiated state. The mental state suggested by Leech has too much of a definite direction, too much of the self-conscious. This gap between Leech's description and the perceived effect of the metaphor may be merely a matter of an appropriate meta-language. At any rate, it is brought out quite clearly if we compare Leech's passage with Reinhart's comments on it.

> Leech's interpretation of the meaning of *bathen* in this context concentrated around two properties: totality and simplicity. The idea of totality is expressed in the first sentence of his analysis in which the key phrases *whole-heartedly, becomes their element, see nothing beyond it* express the idea of a feeling which is total. This property of totality is derived from the connotation associated with *bathen* of being completely (or totally) immersed in water.
> (Reinhart 1976: 396)

Curiously enough, Reinhart attributes her own, more adequate terms, to Leech. She has "extracted" from Leech's phrases the term totality that applies more accurately to the perceived effect of Chaucer's metaphor, discarding those components that introduce mere noisy elements into the description of the metaphor. Now what is wrong with Leech's phrases is that the noisy elements in them direct attention away from the truly descriptive term *totality*. What is even worse, they may easily become "false but obtrusive cues" with the help of which the metaphor may be rapidly (but mistakenly) related to other aspects of the text. To be sure, Leech does not do anything of the sort; his analysis stops at this point, and one must grant him the benefit of doubt. But Reinhart's term *totality* is more accurate and, by the same token, more flexible. A similar tale may be told about the feature [SIMPLICITY] and its relationship to Leech's phrases (where the noisy, potentially misleading elements culminate in *the natural gift of God*). It is Reinhart who has extracted *simplicity* from phrases that contain many other, noisy attributes:

The verbs *steep* and *bathen* share the connotation of being immersed in water, but *bathen* has furthermore the connotations purity and daily activity which *steep* lacks. These connotations are the source of the property of simplicity which is stressed in the second sentence of Leech's analysis ("Their delight is simple, uncomplicated."), and no such property can be attributed to the focus of the metaphor from Othello (ibid, 397).

Richards' analysis would fare only slightly better under such a scrutiny. Unlike Leech, Richards does not introduce phrases that are bundles of (mostly noisy) features. His terms are such abstractions as *deprivation, dessication, superfluity*, which by no means are felt to be irrelevant to Shakespeare's metaphor. There is, however, a feeling that something essential is missing from Richards' account. It would appear that it is a victim of rapid conceptualization. Richards' abstractions form a neat, clear-cut contrast, which can readily be related to Coleridge's famous description of imagination as "the reconcilement of opposite or discordant qualities", while some elusive but no less essential quality seems to be missed. Hence the impression of rapid conceptualization.

Richards' paper on metaphor contains much criticism of Lord Kames's 18th century views expressed in his *Elements of Criticism*. Kames comments on Excerpt 2 as a line isolated from its context: "The resemblance is too faint to be agreeable – poverty must here be conceived to be a fluid which it resembles not in any manner" (Richards 1939: 104). Lord Kames does, then, refer to the sensuous element of the metaphor, but obviously does not know what to do with it. Richards admits that "it is not an easy matter to explain or justify that 'steep'd'" (ibid). So he, too, proceeds to look for the keys to this metaphor where there is more light: in the whole speech which "returns again and again to these liquid images" (10), and in the reconcilement of opposite or discordant qualities: "It's not a case of a lack of resemblance, but of too much diversity, too much oppositeness"; that is, when Richards can't beat Lord Kames in this particular issue, he joins him. Intuitively, however, there appears to be some quality that may justify Excerpts 1 and 2 in their own right.

In order to account for the "missing quality", we must consider the relationship between the implied vehicle *water* and the abstractions *gladness* and *poverty*. *Water* and the abstractions do have one conspicuous quality in common: they can be described in Ehrenzweig's term as "Gestalt-free" entities. One rather widespread but not very illuminating way to handle their fusion would be to say that the verbs *bathen* and *steep'd* implicitly turn their respective indirect objects (*gladness* and *poverty*) into water.

Let us consider an alternative way of handling Chaucer's metaphor, and then apply our findings to Shakespeare's. Being immersed in water (or some other liquid) arouses a sensation in the tactile mode, which is the least differentiated sensory mode. The water envelops the whole outer surface of one's body, so there is a lowly differentiated sensation on the entire surface of the skin. How can one describe the sensory aspect of these metaphors?

Although what we have here cannot be called a synaesthetic metaphor proper, the discussion of the tactile aspect of being immersed in water and its attribution to an abstract noun can benefit from studies in synaesthesia. Ullmann (1957: 266–289) explored the panchronistic tendencies in synaesthesia. His point of departure was a hierarchic conception of the senses, based on their relative differentiation: the visual sense being the most differentiated, the tactile sense being the least differentiated one. Ullmann found that in Romantic and some post-Romantic poetry there was an overwhelming tendency to transfer from the less differentiated senses to the more differentiated ones, the most frequent source-sense being the tactile. From Ullmann's findings one might predict, for instance, that phrases like *soft sounds, warm sounds, soft colours, warm colours* would be judged as more natural than e.g. *loud touch, loud temperature* (or Donne's notorious *loud perfume*), *green touch, green temperature*, or even *minor-scale touch* or *variegated temperature*. At some variance with Ullmann's explanation, I have pointed out that a principle of "the pauper's sheep" is at work here: it is precisely the senses having relatively rich vocabularies that borrow terms from the senses that have relatively poor vocabularies. The reason seems to be that speaking of the more differentiated sensory domain in terms of a less differentiated one is a powerful means of dedifferentiation. Language being a highly categorized conceptual system, it would appear to be impossible to talk about undifferentiated, pre-categorical sensory information. Talking about sounds and colours in terms of the tactile or thermal vocabularies may convey just such an impression of their undifferentiated, pre-categorical sensory aspects. When, as a result of metaphorical contradiction, the abstractions *gladness* and *poverty* cancel the material and tactile components of water, it is precisely this elusive quality of undifferentiatedness that is transferred to them (see Chapter 12).

In Excerpt 1, the temperature or any other property of the implied liquid is not specified. One "default"-effect (that is, "unless otherwise specified") of *gladness* is that it eliminates any possible unpleasurable circumstance (e.g. *bathen in chloric acid*, or *in freezing water*). In other words, the default suggestion of the metaphor would be a pleasurable bath. The verb *bathen* transfers to *gladness* the transfer feature ⟨WATER (or similar liquid)⟩. *Water* and *gladness* are compatible in that they have no characteristic stable visual shapes. They are, however, contrasted in the features [±MATERIAL] and [±TACTILE]. As a result of this contrast, the features [+MATERIAL] and [+TACTILE] are cancelled in *water*. The residual meaning will be something like "being immersed or totally enveloped in a Gestalt-free and thing-free quality that arouses an undifferentiated pleasurable feeling". It is perhaps this feeling that Leech's phrases tried to capture, but contaminated with additional components.

Submitting Chaucer's metaphor to members of a graduate seminar on figurative language, I asked the students to comment on its perceptual quality, relying on introspection. At the beginning responses were characterized by rapid conceptualization, and some of them could be traced back to "false but obtrusive cues". My silence suggesting more could be proposed, there gradually emerged signs of delayed conceptualization, and elements of Noy's interpretation of the "punching" bass and Ehrenzweig's account of the oceanic experience began to crop up. It began with comments like "it's somehow total. it's from all directions. it engulfs you". Later there were comments on feelings of the kind that had been described by Ehrenzweig as the suspension of boundaries between self and not-self, or even between various parts and layers of the self. Finally, there came comments concerning some feeling that is somehow tactile and not-tactile, something that is somehow there and isn't at the same time, that is, an undifferentiated sensation of a Gestalt-free and thing-free quality. The lesson of this exercise is: experience of the undifferentiated thing-free and Gestalt-free quality in question is accessible through careful introspection, if one is not prevented from reaching it by being satisfied with some more easily accessible conceptualization (cf. Chapters 5, 13).

A few years after having completed the present discussion, I came across Werner's paper "A Psychological Analysis of Expressive Language". At one point he reports an experiment carried out with German subjects back in 1932, "who had to report on their physiognomic experience of visually presented words" (Werner, 1978:425). One of his subjects, in response to the word *feucht* ("moist"), gave an exquisite description of the experience we are dealing with:

> In the first moment, an experience of cold-moist, I had the impression of something completely diffuse […] with a suction movement in the middle. This went hand in hand with a change in my bodily state. The surface [of my body] became peculiarly important […] somehow accentuated […] I had the feeling that the inner part of my body was not really inside, but on the periphery, which created a tension directed inwards, a kind of suction. This sensation had something directly to do with the word and its properties. It wasn't as if there were the word outside and my sensation separate from it, but these two things were one and the same. They were not similar or equal, but identical (*idem*, 426).

Before returning to Excerpt 2, let us briefly consider another metaphor by Shakespeare, which Richards quotes in a footnote by way of comparison:

3.   And steep my senses in forgetfulness

(*Henry IV. P. II.*, III. i.).

Richards assumes that here the problem of lack of resemblance between water and an abstraction is the same as in Excerpts 1 and 2. Here, however, says he, "Lethe, by complicating the metaphor removes the difficulty" (p. 103). In other words, we have here something like a metonymic transfer from "the River of Oblivion", in which one could be steeped, literally. Notwithstanding, I claim, the metaphoric contradiction between *steep* and *forgetfulness* works here in a way similar to Excerpt 1. The abstraction cancels in *water* the material components, and leaves an undifferentiated immaterial "mass", which can reinforce the impression of "dullness of senses" which King Henry is seeking in sleep. The allusion to Lethe merely increases the multiple relationship between *steep* and *forgetfulness*, and perhaps further increases the denseness and dullness of the immaterial "mass".

If we return now to Shakespeare's metaphor in Excerpt 2, we may note that being immersed in water may cause a pleasurable sensation as described above, or a disagreeable sensation of suffocation, an experience of being overwhelmed by water. *Steep* adds to the idea of immersion the suggestion of force or suddenness, or, at any rate, of downward movement. These suggestions tend to bias the conception of the state of immersion in the direction of helplessness. Likewise, the "default"-effect of the connotations of poverty is to eliminate possible pleasurable specifications of the state of being immersed. Richards, faithful to his conception of reconcilement of opposite qualities, comments on 2: "In poverty all is outgoing without income; were we 'steeped to the very lips' it would be the incomings that we would have to fight against" (ibid, 105). The feeling of suffocation in both water and poverty might be a much more immediate sensation.[1] Notice that in Excerpt 3 the pleasurable or unpleasurable quality of the experience is determined by whether forgetfulness is considered pleasurable. In Excerpt 2, the suggestion of suffocation is reinforced by *to the very lips*. Apart from this, *Steeped me in poverty* is subject to a process similar to *bathen in gladnesse*: the abstraction cancels in *water* the features [+MATERIAL] and [+TACTILE] and leaves the undifferentiated sensation of a Gestalt-free and thing-free quality, threatening with the suspension of boundaries between self

---

1. Two aspects of the relevance of suffocation should be pointed out. First, suffocation applies literally to "being immersed in water"; to *poverty* it applies only metaphorically. After the deletion of the irrelevant features we get the notion of being deprived of something that is utterly vital; this notion applies to both states literally, and is transferred to *poverty*. Second, *poverty* is a highly abstract state that cannot be immediately experienced, only inferred from a variety of more concrete and specific states. In Shakespeare's metaphor, an immediately experienced physical sensation (of e.g. contracting, panicking muscles desperately struggling to keep oneself alive) may be transferred to *poverty* from *suffocation*.

and not-self. It is an experience that points toward what may be characterized in Ehrenzweig's words as "Oceanic dedifferentiation [that] is felt and feared as death itself".

4.3   Oceanic imagery in *Faust*

In this section I propose to utilize Ehrenzweig against Ehrenzweig in a brief discussion of "oceanic" imagery in *Faust*. Ehrenzweig refers several times to the Homunkulus-episode in *Faust Part Two*. It seems to have an enormous grip on his imagination, because "Nowhere in literature is there a more condensed image of the self-creating and self-scattering womb, or rather the divine parentless child identified with the womb from which he delivers himself in a threefold act of birth, love and death" (Ehrenzweig 1970: 215). Since Homunkulus appears as one of the *dramatis personae* (and not as a figure of language) over substantial stretches of time, engages in dialogues and longer speeches, I shall quote here only one of Ehrenzweig's several summaries of the episode:

> The chemical manikin, Homunkulus, achieves his own suicidal rebirth in love. I have already mentioned the extreme oceanic undifferentiation of the episode. Homunkulus is still unborn, enclosed in a glass phial which can become incandescent and lift itself into the air (this is an additional phallic symbolism). The manikin achieves rebirth by shattering his glass in a fiery explosion at the feet of the sea goddess, Galatea, amidst a general scene of orgiastic self-abandon.
> (Ehrenzweig, 1970: 215)

We must distinguish in this account between the **immediate presentation** of an undifferentiated state, and the **differentiated idea** of an undifferentiated state. Had Ehrenzweig characterized only the events conveyed in the last sentence of this quotation as "oceanic undifferentiation", we may have accepted it as a description of the achievement of such a state. But when he concerns himself with the image suggested in the last sentence but one (including the suggestion of "phallic symbolism"), or when he speaks of Homunkulus as of the man-made manikin "who is still unborn and encased in the glass womb he carries about" (ibid, 199), we may regard it at best as the differentiated idea of an undifferentiated existence in the womb, that is, an allegory of an oceanic state.

This conclusion is warranted by Ehrenzweig's own account of the oceanic experience as quoted in the first section of the present chapter. The crucial point of my argument should rely on the opposition of "oceanic undifferentiation" with "focussed Gestalt". The stable glass case with a characteristic human shape in it may, perhaps, represent a "return to the womb", and thus stand for "oceanic undifferentiation"; but it presents the audience or the reader with some focussed, well differentiated Gestalt. Thus, far from being an "experience of fusion", of suspending "the boundaries between self and not-self", this image of Homunkulus represents a state in which "the objects and self are clearly held apart", the glass case serving to enhance this separation. From such a focussed, stable shape one may perhaps abstract the idea of the "return to the womb", but not perceive the experiencing of fusion and undifferentiation. Hence the allegoric character of the image.

So, there appear to be two alternative ways of getting "oceanic" imagery into a poem. Either some **differentiated stable visual shape**, as in the image of the encased Homunculus, from which a visual resemblance to the unborn child in the womb may be inferred, or some dedifferentiation-process that "suspends many kinds of boundaries and distinctions; at an extreme limit it may remove the boundaries of individual existence and so produce a mystic oceanic feeling" (Ehrenzweig, 1970: 304). The present Chapter has discussed a metaphoric technique of such a suspension of boundaries; and Goethe did have recourse in *Faust* to this technique. In my book (Tsur 1992a: 267–270; 329-344 [2008²: 3005–308; 360–382]) and in a German paper (Tsur, 2006) I discuss at length the imagery of *Faust*, Part I; here I only want to quote a single passage, in which a crucial metaphor concerns immersion in an abstraction, that seems to lead to mystic insight.

> 4. *Die Geisterwelt ist nicht verschlossen;*
> *dein Sinn ist zu, dein Herz ist tot;*
> *Auf! bade, Schuler, unverdrossen,*
> *die ird'sche Brust in Morgenrot;*
>
> (Faust part one, 443–446).

> The spirit-world no closures fasten –
> Thy mind is shut, thy heart is dead;
> Disciple, up! Undaunted, hasten!
> Bathe mortal breast in Dawn's first red!
>
> (trans. Bayard Taylor).

In Excerpt 4, the undifferentiated experience of being immersed in a "thick" thing-free and Gestalt-free entity is reinforced by two of its aspects. First, the abstraction that acts to cancel the material aspects of *water* does have a sensory attribute: colour. Its effect here is to increase the "density" of the "thick texture" of the thing-free entity into which one is to be plunged, and so intensify the resulting undifferentiated sensation. Second, this abstraction itself is part of a large-scale spatial scene. Perhaps the most conspicuous condition in which abstract nouns may assume a lowly-differentiated character is when they occur in the description of a concrete, specific landscape, in which the speaker (or perceiving consciousness) is in an intensive relation to his environment. In Excerpt 4, the redness of the morning both provides the abstraction and indicates the concrete landscape, without mentioning any object that may have some stable characteristic visual shape (cf. Chapter 5).

Here we might pause for a moment and reflect again on my use of psychoanalytical terms. With relation to Excerpt 4, "oceanic undifferentiation" is used as a descriptive term. It refers to the structure of imagery or figurative language and its perceived effects. With relation to Homunkulus encased in the glass phial it is used as an interpretive term. It refers to a well-differentiated image in the text, and indicates its relationship to an undifferentiated experience outside the text, inside the womb, with reference to Freudian theory. Thus – as promised – some care has been taken to emphasize the descriptive content of these terms, and to de-emphasize what the phenomena described may **mean**.

Dedifferentiation and undifferentiation in themselves are cognitive phenomena, as I have shown at length elsewhere (Tsur 1983, 1992a). Such states and processes can be exploited by poetic language and organized in some aesthetic structure; or, the same states and processes can be exploited in the service of personality dynamics and/or psychopathological defenses. When the study of literature shows how cognitive processes and the sequence of words may be related to aesthetic structures, it may be called cognitive poetics. When they are related to the unconscious processes of personality dynamics, it may be called psychoanalytical criticism (cf. Tsur 1992b: Chapter 5).

4.4   Conclusions

Abstract nouns, like *gladness, poverty and forgetfulness* are normally associated with highly-differentiated conceptual thinking, whereas in Excerpts 1, 2 and 3, according to our analysis, they are associated with undifferentiated percepts. My point is that abstract nouns (as well as the process of abstraction itself) are double-edged, that is, in different environments they may give rise to incompatible, or even opposite, qualities (this point is amply exemplified in Chapters 5–6). At present, I wish to illuminate this double-edgedness by way of a final quotation from Ehrenzweig (1969: 124):

> The abstract concept of the creative thinker succeeds in overcoming common-sense differences between ordinary, concrete things. It extracts from these different things a common property which is the new abstract concept. What is not sufficiently realized is that this "seeing together" of concrete things ordinarily held apart again involves a capacity for undifferentiated percepts. The abstract image in the moment of creative insight may appear empty and blank owing to the

conscious incompatibility of the imagery. Creative abstraction differs from truly empty generalization in that it is still infested on a lower mental level with the multitude of visions from which it arose in the first place. Empty generalizations can be handled with such smooth facility because they have cut themselves off from their undifferentiated matrix.

Ehrenzweig distinguishes, then, between "creative abstraction" and "truly empty generalization". In an important sense, the difference between them is quantitative: in the degree of dissociation from the data. In another important respect, the difference is qualitative: that between undifferentiated percepts and highly differentiated concepts. The practical critic, however, cannot be satisfied with such a distinction. If he is to be engaged in something that is more than mere critical impressionism, he must find some answer to the question "How can I know whether an abstract noun is to be treated in a given text as a creative abstraction or as a truly empty generalization"? Chapters 5 and 6 contain an inquiry into the nature of the answers to this question. As for the metaphors by Chaucer, Shakespeare and Goethe discussed in the present chapter, Ehrenzweig's phrase "infested on a lower level" may offer a useful lead. The practical critic, who is confronted with a text that has no mental life of its own, cannot inquire whether *gladness*, or *poverty*, or *forgetfulness*, or the *redness of the morning* are "infested on a lower level" with anything, although he may have some vague intuition that in these metaphors they **are**. He may, however, investigate what is the source of this intuition in the text. In the present instances, the respective abstractions are "infested" by the verbs *bathe* and *steep* with diffuse sensations abstracted from the transfer-feature ⟨WATER⟩, that refers to a substance that has no characteristic stable visual shape. In this respect, *water* fuses imperceptibly with the abstractions, which likewise lack characteristic visual shapes. As a result of the conflict between the features [+MATERIAL + TACTILE] and [−MATERIAL −TACTILE] the former are cancelled, and an undifferentiated sensation (resembling the tactile sense, but dissociated from all the senses) of being totally immersed or wrapped in a Gestalt-free, material-free and thing-free quality is transferred to the abstractions. In other words, by canceling [+MATERIAL +TACTILE] in the experience of being immersed in water, it is the features [LOWER LEVEL MENTAL ACTIVITY] or [UNDIFFERENTIATED SENSATION] that are transferred to, and fused with, the abstractions.

CHAPTER 5

Deixis and abstractions

Adventures in space and time

This chapter tells the tale of my adventures with a special verbal structure in poetry: deixis combined with abstract nouns. *Deixis* is the pointing or specifying function of some words (as definite articles and demonstrative pronouns), tense and a variety of other grammatical and lexical features whose denotation changes from one discourse to another. When one says *I*, or *here*,or *now*, the denotation of these words depends on who the speaker is, and where or when he or she is speaking. By the same token, *there* and *then*, the antonyms of *here* and *now*, change their denotations too. Deixis instructs the reader to construct from the verbal material a situation in which such denotations are pertinent. My adventures began in the late 1960s with a poem called "Shepherd", by the Hebrew poet Abraham Shlonsky:

1. This width, that is spreading its nostrils.
   This height that is yearning for you.
   The light flowing with the whiteness of milk.
   And the smell of wool,
   And the smell of bread.

A more sophisticated version I found in a poem by another great Hebrew poet (of the same school), Nathan Alterman:

2. This night.
   The estrangement of these walls.
   A war of silences, breast to breast.
   The cautious life
   Of the tallow candle.

When I read such poetic texts, I have an intense sensation. As a teacher, I had here two problems. First, how can I explain with words the nature of this sensation? Second, how can I make my students *feel* this sensation, not merely repeat my words? To this end, I have developed the following teaching strategy. I tell my students: "Say about this stanza [or line] anything you feel relevant". I ask no guiding questions. Since it is sometimes difficult to suppress some response of assent,

I add "Whenever I say "yes", it means that I have understood, not necessarily that I agree". At some point they begin to produce responses that witness to perceptions similar to mine. (See also Chapters 4 and 13.).

At first, most students point out that "there is an intense emotional atmosphere" in both stanzas. "In Excerpt 2 the phrase "A war of silences, breast to breast" suggests the presence of some persons facing each other, who are hostile and don't talk"; "In this verse line attention is directed away from the persons to the atmosphere"; "Walls with no decoration may be very unfriendly"; "The phrase "The estrangement of these walls" shifts attention from the walls to the estranged atmosphere in the room". Other relevant responses include such suggestions as "The words evoke [or represent, or can be construed as] some coherent scene"; "The concrete nouns *Shepherd, wool, bread* in Excerpt 1, and *walls, breast to breast,* and *candle* in Excerpt 2 give some vague clues for a reconstruction of the physical situation"; "The deictic devices *this* and *these* have to do with the generation of a coherent scene"; "The deictic devices suggest that there is some perceiving 'I' in the middle of the situation"; "The line 'This height that is yearning for you' reinforces the presence of such a perceiving self"; "The verb *yearning* charges the abstraction with energy, and turns it into some active, invisible presence"; "There are many abstract nouns in this stanza"; "All the sentences of this stanza are elliptic". Sometimes there is even some suggestion that "the elliptic sentences have here a deictic function: they point to the percepts of the immediate situation". "*Width* and *height* are pure geometrical dimensions; but here they are somehow emotionally charged". When encouraged to provide further responses, you may hear such comments as "as if the emotional atmosphere were thick"; "I feel as if I were plunged in this thick atmosphere". Some of those who report the latter feeling say that they feel some faint tactile sensation all over their skin; some others, on the contrary, that the boundary between their body and this thick texture was suspended.

Two unusual grammatical structures are conspicuous in these two excerpts. The first one concerns the noun that occurs in the referential position (that is, syntactic position occupied by a noun phrase that anchors the utterance in extra-linguistic reality). The normal, "unmarked", syntactic structure of such constructions would be that concrete, "spatio-temporally continuous particulars" as "bread", "wool", "walls", "candle" occur in the referential position (Strawson 1967). (By "spatio-temporally continuous particulars" Strawson means objects that are continuous in space, and if you go away and come back they stay unchanged.) Such more abstract or more general qualities as "whiteness", "smell", "estrangement", should occur as attributes or predicates, e.g. "the white milk", or "the milk is white"; "the smelling wool", or "the wool has smell", or "the wool smells"; "the estranged walls", or "the walls are estranged". In these two excerpts, the adjectives are systematically turned into abstract nouns which, in turn, are manipulated into the referential position instead of the spatio-temporally continuous particulars. (I have called such transformations *topicalized attributes*, or *thematized predicate*.) Thus, in these two excerpts, not the concrete objects, but their attributes that have no stable characteristic visual shapes are manipulated into the focus of the perceiving consciousness. Such transformations are quite characteristic of poetry that displays some intense, dense emotionally-charged atmosphere. In everyday life and language we do not usually distinguish between physical objects and their attributes (or perceptual qualities). When we perceive (or speak of) the one, we are inclined automatically to identify it with the other. But the two are far from identical. One of the tasks of the "ABSTRACT of the CONCRETE" genitive phrases ("estrangement of these walls") may be to de-automatize the relationship between the attributes (or perceptual qualities) and the physical object.

The other conspicuous grammatical structure concerns elliptic sentences. Some of my students did discern in them a deictic element. This deictic element may have far-reaching poetic consequences. The function of an indicative predication is to *affect the beliefs* of the addressee, and to connect the utterance to extralinguistic reality (by suggesting "it occurred"). A noun phrase without predication places some event (or state of affairs) at the disposal of one's *perception*, without affecting the addressee's beliefs or attitudes. If the phrase contains deixis it *may*, as we have seen, connect the utterance to extralinguistic reality, without affecting our beliefs.

5.1   Sequential and spatial processing

There is a problem concerning the use of words to convey emotions. Words refer to compact concepts but, apparently, they are capable of conveying diffuse perceptions and emotions. Even such words as "emotion", or "ecstasy" communicate only the compact concepts of emotion and ecstasy, not the diffuse mental processes. We have already seen that such verbal constructs as topicalized attributes may loosen the tight relationship between objects and their attributes, or percepts that convey them. That may be one technique for overcoming this problem. But all the foregoing examples suggested that the deixis too, and the immediate space to which it points, may have to do with rendering conceptual language more diffuse. This led me to ask what is it about space perception that may render an utterance diffuse. Eventually it led me to brain research. Brain scientists claim that the two hemispheres of the human brain have different functions. The right hemisphere controls the left side of the body, while the left hemisphere controls its right side. But they differ in their mode of operation too. The left hemisphere is predominantly involved with analytic, logical thinking, especially in verbal and mathematical functions. Its mode of operation is primarily sequential. The right hemisphere, by contrast,

> seems specialized for holistic mentation. Its language ability is quite limited. This hemisphere is primarily responsible for our orientation in space, artistic endeavour, crafts, body image, recognition of faces. It processes information more diffusely than does the left hemisphere, and its responsibilities demand a ready integration of many inputs at once. If the left hemisphere can be termed analytic and sequential in its operation, then the right hemisphere is more holistic and relational, and more simultaneous in its mode of operation.
>
> (Ornstein 1975: 67–8)

> This mode of information-processing, too, would seem to underlie an "intuitive" rather than "intellectual" integration of complex entities.   (Ornstein 1975: 95)

This is a very rough, imprecise characterization of brain functions. But it may pinpoint the source of our problem. Such experiences as feelings, emotions, intuitions, and orientation are diffuse, global, non-sequential processes, and are related to the right hemisphere, whereas the words that refer to them do so *via* concepts that are compact, analytic, sequential, and are related to the left hemisphere. Telling about diffuse, global, illogical experiences becomes necessarily compact, analytic, logical. It is, however, the nature of the problem that also offers the nature of the poets' solution; and our discussion of Excerpts 1 and 2 appears to supply a typical example of this solution. Since such global activities as emotions and spatial orientation both are intimately associated with the right hemisphere, one might surmise that in these excerpts the definite spatial setting may be an instrument for transferring part of the processing of the verbal message to the right hemisphere.

At least two kinds of information about semantic categories are stored in memory: the *names* of the categories and representations of their *properties*. In the course of normal speech we perceive the representations of these properties *categorically*: we do not perceive the semantic features (or meaning-components), but a single compact semantic entity which they constitute. Ornstein brings some convincing experimental evidence that when some memory image concerning spatial orientation is called up, the right hemisphere may be activated, even though one may be engaged in some verbal activity. "Which direction a person gazes is affected by the question asked. If the question is verbal analytical (such as "Divide 144 by 6, and multiply the answer by 7" or "How do you spell "Mississippi"?"), more eye movements are made to the right than if the question involves spatial mentation (such as "Which way does an Indian face on the nickel?") (Ornstein 1975: 77). When a landscape-description and certain stylistic devices transfer a significant part of the processing of the message to the right hemisphere of the brain, representations of some or many properties of these categories escape the control of categorical perception, and constitute some global, diffuse atmosphere in a concrete landscape.[1] At the extreme of this technique, there may be no stable objects at all in the description, the concrete landscape being compellingly indicated by emphatic deictic devices only. In Excerpts 1 and 2, the abstractions "width", "height", "The light flowing with the whiteness of milk", "smell", "night", "estrangement", "cautious life" and "A war of silences" supply the intense, shape-free, fluid, diffuse input that is processed by the orientation mechanism. Hence the feeling of some thick, supersensuous texture engulfing the perceiving self.

There is no evidence in Ornstein's discussion for my conjecture concerning this effect of the orientation mechanism on poetic language. My rescue came from neuropsychological studies of religious experiences. A dominant purport of Ornstein's book is that meditation is related to the right hemisphere of the brain. At the time of writing the published version of this paper I was engaged in a study of cognitive processes in religious and mystic poetry. I had recourse to the above conception of the orientation mechanism for the solution of another paradoxical state of affairs: some meditation involves voluntary switching to a state of consciousness in which voluntary control is relinquished. At the time of writing I encountered some brain research that may support or refute this conception. Newberg, D'Aquili and Rause (2001) conducted a SPECT camera brain-imaging study (the acronym stands for Single Photon Emission Computed Tomography) of Tibetan meditators and Franciscan nuns at prayer. To my pleasant surprise, these researchers claim that what they call the "orientation association area" (OAA) is "extremely important in the brain's sense of mystical and religious experiences, which often involve altered perceptions of space and time, self and ego" (Newberg et al. 2001: 29). This would massively support my speculations based on the structure of literary texts, introspection, and earlier brain research. The brain scans taken at the peak of their subjects' meditative state, however, show a sharp reduction in the activity levels of the orientation area. These results prove that the orientation mechanism *is* involved; but the changes go opposite to the predicted direction. This was encouraging and dismaying for me, at the same time. But the authors, after gathering all the available information, came to a conclusion that lent, in fact, massive support to my hypothesis.

> We know that the orientation area never rests, so what could account for this unusual drop in activity levels in this small section of the brain? As we pondered the question, a fascinating possibility emerged: What if the orientation area was working as hard as ever, but the incoming flow of sensory information had somehow been blocked? That would explain the drop in brain activity in the region.
> (Newberg et al. 2001: 6)

---

1. A recent summary of research on lateralization with reference to poetic language can be found in Kane 2004 (2007).

Such an explanation seems consistent with our foregoing findings concerning a verbal structure that combines deixis with abstract nouns, or nouns denoting entities that have no characteristic visual shape. The deixis activates the orientation mechanism; but, instead on stable objects, it acts upon abstractions, or at least entities and qualities that are deprived of stable characteristic visual shapes. Not all subjects in this research were found to have a specific decrease in activity in the orientation area. One possible reason the researchers suggest is this: "we were limited in this study by looking only at one time point of the meditation. It is possible that in the early stage of meditation there is actually an increase in activity in the orientation area while the subject begins his focus on a visualized object. Thus, we might capture the orientation area either increased, unchanged, or decreased depending on the stage of meditation the person was actually in" (Newberg et al. 2001:176). Thus, even the conception that the abstractions serve as the rich unstable information processed by the orientation mechanism and may generate some thick, supersensuous texture engulfing the perceiving self is consistent with the findings of this neuropsychological research. We must assume that we are dealing with one of the earlier stages of this kind of information processing.

But the emerging picture is much more complicated than what we had imagined. In a later chapter, these researchers point out that there are two orientation areas, situated at the posterior section of the parietal lobe, one in each hemisphere of the brain:

> The left orientation area is responsible for creating the mental sensation of a limited, physically defined body, while the right orientation area is associated with generating the sense of spatial coordinates that provides the matrix in which the body can be oriented. In simpler terms, the left orientation area creates the brain's spatial sense of self, while the right side creates the physical space in which that self can exist.   (Newberg et al. 2001:28)

To be more precise, then, it was the left orientation association area where a sharp reduction in activity levels was found.

I consider these findings extremely valuable for interpreting the meditative experience. Mystics and meditators of many religions as well as romantic poets aspire to achieve a mental state which they describe as the suspension of the boundaries between self and not self, or the dissolution of the self in infinite space, what Ehrnzweig, following Freud, calls "Oceanic Dedifferentiation" (see above, Chapter 4). William James quotes an illuminating description of such a state from a letter by Tennyson: "all at once, as it were out of the intensity of the consciousness of individuality, individuality itself seemed to dissolve and fade away into boundless being [...] where death was an almost laughable impossibility – the loss of personality (if so it were) seeming no extinction, but the only true life" (James 1902:384n). The information conveyed in Figure 1 and in Newberg et al.'s

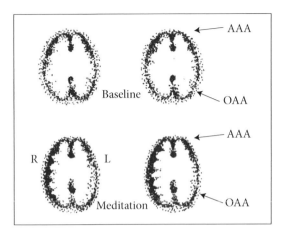

Figure 1. The top row of images shows the meditator's brain at rest and indicates an even distribution of activity throughout the brain. (The top of the image is the front of the brain and part of the attention association area, or AAA, while the bottom of the image is part of the orientation association area, or OAA.) The bottom row of images shows the brain during meditation, in which the left orientation area (on your right) is markedly decreased compared to the right side (from Newberg et al.)

discussion accounts most conspicuously for what Tennyson described as "all at once, as it were out of the intensity of the consciousness of individuality, individuality itself seemed to dissolve and fade away into boundless being" (see additional discussion of this excerpt in Chapter 14).

In this case, the boundaries of the self must be de-emphasized, and the perception of the surrounding space overemphasized. The process must begin, therefore, with activities having opposing effects in the two orientation areas: in the right area "the sense of spatial coordinates that provides the matrix in which the body can be oriented" must be reinforced; in the left area "the mental sensation of a limited, physically defined body" must be reduced. What is more, the diffuse information-processing mode originating in the right hemisphere may help to blur, as an initial step, the mental sensation of a well-defined physical boundary of the body – whatever the later stages of the cognitive and neurological processes. In imaginative processes, objects that have stable characteristic visual shapes enhance the feeling of their separateness and our separateness from them; abstractions as well as Gestalt-free and thing-free qualities enhance a feeling of the suspended boundaries.

5.2   *Time* in poetry

Let us briefly explore now one of the most venerable abstractions in poetry, *time* with its subordinate nouns ("hyponyms"), and see whether they bear out, in changing contexts, the foregoing theoretical considerations. To answer this question, we have to make a few distinctions concerning the meaning of *time*, and then relate them to our foregoing cognitive considerations. *Time* may refer (a) to a sequence (a nonspatial continuum that is measured in terms of events which succeed one another from past through present to future), (b) to the principle of that sequence, or (c) to a specific point in that sequence (see Figure 2). In sense (a), *time* is a mass noun that refuses the indefinite article, but accepts the quantifier *some* (e.g. "some time ago"); in sense (c), it is a count noun in accepting the definite and indefinite articles (e.g. "this time", "once upon a time"); in sense (b) it is usually considered as a mass noun; but, since it denotes a category that denotes a single generic principle, it resembles a proper name in uniquely referring to one referent only (it is quite frequently capitalized; see Excerpts 4 and 8 below).

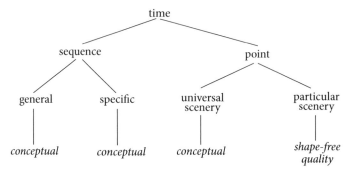

Figure 2. Time may refer to a sequence or to a specific point in that sequence. In some conditions the abstract noun tends to be perceived as a concept; in some as a shape-free perceptual quality

Thus, both in sense (b) and (c) *time* is a singular term but whereas in sense (c) it is frequently individuated in a particular situation, in sense (b) it is necessarily considered as a general object, apart from special circumstances.

Thus, in sense (b) *time* has a somewhat ambiguous status: in some respects it is a mass noun (it could be paraphrased by, e.g. "duration"), in some respects it resembles a proper noun (in uniquely referring to one referent only). In several poems by Shakespeare and Marvell, this ambiguity is resolved in the direction of proper nouns, by attributing to *time* some characteristic visual shape and some visible, often violent action. In this way, *time* becomes a superpersonal agent. By "superpersonal agent" I mean "of the nature of an individual rational being", and "of superhuman dimensions and power". In this capacity, *time* features compact consciousness, definite will, patent purpose and so on. In light of our foregoing cognitive considerations, then, we might expect *time* in these instances to be nearer to the conceptual pole. Since both sequence (of time) and purposeful actions (of a superpersonal agent) are "linear, sequential", both time-as-a-sequence and time-as-a-generic-principle will tend to be perceived as compact concepts, intellectual abstractions. When *time* denotes a particular point in a sequence, part of a situation defined here-and-now, the abstraction may be related to spatial orientation, and perceived as a diffuse quality: a mood, an atmosphere. In such instances *time* has a double function: it defines the immediate situation in time, and provides the abstraction that is to be perceived in it as a diffuse entity (see, for instance, Excerpt 9 below). Universal scenery (as in Excerpt 6 below, for instance, where we do not know where and when it occurs) will reinforce general concepts, a particular immediate scene (located in space and time) will enhance some shape-free quality. Conclusive statements, logical arguments, and clausal (verbal) syntactic structure tend to enhance the definable conceptual entity, whereas descriptive utterances, suspensive (non-conclusive) statements, and phrasal (nominal) syntactic structures tend to reinforce some mood or atmosphere, that is, elusive, sensuous *qualities*.

In some of the excerpts discussed below time generates some vague, diffuse atmosphere; and in some a compact concept or an allegorical representation thereof.

3.   Those hours that with gentle work did frame
     The lovely gaze where every eye doth dwell,
     Will play the tyrants to the very same
     And that unfair which fairly doth excel:
     For never-resting time leads summer on
     To hideous winter and confounds him there […]
                                                  (Shakespeare, Sonnet 5)

4.   Devouring Time, blunt thou the lion's paws […]
                                                  (Shakespeare, Sonnet 19)

5.   Being your slave, what should I do but tend
     Upon the hours and times of your desire?
                                                  (Shakespeare, Sonnet 57)

6.   Since brass, nor stone, nor earth, nor boundless sea,
     But sad mortality o'ersways their power,
     How with this rage shall beauty hold a plea
     Whose action is no stronger than a flower?
     O how shall summer's honey breath hold out
     Against the wreckful siege of battering days,
     When rocks impregnable are not so stout,
     Nor gates of steel so strong but Time decays?
                                                  (Shakespeare, Sonnet 65)

7.   That time of the year thou mayst in me behold
      When yellow leaves, or none, or few do hang
      Upon those boughs which shake against the cold,
      Bare ruined choirs, where late the sweet bird sang; […]
                                    (Shakespeare, Sonnet 73)

8.   But at my back I always hear
      Time's wingéd chariot hurrying near.
                                    (Marvell, "To his Coy Mistress")

9.   It is a beauteous evening, calm and free
      The holy time is quiet as a Nun
      Breathless with adoration; the broad sun
      Is sinking down in its tranquillity;
      The gentleness of heaven broods o'er the Sea.
      Listen! the mighty Being is awake,
      And doth with his eternal motion make
      A sound like thunder – everlastingly.
                      (Wordsworth, "Composed upon the Beach near Calais")

10.   Soul-soothing Art! whom Morning, Noontide, Even,
      Do serve with all their changeful pagentry […]
                      (Wordsworth, "Upon the Sight of a Beautiful Picture")

What arguments can be brought in support of our intuition that in a given passage *time* refers to some (allegorized) compact concept, or some elusive, diffuse quality? In the excerpts by Shakespeare and Marvell above, *time* is placed in what Wilson Knight (1964: 57–8) characterizes as the "eternal now". It should be distinguished from Wordsworth's "immediate now" in Excerpt 9. Whereas Wordsworth implies "at *this* particular time, at *this* particular place", Shakespeare, in speaking of "all those beauties whereof now he's king", implies "at *any* particular moment, at *any* particular place you care to consider", that is, apart from specific circumstances. There *are* instances, as in Excerpt 5, when Shakespeare refers to particular points in time. Here, however, the particular "hours and times of your desire" are in the plural and, again, apart from specific circumstances; so the phrase is turned into a *conceptual summary* of momentary emotional qualities. In Marvell's "To his Coy Mistress" (Excerpt 8), *time* is set in what appears to be a vigorous logical argument that has the psychological atmosphere of patent purpose to persuade his coy mistress to enjoy the present day, trusting as little as possible to the future. The poem plays up, on the one hand, time against timelessness, and on the other hand, sequential time against the eternal now. In Excerpt 8 *time* has been associated with a conventional visual image and an intense action, in a definite direction. Excerpt 8 exhibits the "eternal now" indicated by "always" and by the stable visual shape of "chariot" as well as by the other elements discussed in this paragraph, and *time* is perceived as the allegorical presentation of a compact, near-conceptual entity.

In Shakespeare's sonnets, *time* is frequently associated with logical arguments, occasionally introduced by some causal conjunction (such as "Since" in Excerpt 6). The logical argument also prevails in the sonnets persuading the friend to get married, in which *time* often occurs. Or, consider Excerpt 4. Here *time* acts as a superpersonal agent: two violent actions are attributed to it ("Devouring", "blunt"), the first one being part of a vocative phrase, the other being expressed by an imperative verb. Both these grammatical forms are noted for their psychological atmosphere of definite direction. In addition, there is no definite setting in which the action might take place.

In Excerpt 3, *time* acts as a superpersonal agent, constructive and, in due course, destructive, in a temporal sequence, strongly associated with several actions, partly in a universal setting, and partly in no setting at all, with a causal argument beginning in the fifth line. A different effect is produced in Excerpt 7. Here there is an atmosphere, evoked by the images; there is a prevailing autumnal quality, hovering, as it were, in the quatrain. *Time*, as could be expected, refers to a particular season of the year, not to sequential time. The season is described in spatial terms, which are descriptive rather than persuasive. The setting described fluctuates, so to speak, between a particular landscape and a *typical* representation of Autumn. There is a very detailed description of the landscape, particularizing every subtlety, attempting to achieve maximum accuracy. The four finite verbs (unlike as "blunt", "frame", or "lead" in Excerpts 3 and 4) do not denote any conclusive action of time or related objects. "Behold" denotes an act of perception; "hang" denotes a state rather than an action: "sang" denotes a continuous action that "supplies food to the senses"; "shake", although denoting physical movement, is anything but a conclusive action; furthermore, in a context of bestowing emotions upon a landscape, it suggests a *state of mind* or a *state* of being cold. In neither case it can be described as having a psychological atmosphere of certainty or patent purpose. The auxiliary verb "mayst" in Excerpt 7 is far less conclusive than "did" or "doth" in Excerpt 3. Two prominent phrasal constructions draw attention: "Yellow leaves, or none, or few …", and "Bare ruined choirs", which have no parallel in the former excerpts. The suspensive (non-conclusive) quality of the first phrase is reinforced by the hesitating tone of "…or … or", and, by the same token, by delaying the expected predicate. Thus, the Autumnal mood of decay is abstracted from parallel instances of autumnal decay, subsumed under a coherent landscape, and reinforced by the inconclusive tone of the quatrain.

Now let us return to Excerpt 9. Though a nun has, in principle, a visual shape, here she serves as a simile for *calmness*: she is not really in the scene, and cannot be seen. The "holy time" is invisible, and may show no visible sign of excitement.

In the present context of abstract qualities (no visible parts of the nun are mentioned), the excitement is devoid of physical activity, and all its immense energy is fused, to intensify these abstract qualities, with others of *calm, holiness, tranquillity*, and *solemnity*.

"The holy time" (like "beauteous evening") is, obviously, an abstraction from certain natural objects *at a given time*. It occurs in a fairly particularized situation. It is not sequential time, but a particular *now* in a particular *here*. The immediate subtlety of the minute is reinforced by the particular "tiptoe effect" of "calm excitement", which, as suggested by Cleanth Brooks (1968:6), is dependent on the particular combination of apparently incompatible elements. The abstractness of *time* is reinforced, as we have seen, by the surrounding abstract nouns, even by the adjective "holy". On the other hand, *time* serves here to shift attention away from the perceived objects of the scene to its felt quality. In the physical reality represented, it is not *time* that is quiet, but the natural objects of the landscape seem quiet *at this time*. Thus, "the holy time" is perceived as a thing-free quality hovering in a concrete land-scape. The nun may be "breathless with adoration", but this meaning does not come into full focus. "Breathless" may apply to a landscape as well, in the sense of "there is not the slightest current of air". This is corroborated, in retrospect, by one of the meanings of *calm* – "not windy". Similarly to the invisible presence of "breathless" air and the "mighty being" – thing-free qualities such as holiness, adoration, tranquillity, solemnity are intensely present. The nominal style of the quatrain is remarkable. There are only three finite verbs in four lines, only one that denotes spatial motion ("is sinking down"*)*, the verb "is" twice, once as a copula, and once denoting existence in a deictic phrase. Time is not associated with violent actions (as in so many of Shakespeare's sonnets), but with states and shape-free qualities.

Although the atmosphere of the sonnet has been subsumed under a well-defined scene, this has been indicated only in the title in some editions ("Composed upon the Beach near Calais"), and by two concrete nouns: "sun", "sea". What is important here is not the landscape but the atmosphere, the impressive solemnity hovering over it. Instead of talking about natural objects in the landscape – as usual with Wordsworth – he talks about the spirit that informs them, by turning some attributes and circumstances of the possible landscape into abstract nouns, which have a strong cumulative impact of thing-free qualities, together with some other abstract nouns: "evening" (with *time* as its synonym), "the gentleness of heaven", "adoration", "tranquillity". The phrase "gentleness of heaven" is noteworthy in this respect, especially if one compares it to a possible alternative phrasing: "the gentle heaven broods o'er the sea". Wordsworth resorts here to the poetic device which I have called "topicalized attribute", or "nominalized predicate", or simply the-ABSTRACT-of-the-CONCRETE metaphor. This, as I said, is a conspicuous device to direct attention *away from* the objects and concepts *to* their felt qualities (see more below).

I wish to make three further comments on lines 6–8. First, "Listen!" shifts the mood of the poem from description to the imperative; this is a vigorous deictic device to place the perceiving consciousness right in the midst of the situation, activating its "emotional" mechanism of locating itself in its environment with reference to time and space. Second, some important aspects of the object of "listen" are inaudible. "The mighty Being" may be an abstract periphrasis for "God", imperceptible to the senses. "Is awake" denotes a state, and suggests activity; but the sense-data that might indicate it are not specified at this stage. Thus, again, a more refined sensation of a supersensuous presence is evoked, possibly intimating a pantheistic deity. "A sound like thunder" is introduced only two lines after "listen". Third, the thing-free sound-perception of line 6, then, gets belatedly a "thingy" (though shape-free) motivation in lines 7–8. It should be noticed, however, that "And doth with his eternal motion make/A sound like thunder – everlastingly" is to be attributed to the sea more suitably than to an abstraction. One could suggest, therefore, that lines 7–8 as well comprise intense, thing-free sound-perceptions, a supersensuous atmosphere which has, in line 5, nonetheless, a motivation – displaced from "mighty Being" to "sea". This displacement is, of course, "mitigated" by an animistic pantheistic view, informing this and some other poems by Wordsworth.

This style of cumulating emotionally-loaded abstract nouns is less common in Wordsworth's poetry than in Keats's. Even when Wordsworth writes a sonnet on a typically Keatsean theme, "Upon the Sight of a Beautiful Picture", his abstract nouns tend to the conceptual pole. Compare the perceived effect of Excerpt 10 to Keats's "On Seeing the Elgin Marbles", for instance. Both sonnets purport to express an emotional response to some work(s) of art. But in "Mortality/Weighs heavily on me like unwilling sleep" the verb "Weighs" transfers mass and weight to the abstraction "Mortality", and the description is perceived as some undifferentiated, diffuse though intense essence (see Chapter 6), whereas in Excerpt 10 all the abstract nouns remain compact, conceptual, anything but diffuse. Hence, the two lines are perceived as "rhetorical" rather than emotional.

The first thing that strikes the reader is that at this point of the sonnet, the beginning of the sestet, it invokes art *in general*, transferring the discourse to a highly generalized level, with no attempt to create a particular situation defined here-and-now. Second, the hyponyms of Time, "Morning", "Noon-tide", "Even", constitute a linear sequence, and thus, according to our foregoing assumptions, they assume a compact conceptual character, and even tend to reinforce the conceptual character of any other part of the discourse. Third, the temporal sequence, as in Shakespeare, is associated with a verb of action, but, unlike in Shakespeare, the verb ("do serve") is highly generic and tends to present the abstractions as "merely conceptual" rather than poetic. Fourth, "Pageantry", too, suggests a succession, and so it has a grain of linearity. It *may* refer to some colourful succession, but it merely summarizes it on a highly conceptual level. Fifth, a vocative phrase may have an ingredient of a specific direction (in being directed to its addressee), or may have the potential of a powerful deictic device. Here (as in Shakespeare's "Devouring Time") the vocative phrase strengthens the linear conclusive tone of the poem, and – in the absence of an immediate situation – it does not act as a deictic device as in Excerpt 9.

One notable way in which Excerpt 10 attempts to achieve poeticity is the peculiar use of the epithet in "Soul-soothing Art" and "changeful pageantry". These adjectives are non-restrictive (the poem does not distinguish art that soothes the soul from art that does not), and they act here in a way that is similar to stock epithets in classical and neoclassical poetry. As Riffaterre (1978: 28) has pointed out, in such phrases "the agent of poeticity is a specific relationship between epithet and noun, which designates a quality of the noun's referent […] as characteristic or basic", where the adjective's meaning "is represented *a priori* as a permanent feature"; "in one way or another they must be *exemplary*, strikingly representative" (Riffaterre 1978: 28–9). So, whereas in Excerpt 9 we have an elusive quality in an immediate situation, in 10 one may regard the epithets "Soul-soothing" or "changeful" as reverse kinds of deictic devices, that "shift" their respective nouns to an "eternal now" rather than to an "immediate now". The nouns thus qualified become instances of general ideas, apart from specific circumstances, even when they happen to occur in some particular situation; they tend to focus on stable and permanent properties, rather than on fleeting, elusive qualities. In Excerpt 10, at any rate, they tend to reinforce the conceptual nature of the whole discourse.

The following comment has been made – by a sympathetic but critical reader – on an earlier version of my discussion of *time* in poetry. "In the lines of Wordsworth and Marvell, we have not only two different senses of 'time', but two different words, one a mass noun and one a count noun. How much of the poetic difference (concept and mood, etc.) is just a consequence of this grammatical fact?" In the concrete realm, at least, mass nouns tend to designate undifferentiated, diffuse entities, some general extended substance, whereas count nouns tend to designate differentiated entities with stable visual shapes. So we might expect mass nouns to be the source of undifferentiated moods, and count nouns the source of (allegorized) differentiated concepts. In our poetic sample, however, we find that the reverse is the case. *Time* as a count noun helps to define the immediate situation in time and provides, by the same token, the abstraction that is to be perceived in it as a diffuse entity. Time as a sequence, on the other hand, is a mass noun. It designates a general extended entity, but it is extended in one specific direction, from the past (and/or present) to the future: so it is linear time and tends to be conceptual. *Time* as a general principle is, on the one hand, a mass noun, but, on the other hand – being a general principle – it is a concept. So, it occupies a somewhat ambiguous position between an undifferentiated mass and a differentiated concept. Shakespeare and Marvell disambiguate *time* (in the differentiated direction) by endowing it with a particular identity, a personal will, purposeful actions, and characteristic visual shapes. *Time* both as a count noun and a mass noun designates a concept; and both have definite elements (a definite point or a definite direction); the poetic difference arises from the different exploitations of these definite elements. The "definite" character acts in different ways against a generalized background and in a specific situation. In the former it counts toward a conceptual entity; in the latter it may help to define it in time (and space), so that an abstraction may be perceived in it as a diffuse entity. Thus, the poetic quality of *Time* is determined by its SEQUENTIAL or SPATIAL PROCESSING rather than its being a MASS or COUNT NOUN.

5.3   More on the ABSTRACT of the CONCRETE

In Chapter 1 I mentioned that "concrete" is derived from a word meaning "grown together", "abstract" from "take away". Concrete objects are bundles of attributes "grown together"; isolated attributes are usually denoted by abstract nouns or adjectives. One cannot perceive isolated attributes, unless when they are grown together in a concrete object. In the present section I will further elaborate on the linguistic device already mentioned above, the "ABSTRACT of the CONCRETE" construction. I suggested that its conspicuous purpose is to loosen the relationship between an attribute and the concrete object of which it is an attribute. When we use an abstract noun, we usually denote an abstract *category*; here I explore this linguistic device as suggesting a precategorial attribute. I am going to recapitulate my explanation of the effect of this device in light of Strawson's distinction between *singular terms* and *general terms in predicative position*. Consider, then, the following three phrases:

13.   a.   high hills
      b.   the hills are high
      c.   the height of the hills

I cannot tell which one is *the* deep structure of these utterances; but a transformational terminology makes it possible to compare the stylistic effects of possible alternative formulations. In fact, a terminology derived from philosophical logic might be even more illuminating here. The normal, "unmarked", syntactic structure of such constructions, says Strawson (1967), would be that concrete, "spatio-temporally continuous particulars" as "hills" occur in the referential position. By "spatio-temporally continuous particulars" Strawson means objects that are continuous in space, and if you go away and come back after ten minutes, an hour, a week, or a year they still have the same shape. Such more abstract or more general qualities as "height" should occur as attributes or predicates, e.g. "high hills", or "the hills are high". In such phrases as "the height of the hills", the adjectives are turned into abstract nouns, and the abstract nouns are manipulated into the referential position instead the spatio-temporally continuous particulars. In light of Strawson's conception, 13a and b would be unmarked constructions, 13c a marked construction. As to the relationship of adjectives and abstract nouns, Strawson (1967: 82n) says: "The variation in form from "pretty" to "prettiness" [or, in the present instance, from "high" to "height"] supplies the substantive which is grammatically typical for referential position". Apart from this, there is little semantic difference between them: both abstract nouns and adjectives serve to denote properties that may be *grown together* in concrete nouns. I have called such transformations *thematized predicates* or *topicalized attributes*. "We may think of this", says Halliday (1970: 159) "as governed by a "good reason" principle: many linguistic systems are based on this principle, wherein one option [the "unmarked" option – R.T,] will always be selected unless there are good reasons for selecting otherwise". Here the "good reason" for selecting the "marked" option is to turn the attribute into the *theme*, that is, what Halliday calls the "psychological subject" of the utterance, and thus loosen the relationship between the object and its attribute.

Thus, not the concrete objects, but their attributes that have no stable characteristic visual shapes are manipulated into the psychological centre of the message. In this fashion, the psychological centre is directed **away** from the solid physical objects **to** some thing-free and Gestalt-free quality. Such syntactic constructions (i.e. the ABSTRACT of the CONCRETE) may serve as a convenient tool for the separation between sense-data (or perceptual qualities) and physical objects. In everyday life and language we do not usually distinguish one from the other. As I said, one of the tasks of the ABSTRACT of the CONCRETE genitive phrases ("the height of the hills") may be to de-automatise the relationship between the attributes (or perceptual qualities) and the physical object.

This analysis might account for the fact that such verbal structures are quite common in seventeenth-century instructions for Jesuit meditation and meditative poetry, as well as in Romantic, Symbolist, and post-Symbolist poetry: they draw attention to the surrounding space, but focus on thing-free and Gestalt-free entities (such as abstractions) rather than on stable characteristic visual shapes. Consider, for instance, the following phrase from a passage by the Jesuit writer, Dawson: "to have noted well the distance from one place to another, the height of the hills, and the situation of the townes and villages", or Ignatius' "the length, breadth and depth of Hell". Here the psychological focus is shifted from spatio-temporally continuous objects to certain abstract relations: *distance... height... situation*, or *length, breadth* and *depth*, manipulated into the referential position. As will be seen in Chapter 12, such ABSTRACT of the CONCRETE genitive phrases abound in Rimbaud's "Voyelles".

As I said earlier, such abstractions and Gestalt-free qualities are particularly suitable to suggest suspension of boundaries, and thus contribute to the perception of structural similarity between a poetic text and the meditative experience – by virtue of their lack of stable contours. According to this interpretation, in the context of meditation and related mental states they are perceived differently by the two orientation association areas. I quoted above Newberg et al. saying that "the left orientation area is responsible for creating the mental sensation of a limited, physically defined body", and that during meditation activity is drastically reduced in it. Thus, in the left area they enhance a feeling of the blurring of boundaries; in the right area they are perceived as unstable, fluid information, comparable to the fast-integrated output of right-hemisphere orientation processes that cannot settle as solid objects.

Let us consider at some length a similar construction in a poetic context, in line 5 of Wordsworth's Sonnet "Composed upon the Beach Near Calais":

14.   The gentleness of heaven broods o'er the Sea.

Here too we have the result of the same kinds of transformations as in Dawson's "the height of the hills", and Ignatius' "the length, breadth and depth of Hell", that is, nominalization and thematization, which enable us to compare Wordsworth's line to a different phrase structure:

15.   The gentle heaven broods o'er the Sea.

The difference between the two formulations is, again, the difference between a sentence in which a *spatio-temporally continuous particular* is in the referential position, and one in which an *abstract property of a spatio-temporally continuous particular* is in the referential position. Now I wish to point out three significant aspects of this line. First, the spatio-temporally continuous particular in Wordsworth's phrase, *heaven*, is a thing-free and Gestalt-free entity. Second, in Wordsworth's phrase both the spatio-temporally continuous particular and its abstract property (that is, both *heaven* and *gentleness*) are **simultaneously present**. Third, in Wordsworth's phrase the spatio-temporally continuous particular exceeds the capacity of imagination to comprehend or encompass its whole representation in a single intuition. As a result, *gentleness* is perceived as a diffuse but intense quality infusing the whole perceptual field. This diffuseness is reinforced by "o'er the Sea" which, again, designates a limitless, Gestalt-free particular.

To explore the intense effect of *gentleness* in this line, let us corrupt for a moment the predicate:

16.   The gentleness of heaven *rests* o'er the Sea.

In this corrupt line, I suggest, the affect under discussion is much weakened. What is the source of this difference? Some people would say that whereas *rests* is plain nonfigurative language, *broods* personifies *gentleness*. Suppose that we accept this account, we will have called the phenomenon by a name, but explained nothing. "The gentleness of heaven" will be positioned "o'er the Sea" in the same way, with both predicates. A much more illuminating way would be to distinguish, semantically, between three kinds of predicate: **predicate of state, predicate of process**, and **predicate of action**. Such sentences as *John is tall, This coat is dry, Peter is weak, This house smells,* contain **predicates of state**. Such sentences as *John became tall, The grass grew, The coat dried, Churchill died,* contain **predicates of process**. Such sentences as *She laughed, The children became aggressive, The animals scattered,* contain **predicates of action**. A **predicate of state** indicates that an associated noun is in a certain state. A **predicate of process** indicates a **change of state**. A **predicate of action** indicates a process that is self-arising, subject to voluntary control, and may be purposeful (cf. Fowler 1974:80–82). **Predicates of action** are predicated only of **voluntary agents**, felt to have some intrinsic, independent "force".

It will be noticed that the three kinds of predicates are arranged above in an order of mounting amount and kind of energy. It will also be noticed that when a "higher" kind of predicate is applied instead of a lower one (that is, a predicate of process instead of a predicate of state, or a predicate of action instead of a predicate of process or state), the "extra" energy conveyed by the predicate is perceived as an amplification of the *vividness* of the description. This is what Aristotle called *"energeia"*, vividness. If we return now to Wordsworth's line and to its corrupted version, we may notice that *rests* and *broods* suggest **the same state**. The difference between them is that whereas the former designates a **physical state**, the latter designates a mental **action**, infusing the diffuse thing-free quality *gentleness* with a high level of energy, increasing its impact upon perception.

Semantically, "brood" suggests both a physical and a mental action. The former indicates spreading the wings over the young (as a bird); the latter suggests pondering, sitting quietly and thoughtfully. The former meaning suggests a visual image of the heaven spread over the sea; the latter evokes no visual image – it intensifies the all-pervasive presence of the quality "gentleness". *Gentleness* suggests softness. delicateness; thus, "gentleness [...] broods o'er the Sea" suggests an intense *moderate* quality.

Let us go one step further. I have mentioned that in Wordsworth's line both members of the genitive phrase, *gentleness* and *heaven* are **simultaneously present**. In order to better understand the effect of this simultaneous presence, let us consider the following two lines from Keats *(Isabella*: XLIX):

17.　O for the gentleness of old Romance,
　　　The simple plaining of a minstrel's song!

and compare them to Wordsworth's line which we have already discussed at length, and to the following lines by T. S. Eliot:

18.　　　　　　　　　　I sometimes hear
　　　Behind a public bar in Lower Thames Street
　　　The pleasant whining of a mandolin.
　　　　　　　　　　　　The Waste Land

Let us compare the line "The pleasant whining of a mandolin" to "The simple plaining of a minstrel's song". *Plaining* means here "complaining"; *whining* means "a high-pitched complaining cry". For the sake of comparison, then, *whining* and *plaining* are sufficiently similar from the semantic point of view, and both are "thematized predicates". Moreover, both are used to characterize music in their respective lines. Nevertheless, there is an enormous difference between them. One major difference is this: in Keats's line, as in Wordsworth's, both the entity designated by the prepositional phrase and its abstract property are simultaneously present, at the same time and place; whereas in the passage from Eliot, the spatio-temporally continuous particular (the "mandolin") and its thing-free property ("The pleasant whining") are not necessarily perceived at the same time and place. You can perceive "The pleasant whining" ("in Lower Thames Street"), without seeing the "mandolin" (which is in "a public bar"). But in Keats's verses you cannot perceive "The simple plaining" (or "the gentleness") without perceiving the "minstrel's song" (or the "old Romance"), just as you cannot perceive "the gentleness" without perceiving "heaven" in Wordsworth's line. In other words, when Eliot says "I sometimes hear [...] the pleasant whining", *pleasant whining* may be regarded as a particular in its own right, and not just an aspect of another entity. When Keats says "The simple plaining of a minstrel's song", *simple plaining* must be regarded as an attribute, or property, or aspect of *a minstrel's song*, in which it is "grown together" with other properties or attributes, and from which it must be **abstracted**; consequently, its transmutation into the referential position serves, *inter alia*, to destroy the **thing** and to create sets of loosely connected qualities; that is, to de-automatize the relationship between the perceptual quality and the thing "of" which a perceptual quality it is. The same is true of *gentleness* in the poems by Keats and Wordsworth. Yet here, too, there is an (other) enormous difference.

"A minstrel's song" has no spatial expansion in the sense e.g. "heaven" has; and as I have suggested, the spatial expansion of "heaven" exceeds one's capacity to encompass it in one act of perception. On closer inspection, this difference is reinforced by a further difference: both "whining" and "plaining" suggest some sound, and some emotional element at the same time. In "whining" the sound element is more emphasized; in "plaining", the emotional quality. This is an elusive, "just noticeable difference"; but, as a result, "whining" is felt to be more concrete than "plaining", and is more prone to be perceived as a "thing out there".

Note that this analysis applies to "the gentleness of heaven" only if you understand "heaven" as "firmament", not in the various religious senses of the word. If you understand it as "God" or "the dwelling place of the Deity and the blessed dead", "gentleness" is perceived as a thing out there. However, if you understand it in both senses, they will tend to blur each other generating soft focus, and "gentleness" becomes even more elusive.

We may make, then, the following interim summary of the foregoing discussion. Genitive phrases of "the ABSTRACT of the CONCRETE" form, which are the result of a **nominalized** and **thematized predicate**, that is, of a **topicalized attribute**, tend to de-automatize the relationship between sense data or perceptual qualities and the things "of" which the sense data or perceptual qualities they are. Sometimes the transformational process is reinforced by some figurative and syntactic process as well. In such cases, the result may be the "destruction" of the physical object in which the various abstract qualities are "grown together", and a set of diffuse, loosely related abstract qualities is generated. There is a series of conditions that tend to amplify this process: first, when the second notion of the genitive phrase, the spatio-temporally continuous particular in the CONCRETE position is itself a thing-free and Gestalt-free entity; second, when the attribute topicalized in the phrase cannot be perceived apart from the particular of which it is an attribute; third, when the particular notion in the second Noun Phrase has unlimited spatial expansion, so that the topicalized attribute itself is perceived as diffused over considerable space, amplifying the impression of some lowly-differentiated, diffuse, dense percept. The more advanced the expression in this series, the more evasive and intense the impression appears to be, inducing a feeling that "the surface of one's body becomes peculiarly important, somehow accentuated".

Let us consider now a sixteenth-century example, from Thomas Nashe's "Litany in Time of Plague":

19.   Brightness falls from the air

Both *brightness* and *the air* are thing-free and Gestalt-free entities. *Brightness* is, typically, a quality of other qualities. Thus, we may speak of, e.g. *bright colours*. In Nashe's line it is a topicalized attribute, derived from, e.g. *the bright air*. It should be noted that had we substituted for *brightness* a noun that typically does occur in referential position, such as *"Light* falls from the air", the effect would have been incomparably weaker. In the world of referents, *brightness* cannot be perceived without the particular or the property "of" which it is an attribute or property, the air, or the light, or the colour. The affect of this isolated topicalized attribute is further amplified by four factors. First, both the air and brightness have unlimited spatial expansion, and the present tense suggests here an immediate situation. Second, "air" is the archetypal thing-free, imperceptible entity that is present everywhere. Third, instead of the genitive link *of*, we have here a verb, that emphasizes the separateness of the attribute in the referential position, which thus gains relative independence from the entity of which an attribute it is. Fourth, *brightness* designates a **state**, but a **predicate of process**, *falls*, is applied to it; the substitution of a predicate of process for a predicate of state amplifies the effectiveness of the former two factors. Thus, the "mass" of "brightness" and "air" is strongly amplified into some condensed presence.

Or, consider an excerpt from Wordsworth's "Westminster Bridge" sonnet:

20.   This City now doth, like a garment, wear
      The beauty of the morning;

Wordsworth

Again, both *beauty* and *morning* are abstract nouns, and both are simultaneously present. The morning fills the entire perceived space; and its attribute, *beauty*, is permuted into the referential position. Moreover, the co-presence of *beauty* and *morning* suggests a state; but is expressed by a predicate of action, *wear*, turning the pure abstraction into a thick texture.

Or let us consider a piece of French Symbolist poetry, from Paul Verlaine's sonnet "Langueur":

21.   *En composant des acrostiches indolents*
      D'un style d'or où la langueur du soleil danse.

         Composing indolent acrostics
         Of a golden style in which the languor of the sun dances.

Languor (that is, fatigue, weakness, weariness) is perceived here as a property of the sunbeams. The locution loosens the relationship between the property and the entity of which a property it is. *Languor* is both the grammatical and the psychological subject of the clause. **Dances** is a predicate of *action* applied to a languid *state*, amplifying the felt presence of the languor. Thus, the intense presence of an enfeebled atmosphere is perceived in these lines. This might be regarded as an epitome of Verlaine's poetry, marked by the intense perception of emasculate qualities. Characteristically enough, e.g. Gertrude Hall, in her English translation of this sonnet, "corrects" this locution, and adjusts it to Strawson's principle: "with languid sunshine dancing in each line" (http://poetry.poetryx.com/poems/15302/). Here the "sunshine", and not its attribute "languid" is dancing. "Languid sunshine" offers a stylistic alternative to which Verlaine's locution can be compared. A.S. Kline, by contrast, translating "where the sun's languor plays", manipulates the abstract property, "languor", into the referential position.

The word "langueur" means, as I said, feebleness, fatigue, weariness; but has a rather positive meaning too: sweet and dreamy melancholy. The entire sonnet under discussion is about ennui, extremely helpless fatigue, feebleness, weariness, satiety, nausea. Such a context foregrounds the senses related to feebleness, fatigue. Notwithstanding, the verse line under discussion is perceived as rather pleasant, mainly because the ABSTRACT OF THE CONCRETE metaphor, especially when amplified by a predicate of action, may evoke some supersensuous presense, escaping to some extent from the tyranny of categories. Thus, it tends to be exceptionally pleasant, irrespective of how unpleasant the elements in it are. So, it is possible that the pleasant figurative construction activates the pleasant connotations of the word too. In "Langueur" of the sonnet's title, by contrast, the pleasant connotation seems to remain dormant.

(http://www.poetryintranslation.com/PITBR/French/Verlaine.htm#_Toc 263756551).

Whitman's catalogue techniques may well illuminate how verbal structures may manipulate our cognitive strategies in handling information. In my *Toward a Theory of Cognitive Poetics* I compare at length two types of catalogues in Whitman's poetry, distinguished by Chanita Goodblatt as "illustrative" and "meditative". As an example of the former, Goodblatt quotes some lines from Section 5 of "A Song for Occupations", in which the reader's response to a list of occupations is "to conceptualize the items as a particular statement or category. [...] As such, this catalog can be considered to fulfill an illustrative function" (Goodblatt 1990). In contrast to the illustrative function, Goodblatt distinguishes a meditative catalogue technique, whose function is to emphasize sensory experience (ibid). Goodblatt and Glicksohn (1986) give a good example of this from Whitman's "Song of Myself". I have discussed the two types of catalogues at great length; here I will reproduce, with the necessary changes, a small part of it.

From the stylistic point of view, I have pointed out three main differences between the two types of catalogues: 1. the semantic field(s) from which the catalogue items are drawn; 2. the use of concrete or abstract nouns; and 3. the kind of noun that occurs in the referential position. Consider the contexts in which the word *vine* occurs in each of the two catalogs. In the meditative catalogue it occurs in the context of

22.   Echoes, ripples, and buzzed whispers….loveroot, silkthread, crotch and vine,

whereas in the illustrative catalogue it occurs in the context

23.   The plum-orchard and apple-orchard….gardening….seedlings, cuttings, flowers and vines,

Notice this. "Echoes, ripples, and buzzed whispers" are not more sensuous than "plum-orchard and apple-orchard". More subtle distinctions must be made, as the ones suggested above. While all the items in Excerpt 23 clearly belong to the same semantic field (of plants or agriculture), the items in Excerpt 22 (and, in fact, in the whole passage quoted by Goodblatt and Glicksohn) belong to a diversity of fields. Consequently, the load of Excerpt 23 on the cognitive system can be alleviated by recoding its items in one easily-manipulable category. The load of Excerpt 22 must be handled, as we shall see, in a different way.

There is another conspicuous difference between the two types of catalogues. Most items in the meditative catalogue designate what in Ehrenzweig's terminology may be called **thing-free** and **Gestalt-free** qualities, such as "The smoke of my own breath, echoes, ripples, and buzzed whispers, […] My respiration and inspiration …", whereas most of the items in the illustrative catalogue designate objects that have stable, and sometimes even characteristic, visual shapes that seem to resist the kind of fusion that Bergson mentions (see Chapter 6; as I have emphasized in Chapters 1 and 2, perceptual and imaginary boundaries typically resist fusion, just like physical boundaries). Consider, for instance, the verse

24.   The anvil and tongs and hammer..the axe and the wedge..the square and mitre and jointer and smoothing plane;

in which both qualities are present: the tools are taken from one semantic field (carpentry), and have well-defined boundaries that resist fusion. Thus, the items in the illustrative catalogue indicate, in Bergson's words, perceptions that "are clear, distinct, juxtaposed or juxtaposable one with another", and that "tend to group themselves into objects". Most items in the meditative catalogue, by contrast, have no stable boundaries, and thus *can* at least be fused, and treated as "a succession of states each of which announces that which follows and contains that which precedes it. In reality no one begins or ends, but all extend into each other" – again, in Bergson's words. The impression of such a succession of states is further reinforced by a phrase like

25.   The sniff of green leaves and dry leaves, and of the shore and dark-colored sea-rocks, and of hay in the barn,

which is of the shape [SENSE-IMPRESSION of A and B and C and D and E], where A, B, C, D, and E designate a diversity of objects, fused in a single, momentary, lowly-differentiated sense-impression. One would readily recognize here the grammatical structure of the ABSTRACT of the CONCRETE.

When we first started to discuss these matters of the "itemization" of meditative and illustrative catalogues,[2] some people pointed out that a succession of items like the one pointed out in our illustrative catalogue does have a structure, since the items in each line belong to the same restricted field. We regarded this as a feature contributing to poetic structure. Later, by way of comparison to our sample of meditative catalogue, we realized that on the contrary, it is precisely the arrangement of items in fairly homogeneous groups that induces consciousness into what may be termed "conceptual categorization". Hence it is this very kind of structure that accounts, to a considerable extent, for the conspicuous conceptual – and apparently non-poetic – nature of this kind of catalogue. We are confronted with two alternative strategies of handling excess information. The illustrative catalogue induces conceptual categorization to alleviate the burden on the cognitive system. The meditative catalogue induces the reader to fuse the excess information and dump it in an undifferentiated background texture, very much like in painting and polyphonic music.

5.4   "Total Complexes" and "Just Noticeable Differences"

Finally, conceptual language serves to refer to, and describe, things "out there"; adjectives normally *enumerate the abstract properties* of an object, do not *evoke its felt qualities*. Our discussion of Excerpts 17–18 suggests that "The simple plaining of a minstrel's song" is somehow perceived as less conceptual, more perceptual, than "The pleasant whining of a mandolin". I have given ample reasons for that impression. We should bear in mind, nevertheless, that "pleasant whining" and "simple plaining" are equally conceptual language. I propose to make here two additional comments in order to further clarify the issue. First, in Chapter 10 below I put the question: "How do systems of music-sounds and verbal signs assume perceptual qualities endemic to other systems, such as human emotions?" I propose there the following answer: "Usually only very few features or configurations thereof are available in the target systems that may be shared with the source phenomena. So, the best one can do is to choose the nearest options available in the target system". What is the nearest option for conveying non-conceptual perceptions when using the basically conceptual construction "the ABSTRACT of

---

2.   In the Cognitive Poetics workshop at the Katz Research Institute for Hebrew Literature, Tel Aviv University.

the CONCRETE"? I have given above the following answer to this question: when the attribute topicalized *can* be perceived apart from the particular of which it is an attribute, as in "The pleasant whining of a mandolin", it is perceived as a "thing out there" in its own right; when the attribute topicalized cannot be perceived apart from the particular of which it is an attribute, as in "The simple plaining of a minstrel's song", it is perceived as an elusive quality of the "song".

Secondly, an analogy with overtones in music and phonetics may clarify this issue (as discussed above, in Chapter 2). Fundamental frequencies (pitches, melodies) are perceived as "things out there"; overtones generate their felt qualities. "Overtone" is defined by the Merriam-Webster Dictionary as "one of the higher tones produced simultaneously with the fundamental and that with the fundamental comprise a complex musical tone". When the same melody is recorded on a CD by a flute and a violin, the ear can tell them apart from what it hears, with no need for the eye to see the instruments. It is the overtone structure that gives the various music instruments their peculiar quality. The human ear cannot discern the separate overtones, but fuses them into a "tone colour" (timbre[3]). Likewise, it is the concentrations of overtones (called "formants") that uniquely determine the various vowels in speech. The same speech sounds may be uttered by a female with a high voice and a male with a low voice, because their unique quality is determined not by their fundamental pitch, but their overtone structure.

Overtones are, then, higher tones produced *simultaneously* with the fundamental, with which they are "grown together" into a *complex* musical tone. If, however, we isolate one overtone from the complex and play it alone, it becomes the fundamental. In Chapter 11 we shall see that formant transitions usually integrated in the unitary phoneme become independent entities out there, perceived as glides and whistles, when isolated form the whole. Turning now to semantics, several abstract qualities are grown together into a concrete noun. If we isolate a "topicalized attribute" from a complex noun, its referent is perceived as a thing out there, as in "The pleasant whining of a mandolin"; if, however, the "topicalized attribute" is presented as simultaneously perceived with the object of which it is an attribute, it may become the nearest option in conceptual language to suggest a non-conceptual, *felt quality.*

I have been wondering why should such minimal distinctions make such enormous differences as, e.g. between "a thing out there" and a "felt quality" of a thing out there? It would appear that this phenomenon makes use of

---

3.   TIMBRE the characteristic quality of a sound, independent of pitch and loudness but dependent on the relative strengths of the components of different frequencies, determined by resonance. (*The Random House College Dictionary*)

a psychological mechanism of considerable survival value. As Krueger (1968: 100–101) observed, the overall perceived qualities of "total complexes" is determined by minute, "just noticeable", differences: "It has been observed over and over that the smallest changes in experience are felt emotionally long before the change can be exactly described" (cf. Chapter 9, below). A friend of mine was greatly amused by the following incident. He met a friend and noticed some change in his face. "What happened to your glasses?", he asked. "Nothing. I have shaved off my mustache". A similar story I heard from another friend about "misreading" the change in his own brother's face who had shaved his beard.

In our Western culture we are educated to make decisions only after rigorous analysis of available facts. This is indispensable in, e.g. scientific research. But in circumstances where survival is at stake, a different kind of decision-making is more serviceable. If we analyze all the available signs that, e.g. a predator is near before deciding to run, we may well be unable to complete the analysis. In certain circumstances, a crude but fast integration of available signs cognizable only emotionally, not intellectually, may be vital. In complex, modern societies too, fast, intuitive situation-appraisals may be of immense value.

Again, the perception of overtones may illuminate the issue. When I hear an object struck by another object, I can easily tell whether it's a wooden or metallic object, without seeing it – all thanks to their different sound colors, determined by their different overtone structures. Consider the following description by William Gaver of how we hear in the world: "The sounds made by vibrating wood decay quickly, with low frequencies lasting longer than high ones, whereas the sounds made by vibrating metal decay slowly, with high-frequency showing less damping than low ones. In addition, metal sounds have partials [=overtones – R.T.] with well-defined frequency peaks, whereas wooden sound partials are smeared over frequency space" (Gaver, 1993: 293–294).

As I have said in Chapter 1, the discrimination of overtones exceeds the resolving power of the human ear, which fuses them into a unified percept of tone color. But suppose we could consciously discern the relative duration of high- and low-frequency overtones, and the frequency space over which the overtones are "smeared". This would be time- and energy-consuming. Considering that having heard a wooden or metallic noise may also have considerable survival value, such careful conscious deliberations too may be fatal.

There is, however, an all-important difference between our overtone fusion and perceiving "simple plaining" as a felt quality of the "minstrel's song". While we have no choice but to fuse overtones into felt sound colors, we do have some freedom to switch at will between perceiving "simple plaining" as a felt quality or a "thing out there".

Only now, when making the cross-references between the chapters of the present book, I became aware that the brain mechanism described above may, perhaps, also account for the Oceanic-dedifferentiation effect generated by the IMMERSION-in-an-ABSTRACTION metaphor (cf. Chapter 4). So far I had a Freudian and a Gestaltistic explanation for Oceanic dedifferentiation. But frequently I asked myself what arguments can be given in support of the claim that IMMERSION-in-an-ABSTRACTION metaphors may generate a perception of an Oceanic quality in a poem. The orientation mechanism has been described as the "left orientation area is responsible for creating the mental sensation of a limited, physically defined body, while the right orientation area is associated with generating the sense of spatial coordinates that provides the matrix in which the body can be oriented." Immersion in water arouses a feeling of the suspension of boundaries between one's "limited, physically defined body" and the surrounding liquid. "Immersion" transfers the transfer feature <+LIQUID> to the abstraction and, by the same token, suggests suspension of boundaries. This the orientation mechanism interprets as a "Just Noticeable Difference" indicating Oceanic dedifferentiation.

5.5 Feeling and knowing

Following Marcel Kinsbourne (1982) and other brain scientists I insisted above that right-hemisphere mentation (emotions, intuitions, mystic experiences, etc.) may involve the same features as left-hemisphere mentation (conceptual and logical thinking). The main difference seems to be not in the kinds of features involved, but in their organization: the former, e.g., is typically diffuse and simultaneous, whereas the latter typically compact and linear. We have direct access to an extreme instance of the compact ~ diffuse opposition in the verbal medium in the TOT phenomenon; that is, when we have a word at the tip of our tongue but would not come to mind (Chapter 3). In this state we experience an intense, dense, undifferentiated mass that tends even to have spatial expansion. We seem to have quite precise information both about the semantic and phonetic features of the word, but can experience them only as part of that dense but diffuse, undifferentiated mass. When those features integrate in a compact entity, we suddenly become aware of the word. In one state we *feel* those features, in the other we *know* them. In some instances we speak of a concept ~ percept opposition; and in some of a categorial ~ precategorial opposition.

Psychologists had a real problem with such dichotomies. How can we know when the responses of experimental subjects result from conceptual when from perceptual categorization? This problem is particularly acute in intercultural comparative research.

The present chapter has, in fact, explored the concept ~ percept opposition in the verbal art. We have found that both the deixis plus abstraction construct and the ABSTRACT of the CONCRETE construct are effective devices of diffusing information and generating relatively vague percepts. We have found the same with reference to the IMMERSION in an ABSTRACTION construct in Chapter 4 (on Oceanic Dedifferentiation). One may say that in comparing Excerpts 17 and 18 the opposition between the perceived qualities of the two metaphors is less clear-cut than the concept ~ percept opposition. Nevertheless, they may be located at two different points on the percept–concept continuum, Excerpt 18 being nearer to the concept-end, Excerpt 17 to the percept-end. Such a description presupposes that there be, in spite of the differences in the unique conscious qualities, a continuum between perception and cognition (or, percept and concept).

In her intercultural studies, Barbara B. Lloyd (1972:19) quotes French on the nature of such a continuum:

> Perception can be defined as the process of immediate experience in organisms. This links perception with sensation; such primitive terms as "seeing", "tasting" and "feeling" are refinable into perceptual processes. As experience becomes less immediate and the amount of inference by the organism increases, processes of cognition[4] have become involved. Among the primitive terms are "knowing" and "thinking".

Lloyd, further, refers to Tajfel, who adopted the notion of immediacy in defining perception, but specified four necessary qualifications:

> These required that the stimulus material allow the possibility of only one correct response, that responses must occur at the time the sensory material is received, and must not be based on complex and abstract inferences, nor on an awareness by the perceiver of alternatives (ibid).

The phrase "nor an awareness of" in the last qualification ought to bear on some of the other ones too. Thus, for instance, according to the present view, perception is based on the forming and testing of hypotheses, but it is performed with such immediacy that the perceiver is not aware of it.

In relation to "feeling" in French's description the following two definitions from the *Random House College Dictionary* are, I would suggest, relevant: "physical sensation not connected with sight, hearing, taste, or smell" and "consciousness

---

4.   Lloyd uses the term "cognition" in a sense that is different from the one used throughout the present study. She uses the term in the sense "thought processes (as opposed to perceptual and emotional processes) are involved", whereas I am using it as in the phrase "cognitive psychology", which includes perceptual and emotional processes as well.

itself without regard to thought or a perceived object, as excitement-calm, strain-relaxation".

In the case studies of the next chapter we will see that such distinctions may be useful in distinguishing quite sophisticated poetic qualities, such as symbol and allegory, or some altered state of consciousness conveyed by the verbal arts by way of *feeling*, not merely *knowing*.

5.6   Conclusion

Lateralization and ever-refined distinctions in brain structure may, perhaps, account for distinctions between perceptual qualities; but we need much more than that. What we need is a tool to make distinctions within a text between perceptual qualities of individual stylistic devices. We are at a level of delicacy when it makes all the difference whether the text says *"languid sunshine"* or "the *languor of the sunshine"* "dancing in each line". Even the most thorough mapping of the brain cannot provide that. I had the good luck to have begun at the opposite end, with a set of stylistic devices that display insufficiently-explained perceptual qualities: ABSTRACT of the CONCRETE genitive phrases, and the co-presence of deictic devices with abstract nouns – sometimes a combination of the two. After years of agonizing search I found that some of those effects can be accounted for, quite plausibly, with reference to certain brain structures and brain processes. The explanation found would also account for the occurrence of such expressions in varieties of Romantic "meditative poems", in seventeenth-century Jesuit instructions for meditation, and in poems that suggest invisible presences. In Whitman's poetry, for instance, critics have intuitively distinguished between "illustrative" and "meditative" catalogues. Both types consist of lists of extremely complex noun phrases. I have shown that one of the crucial differences between them is that while the "illustrative" catalogue manipulates a concrete noun into the referential position, the "meditative" catalogue makes use of abstract nouns and "topicalized attributes". Briefly, the application of brain science and psychological categories to poetry is useful only if there is a mediating set of terms that have sufficient descriptive contents to make subtle distinctions between and within texts. Those terms, in turn, may gain their *significance* from the generalizations of brain science and psychology.

CHAPTER 6

Three case studies – Keats, Spenser, Baudelaire

6.1 Poetry and altered states of consciousness

One of man's greatest achievements is personal consciousness.[1] At a very early age he learns to construct stable categories that make a stable world from streams of sensory information that flood his senses. We have encountered in Chapter 1 the relative advantages and disadvantages of rapid and delayed categorization. Well-organized categories constitute a relatively easily manipulable small load of information on one's cognitive system; on the other hand, they entail the loss of important sensory information that might be crucial for the process of accurate adaptation. Exposure to fluid precategorial information, by contrast, may burden the human memory system with too much sensory load that may be available for adaptive purposes and afford great flexibility, but may be time-and-energy consuming, and occupy too much mental processing space. Delayed categorization may involve a period of uncertainty that may be quite unpleasant, or even intolerable for some individuals. The solution to this catch appears to be what Ehrenzweig (1970: 135) describes (see above, Chapter 4) as "a creative ego rhythm that swings between focussed Gestalt and an oceanic undifferentiation" and "the importance for a creative ego to be able to suspend the boundaries between self and not-self in order to become more at home in the world of reality where the objects and self are clearly held apart" (ibid). In that chapter I argue that in some people's responses to the "IMMERSION in an ABSTRACTION" kind of metaphor one may detect precisely such an element of the suspension of boundaries between self and not-self, of immersion in a thing-free and Gestalt-free quality. A similar tendency may be detected, as suggested in Chapter 5, in such linguistic constructs as deixis plus abstract nouns, or the ABSTRACT of the CONCRETE genitive phrases.

Altered states of consciousness are states in which one is exposed for extended periods of time to precategorial, or lowly-categorized information of varying sorts. These would include a wide range of states in which the actively organizing mind

---

1. I have elsewhere discussed poetry and altered states of consciousness at very great length (Tsur 1992: 411–470 [2008[2]] 451–510).

is not in full control, ranging from hypnagogic or hypnopompic states (the semi-consciousness preceding sleep or waking respectively), through hypnotic state, to varieties of religious experience, most notably mystic and ecstatic. In the creative process, moments of "inspiration" or of "insight" too may involve such altered state of consciousness, though less readily recognized as such.

Since much Romantic and Symbolist poetry on the one hand and religious poetry of most styles on the other seek to be exposed to rich precategorial information, we might expect to find in these styles and genres poems that attempt to achieve, or to display some altered state of consciousness as a regional quality.

6.2   "On Seeing the Elgin Marbles"

In the next five sections, I am going to discuss at some length Keats's sonnet "On Seeing the Elgin Marbles".

1.   My spirit is too week – mortality
      Weighs heavily on me like unwilling sleep,
      And each imagined pinnacle and steep
      Of godlike hardship, tell me I must die
      Like a sick Eagle looking at the sky.
      Yet 'tis a gentle luxury to weep
      That I have not the cloudy winds to keep
      Fresh for the opening of the morning's eye.
      Such dim-conceivèd glories of the brain
      Bring round the heart an indescribable feud;
      So do these wonders a most dizzy pain,
      That mingles Grecian grandeur with the rude
      Wasting of old Time – with a billowy main –
      A sun – a shadow of a magnitude.

This sonnet is quite remarkable in the poetry of altered states of consciousness. This is one of the exquisite instances in which Keats achieves one of his "many havens of intensity". This suggests a kind of "peak experience", similar to ecstasy; and it is, definitely, a prominent kind of "altered state of consciousness". In what follows I shall try to trace, briefly, the cumulative impact of elements that contribute to it. A unique feature of this poem is that it begins with a direct reference to a rather common kind of altered state of consciousness, "unwilling sleep", whether unwilling to come or to go.

There is an overwhelming experience arousing in the experiencer a sense of finitude, a sense of mortality: "mortality weighs heavily on me", and "I must die". Man's sense of finitude and limitedness is sometimes expressed by presenting him as infinitely small, or insignificant, or of limited faculties. The first element Rudolf Otto points out in the numinous is what he calls "creature-feeling" or "feeling of dependence": "It is the emotion of a creature, submerged and overwhelmed by its own nothingness in contrast to that which is supreme above all creatures". (Otto 1959:24). This "creature-feeling" is Keats's experience in front of Grecian art. I would point out two aspects of this emotional state: passive emotional receptivity, far away from the "actively organizing mind"; and a state describable as "awe": an overwhelming feeling of reverence, admiration, fear, produced by that which is grand, sublime, extremely powerful, or the like. In Keats's sonnet, "My spirit is too weak" is a straightforward enough conceptual statement of an emotional state suggesting a relaxation of volitional control; while the landscape descriptions "each imagined pinnacle and steep / Of godlike hardship… / a billowy main – / A sun – a shadow of a magnitude", as well as "wonders… Grecian grandeur" can be characterized as "grand, sublime, extremely powerful".

This sonnet contains a considerable number of abstractions and thing-free qualities that are the source of emotionally loaded, undifferentiated perceptions. Here, I want to point out that *mortality* in line 1 makes an impression that may be described as a diffuse though intense essence or quality. The sonnet begins in a way that could be perceived as almost plain conceptual language. "My spirit is too weak" is, as I said, a straightforward conceptual statement. "Weighs heavily on me" is, in ordinary language, a dead metaphor, in the sense 'troubles me'. Nevertheless, the first two lines are rather perceived as undifferentiated and nonconceptual. Why? One reason could be the peculiar tension between the abstract and the concrete in the sentence "Mortality weighs heavily on me like unwilling sleep". Another reason may be the peculiar nature of the concrete element in this tension. Finally, the perceived quality generated in this way is reinforced by the relation of this phrase to the surrounding phrases.

Let me spell this out. If one may speak of relatively more and less abstract nouns, *mortality* is more abstract than *death* in the sense that the potential is more abstract than the actual. Besides, we are accustomed to personifications of *Death* in poetry, myth, and even our every-day thought, to the extent that we no longer associate such personifications with pure abstractions; by contrast, *mortality* is shape-free in our awareness. In this sense, *mortality* stretches the expression into the abstract direction. *Weighs*, on the other hand, attributes to *mortality* a property which is exclusive of physical objects. Now, when an abstraction is associated with a physical object that has a characteristic visual shape, the typical result is a figurative expression in which the abstraction has a compact, differentiated, conceptual character. When, however, the abstraction is associated with a physical quality that belongs to the domain of one of the least differentiated senses, such as the tactile or thermal sense, or the sense of weight, it tends to be registered as a diffuse, undifferentiated though intense and saturated percept (see Chapter 12). By attributing weight to *mortality*, one endows it with potency, or power. In this way, the present metaphor joins a highly abstract (differentiated) noun with a very lowly-differentiated predicate; there is a "hole" left at what Wimsatt (1954) calls **the substantive level** (that is to say, the expression suggests the kind of feeling for which our vocabulary has no name). In the present case, inasmuch as the metaphor is immediately preceded by a direct expression "My spirit is too weak" on the substantive level, it serves as a standard for deviation in either direction. Notice that this analysis depends on a certain mental performance: it takes for granted that the predicate *weighs* is not taken in the straightforward idiomatic sense of "troubles me". But the qualities that are suggested here as inherent in the predicate can be detected only if one understands *weighs* as a physical attribute proper, and conceives of the term as allowing, at one and the same time, for a more abstract and a more concrete interpretation of the expression on the substantive level than it, taken by itself, would suggest. Here, such a reading is encouraged by the sequel, "like unwilling sleep", which metonymically transfers an undifferentiated sense of heaviness from the limbs to *mortality*, the abstraction being related to the speaker from the outside, as it were.

6.3   Alternative mental performances

The perceived effect of a poem depends both on its structure and the reader's mental performance of it. Alternative performances of the same poem may yield different perceived effects. In the following, I shall propose two alternative mental performances of the poem's ensuing landscape description. According to the assumption concerning the relationship between landscape descriptions and emotional qualities in poetry expounded in Chapter 5, one might expect that the "pinnacles and steeps" amplify the emotional quality of *mortality*, by increasing its diffuseness. This, however, is not necessarily the case. Alternative mental performances may be involved, and the reader may switch back and forth between them. Horizontally, "Each imagined pinnacle and steep" may be conceived of as of part of an actual, continuous landscape; vertically, as of strikingly representative examples of "godlike hardship", that is, of a circumstance in which excessive and painful effort of some kind is required. Qua *exemplary*, the landscape tends to bring the conceptual nature of *hardship* into sharp focus. Now, the more emphasis is placed on the *actual* (rather than the exemplary) nature of the landscape, the softer (the more diffuse) becomes the focus of perception of the abstraction *hardship*. Alternatively, the more our awareness is focused on the *shapes* of the "pinnacles and steeps", the sharper the definition gets of the conceptual quality; and, conversely, the more one's awareness is focussed on **locating oneself in space and time** with reference to the pinnacles and steeps, the more diffuse (the more 'perceptual') the concept becomes. All this is implied by our discussion of orientation in Chapter 5.

The line "Like a sick eagle looking at the sky" has a multiple relationship to the preceding utterance. First, the eagle reinforces connotations of loftiness in "pinnacles and steeps". Second, the eagle enacts the sense of desperate helplessness; it combines in one visual image impending death with what the eagle *might* be in the sky, and thus reinforces a tragic feeling. Third, the mere appearance of the eagle enhances the suggestion that the "pinnacles and steeps" may constitute an actual landscape. Fourth, the eagle "looking at the sky" represents a consciousness in the very act of locating itself with reference to space, that is, it emphasizes the aspect of spatial orientation, rather than the exemplary aspect in "each pinnacle and steep", and thus increases the diffuse, rather than the compact perception of *mortality* and, also, of *hardship*.

6.4   Symbol and allegory

Our discussion of the two aspects of "each imagined pinnacle and steep" upon which awareness may be focused, raises an additional issue of the utmost importance. The theoretical equipment introduced here can help to discern some crucial respects in which allegory is distinguished from symbol. Traditionally, both suggest a kind of 'double-talk': talking of some concrete entities and implying some abstract ones. But whereas in allegory the concrete or material forms are considered as the "mere" guise of some well-defined abstract or spiritual meaning, the symbol is conceived to have an existence independent from the abstractions, and to suggest, "somehow", the ineffable, some reality, or quality, or feeling, that cannot be expressed in ordinary, conceptual language. The landscape in Keats's sonnet can be perceived as allegorical, strikingly representative of "godlike hardship", or as symbolic, suggesting certain feelings that tend to elude words. Now, ineffable experiences are ineffable precisely because they are related to right-hemisphere brain activities, in which information is diffuse, undifferentiated, global, whereas the language which seeks to express those experiences is a typical left-hemisphere brain-activity, in which information is compact, well-differentiated, and linear. Traditional allegory bestows well-differentiated physical shapes and human actions upon clear-cut ideas, which can be represented in clear, conceptual language as well; by contrast, the symbol manipulates information in such a way that some (or most) of it is perceived as diffuse, undifferentiated, global. The symbol does this by associating information with the cognitive mechanism of spatial orientation, or by treating it in terms of the least differentiated senses, or by presenting its elements in multiple relationships (cf. Tsur 1987: 1–4); all these techniques can be reinforced by what I have called "divergent structures". (see Chapter 9).

6.5   Keats and Marlowe

One might further highlight the peculiar semantic nature of the present sonnet by comparing its lines 9–10 to three lines from Marlowe's tragedy "Tamburlaine".

2.   Such dim-conceivèd glories of the brain
     Bring round the heart an indescribable feud …

3.   Nature that framed us of four elements,
     Warring within our breasts for regiment,
     Doth teach us all to have aspiring minds.

In spite of Tamburlaine's and Faustus' notorious craving for infinite things in Marlowe's tragedies, we may expect, from a common sweeping generalization, Keats's poetry to be of a more romantic, more affective mood than Marlowe's. It would be interesting to see whether and how the two passages bear out such pieces of "common knowledge".

The two passages have a considerable number of elements in common. Both refer, in a fairly direct way, to an undifferentiable feeling, in terms of a "Gestalt-free" quality, by linguistic terms that are near-synonyms: a *war* "within our breasts", and a *feud* "round the heart", and its relation to what happens in our minds (or in the brain). For Keats, as a true Romanticist, this is an intense passion at unique moments; it is so intense that it cannot be sustained for a considerable period. For Marlowe, this feeling is a more or less permanent disposition. Some readers report that they perceive a heightened affective quality in Excerpt 2, as compared to Excerpt 3. One possible explanation for this may rely on the different connotations of *warring* and *feud*. But far more significant seems to be the fact that whereas in Marlowe's passage it is the clearly differentiated "four elements" that are "warring within our breasts", Keats's "feud" around the heart is not only undifferentiated and Gestalt-free, but *thing-free* too: in ordinary referential language we expect to be told the feud is taking place *between whom* or *what*. Moreover, the location *"round the heart"* is clearly included in *"within* our breasts"; but as for their psychological atmosphere, the former phrase is perceived as vague, indistinct, whereas the latter as contained within clear boundaries. Thus, the more passionate impact of Keats's lines has to do with the fact that they are focused on violent actions, stripped of things that might carry them. Furthermore, although both metaphors seem to refer to some kind of emotional turbulence, Marlowe uses rhetorical devices to heighten its conscious "linear" quality, whereas Keats uses devices to mute, or obscure, this conscious quality. Marlowe's "warring within our breasts" is endowed with the psychological atmosphere of *patent purpose*, generated by the purposive ingredient in the words and phrases "for regiment", "teach", "aspiring minds", as well as by the conclusive nature of *all*. One interesting contrast between the two passages concerns the explicit use of the personal pronoun "our" by Marlowe, and the conspicuously impersonal constructs in Keats's two verses, de-emphasizing the involvement of a purposeful agent (I shall return to this point).

Keats, by contrast, emphasizes the undifferentiated character of the passion by the adjectives "*indescribable* feud", and "*dim*-conceivèd glories". I shall refrain from discussing all the aspects relevant to this comparison. I only want to discuss here the phrase "glories of the brain", recapitulating (from Chapter 5) my discussion of the ABSTRACT of the CONCRETE genitive phrases. In ordinary speech, the most natural order in such phrases is, according to Strawson (1967), when the more concrete noun occurs in the referring position, the less concrete one in the predicative position as, for instance, when a *spatio-temporally continuous particular* occurs in the referring position, whereas a *property* of a spatio-temporally continuous particular is assigned to the predicative position, in such sentences, for instance, as "the brain has glories" and "the brain is glorious". In these two phrases, *brain* is the referring expression, and *glories* or *glorious* denote a property attributed to the brain. The phrase "glories of the brain" can be thought of in a somewhat antiquated framework, as derived from the other two phrases through two transformations: the nominalization of the "deep" predicate, and its permutation into the referring position in the surface phrase. I called such genitive phrases "nominalized predicates" or "topicalized attributes". They shift the focus of attention from "things as bundles of properties" to their "sensed properties", dissociated to some degree from the things. In the present context, this can be regarded as a kind of regression to a "pre-thing" state, reinforcing the thing-free quality encountered in *feud*.

This comparison of the two passages does not greatly differ from the usual techniques of close reading. Nonetheless, our discussion of consciousness and of the categorization of information conveys several significant contributions. Theories of metaphor explore, typically, such issues as how to furnish the best possible paraphrase for a metaphor, or how people understand novel metaphors. Here we have two metaphors that do not differ significantly in their meanings, but rather in their perceived effects. The cognitive frame of reference has contributed to an explanation of this difference: It has explained the relationship between certain linguistic structures and the "regression" to a low-category mode of perception; it has also explained, in turn, the relationship of such regression to the affective quality of the text, as well as to our cognitive characterization of poetry. We have also indicated how these relationships can be further pursued, so as to relate the texts to the effects of period and style, such as Classic/Romantic. In the present context, it also suggests how this difference may contribute to a distinction between some permanent mood and an altered state of consciousness. One may, further, claim that it was the cognitive framework that suggested these linguistic tools for description; in a different frame of reference these descriptions would have appeared little more than trivial.

6.6   Ambiguity and soft focus

Presenting semantic elements in multiple relationships is the favorite object of New Criticism's ambiguity-hunting (e.g. Empson 1955). Consider, for instance, "Such dim-conceivèd glories of the brain". "Glory" is a fairly clear-cut notion, denoting, for our purpose, 'exalted or adoring praise', or 'an object of pride', or 'splendour, brilliance, halo'. "Glories of the brain" may mean, accordingly, either 'adoring glories given to the object of Greek Art' (the glories of the onlooker's brain); or '"The Elgin Marbles" are objects of pride, the glories of the creator's brain'. "Dim" as a muting adjective brings out the brilliance aspect of "glory". Thus, again we have a sensuous presentation of the irrational response: sight is the most differentiated of the senses (see below, Chapter 12), hence serving conventionally as metaphor for rational faculties. Though "dim" turns "glories", implicitly, into light, it is "dim" that makes the light less distinct, less differentiable. Similarly, the "dim-conceivèd glories" of the creator's brain stem from the *dark layers* of the unconscious mind. Now consider "dim-*conceivèd*". Which one of its possible meanings would be relevant to the poem? "To conceive of" means 'To comprehend through the intellect something not perceived through the senses'. "To conceive" means 'to relate ideas or feelings to one another in a pattern'; or, in a different sense, 'to become pregnant' – yielding a fairly physical metaphor for irrational *bringing forth*. At any rate, "dim" and "glories" *foreshadow*, as it were, the more objectively presented "sun" and "shadow" in the last line. Thus, paraphrasing Arthur Mizener (1964: 142) who, in turn, echoes Bergson on "metaphysical intuition", no single meaning of these words will these lines work out completely, nor will the language allow any one of the several emergent figures to usurp our attention (cf. Chapter 1). Thus, the blurred meanings contribute to the diffuse perception of the sonnet. In cognitive terms we might speak of overloading the cognitive system with these rival meanings. In terms of figure-ground relationship we might say that we handle the potentially well-defined meanings by "dumping" them in an undifferentiated "ground".[2] The process is very similar to that in the visual mode, where well-defined shapes, when overlapping or endlessly repeated, are perceived as undifferentiated ground.[3]

---

2.   This is a cognitive approach to ambiguity. Kris and Kaplan (1965) offer a psychoanalytic explanation of aesthetic ambiguity. In Chapter 1 I quote Semir Zeki's (2004) neurological study of ambiguity.

3.   I suggested in Chapter 3 with reference to the Stroop test that abstractions extracted from parallel entities have considerable adaptation value: they facilitate the preservation of such parallel entities in active memory. Damping visual or verbal information in an undifferentiated ground is another technique for alleviating the load on the cognitive system (cf. Whitman's "illustrative" and "meditative" catalogues in Chapter 5).

The adjective in "Of *godlike* hardship" means 'like, or befitting a god'; and it may suggest either 'hardship that only a god can endure', or 'hardship that only a god can inflict'. In this way, the word *godlike* fuses two plains of reality: that of the experiencing subject, and of the external object. There is a similar ambiguity in *wonders* in line 11, meaning either 'something that *causes* astonishment, admiration, astonishment or awe', or 'the emotion *excited* by what is strange, admirable or surprising'. In such ambiguities (of which there are quite a few in this sonnet) the various meanings are simultaneously active, and tend to blur each other, preventing each other from usurping the entire available mental space. That is how a soft, integrated focus of meanings is achieved in this poem, underlying its intense emotional quality. In my discussion of "each imagined pinnacle and steep" I suggested two alternative mental performances, a vertical and a horizontal one: the former suggesting strikingly representative examples of "godlike hardship", the latter suggesting an actual, continuous landscape.

I have described the synchronic effect of images hovering between a subjective and an objective existence. They have, however, a diachronic aspect too. The octet is dominated by first person singular pronouns; they disappear in the sestet all in all. Most conspicuous are the impersonal constructs "glories of *the* brain" and "round *the* heart", instead "glories of *my* brain", and "round *my* heart". *Pain* (in line 11) too is a psychological abstraction which, again, seems to be unrelated to any individual consciousness. The above ambiguous phrases serve as transition from the "I", the enduring, conscious element that knows experience to a less conscious state; that is, they serve as transition from a state of individual consciousness to an altered state of consciousness.[4] In this state there is an awareness of a stream of images, but no awareness of the self as thinking, feeling, and willing, and distinguishing itself from selves of others and from objects of its thought. It concerns an "ability to make up one's mind about nothing – to let the mind be a thoroughfare for all thoughts" (Keats 1956: 26). This stream of images, dissociated from the self as thinking, feeling, and willing, and distinguishing itself from other selves and from objects of its thought, leads to a state of consciousness designated

---

4.   Recent neuropsychological studies of altered states of consciousness support this conception: "Selfhood then seems to have evolved along lines suggesting at least in shorthand the operations of a kind of 'I–Me–Mine' complex. But what happens when this egocentric triad briefly dissolves? Novel states of consciousness emerge" (Austin 2000: 209). Michael A. Persinger (1987) claims that God experiences (as well as some pathological conditions) are associated with *temporal lobe transients*, which are electrical perturbations of the temporal lobe in the human brain (16). A characteristic of such states "is an alteration in the description of the self. Depersonalization is typical" (Persinger 1987: 18; see also Hopkins' "The Windhover", Chapter 7).

as "a most dizzy pain". "Pain" merely names an acute but undifferentiated feeling. While not diminishing the intensity of pain, "dizzy" blurs its contours. "Dizzy" refers to a whirling state of uneasy feeling, sometimes extremely intense, blurring one's perception of the external world. The very presence of "dizzy" contributes to the structural resemblance of Keats's poem to an altered state of consciousness. As Michael A. Persinger says in his study of the neuropsychological bases of God beliefs, "Few people appear to acknowledge the role of vestibular sensations in the God Experience. However, in light of the temporal lobe's role in the sensation of balance and movement, these experiences are expected. [...] Literature concerned with the God Experiences are full of metaphors describing essential vestibular inputs. Sensations of 'being lifted', 'feeling light', or even 'spinning, like being intoxicated', are common" (Persinger 1987:26).

The last tercet gives us the "chemical makeup" of this "dizzy pain": it "mingles Grecian grandeur with the rude wasting of old Time – with a billowy main – a sun – a shadow of a magnitude". In this list the syntactic structure dissolves, reinforcing a significant semantic aspect. In an attempt to understand the poetic significance of this structure, let us repeat (from Chapter 1) Bergson's comment on "metaphysical intuition", as quoted by Ehrenzweig, who regards it as a Gestalt-free vision:

> "When I direct my attention inward to contemplate my own self [...] I perceive at first, as a crust solidified at the surface, all the perceptions which come to it from the material world. These perceptions are clear, distinct, juxtaposed or juxtaposable one with another; they tend to group themselves into objects. [...] But if I draw myself in from the periphery towards the centre [...] I find an altogether different thing. There is beneath these sharply cut crystals and this frozen surface a continuous flux which is not comparable to any flux I have ever seen. There is a succession of states each of which announces that which follows and contains that which precedes it. In reality no one begins or ends, but all extend into each other".
> (Ehrenzweig l965:34–35)

In Keats's sonnet, the constituents of the "dizzy pain" are expressed by syntactically juxtaposed phrases. You cannot escape juxtaposition in language; but the dissolution of syntax relaxes its logical organization. Furthermore, the *referents* of those phrases are said to be "mingled". In addition, with the exception of "A sun", they don't "group themselves into objects", into "sharply cut crystals and [...] frozen surface"; all the rest are thing-free and Gestalt-free entities, which have no clear-cut solid boundaries, so that they don't resist entering the "succession of states" in which "no one begins or ends, but all extend into each other". The notorious 18th-century diction embodied in "billowy main" has in this context a special effect. This kind of diction makes use, as Wimsatt (1954) pointed out, of a general term as "main" (in the sense of 'broad expanse') with an epithet denoting one of its concrete attributes, "billowy", skipping the straightforward term on the "substantive level", "ocean" or "high sea", generating tension between the more than usually abstract and the more than usually concrete. Both terms of the phrase designate Gestalt-free entities, and in the present context suggest enormous energy.

Grandeur and *magnitude* are etymologically synonymous: both are derived from adjectives that mean "big". Nonetheless, they have acquired different senses: the former applies to the impressive, the latter to the measurable qualities of things (in this sense, too, the sonnet moves from the subjective towards the more objective). Their sublime effect is cumulative. The sun and the shadow are clear opposites fit for a forceful ending of a sonnet dominated by indistinct – though sublime – passions. Nonetheless, "a shadow of a magnitude" intimates some essence beyond the perceptible realm. Both shadow and magnitude are attributes of physical objects. The shadow is but a reflection of an object; magnitude is an abstraction from an object; the "object" itself, which remains unnamed, has been skipped – generating high metaphoric tension between both sides of the omitted "substantive level". The magnitude is here a *thing-free* abstraction – casting a visible shadow; and here we have the sun that gives the light – to make the shadow-casting more real. Does this not suggest, even make us visualise, so to speak, a most intense, supersensuous reality beyond the "cave" we are bound to live in?

Thus, Keats's sonnet begins with a rather trivial kind of altered state of consciousness, suggested by the lowly-differentiated predicate "weighs" applied to the abstract subject "mortality" on the one hand, and the hypnagogic state "unwilling sleep" on the other. It moves through successions of sublime entities beginning with a concrete landscape and culminating in a most intense lowly-differentiated, diffuse "peak experience" affording an insight into an imperceptible world "beyond". The peculiar rhyme-structure of the sestet in this sonnet makes a unique contribution to this diffuse "open" ending. The so-called Italian Sonnet may have a variety of rhyme-patterns in its sestet; in this sonnet the rhyme pattern is: **ababab**. Suppose the poem ended with an **abab** quatrain, say

4.   Such dim-conceivèd glories of the brain
     Bring round the heart an indescribable feud;
     So do these wonders a most dizzy pain,
     A sun – a shadow of a magnitude.

Irrespective of the illogical linking of the last line to the preceding ones, such a structure generates a symmetrical, stable ending. The fourth line of the unit constitutes a highly *required* closure. Now when you have not four but six lines, in an **ababab** pattern, instead a stable closure, you obtain a fluid pattern. You

may conceive of this fluid pattern in different ways: as, e.g. of a closed quatrain – reopened by an additional pair of **ab**-rhymes; this would yield an effective closure, grossly sabotaged. Or, alternatively, you may conceive of it as of an
indefinitely repeatable pair of **ab**-rhymes, yielding a smooth, open-ended fluid
structure. The fluidity of this pattern is further heightened by the tense enjambment "with the rude/Wasting of old Time". If the closed ending of Excerpt 4 has
a highly-differentiated symmetrical shape, inducing a rational perceptual quality, the open ending of Excerpt 1 has a fluid, lowly-differentiated, diffuse quality,
reinforcing the lowly-differentiated, diffuse state of consciousness indicated at
the semantic and thematic level of the sonnet.

Now consider this. The present sonnet is exceptional in an important sense
even among Keats's "ecstatic" poems. In the best of romantic ecstatic poetry, we
find sometimes that inactivity through death is counterbalanced by some intense
activity, or immense sublimity (connoting intensity). Thus we find that in some of
Keats's poems ecstasy is achieved by using death-imagery in a context of intense
passion. Consider the endings of some of the sonnets in which Keats is said to
achieve his "many havens of intensity".

> 5.   …then on the shore
>   Of the wide world I stand alone and think
>   Till Love and Fame to nothingness do sink.   (Keats, "When I have fears")
>
> 6. Still, still to hear her tender-taken breath,
>   And so live ever – or else swoon to death.   (Keats, "Bright Star")
>
> 7. Love, Fame and Beauty are intense indeed,
>   But death intenser; Death is Life's high meed.   (Keats, "Why did I laugh?")

According to Barbara Herrnstein-Smith (1968: 172–182), the mention of death
or nothingness at the end of such a poem constitutes a "closural allusion", arousing a vague feeling that there is nothing after this. The couplet following the
quatrains reinforces this feeling of closure. Thus, in these sonnets, the mention of death (coupled with intense passion) generates a feeling of ecstasy, or
"peak experience"; this feeling of "peak" is reinforced by the structural closure
of the couplet, generating a *conclusive* tone. In Keats's Elgin-Marbles sonnet,
by contrast, there is no such mention of death, or structural closure. On the
contrary rather, the **ababab** rhyme-pattern commits a "sabotage" against the
symmetrical **abab** grouping, while the run-on line toward the end commits
another "sabotage", against the two-line groupings of **ab**. Furthermore, while
the juxtaposed phrases divide the last but one line into two symmetrical halves,
5 + 5, the last line is divided into two assymmetrical parts, 2 + 8 – yet another
"sabotage" against closure. In this way, in spite of the rigorous rhyme pattern,

there is here a feeling of dissolving shapes reinforcing any impression of dissolving consciousness suggested by the contents and the semantic structure. The possible Platonic allusion in "a shadow of a magnitude" suggests the possibility of having caught some vague knowledge of some world inaccessible to the senses.

Now a final comment on this sonnet and other similar ones. According to the conception propounded here, it does not *arouse* an ecstatic experience in the reader; it displays a regional quality which the reader recognizes as ecstatic. We have followed at some length the verbal means which contribute to the perception of such an ecstatic regional quality.

In the discussion above, I made use of the fairly traditional tools of New Criticism, Structuralism, and linguistics on the one hand, and of Cognitive poetics on the other. At this point I would like to make a comment on the relationship between New Criticism and Structuralism on the one hand, and Cognitive Poetics on the other. The former use critical terms with great descriptive contents, that are capable of making fine distinctions within a text or between texts. But when the job is done, the "so-what" question inevitably arises. My discussion of the phrase "billowy main" as an instance of the notorious 18th-century poetic diction and of a genitive phrase that skips "the substantive level" may be illuminating here. It becomes significant in a way that is very far from, e.g. Pope's poetic ideals – rather as part of a verbal structure that conforms with Bergson's description of "metaphysical intuition". It is the "perceived effect" of the text that confers significance upon these detailed descriptions. And it is Cognitive Poetics that provides the best way to handle perceived effects in a principled manner. On the other hand, the terms of Cognitive Science have little descriptive contents to make fine distinctions within and between poetic texts; so they are crucially dependent on the terms developed by New Criticism and Structuralism, or even 18th-century poetic theory.

In the rest of this chapter, I am going to compare a short passage from Spenser with a sonnet by Baudelaire.

6.7   Chearlesse Night in Spenser and Baudelaire

8.   Tho when as chearlesse Night ycovered had
     Faire heaven with an Universal cloud,
     And every wight dismayd with darkness sad,
     In silence and in sleepe themselves did shroud,
     She heard a shrilling Trompet sound aloud …

               (Spenser, *The Fairie Qvene*, III. xii. 1.).

9.   *Recueillement*
        Sois sage, ô ma Douleur, et tiens-toi plus tranquille.
        Tu réclamais le Soir; il descend; le voici:
        Une atmosphère obscure envelope la ville,
        Aux uns portant la paix, aux autres le souci.

        Pendent que des mortels la multitude vile,
        Sous le fouet du Plaisir, ce bourreau sans merci,
        Va cueillir des remords dans la fête servile,
        Ma Douleur, donne-moi la main; viens par ici,

        Loin d'eux. Vois se pencher les défuntes Années,
        Sur les balcons du ciel, en robes surannées;
        Surgir du fond des eaux le Regret souriant;

        Le Soleil moribond s'endormir sous un arche,
        Et, comme un long linceul traînant à l'Orient,
        Entends ma chère, entends la douce Nuit qui marche.   (Charles Baudelaire)

Spenser's is, undoubtedly, an allegoric night. Nevertheless, it is not pure allegory, in the sense that – as Legouis and Cazamian (1935) and others have suggested – one may well enjoy the poem even when missing most of the allegory, if one feeds the senses of his mind on the rich, sensuous descriptions. Therefore, when comparing this description to Baudelaire's poem, the factor of *other things being equal* is far more striking than one might expect. Indeed, some things are almost identical, and the differences – though unmistakable – are almost hopelessly evasive.

Spenser's stanza is informed by an atmosphere generated by the co-occurrence of nouns such as *Night, darkness* and adjectives as *chearlesse, sad*. Similarly, in Baudelaire's sonnet we find "*Douleur, Soir, Nuit, obscure*". Furthermore, for Spenser's *shroud* we find "*linceul*" in Baudelaire's sonnet. In one poem people are "dismayd with darkness", "In silence and in sleepe themselves did shroud"; in the other one darkness brings to some "*la paix*", and to some "*le souci*". Characteristically, in one poem we find the verb *ycovered*, in the other *enveloppe*, both having an abstract noun for subject.

It is undeniable that Spenser's poem induces some atmosphere, quite dispensable in an allegory; whereas in Baudelaire's prevailingly symbolist-impressionist sonnet there is an allegoric machinery, more elaborate than in Spenser's present stanza. There is a long series of abstract nouns capitalized (and all but *l'Orient* personified): "*Douleur, Soir, Plaisir, les défuntes Années, le Regret souriant, la douce Nuit qui marche*"; and a concrete noun capitalized and personified: "*le Soleil moribond*". In addition, there is in the sonnet a long series of nouns, most of them abstract, some of them collective, or denoting some substance that lacks characteristic visual shape, such as *"atmosphère, la ville, la paix, le souci, des mortels la multitudes vile, des remords, la fête, du ciel, du fond des eaux".*

The issue at stake is that of the whole that determines the character of its parts. In the passage from *The Fairie Qvene* the abstractions tend toward a compact, conceptual character under which a mood is subsumed, whereas in *"Recueillement"* it is the diffuse mood, the atmosphere, that is dominant, and the allegorical figures interplay and join forces to induce it. According to our foregoing assumptions, the reader is supposed directly to perceive this difference. After the event, however, he is entitled to get a reasoned account of the source of this difference. What reasons can be brought, then, in favour of the respective qualities perceived in the two poems? No doubt, some of our different impressions are due to our different expectations: if we know that we are going to read Spenser, or Baudelaire, we may be inclined to perceive an allegoric-conceptual character, or a symbolic-perceptual character in their respective poems.

But even after making these allowances, some people feel there is an unmistakable – if evasive – difference between the two poems. We feel that in Baudelaire some concepts have been attenuated to their utmost, fused into each other, generating an extremely dense, thing-free and concept-free atmosphere inducing a feeling of having perceived an infinitely subtle sense-perception. Whereas in Spenser, the concepts as well as the percepts are "hard", well-distinguished.

This difference may be accounted for in terms of the distinctions propounded in the preceding chapter. First, Baudelaire activates the mechanisms of spatial orientation in an immediate situation defined here-and-now, by using a great number of vigorous deictic devices; this, as we have seen, may have a decisive effect on processing information in a more diffuse (that is, more emotional) manner. The vocative phrases in lines 1, 8 and 14 (*"ô ma Douleur, ma Douleur"*, and *"ma chère"*), and the imperatives in lines 1, 8, 9 and 14 (*"Sois sage, tiens-toi, donnes-moi, viens, vois, entends"*) are effective deictic devices implicit in words and phrases that carry additional information, and create an "immediate", "vivid" situation; their effect is enhanced by a few explicit deictic devices, such as *"le voici"* (line 2), and *"viens par ici/Loin d'eux"* (lines 8–9). One possible source of the intense feeling perceived is the tension between the cumulation of abstractions and the concrete situation defined by deictic devices mainly.

Spenser, on the contrary, employs all available devices to shift the situation to a general rather than a specific scene. The cloud that covers heaven is an "Universal cloud"; and the situation is defined with reference to time not by deixis but a temporal clause (introduced by *when*).

Second, Spenser uses such all-inclusive "universals and absolutes" as *"universal* cloud" and *"every* wight", suggesting "a sense of control, security and authority", and thus reinforces the conceptual character of his description. Baudelaire, on the contrary, makes fine distinctions within his population: "*Aux uns portant la paix, aux autres le souci*", reinforcing the psychological atmosphere of uncertainty in the poem.

Third, Spenser uses his adjectives as epithets, that is, they represent **cheerlessness** as a permanent, characteristic and basic feature of *Night*, **sadness** – of *darkness* and **fairness** of *heaven*. Moreover, *Night, darkness* and *heaven* are conceived of as of strikingly representative exemplars of cheerlessness, sadness and fairness respectively. The permanent, basic and exemplary nature of the qualities designated becomes clear from the observation that "poeticity disappears when the adjective is modified or qualified or enters into a predicative relationship – in short, when it ceases to be an epithet" (Riffaterre 1978: 28), in constructions as "very sad darkness", or "darkness is sad", "Night is cheerless", etc. The point is that for Spenser darkness is sad evidently and absolutely (that is, in an unqualified manner); sadness is inherent in, hence need not be attributed to, darkness. In other words, the adjectives in *chearlesse Night* and *darkness sad* are nonrestrictive: they denote an attribute inherent in the noun, and do not distinguish between sad darkness and, say, cheerful or comforting darkness. In the light of the foregoing discussions, one may suggest that a restrictive adjective particularizes the noun, whereas a nonrestrictive adjective keeps it on a general level.

These suggestions are corroborated, from a different angle, and in a wider perspective, by C.S. Lewis' classical study (1936: 313):

> Like the writers of the New Testament [...] he is endlessly preoccupied with such ultimate antitheses as Light and Darkness of Life and Death. It has not often been noticed [...] that night is hardly even mentioned by Spenser without aversion. His story leads him to describe innumerable nightfalls, and his feeling about them is always the same.

Baudelaire's darkness differs from Spenser's not only in the poet's gentle feeling towards it: it is an accidental – local rather than universal – "*atmosphère obscure*" that envelops the city; and *obscure* is a nonrestrictive adjective of "*atmosphère*". In other words, obscurity is not an inherent, permanent quality of the atmosphere that envelops the city; indeed, lighting is typically changing from moment to moment.

Now it is illuminating to see what happens to the adjectives *faire* and *obscure*, which in one of their main senses are exact antonyms, and as such **ought to** behave in a similar manner. Both adjectives have several meanings relevant to their contexts, but whereas the meanings of Spenser's epithet yield a complex of compact, conceptual entities perceived in sharp focus, those of

Baudelaire's restrictive adjective yield a diffuse, perceptual entity, perceived in a soft focus. The plurisignation of *Fair* seems to be essential here for Spenser's allegorical method. It denotes (a) free from bias, dishonesty or injustice; (b) bright; (c) beautiful. Its first meaning corroborates the allegoric contrast between the moral qualities intimated by the canto. The second meaning enables to state the sharp contrast between brightness and darkness. Whereas the third meaning reinforces in an allegoric manner the first two. Both words that constitute the phrase "*atmosphère*" *obscure* are ambiguous. "*Atmosphère*" may either mean "air" which, we all know, envelops the city; or, a quality that produces a mood or impression. Similarly, in connection with the first sense of "*atmosphère*", "*obscure*" means "dusk, evening twilight" (contributing to the specific, immediate situation); in connection with the second sense it may mean something like mysterious, giving the mood or impression its peculiar emotional "colouring". In accordance with the central claim of the present chapter, "*une atmosphère obscure*" denotes a visible but intangible substance – a perceptible feeling, so to speak, particularizing and informing the scenery of the sonnet. This difference may be regarded as a consequence of the restrictive ~ nonrestrictive opposition of these adjectives.

C.S. Lewis' passage is relevant in an additional respect: Spenser "is endlessly preoccupied with such ultimate antitheses as Light and Darkness of Life and Death". According to Gestalt theory, clear-cut contrasts tend to assume some logical organization, with a psychological atmosphere of certainty and patent purpose, whereas finer distinctions, by amassing overwhelming information, may produce a threat of chaos. Such chaos is more readily controlled when processed in relation to the "integration of diffuse input, such as orienting oneself is space", resulting in some vague, elusive, emotionally loaded atmosphere perceived in a concrete landscape.

In Excerpt 8 we have the indication of such "ultimate antitheses" in the sensory domains, in the opposition between "faire heaven" and "universal cloud", and between "silence and sleepe" and "she heard a shrilling Trompet sound aloud". In the emotional domain, *chearlesse* and *sad* are synonymous; however, in the former adjective (but not in the latter) the emotional colour is obtained by negating its opposite (*chear*); so it implies a sharp opposition. How different are Baudelaire's **nuances**! He does not contrast light with darkness, but "*Soir*" (line 2) with "*Nuit*" (line 14). The contrast between silence and sound is strikingly subtle. Only the last line of this sonnet appeals to the auditory sense. The perception of the marching Night's paths suggests either some infinitely subtle, supersensuous sound, or, by way of hyperbole, an all-pervasive silence, in which one may hear even the marching of the night. If in Spenser's poem silence and sleep are to be distinguished from

10.   With that, an hideous storme of winds arose,
       With dreadful thunder and lightning atwixt,
       And an earth-quake, as if it straight would lose
       The worlds foundation from his center fixt;

the first line of "*Recueillement*" implies a distinction between "tranquille" and "plus tranquille".

We have seen in Spenser the epithets *chearlesse* and *sad* attributed, almost *a priori*, to *Night* and *darknesse*. They have emphasized, unambiguously, some conventional, spiritual aspects of the nouns. *Chearlesse* and *sad* denote some unambiguously undesirable qualities. But what about "*Douleur*" in Excerpt 9? Although the word itself denotes some undesirable quality nowhere does the sonnet state that it *is* desirable, the speaker invokes it in a tone of intimacy and affection. Consider "*O ma Douleur*" and "*Ma Douleur, donnes-moi la main*". The passionate tone indicated by the interjection *O* becomes affectionate, by virtue of "give me your hand" – a gesture intended to bestow a feeling of assurance upon a child (cf. "*sois sage*" in line 1, implying a tone of comforting a child). Now, is darkness in Excerpt 9 as undesirable as in *The Fairie Qvene*, or, on the contrary, does it bring relief as, say, in Coleridge's "Ancient Mariner"? Darkness has been explicitly desired by "*Douleur*"; but is "*douleur*" itself desirable? This ambiguous character has not been resolved, but rather reinforced, by the fact that Night falls "*Aux uns portant la paix, aux autres le souci*".

Or, consider the subtleness of a phrase like "*le Regret souriant*". In an allegory we might expect *Regret* to assume almost any expression but smiling; its face would express sorrow, or gravity, but not a smile. The present sonnet has acquired some mood that avoids any extremities. Of *Regret* one may conceive as more moderate than sorrow, of "*souriant*" as more moderate than "laughing". The paradoxical combination need not be perceived as paradoxical at all, but as a subtle (or even gentle) feeling, in which there is an emphasis on the common bearing of both of its elements on some process of spiritual cleansing and refreshing (cf. discussion in Chapter 14). Or again, if at the beginning of the sonnet we have found some affinity between "*Douleur*" and the dusk of evening, the arrival of night should suggest some extreme grief or distress. This is reinforced by death-imagery, such as "*défuntes, moribond, linceul*". In this sense, the last line is a culmination of a death-process. On the other hand, Night is called here "*la douce Nuit*", and "*qui marche*" echoes in its consonants "*ma chère*". This last line is, then, really ambivalent, accomplishing the process of death and bringing relief, suggesting the beginning of a process of "rebirth".[5]

---

5.   I have elsewhere discussed at considerable length the The Death-and-Rebirth Archetype in this sonnet (see Tsur, online).

In the passage from *The Fairie Qvene* the relationship between *Night* and *chearlesse, darkness* and *sad* is made unambiguous, by means of their grammatical connection. In *"Recueillement"*, on the other hand, *Sorrow* is not attributed to *Evening*. It has been personified, and had called for the evening. The reader is left in uncertainty whether Sorrow and Evening are disconnected entities, or are to be treated as metonymically related. If they explain and qualify each other, one may assume that *"ma Douleur"* has called precisely for the evening because "she" resembles it in some sense; it is a "twilight" mood, a nuance, in between identifiable extremes; *"ma Douleur"* stresses the emotional quality of the evening atmosphere, whereas the dusk presents Sorrow as gloomy, dusky, unlike **dark** distress.

"Il descend", as predicated of *"Soir"*, may mean one of two things. In an allegoric context, it might refer to some personification of the evening, descending from Heaven (like some angel). In an impressionist poem like this, the evening descending from nowhere is diffuse, spread all over the visible space and beyond, and enhances the thing-free quality presented by *"une atmosphère obscure"*. This all-pervasive quality, substantial and insubstantial at once, is reinforced by *"Et, comme un long linceul traînant à l'Orient"*. There seems to be some dark substance spreading toward the East; it is evenly spread like some solid stuff, yet intangible. It seems to be "long": its end appears to be lost beyond the horizon.

The syntactic structures of the two passages, too, contribute to the perceived difference between one clear, over-all opposition in Excerpt 8, and a multidirectional set of oppositions based on minute distinctions in Excerpt 9. Spenser's stanza, the first in its canto, begins with a connective heralding hypotaxis: "Tho when as …" indicates that the following description is to be conceived as opposed to something else. This expectation is amply fulfilled in "She heard …" etc. A similar construction we have in Excerpt 13, *"Pendant que …"*. But whereas Spenser's complex sentence presents two opposites, *Silence* and *shrill of Trompets*, against each other, in Baudelaire's sonnet the syntactic structure has been exploited to an even more complex effect. *"Pendant que"* introducing the hypotactic sentence appears at the beginning of Quatrain 2. "While the vile multitude of mortals is doing one thing, let's separate us from them, and do something that opposes their action". But one of the main effects of this hypotactic sentence is a contrast with the parataxis in the former quatrain. One of the effects of the more relaxed paratactic structure in the first quatrain and parts of the sestet is to carry and articulate the parallel events that constitute the process (emphasizing this leisure by contrast to the second quatrain), whereas when reading Spenser's stanza, one must look forward to the clear, unambiguous opposite.

6.8   To sum up

Abstract nouns may refer to more or less clear-cut concepts or more or less diffuse percepts. When those diffuse percepts are loaded with energy, they are experienced as emotions. By default the abstract noun refer to concepts; but in certain circumstances they tend more toward the perceptual pole. There is a wide range of dichotomies or dichotomic spectra that may tilt the balance in one or the other direction. They may act on very minute scales and simultaneously. From such interactions the overall perceived quality of the *whole* emerges. In some instances different relative weight may be assigned to the various elements, resulting in alternative mental performances that generate alternative perceived qualities. In Keats's Elgin-Marbles sonnet, "each imagined pinnacle and steep" may be treated as strikingly representative examples of "godlike hardship", or as part of a coherent landscape, activating alternative cognitive mechanisms that tend toward the conceptual or the perceptual pole, respectively. The cumulative impact of such mechanisms may account for the evasive difference between symbol and allegory, or between the perceived effects of various period styles. I have compared on a minute scale two nineteenth-century sonnets to short excerpts from two longer sixteenth-century works, Keats to Marlowe, and Baudelaire to Spenser. I have pointed out some very conspicuous similarities in these pairs, and demonstrated how in Keats and Baudelaire the minute-scale differences tilt the balance in the perceptual-emotive direction, in Marlowe and Spenser in the conceptual direction.

The last section of the present chapter focuses the discussion on an inquiry into the relationship between an "extreme" kind of symbol and "good old allegory of our fathers".[6] We have found some evidence that traditional critical terminology such as "personification", "extended comparison", "the first and second term (or tenor and vehicle) of the metaphor" may, at best, point at the similarity of the two figures, but can do little justice to the intuitively felt immense difference between, e.g. Spenser and Baudelaire. The theoretical frame of reference and critical apparatus expounded in this and the preceding chapter seem to be appropriate to handle this difference. It has been assumed here that the critic must rely on the aesthetic qualities of the poems directly perceived and reported by a variety of readers. In case of disagreement, one may attempt to account for conflicting

---

6.   In 1888 an adverse critic, Jules Lemaître, attempted to debunk French Symbolism: "*Un symbole est, en somme, une comparaison prolongée dont ne nous donne que le second terme, un système de métaphores suivies. Bref, le symbole, c'est la vieille 'allégories' de nos pères*" [A symbol, in sum, is nothing but an extended comparison in which only the second term is given, a system of sustained metaphors. Briefly, it is the old 'allegory' of our fathers" (quoted by Brooke-Rose 1958:32).

intuitions in terms of differences in the relative weight assigned to the various variables that determine the effect of the whole in one's "mental performance". Further, one may assume that in such cases as Excerpts 8 and 9 the same kind of information is processed in two different ways, and categorized in a way that is nearer to the conceptual or to the perceptual pole, respectively. In the case of allegory, information is perceived as typically conceptual and compact; in the case of 19th century symbolism – as perceptual and diffuse. We have also identified a few variables in the text that influence the intuitive decision of the readers whether to categorize information as compact or diffuse entities. This influence of linguistic and thematic devices on the organization of the perceived effects can be explained only *via* the putative cognitive mechanisms activated by them. Most notable among them is the correlation between emphatic deictic devices and specific landscape descriptions on the one hand, and the diffuse, undifferentiated vision induced by abstract nouns. Because there appears to be little structural resemblance between these devices and that kind of vision, here we must go outside the domain of literary criticism or linguistic description, or even cognitive theory proper, to the different modes of functioning of the two hemispheres of the human brain. Only an understanding of the linear nature of the activities of the language-hemisphere, and the global and diffuse nature of the activities usually associated with the other hemisphere can account for the relationship between spatial orientation and the undifferentiated vision aroused by abstract nouns. But this should be noted: this conception is a far cry from what Fodor (1979: 18) called "Psychological Reductionism", that is, "the doctrine that every psychological natural kind is, or is coextensive with, a neurological natural kind". The doctrine expounded here, on the contrary, attempts to account for the correlation between certain linguistic and thematic devices and certain perceived aesthetic qualities consistently reported by various readers, by focussing on the point of intersection of two *apparently* unrelated kinds of brain-processes (i.e. emotions and spatial orientation). As a result, the perceived qualities of poetic passages like Excerpts 8 and 9 became susceptible to meaningful public debate.

CHAPTER 7

Linguistic devices and ecstatic poetry

"The Windhover" – tongue-twisters and cognitive processes

7.1   Ecstatic quality, linguistic devices, and cognitive processes

Hopkins is a difficult poet. It is almost impossible to imagine a spontaneous "first reading" of any of his poems. It is more reasonable to assume that "spontaneous" response to a poem by Hopkins becomes possible only after the studious internalization of research done (independently, or by reading footnotes) on his language, imagery and theological conceptions. After the assimilation of all this knowledge, there *may* be a smooth, "spontaneous" response to the mystic or ecstatic experience conveyed by such a poem.

   In the first part of this chapter I will investigate two conspicuous linguistic features in Hopkins' poetry, and their possible contribution to its ecstatic quality. I will explore, in light of the theory expounded in Chapter 2, how such tongue-twister phrases as "dapple-dawn-drawn falcon" may activate both phonetic and semantic precategorial information; and, in light of my analysis in Chapters 5 and 6 – the depersonalizing effect of the relative scarcity of finite verbs. In the second part I will explore how, by applying certain vocal strategies, a performer may enhance or inhibit the interaction of precategorial information. The discussion will be focused on "The Windhover". As to this poem's specific imagery, I will inquire, again in light of Chapter 6, into the question how such images as "The Windhover" and "As a skate's heel sweeps smooth on a bow-bend" may suggest an ecstatic experience. In other words, this is not a close reading of the poem, but an exploration of certain theoretical issues. (An excellent word-by-word explication of the poem can be found in Landow, Online).

> I caught this morning morning's minion, king-
> dom of daylight's dauphin, dapple-dawn-drawn Falcon, in his riding
> Of the rolling level underneath him steady air, and striding
> High there, how he rung upon the rein of a wimpling wing

In his ecstasy! then off, off forth on swing,
    As a skate's heel sweeps smooth on a bow-bend: the hurl and gliding
        Rebuffed the big wind. My heart in hiding
Stirred for a bird, – the achieve of, the mastery of the thing!

Brute beauty and valour and act, oh, air, pride, plume, here
    Buckle! AND the fire that breaks from thee then, a billion
Times told lovelier, more dangerous, O my chevalier!
    No wonder of it: shéer plód makes plough down sillion
Shine, and blue-bleak embers, ah my dear,
    Fall, gall themselves, and gash gold-vermilion.

This issue, however, arouses a much wider problem. Language is, by its nature, conceptual and logical. According to the semiotician Manfred Bierwisch, "The dictionary of a language is [...] a system of concepts in which a phonological form and certain syntactic and morphological characteristics are assigned to each concept" (1970: 172). Syntactic structures establish certain logical relationships between the words of a discourse. Mystic experience in general, and ecstasy in particular, by contrast, are altered states of consciousness, nonconceptual and illogical in nature. Language appears, then, particularly ill-suited to convey mystic-ecstatic experiences. Nevertheless, as we know, in a wide variety of cultures there exist rich corpora of mystic-ecstatic poetry. How do poets attempt to overcome this limitation of language? The present book is an extended inquiry into certain aspects of precisely that question. In my various writings I have explored this issue, following a variety of paths. In Chapter 1 I quoted Bergson's description of an incommunicable altered state of consciousness. Here I will reproduce it, and then explore how it works both in the semantic and the phonetic dimension of the phrase "dapple-dawn-drawn falcon" in Hopkins' poem. Then I will explore the contribution of additional linguistic devices to the ecstatic quality of the poem.

Consider, then, Bergson's following description of "metaphysical intuition" (quoted by Ehrenzweig):

What Bergson calls metaphysical intuition is a Gestalt-free vision, capable of superimposed perception. Let us hear his own masterful description of surface and depth vision:

"When I direct my attention inward to contemplate my own self [...] I perceive at first, as a crust solidified at the surface, all the perceptions which come to it from the material world. These perceptions are clear, distinct, juxtaposed or juxtaposable one with another; they tend to group themselves into objects. [...] But if I draw myself in from the periphery towards the centre [...] I find an altogether different thing. There is beneath these sharply cut crystals and this frozen surface

> a continuous flux which is not comparable to any flux I have ever seen. There is
> a succession of states each of which announces that which follows and contains
> that which precedes it. In reality no one begins or ends, but all extend into each
> other".
> (Ehrenzweig 1965: 34–35)

Bergson recognizes that juxtaposition is essential for surface perception,
but not for depth perception. He gives a practical recipe to achieve intuition:
he recommends one to visualize at the same time a diversity of objects in
superimposition.

> "By choosing images as dissimilar as possible, we shall prevent any one of them
> from usurping the place of the intuition it is intended to call up, since it would
> then be driven away at once by its rivals. By providing that, in spite of their
> differences of aspects, they all require from the mind the same kind of attention
> […] we shall gradually accustom consciousness to a particular and clearly defined
> disposition".
> (ibid.)

Now, linguistic structures do not conform with the structure of complex objects
in reality, and much less with the Bergsonian "flux". When you say "a green round
table", you use three juxtaposed words, but refer to a unitary object. So, let us
consider first how Bergson's "succession of states [in which] no one begins or
ends, but all extend into each other" works in the semantic dimension of the
epithet in the phrase "*dapple-dawn-drawn* Falcon". It appears to be a rather elaborate description contracted into a three-word nominal phrase. But what is the
elaborate description suggested? Owing to the contracted structure, the relationship between the two nouns and the past participle remains ambiguous in the
sequence. As George P. Landow (online) observes, the phrase can have several
meanings:

1. the dappled (or spotted or variegated) dawn[light] draws the falcon [so the
    speaker can see it]; or
2. the dappled dawn draws (or attracts) the falcon; or
3. the dappled falcon is drawn (attracted) by the dawn.

But in his "interlinear translation" of the poem he offers a fourth paraphrase:
"a falcon spotted or dappled by the dawn". The linguistic difference between
Paraphrases 2 and 3 can be accounted for in terms of different phrase-structure
parsings: "[dapple dawn] [drawn] falcon", and "[dapple] [dawn drawn] falcon".
The difference between Paraphrases 1 and 2 can be accounted for in terms of different kinds of metaphor: Paraphrase 1 suggests a "sensuous metaphor", referring
to the falcon's spatial movement as seen by the perceiver; Paraphrase 2 suggests a
"functional metaphor", referring to the falcon's mental process. The fourth paraphrase explicitly suggests that it is a "dappled falcon", and that it is "drawn" by

dawn; but that it is "dappled by the dawn" is based on an inference, not necessarily on a metaphoric construal. Landow further observes: "Although these various readings do not make the phrase mean the same thing, none of them much changes the meaning of the poem or really conflicts with the others, which suggests that Hopkins wished the reader to reach for all them. What does this kind of phrasing tell us about Hopkins' conception of language? reality? poetry? the way poetry should be read?"

I submit that the importance of this kind of ambiguities lies not so much in the enrichment of its meaning, but in what it does to meaning. Arthur Mizener's (1964: 142) exposition of "soft focus" in Shakespeare's sonnets (using the verb *usurp*) echoes Bergson on "metaphysical intuition". Paraphrasing Mizener, "no single meaning of this cluster of words will the poem work out completely, nor will the language allow any one of the several emergent figures to usurp our attention". The various meanings blur each other or, using Bergson's words, "extend into each other".

The paraphrases use prepositions and finite verbs to make logical relationships explicit. The "pileup of adjectives", by contrast, relies on the implicit, structural meanings of the collocations. Unable to disambiguate logical relationships, it generates a "pileup" of meanings. The adjectives do not merely convey a juxtaposed accumulation of meanings, but a jammed tangled mass of variously-paraphrasable meanings resulting from collision. By the same token, they generate a jam of sound clusters which, in light of Bergson's formulation, has a similar effect.

The process in the phonetic dimension requires a more elaborate explanation. As I argued in Chapter 2, speech consists of strings of abstract phonetic categories. The precategorial acoustic information that carries them is normally shut out of consciousness. Still, perceived poetic effects on the one hand, and the facilitation of certain cognitive tasks on the other, indicate that some of this information lingers on subliminally in active memory, and is available for certain cognitive tasks and aesthetic effects. It is active, usually, in the background, unnoticed; but rhyme and alliteration may direct attention to it, turning it to aesthetic end in that it is perceived as musicality. The sound patterns of poetry in general, and rhyme in particular, typically exploit this precategorial acoustic information and, actually, enhance its memory traces. In Chapter 2 I quote a series of experiments with efficient and poor readers which strongly suggest that lingering precategorial auditory information substantially improves reading performance. In nonaesthetic memory experiments, reliance on lingering auditory information reveals two typical effects. It enables verbal material to linger for some time in short-term memory for more efficient processing, but also may cause acoustic confusion in certain circumstances. What in the nonaesthetic memory experiments is called acoustic *confusion*, in an aesthetic context co-occurs with a continuous text, and may be perceived in the background as "harmonious *fusion*", "musicality".

What can we learn from these experiments and their interpretation about the relationship between mystic poetry and Hopkins' "tongue-twisters"? Language consists of "juxtaposable" sound clusters attached to concepts (called "words"). Syntactic structures establish certain logical relationships between those juxtaposed words. Such a system would appear particularly unsuitable to convey intuitions based on the flux described by Bergson. Not only the concepts, but also the sound clusters denoting them are juxtaposed. As Crowder (1983:255) suggests in the set of experiments quoted in Chapter 2, "if the two units are too close together, they will integrate rather than inhibit. If they integrate, the subject will lose valuable information". In Hopkins' poem, the pileup of exceptionally similar sound clusters in close succession may have the following effect: it may reinforce the lingering rich precategorial auditory information in active memory, and may enhance its interaction, causing fusion (or confusion). Thus, though the phonetic categories and their clusters are juxtaposed, "in reality no one begins or ends, but all extend into each other". Normally, rhymes break up a longer text into easily-remembered chunks. At the same time, the reverberating similar sounds unify the segmented text, and also enlist auditory memory in the service of remembering. In Hopkins' pileup of sound clusters, where there is no intervening text, the reverberating similar sounds extend into each other, fusing the discrete phonetic units, so as to contribute to the perception of a flux. In such instances there is a greater sense of violence in the coalescence of similar sound clusters than in ordinary rhyme or alliteration, where the effect may be smooth, or "clicking". As to the pileup of adjectives, no single meaning of these words will the poem work out completely, nor will the language allow any one of the several emergent figures to usurp our attention – their meaning components are simultaneously present.

Thus, in the sequence "dapple-dawn-drawn falcon", the principle of juxtaposition has been blatantly violated both in the phonetic and semantic dimension of the phonological clusters attached to concepts (called "words"), generating a jammed tangled mass of meanings and sound clusters resulting from collision.

One can easily make out a case for the falcon's ascent as a metaphor for ecstasy. But what about the other aspects of the falcon image so carefully emphasized? Are they "irrelevant texture" for the tenor suggested by the image, or do they contribute too to a drawn-out metaphor for an ecstatic experience? What about, e.g. "how he rung upon the rein", or "riding/Of the rolling level underneath him steady air", or the simile "As a skate's heel sweeps smooth on a bow-bend"? While ascent may be regarded as a well-worn conventional metaphor for a variety of God experiences, skating and the technicalities of falconry are usually not. This poem has another intriguing aspect: "lack of verbs used as verbs (only four or five active verbs in eight lines – the rest are used as other parts of speech)". This feature is conspicuous in the sestet too. Does it too contribute to the God experience? I will explore such features of the poem's imagery in light of two comments, one by Maud Bodkin on Dante's "Paradiso", and one by Michael Persinger on the neuropsychology of God Experiences.

In her discussion of Dante's "Paradiso", Maud Bodkin observes that in her own experience, "imaginative realization of the ascent thus indicated is inseparable from the recall [...] of flight as it is known in dreams". She comments on a very different image, characterizing its effect as "the absence of any sensation of effort, the wonder at effortless attainment of a new sphere" (Bodkin 1963: 143). Such "absence of any sensation of effort" may account for the occurrence of "floating" and "hovering" imagery in ecstatic poetry. To take some "floating" imagery in prominent English ecstatic poems: the "cloud/That floats on high, o'er vales and hills" in Wordsworth's "Daffodils", and the "shadow of the dome of pleasure/Floated midway on the waves" and, in a somewhat different sense, the expression "Beware! Beware!/His flashing eyes, his floating hair!" in Coleridge's "Kubla Khan". These are natural symbols for precisely such effortless movement. The noun "windhover" (as opposed to "falcon" or "hawk") suggests a bird hovering on the wind. And quite a few additional images in this poem suggest movement in the unsteady element of wind or air, as in "riding/Of the rolling level underneath him steady air" (paraphrased by some commentators as "the steady air rolling level underneath him"). In this perspective, "As a skate's heel sweeps smooth on a bow-bend" is just another striking image of effortless movement in space, drawing a wide smooth arc.

Maud Bodkin applied Jungian archetypes in literary criticism. But her above insight gets support from more recent studies in what nowadays is called "neuro-theology". Michael A. Persinger's (1987) neuropsychological study may illuminate this kind of imagery from a different angle. He observes that God Experiences (as well as some pathological conditions) are associated with *temporal lobe transients*, electrical perturbations of the temporal lobe in the human brain (16). I assume that, psychologically, "God Experience involving temporal lobe instability" (26) is relevant to ecstatic poetry too. I will explore the relevance of two characteristics of such states: depersonalization and vestibular sensations (that is, of, relating to, or affecting the perception of body position and movement). As to the relevance of "floating"-imagery to "Daffodils" and "Kubla Khan", the following observation may help to integrate it into the ecstatic experience suggested by these poems: "Few people appear to acknowledge the role of vestibular sensations in the God Experience. However, in light of the temporal lobe's role in the sensation of balance and movement, these experiences are expected. [...] Literature concerned with the God Experiences are full of metaphors describing essential vestibular inputs. Sensations of 'being lifted', 'feeling light', or even 'spinning, like being intoxicated', are common" (Persinger 1987: 26). After quoting an account of such an experience, he observes: "Note the repeated references to vestibular sensations: 'floating,' 'lifted,' 'moving,' 'spinning'" (27). I appealed to the same mechanism in my discussion of the phrase "a most dizzy pain" in Keats's "On Seeing the Elgin Marbles") as well (see above, Chapter 6).

I would include under "references to vestibular sensations" such expressions too as "how he rung upon the rein of a wimpling wing". Consider e.g. the following elucidation: "To 'ring' in falconry means to ascend spirally. So, the image here is of the falcon [ringing] on the rein of a [single] wimpling (rippling) wing"; and then, "The falcon rises in the sky in a spiral and then breaks off, using the momentum of his spiral (off, off forth on swing), in a long arc" (Landow, online).

Now we turn to the other feature mentioned in the exposition: the scarcity of finite verbs. What has this feature to do with ecstatic poetry? I claim that it is intimately related to two issues of basic importance for mystic-ecstatic poetry: depersonalization and what I have called "thematized predicate" or "topicalized attribute" (see above, Chapter 5).

Let us begin with Persinger's claim that such states of consciousness involve "an alteration in the description of the self. Depersonalization is typical" (Persinger 1987: 18). The most conspicuous linguistic devices of personalization are, of course, personal pronouns, or the naming of the agents to whom those pronouns apply. Finite verbs are another conspicuous device of personalization: they indicate the agent, recipient and time of the action expressed by the verb. Another conspicuous personalization device is the addressing of a present or absent person.

In "The Windhover", personalization is very much in evidence. The poem begins with a first personal pronoun: "I caught" (="I caught [sight of]"). Such phrases that are at once apostrophes and exclamations as "O my chevalier!" and "ah my dear" are even more effective personalization devices. At the same time, depersonalization too is very much in evidence. The most conspicuous device concerns the nominalization of verbs. Consider, for instance, the collocation "the hurl and gliding". When Milton says "Him the Almighty Power/Hurl'd headlong, flaming, from th'ethereal sky", he explicitly says who hurled whom, when, how, wherefrom and whereto. The verb "hurled" denotes vigorous or violent propulsive movement in space, and serves, among other things, to establish a relationship between the referring expressions "Him" and "the Almighty Power". In Hopkins' poem, the phrase "the hurl" places at the immediate disposal of the reader's awareness a state of affairs characterized as "vigorous or violent propulsive movement in space". It becomes a disembodied referring expression, the psychological center of the utterance. The phrase "riding/Of the rolling level underneath him steady air" is a more elaborate instance of the same principle.

We have seen exclamations associated with apostrophes and interjections which typically enhance personalization. Now consider the sequence "Brute beauty and valour and act, oh, air, pride, plume". The whole sequence consists of a series of exclamations of wonder. Apart from the first phrase, it is a series of isolated words, all but one monosyllabic; and all but one abstract nouns. In the middle of the series there is a monosyllabic interjection. The isolated words (and phrase) refer to emotionally indifferent entities; but being used as exclamations, they are charged with great emotional load. As Landow (online) rightly observes, his interlinear translation of Hopkins's "The Windhover" into simpler, if vastly less interesting or effective, language should help us follow Hopkins's argument: "Then, at this point, all the bird's brute, animal beauty, courage, and – oh! – his proud air and feathers [buckle or crumple!]" Comparing the simplified version to the original points up the unique effect of the latter. Instead of a coherent discourse we have a series of disconnected nouns and noun phrase, whose cumulative impact is a transport of amazed admiration. But notice this: the succession of nouns enumerates only the things perceived, not the experiencer.

Compare the phrase "Brute beauty" to "beautiful brute" (animal). Both may serve as exclamations of wonder. In the latter phrase a concrete noun is in the referring position ("brute"). The adjective "beautiful" refers to an attribute of brute. In the former phrase, the adjective has been nominalized (turned into an abstract noun), and topicalized (that is, manipulated into the referring position). Thus it becomes the psychological subject of the utterance. "Brute", in turn, is turned into an adjective and comes to mean "characteristic of an animal in quality, action, or instinct". While "beautiful brute" refers to a stable object, "Brute beauty" to an elusive *quality*. By the same token, phonetically, the phrase "Brute beauty" manipulates two tokens of the sound sequence [b...uːt] into close proximity, effecting acoustic confusion; and generates a string of two consecutive stressed syllables, blurring the metric pattern.

In the phrase "the achieve of, the mastery of the thing!", at least "achieve" is a verb turned abstract noun. As I suggested in Chapter 5, in such "ABSTRACT of the CONCRETE" constructions attention is conspicuously shifted away from the concrete thing to its abstract attributes. As I have suggested, such constructions loosen the relations between the attributes "grown together" in the concrete noun, and render them more like the stream of information in emotions. Bergson's conception of what he calls "surface" and "depth" perception may throw some interesting light on such grammatical transformations. Things that have stable characteristic visual shapes are "juxtaposable", and resist fusion. Abstractions, or thing-free and Gestalt-free qualities have no stable boundaries. Shifting attention to them facilitates their fusion, their "extending into each other". Such constructions are prevalent in poems that display strong emotional qualities or suggest some altered state of consciousness. As I mentioned in Chapter 5, in sixteenth-century Jesuit instructions for meditation too attention is frequently directed away by such grammatical means from stable sceneries to abstract relations (like length, breadth, depth, and height) manipulated into the referring position. Chanita Goodblatt distinguished between "illustrative" and "meditative" catalogues in Whitman's poetry. I have shown that one of the conspicuous linguistic differences between them is that the "ABSTRACT of the CONCRETE" constructions abound in the "meditative" catalogues, directing attention away from the stable objects to their Gestalt-free and thing-free attributes; in the "illustrative" catalogues stable objects are in the referring position (Tsur 2008: 456–468).

This chapter does not presume to offer a comprehensive reading of "The Windhover". Its explicit purpose is to point out certain linguistic devices that are conspicuous in the poem, and explore how certain cognitive theories can account for their possible contribution to an ecstatic quality.

7.2   Vocal performance and lingering precategorial auditory information

In Chapter 2 I discussed experiments concerning lateral inhibition and the fusion of lingering precategorial auditory information in the verbal media. I also discussed the issue of colour or overtone interaction across Gestalt boundaries. In what follows I will explore the vocal strategies by which a performer may boost or inhibit the interaction of such precategorial auditory information across word and phrase boundaries in the verbal medium. Richard Austin provides online a beautiful reading of Hopkins' "The Windhover". As we shall see, however, I would prefer if he leveled intonation leaps at certain points, so as to articulate word boundaries less clearly. This is by no means a mistake I am trying to correct. We seem to be at cross-purposes. While Austin's purpose seems to be to overarticulate boundaries so as to disambiguate the syntactic structure of obscure pileups, my purpose is to weaken boundaries, so as to boost overtone interaction.

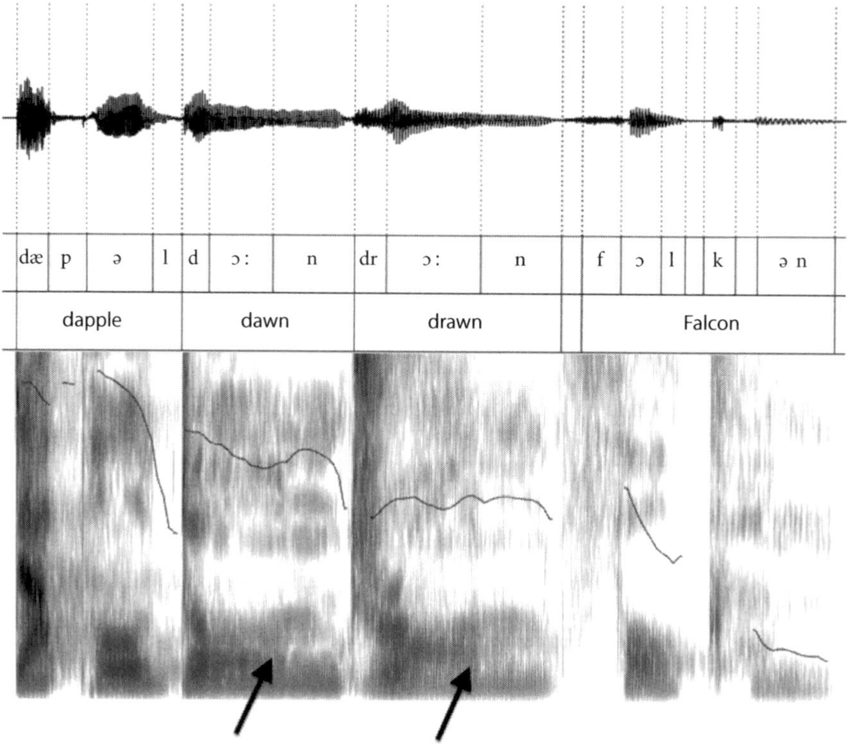

Figure 1. Wave plot, pitch contour and spectrogram of the phrase "dapple-dawn-drawn-Falcon", read by Richard Austin. The upper window presents the wave plot display, which shows a plot of the wave amplitude (in volts) on the vertical axis, as a function of time (in milliseconds) on the horizontal axis. The lowest window presents a spectrogram, which displays relative intensity as a function of time (horizontal axis) and frequency (vertical axis); as well as a fundamental frequency (pitch) plot, displaying time on the horizontal axis and the estimated glottal frequency in Hz on the vertical axis

    Figure 1 gives phonetic information about the phrase "dapple-dawn-drawn-Falcon", excised from this reading. Similarity of overtone concentrations (shown by the spectrograms) obviously reflect the similar phonetic structures of words. Similarity of durations, pitch contours and amplitudes are largely due to the performer's manipulation.

    The arrows in Figure 1 point at the first and second formant, at the point where the vowel and [n] meet in "dawn" and "drawn" (formants are concentrations of overtones that uniquely determine speech sounds; the first and second formants being the crucial ones). The shape of the three plots are very similar for the words "dawn" and "drawn", sufficiently similar to enhance the lingering precategorial auditory information in each other. It should be noted that there is a gradual loss of pitch and amplitude from word to word. This is due to a gradual loss of subglottal air pressure while uttering the breath group (this is the unmarked possibility).

There is precedent from colour interaction in visual perception and overtone interaction in polyphonic music that the weaker the perceptual boundaries, the stronger the interaction of Gestalt-free elements across them (Ehrenzweig 1970: 170–172; see Chapter 2 above). The refractory period required for articulating two successive very similar sound clusters in the "pileup" generates a well-articulated boundary between the two words. I had the impression that the distinct downstep from the pitch of "dawn" to that of "drawn" enhances this boundary, obstructing the interaction of lingering precategorial auditory information. So, I used the speech processor Praat to lower the pitch of "dawn" to equalize it with "drawn", blurring the distinct boundary between the two words, so as to boost the fusion of precategorial information.   (4)

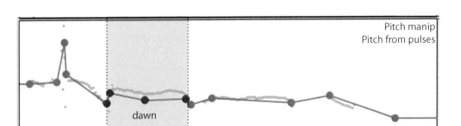

Figure 2. The genuine and "doctored" pitch contour of *dapple dawn drawn Falcon*. The higher, dim curve reflects the genuine reading, the lower curve with the "pitch dots" reflects the manipulated reading

The difference between the two versions will be better discerned when listening to them in close succession. Regarding background reverberation, (5) some listeners distinguish a clear difference; but some can hear no difference at all. This should by no means surprise us. The experiments with efficient and poor readers (in Chapter 2) suggest that people differ regarding their reliance on phonetic coding in verbal tasks. It would now appear that this is not an either/or, but a more/less difference. Finally, let us listen to the first few lines of the poem with the doctored intonation contour substituted for the genuine one.   (6)

A similar problem arises, with the necessary changes, at other points of this performance, such as in "this morning morning's minion". Here too the boundary of the first token of "morning" is enhanced by pitch movement, obstructing the interaction of lingering precategorial auditory information of the two tokens of the same word. But while in the foregoing case the relevant feature of the pitch movement was a distinct downstep at the onset of the similar words, here the relevant features involve terminal contour followed by a pitch reset.

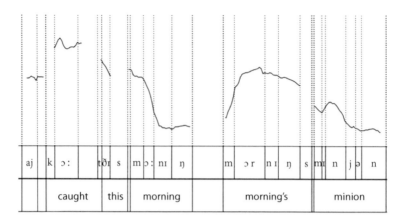

aj	k	ɔː		tŏɪ	s		mɒː	nɪ	ŋ		m	ɔ r	nɪ	ŋ	s	mɪ	n	j ə	n
		caught			this			morning					morning's					minion	

Figure 3. Pitch contour of "I caught this morning morning's minion". The terminal contour of the first token of "morning" steeply falls to the base pitch, like the terminal intonation contour of "minion". The fall is followed by a pitch reset on the second token

The terminal contour of the first token of "morning" falls to the base pitch just like the terminal contour of "minion", but is considerably steeper. This generates two problems. The terminal contour of the first token is not similar to the second token's, but to that of "minion"; and the steep fall to the base line suggests discontinuity, enhancing the boundary between the two tokens. This is further reinforced by a longish pause (305 msec) between the two tokens, and a (7) pitch reset at the beginning of the second token, This clearly articulates syntax, but obstructs the interaction of Gestalt-free elements across the boundary. To mitigate this effect, I slightly raised the last two "pitch points" in the intonation curve of the first "morning". A terminal contour that fails to fall to the base line (8) is perceived as less *final*. The result is visually represented in Figure 4.[1]

---

1.   The pitch manipulation feature of the speech processor *Praat* involves "stylization" of the pitch plot, that is, rendering it less fine-grained by omitting "pitch points" (cf. Figure 2 above). This constrains the fine-grainedness of the manipulations as well. Hence the differences between the pitch plots of words that were not manipulated, in Figure 3 on the one hand, and Figures 4–5 on the other.

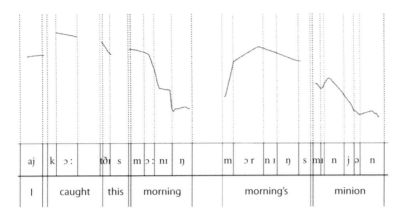

aj	k	ɔ :	tðɪ	s	m	ɒ ː	nɪ	ŋ		m	ɔ r	nɪ	ŋ	s	mɪ	n	j ə	n
I		caught		this		morning					morning's					minion		

Figure 4. Pitch contour, manipulated, of "I caught this morning morning's minion". The pitch on -*ning* has been slightly raised, in order to weaken the word boundary

The raising of pitch on ŋ is negligible; the manipulation mainly affects -*ni*-. The pitch measurements for -*ni*- in the genuine version can be profitably compared to the measurements of "minion" in the same version, and to the pitches of the same speech sounds in the manipulated version. We have the following pitch measurements for -*ni*- in the genuine version (in semitones):

mean pitch: 74.02 st
maximum pitch: 75.88 st
minimum pitch: 73.39 st

The measurements for -*io*- (in "minion") are quite similar:

mean pitch: 74.02 st
maximum pitch: 75.21 st
minimum pitch: 73.23 st

Thus, the two terminal contours have similar "concluding" effects, suggesting disconituity. In the manipulated version, the mean and maximum pitches for -*ni*- are 2–3 semitones higher:

mean pitch: 76.75 st
maximum pitch: 78.48 st
minimum pitch: 73.63 st

Such manipulation, then, weakens the boundary between the two tokens of "morning", facilitating the interaction of precategorial auditory information across it. Later I shortened the pause between the two tokens of "morning". I also found that the high rise of intonation on the second token of "morning" suggests a new beginning, further enhancing the sense of discontinuity between the two tokens; so, I lowered the pitch onset of this word, to smooth it out with the onset of "minion" on the one hand, and with the lower end of the first "morning", on the other. Finally, for similar reasons, I slightly lowered the jutting pitch peak on "minion" too. The resulting intonation contours are shown in Figure 5. So, let us listen in succession to the three versions of the phrase. Finally, let us listen again to the first few lines with all the manipulated parts substituted for their genuine counterparts.

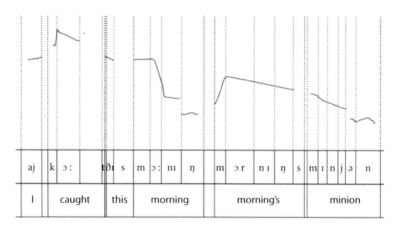

Figure 5. Further manipulation of "I caught this morning morning's minion". The pitch contour of "morning's minion" has been smoothened out, and the huge pause between the two tokens of "morning" shortened

As I have emphasized in many of my writings, the issue at stake in this doctoring exercise is not which one is the correct performance, but whether we can imagine or secure a reading that boosts rather than hinders the fusion of lingering precategorial auditory information within the pileup. There are almost insurmountable difficulties in eliciting rhythmicality or musicality judgments in experimental situations. But, in principle at least, one may submit to panels of judges pairs of genuine and doctored versions and decide whether one of them solves the rhythmic problem in hand, or whether it is conducive to the fusion of lingering precategorial information. In this respect, the purpose of the foregoing exercise was to explore the vocal strategies by which a performer may boost or inhibit the interaction of Gestalt-free elements across word and phrase boundaries.

CHAPTER 8

Defamiliarization revisited

This chapter is devoted to a kind of low categorization that does not involve "precategorial" information proper: I will briefly revisit "defamiliarization". Defamiliarization ("making it strange") is an effective stylistic device resulting from a disturbance of the process of categorization. It results, however, not in precategorial information, but in hard and fast categories of a lower rank than the appropriate ones. In many respects, the two phenomena are deceptively alike, and hard to distinguish. As will be seen in Chapter 13, two anonymous reviewers asked for an explicit distinction between delayed categorization as expounded in Chapter 1, and defamiliarization.

Shklovsky's "Art as Technique" is one of the most illustrious ancestors of Cognitive Poetics. Shklovsky assigns defamiliarization a general purpose: In art, it is our experience of the process of construction that counts, not the finished product.

> The process of algebrization, the over-automatization of an object, permits the greatest economy of perceptive effort. Either objects are assigned only one feature – a number, for example – or else they function as though by formula and do not even appear in cognition [...]. Habituation devours works, cloths, furniture, one's wife, and the fear of war. "If the whole complex lives of many people go on unconsciously, then such lives are as if they had never been" [Leo Tolstoy's *Diary*, 1897]. And art exists that one may recover the sensation of life; it exists to make one feel things, to make the stone *stony*. The purpose of art is to impart the sensation of things as they are perceived and not as they are known. The technique of art is to make the object "unfamiliar", to make forms difficult, to increase the difficulty and length of perception because the process of perception is an aesthetic end in itself and must be prolonged." (Shklovsky 1965: 12)

Shklovsky too, then, speaks of the disturbance of cognitive processes. In what follows, I will briefly explore this process. I will also suggest that various instances of defamiliarization may manipulate the implied reader to assume a variety of cognitive positions, resulting in varying poetic effects. Furthermore, defamiliarization may illuminate the cognitive phenomenon of "aesthetic distance".

In everyday life we frequently are unaware of a distinction between an overall context and its perceived parts. When he was old and his eyes grew dim, Isaak used to hear his sons' voices or feel the surface of their skin. A certain voice quality, with hairy skin, he used to interpret as Esau; a different voice quality, with a smooth skin – as Jacob. A fairly automatic way of "completing" the context "worked" in ordinary situations implacably, until an unusual situation occurred: "The voice is Jacob's voice but the hands are hands of Esau" (*Genesis* 7.22). With such an ambiguous situation one may deal in one of two ways: (1) may suppress some of the incompatible percepts, and give or retain one's blessings on the evidence of *one* consistent set of percepts (the hands *or* the voice). (2) postulate a fairly complex hypothesis to account for the discrepancy of percepts, e.g. that Rebekah put the skin of the kids on Jacob's hands and upon the smooth parts of his neck. Isaak, who *was* expecting Esau, suppressed the voice-percepts, inconsistent with Esau's hands, and the resulting fatal error is well-known.

Jumping to premature conclusions on the evidence of insufficient percepts may work in many cases, but in some it may prove disastrous indeed. Likewise, Gombrich (1963) observed in his "Meditations on a Hobby-Horse": "Certain young fishes can even be deceived by two simple dots arranged horizontally to be the eyes of the mother fish in whose mouth they are accustomed to shelter against danger".

I submit that in poetry-reading as well as in everyday life it is vital to be on the alert regarding the relationship between percepts and interpretive hypotheses. When our hypotheses are too "strong," as in Isaak's, or the young fishes' case, we are inclined to suppress those attributes of the objects and situations which do not conform with them. When, on the other hand, we encounter some deviation from the familiar, the best way to handle it, in poetry as in life, is by formulating a more complex hypothesis, i.e. by supposing some situation in which the unlikely percepts and/or attributes become plausible; we "verify" our hypotheses by finding some additional confirming or infirming details in the poem.

The relationship between the perception of details and forming hypotheses affects our discussion in two different respects. On the one hand, it is a question of accuracy in actualizing a literary work of art; on the other hand, it may be a matter of style: whether the work conceptualizes situations, or offers rather particular attributes, fragments of situations, and leaves integration to the reader.

Excessive dwelling on percepts *before* interpretation is characteristic of the uninitiated (children, freshmen, strangers). Therefore it readily lends itself for ironical use; that is why ironic literature, e.g. paradoxes, absurd plays and satirical novels are inclined to use some extreme situation, unusual point of view, or unfamiliar society. A naïve observer is inclined to observe a larger number of physical details and is, on the other hand, slower to conceptualize. Such a description in a literary work sometimes makes the reader feel superior, hence his ironic attitude. This is, as well, a way to induce the reader to formulate fairly complex and elaborate hypotheses which may form an indispensable part of his appreciating the work. The relationship between sense-perceptions and their interpretation as objects becomes very significant in literary practice and criticism, when we come to the device which the Russian formalists call "defamiliarizing" ("making it strange.") The "school-example" for this device is, of course, Tolstoy's description of what Natasha (in *War and Peace*) sees at the opera performance:

> Smooth boards formed the centre of the stage, at the sides stood painted canvases representing trees, and in the background was a cloth stretched over boards. In the middle of the stage sat some girls in red bodices and white petticoats. The extremely fat girl in a white silk dress was sitting apart on a low bench, to the back of which a piece of green cardboard was glued. They were all singing something. When they had finished their chorus, the girl in white advanced towards the prompter's box, and a man with stout legs encased in silk tights, a plume in his cap and a dagger at his waist, went up to her and began to sing and wave his arms about. First the man in tights sang alone, then she sang, then they both paused while the orchestra played and the man fingered the hand of the girl in white, obviously waiting for the beat when they should start singing again. They sang a duet and everyone in the theatre began clapping and shouting, while the man and woman on stage, who were playing a pair of lovers, began smiling, spreading out their arms and bowing. (trans. Rosemary Edmonds, vol. 1, p. 663)

Tolstoy's passage gives us only what Natasha perceives, but leaves on a lower level of conceptualization; integration is left for the reader. Such a description lets the reader "recover the sensation of" the absurdity of the grand operatic style; but, by the same token, reflects the dissolution of Natasha's dramatic illusion. Thus, the disturbance of integration in this passage may also serve as a "school-example" for another cognitive phenomenon involved in the aesthetic experience. Edward Bullough (1913) speaks of "psychic" or "aesthetic distance". Both "aesthetic under-distance" and "overdistance" sabotage "dramatic illusion"; in this case Natasha's overdistance causes her to see, e.g., "painted canvases representing trees" instead 'trees'. The result is obviously ironical.

Comparing this passage to another one conveying a similar situation would suggest that there may be a difference of degree, too, in 'de-automatization' of interpretation. In Borges's short story "Averroes's search" the traveler Abulcasim Al-Ashari tells the following story about the 'wonders' of far-away China:

> "'One afternoon, the Moslem merchants of Sin Kalan took me to a house of painted wood where many people lived. It is impossible to describe the house, which was rather a single room, with rows of cabinets or balconies on top of each other. In these cavities there were people who were eating and drinking, and also on a floor, and also on a terrace. The persons on this terrace were playing

the drum and the lute, save for some fifteen or twenty (with crimson-colored masks) who were praying, singing and conversing. They suffered prison, but no one could see the jail; they travelled on horseback, but no one could see the horse; they fought, but the swords were of reed; they died and then stood up again.

'The acts of madmen,' said Farach, 'exceed the previsions of the sane'. 'These were no madmen,' Abulcasim had to explain. 'They were representing a story, a merchant told me.'" (*Labyrinths*, p. 184)

In both stories the *personae* are unable to categorize details on a higher level, and so integrate them into 'dramatic illusion'. There are, however, two remarkable differences between the two descriptions. First, in Natasha's case it is a failure of perceptual integration, whereas in Abulcasim's case it is failure of conceptual integration. Second, it is not only that Abulcasim and his audience are more naïve than Natasha (with whom aesthetic overdistance is only a passing mood). It is rather that Borges' reader is left in ignorance for relatively long, just as the personae of the story. For him, too, the interpretation of the "house of painted wood" comes as a sudden revelation, a sudden change of sets, resulting in wit. Tolstoy takes the reader into his confidence from the very beginning. The ironic tone pervading this passage is derived from the discrepancy between Natasha's failure to integrate, and the ease with which the reader conceptualizes, at the same time, the data provided to him through her eyes.

Borges' short story is very short and bewilderingly sophisticated. It contains irony upon irony, and defamiliarization upon defamiliarization. At the end of his search, in his commentary on Aristotle, Averroes arrives at the following conclusion: "Aristu (Aristotle) gives the name of tragedy to panegyrics and that of comedy to satires and anathemas. Admirable tragedies and comedies abound in the pages of the Koran …".

Then the real author steps in, breaking the aesthetic distance:

In the foregoing story, I tried to narrate the process of a defeat. […] I remembered Averroes who, closed within the orb of Islam, could never know the meaning of the terms tragedy and comedy. […] I felt that Averroes, wanting to imagine what a drama is without ever having suspected what a theatre is, was no more absurd than I, wanting to imagine Averroes with no other sources than a few fragments from Renan, Lane and Asín Palacios".

Beyond the immediate ironic effect of the defamiliarization of the theater, it explains Averroes' failure to understand tragedy and comedy; but, at the same time, defamiliarizes the author's patronizing attitude in observing Averroes' failure. Finally, the reader not only receives an ironic point of view on not knowing what a theater performance is; he experiences the shock of not knowing that the description refers to a theater performance.

There are, however, instances in which the device of "defamiliarization" is put to a more sympathetic use. It may be particularly effective with the technique of the stream of consciousness, where the effect, rather than ironic, is emotional or suggests a different state of consciousness. Or consider Yeats's "Leda and the Swan":

> A sudden blow: the great wings beating still
> Above the staggering girl, her thighs caressed
> By the dark webs, her nape caught in his bill,
> He holds her helpless breast upon his breast.
>
> How can those terrified vague fingers push
> The feathered glory from her loosening thighs?
> And how can body, laid in that white rush,
> But feel the strange heart beating where it lies?
>
> A shudder in the loins engenders there
> The broken wall, the burning roof and tower
> And Agamemnon dead.
>   Being so caught up,
> So mastered by the brute blood of the air,
> Did she put on his knowledge with his power
> Before the indifferent beak could let her drop?

The sonnet is, of course, far more complex than I shall show here (a masterful analysis is in Spitzer 1962: 3–13). What concerns us here is that the two quatrains offer us a series of sensations the astounded "staggering girl" may have felt. She is so bewildered that she can understand nothing (in other words, she cannot interpret her sensations). Only the reader, who has the clue in the title, may have a "double vision": he has Leda's confounded point of view, the "immediate" perception of a meaningless, overwhelming experience of "great wings beating still above", "her thighs caressed", "her nape caught in his bill", but no swan. At the same time he may integrate the sensations in a meaningful situation: a *swan* raping a girl.

> The expressions "feathered glory" and "white rush" must be admired, not only because of their denotation of sublime aspects of the swan–god, but because the transposition of terms (= glorious feathers, a rushing white thing) suggests the way in which Leda's first impressions have recorded themselves: central is the glory and the rush, the forces that overpower her (beauty, movement); marginal the feathers and the whiteness, the concrete elements. (Spitzer 1962: 7)

Here, defamiliarized percepts are part of a much wider meaning structure. Leda's rape by Zeus engendered Helen of Troy who, in turn, caused the Trojan war which, by an intricate chain of events, caused Agamemnon's death. Yeats yokes together by violence and immediacy two remote defamiliarized situations: the sexual act is defamiliarized as "A shudder in the loins"; the Trojan war as "The broken wall, the burning roof and tower". "Agamemnon dead" involves an additional leap, but provides a clue for the integration of the lowly-categorized items. The meaningless, minute "shudder in the loins" had overwhelming consequences: "broken wall, [...] burning roof and tower". These apparently unrelated events, however, when integrated, make up an event that shook the world and the entire human history. Thus, Yeats plays up minute meaningless sensations against all-embracing knowledge, epitomized as "Did she put on his knowledge with his power/Before the indifferent beak could let her drop?"

Though Spitzer objects to a "Longinian analysis" of this poem, Longinus' following passage may account for the substantial difference between the defamiliarization effect in the Tolstoy and Borges passages on the one hand, and Yeats's sonnet on the other:

> For it is the nature of the passions, in their vehement rush, to sweep and thrust everything before them, or rather to demand hazardous turns as altogether indispensable. They do not allow the hearer leisure to criticise the number of the metaphors because he is carried away ...

All three texts present to the mind disconnected rather than integrated percepts. One crucial element pointed out by psychologists in emotions is deviation from normal energy level. Tolstoy's and Borges' passages leave the reader with sufficient leisure to observe the disconnected, meaningless percepts. In Leda's overpowering experience the "vehement rush" becomes an overwhelming emotional experience. In Polányi's term, the reader is forced to "attend away" from the meaningless, disconnected details to their overall "joint effect". Spitzer points out how Yeats exploits a rather trivial rhetorical device to promote this process of "attending away". By having recourse to "transferred epithet", he directs attention away from the glorious *feathers* to the abstraction "feathered *glory*", and from "a rushing white thing" to the overall quality "white *rush*". By this observation, Spitzer anticipates my conception of "topicalized attribute" (cf. Chapter 5). Yeats manipulates *glory* and *rush* into the position of the psychological subject. Here the glorious, rushing swan categorized as *glory* and *rush*, is "thing-free" and "Gestalt-free", and of very high "potency", constituting an overwhelming experience, rather than mere failure of conceptualization or perceptual integration.

In my theory, Shklovsky's defamiliarization represents a wider principle, that poetic effects are generated by a disturbance of, or delay in, a wide range of cognitive porcesses. Consider speech perception. Speech sounds are transmitted by an enormous amount of precategorial acoustic information, which is immediately recoded into phonetic categories, and excluded from awareness. We perceive only a unitary phonetic category as [i] or [u]. But, in what I call "the poetic mode of speech perception", we can tell that [u] is "somehow" lower and darker than [i].

This is because recoding has been delayed, and some of the precategorial acoustic information subliminally reaches awareness: the second formant (overtone concentration) of [u] is lower than that of [i]; and the first two formants of [u] are nearer to one another, less easily discernible, than those of [i]. This aesthetic quality would hardly be called "making it strange"; but it, too, is generated by the cognitive mechanism of delaying categorization. Thus, defamiliarization and the poetic mode of speech perception are subsumed under the same aesthetic principle, but while the former is of macro-scale, the latter is of very minute scale, generating very different qualities as they appear to consciousness.

CHAPTER 9

Aesthetic qualities as structural resemblance

Divergence and perceptual forces in poetry

As I said in Chapter 1, in this chapter I am dealing with issues that display differences in degree, but may generate a variety of intense perceptual qualities. I will explore two sets of related features of poetic structure, which run all through my work, since my first English publication to my latest articles: convergence-and-divergence, and perceptual forces. I will mention convergence for the sake of comparison only, and concentrate on divergence and perceptual forces.

9.1   Emotional qualities and onomatopoeia

Traditional poetics has largely described the structures underlying these features, but had to resort to impressionistic means to point out their contribution to emotional qualities. Cognitive Poetics, by contrast, is tailor-made to deal with that aspect of poetry in a principled manner. As to aesthetic qualities, the following example may illuminate their nature. The adjective "sad" has different meanings in the sentences "My sister is sad", and "The music is sad". In the former, it refers to the mental processes of a flesh-and-blood person. In the latter it does not refer to the mental processes of the sound sequence. Nor does it refer to the mental processes the music arouses in the listener. One can be perfectly consistent when saying "That sad piece of music inspired me with happiness". It reports, rather, that the listener has detected some structural resemblance between the music and an emotion, such as low energy level, slow movement, and a withdrawn, unassertive attitude suggested by the minor key.[1] In this sense, "sad" refers to an aesthetic

---

1.   For a cognitive explanation (in an evolutionary perspective) of the "withdrawn, unassertive" affective character of the minor key see, e.g. Cook and Fujisawa 2006: 9–16; Cook and Hayashi 2008: 318–319. They invoke John Ohala's conception of a cross-species "frequency code" expounded in Chapter 11 below. As to the affective character of the major and minor modes, Cook and Hayashi (2008: 311) quote Jean-Philippe Rameau, the French composer and author of an influential book on harmony, who wrote in 1722: "'The major mode is suitable

quality of the music. Cognitive Poetics provides a conceptual system that allows to explore similar aesthetic qualities in specific instances of poetry. We will isolate two structural aspects of emotions: relative disorganization and deviation from normal energy level.

How do systems of music-sounds and verbal signs assume perceptual qualities endemic to other systems, such as human emotions or animal calls? At the present stage of my argument I only want to point out that the resources available in the target systems impose severe strictures on the process. Usually only very few features or configurations thereof are available in the target systems that may be shared with the source phenomena. So, the best one can do is to choose the nearest options available in the target system. Minute differences may suffice to transform the perceived character of a complex whole. As Krueger (1968:100–101) observed, the overall perceived qualities of "total complexes" is determined by minute differences: "It has been observed over and over that the smallest changes in experience are felt emotionally long before the change can be exactly described" (cf. Chapter 5).

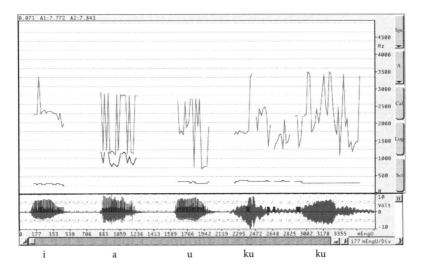

i   a   u   ku   ku

Figure 1. Wave plot, and the first and second formants of the cardinal vowels i-a-u, and of the European cuckoo's call. (Formants are concentrations of overtones that determine vowels and sound colour). Note that the formants of the bird's call are most similar to, but not identical with, the vowel [u] (produced on SoundScope)

for songs of mirth and rejoicing,' sometimes 'tempests and furies,' [...] as well as 'grandeur and magnificence.' The minor mode, on the other hand, is suitable for 'sweetness or tenderness, plaints, and mournful songs" (see Chapter 14).

In onomatopoeia, the phonological system of a language cannot reproduce the actual sounds of, e.g. the cuckoo's call: neither the minor-third interval, nor the sound quality, nor the abrupt onset. The bird says neither [k] nor [u]. The only thing one can do is to choose the speech sounds with the nearest formant structure (see Figure 1). A symphony orchestra, by contrast, can reproduce the minor-third interval, but not the formant structure of the call (cf. Chapter 11).

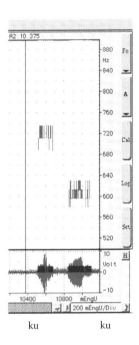 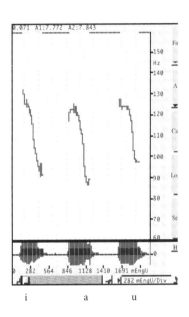

Figure 2. Wave plot and pitch abstract of the European cuckoo's call and of the cardinal vowels read by a professional reader

The nearest option to codify in human speech the abrupt onset of the call is the abrupt consonant [k] – all the other features of [k] are irrelevant. This use of voiceless stops to indicate abrupt onset appears to have some intercultural validity. The Chinese word for "cuckoo" is "pu-ku". In Japanese we have "Hatodokei" = dove + clock, but also "poppoo", "kokyu" and "kakkou". In the orchestra, the abrupt onset is indicated more directly (see Figure 3). Thus, the voiceless plosive [k] is a bundle of perceptual features, a subset of which is frequently exploited by the context to suggest some abrupt metallic noises as "ticktack" or "click"; but in the case of "cuckoo" only the perceptual feature [+ABRUPT] is utilized. Thus, the same elements or configurations in a target system may serve as the "nearest option" for a wide range of source phenomena.

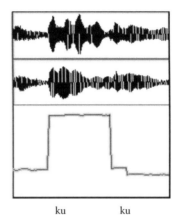

ku   ku

Figure 3. Sound waves and pitch extract of the imitation of the cuckoo's call in L. Mozart's "Toy Symphony" (produced on Praat)

In a recent paper (2007; see now Tsur 2012) I discuss Milton's verse line

1.   And sát as prínces, whom the supréme kíng
     w   s   w   s   w   s   w   s   w   s

and quote Milton's 1809 editor, Henry J. Todd's comment: "I conceive that Milton also intended the last foot of [this] verse to be a spondee, as more digni-fied and impressive than the accentuation […] of *súpreme* on the first syllable" (Todd 1970:199). As a side issue, I raise the question what "dignified" may mean with reference to metric structures. It suggests, I claim, that the listener may detect some structural resemblance between the consecutive heavy stresses and the outward manifestations of dignity in humans, such as weightiness, reserve of manner, and clearly-articulated gestures. "Weightiness" in a context of two consecutive stressed syllables encumbered by an unstressed syllable of a disyllable in a strong position suggests "massive", "hard to deal with" or "demanding great effort". In a context of dignified human behavior it suggests "of much importance or consequence". As to "reserve", a stressed syllable in a weak position (followed by another stressed syllable) "holds back" the rhythmic movement of the line, whereas a dignified person "holds back", "controls" his responses, the expression of his emotions or thoughts. As to "clearly articulated gestures" in poetry, I argue in that paper that the rhythmical performance of such constructs as a disyllable with its second, stressed, syllable in a weak position requires exceptionally clear artic-ulation. According to the foregoing analysis, then, within the limited resources of metric structures, consecutive stresses with some additional difficulty are the nearest perceptual options for suggesting a general quality of muchness, slow-ness and articulateness that can be individuated through the meaning of words as expressing dignity. But notice this. There is no iconic relationship here between metric structure and contents. Rather, the contents individuates as dignified the generalized qualities suggested by the metric structure. Pope's

2.   And ten low words oft creep in one dull line

is not perceived as "dignified"; rather, the two verse lines exploit different potentials of slowness suggested by successive stressed syllables.[2]

9.2   Convergent and divergent style

The terms "convergent" and "divergent" are taken from optics where they are applied to rays of light which meet or tend to meet in a focus, and to rays which continually depart from one another. Guilford (1970 [1959[1]]) adopted those terms in the phrases "convergent-thinking" and "divergent-thinking abilities", referring by them to logical and creative thinking, respectively. One may add that emotional processes are typically more divergent than non-emotional mental processes. This suggests a spectrum: LOGICAL THINKING→CREATIVE THINKING→EMOTIONAL PROCESSES. Emotional and non-emotional processes do not constitute a rigid dichotomy, but a continuum. "There is no point on this continuum", says Elizabeth Duffy (1968: 138), "where a 'non-emotional' degree of disorganization of response changes suddenly to an 'emotional' degree of disorganization; and there is no point at which a 'non-emotional' conscious state changes suddenly to an 'emotional' one. These characteristics of experience and behavior show continuous variation rather than separation into hard and fast categories". The same holds true of the energy-level continuum. I borrowed Guilford's terms to describe the structural resemblance between certain poetic structures on the one hand, and convergent and divergent mental processes on the other. Now notice this: "disorganization" in divergent poetry is, still, severely constrained by regular meter.

    I propose to introduce the distinction "convergence vs. divergence" by comparing two passages in which other things are really equal, in fact, *literally* identical, where the only difference is the line division:

---

2.   As to the desirable potential of slowness see, e.g. Shakespeare's Sonnet 94:

    They that have power to hurt and will do none,
    That do not do the thing they most do show,
    Who, moving others, are themselves as stone,
    Unmoved, cold, and to temptation slow,
    They rightly do inherit heaven's graces...

3. But wherefore thou alone? Wherefore with thee
   Came not all Hell broke loose? Is pain to them
   Less pain, less to be fled, or thou than they
   Less hardy to endure? Courageous Chief,
   The first in flight from pain, had'st thou alleg'd
   To thy deserted host this cause of flight,
   Thou surely had'st not come sole fugitive.

   (*Paradise Lost* IV. 917–923)

4.   But wherefore thou alone?
   Wherefore with thee came not all Hell broke loose?
   Is pain to them less pain, less to be fled,
   Or thou than they less hardy to endure?
   Courageous Chief, the first in flight from pain,
   Had'st thou alleg'd to thy deserted host
   This cause of flight, thou surely had'st not come
   Sole fugitive.

Excerpt 3 consists of a series of "straddled lines". These are sentences run-on from one line to another which themselves, when isolated, form an iambic pentameter line. The run-on lines of Excerpt 3 are rearranged (by James Whaler 1956) into end-stopped lines in Excerpt 4. This rearrangement affects the perceived quality of the passage. Excerpt 3 is perceived as fluid, whereas Excerpt 4 as more stable. When the syntactic unit and the verse line coincide, they reinforce each other's shape, yielding "strong Gestalts". When the syntactic unit is run on from one line to another, they blur each other, yielding "weak Gestalts". I've asked students "Is irony equally subtle in the two passages?" Some students could discern no significant difference. But the rest were in agreement that irony seems to be 'somehow subtler' in Excerpt 3. How can we explain this? Semantically and syntactically the two passages are identical.

Gestalt psychologists have produced evidence that strong Gestalts are typically perceived as rational, non-emotional, whereas weak Gestalts typically display an emotional quality. A similar correlation emerges from findings of the Rorschach inkblot test (Rorschach 1951; Alcock 1963). In Excerpt 3, the sentences run on from line to line, and the line boundaries intruding upon the sentences blur each other, weakening each other's shape.

Leonard B. Meyer, who applies Gestalt theory to music, accounts for the association of weak and strong Gestalts with emotional and intellectual qualities as follows. "Because good shape is intelligible in this sense, it creates a psychological atmosphere of certainty, security, and patent purpose, in which the listener feels a sense of control and power as well as a sense of specific tendency and definite direction" (Meyer 1956: 160). Poor shapes generate an opposite atmosphere.

We have noted, however, that the divergent structure in Excerpt 3 seems to affect not only emotional qualities, but irony too, rendering it subtler. Meyer's formulation may account for this effect too, precisely because it refers to a general psychological atmosphere, rather than a specific attitude.

The ironic attitude typically involves some kind of pretended ignorance, pretending to have no specific intentions. The "psychological atmosphere of patent purpose" inspired by the stronger Gestalts in Excerpt 4 subverts, therefore, the tone of elusive ignorance in irony. Weak Gestalts, divergent structures, may enhance, then, quite diverse attitudes. Rather than indicating an iconic relationship between form and content, divergent structures generate a "a psychological atmosphere of uncertainty, lack of patent purpose and definite direction", concreted by various kinds of contents in a variety of more specific attitudes.

9.3 Perceptual forces (large scale)

Our other term is "perceptual forces". At the beginning of his book *Art and Visual Perception*, Arnheim demonstrates "the hidden structure of a square" by placing a black cardboard disk in various positions on a white square.

Figures 4–5 Perceptual forces: the disks display restlessness experienced as a tendency to get away from where they are placed, toward the middle or toward the boundary

Thus he "maps out" regions of tension and balance. In Figure 4, the disk lies slightly off the centre. "In looking at the disk" he says "we may find that it does not merely occupy a certain place but exhibits restlessness. This restlessness may be experienced as a tendency of the disk to get away from where it is placed or, more specifically, as a pull in a particular direction – for example, toward the center" (Arnheim 1967: 2).

"Psychologically", says Arnheim, "the pulls in the disk exist in the experience of any person who looks at it" (idem, 6). "There is no point in calling these forces 'illusions' [he says]. They are no more illusory than colors, which are attributed to the objects themselves, although they are actually nothing but the reactions of the nervous system to light of particular wave lengths" (idem, 8). "The disk is most stably settled when its center coincides with the center of the square. In Figure 5 it may be seen as drawn toward the contour to the right. With changing distance this effect will weaken or even turn into its opposite" (idem, 3).

Do perceptual forces exist in verbal structures as well? Fodor and his colleagues used this principle to test the psychological reality of constituent or phrase structure of sentences. The technique is based on the Gestalt assumption that a perceptual unit tends "to preserve its integrity by resisting interruptions" (Fodor & Bever 1965: 415). In the experiment, subjects listened to a sentence during which a click occurred, and immediately afterward were required to write down the sentence and indicate where the click had occurred. If a phrase is a perceptual unit, subjects should tend to hear a click which occurred during a phrase as having occurred between the phrases. One of their sentences was "That he was happy was evident from the way he smiled". This sentence has a major break between "happy" and "was". A click was placed at various positions in this sentence. [...] Each subject heard the sentence with only one click on it. Fodor and Bever found that subjects were most accurate in locating the click which occurred between the two major phrases of the sentence – i.e. between "happy" and "was" in the above example. Clicks occurring before this break tended to be displaced towards the right (i.e. into the break), and those occurring after the break towards the left (i.e. again into the break). A later experiment indicates that even where there can be no acoustic cues for a break, mere syntactic knowledge may evoke such perceptual forces (see Appendix). Fodor et al. however, overlooked one crucial point. If the intrusion occurs in the middle of a perceptual unit, it induces balance and stability; it is only when it occurs between the middle and the boundary that it induces perceptual forces.

For our present purpose, these results have two important implications: first, that perceptual forces do exist in a linguistic environment; second, that perceptual forces in a linguistic environment are crucially influenced by the placement of the intruding event relative to the boundary of the perceptual unit. In poetic prosody there is a further complication. One cannot elicit perceptual forces with the help of some extralinguistic click. However, syntactic boundaries may intrude upon verse lines perceived as *wholes*; and line boundaries may intrude upon syntactic units. Here the exponents of both the intruding and the disrupted events are conveyed by the same noises, by the *same* words.

In a verse line, a syntactic break at the caesura reinforces balance and symmetry; the nearer to the end of the line, the more it presses toward the end for completion. Consequently, our relief will be greater when the missing part is supplied. This may generate, in certain circumstances, a sharp, witty effect, turning the last string of syllables into a "punch-phrase", so to speak. In Excerpt 5, from Pope's *An Essay on Criticism*, there is little that can account for the wit of the second line, except the requiredness of the last word:

5.   Some foreign writers, some our own despise,
      The ancients only, or the moderns, prize.

This is a characteristic feature of Pope's wit. In divergent poetry, the effect is much more sophisticated. A syntactic break near the line boundary exerts pressure toward the boundary; but the verse line is not end-stopped: the sentence runs on to the next line. In such cases a sense of sweeping movement may be generated. Consider, for instance, the following excerpt from Milton's "On his blindness", and note the placement of the two tokens of "best".

6.   "God doth not need
      Either man's work, nor his own gifts. Who best
      Bear his mild yoke, they serve him best. His state
      Is kingly: thousands at his bidding speed,
      And post o'er land and ocean without rest;
      They also serve who only stand and wait."

The sentence "Who best bear his mild yoke, they serve him best" could constitute an iambic pentameter line, and the repeated "best" would enhance the symmetry and stability of its segments. Had Milton divided this run-on line into 6+4 syllables,

7.   Who best bear his mild yoke,
      They serve him best,

he would have generated a relatively mild divergent movement. As it stands, straddled over two lines, beginning in the ninth position and ending in the eighth position of the next line, the repeated pair of words introduces asymmetry and great instability into the sequence. The nearer an intruding break to the middle of a perceptual unit, the more it enhances symmetry; the nearer to its boundary, the more it enhances asymmetry and instability. Here the straddled line begins near the line boundary and ends just before the next line boundary. The first token of "best" occurs at the line boundary which, in turn, intrudes upon the complex sentence near its beginning; the second token of "best" occurs at the sentence boundary which, in turn, intrudes upon the line near its end.

Now compare this to the following excerpt from Coleridge's "The Rime of the Ancient Mariner";

8.   Farewell, farewell! but this I tell
            To thee, thou Wedding-Guest!
      He prayeth well, who loveth well
            Both man and bird and beast.

      He prayeth best, who loveth best
            All things both great and small;
      For the dear God who loveth us,
            He made and loveth all.

While in Milton's sonnet the two tokens of "best" disturb the balance and induce fluidity, Coleridge's repeated "well" and "best" generate stability: their two tokens occur at the precise middle and end of the line, generating a sharp, epigrammatic quality. The two syntactic units (ending with "well" or "best") converge with the two half-lines; in Milton, they diverge. Furthermore, while in Coleridge the relative clause *follows* the main clause: "He prayeth best, who loveth best", Milton inverts this order, so as to increase the predictive load of syntax, generating suspense: "Who best bear his mild yoke, they serve him best". Milton's poem conveys a theologically-laden inner struggle. The theological *ideas* assume an emotional character, the sententious tone of the dictum becomes affectionate, owing to the highly divergent structure of the text, suffused with impetuous perceptual forces, generating a perceptual quality that bears a structural resemblance to powerful emotions. The adjective "mild" softens the utterance both by its meaning, and by blurring the iambic metre.

   We have contrasted Milton's divergent sentence-and-versification structure to a similar but convergent structure in "The Ancient Mariner". We may, however, contrast it more immediately to the structure of the last line in the same poem: "They also serve who only stand and wait". Here the elements of language and versification act in consonance to generate an atmosphere of stability: as in Coleridge, the relative clause comes last; this is the only case in this divergent poem in which a whole sentence entirely converges with the line; and one of the exceptional cases in Milton in which stressed syllables occur only in strong positions, and in all strong positions. Thus, the juxtaposition of diametrically different configurations of language and versification points up the contrast between them, generating a powerful sense of fluidity leading up to an intense sense of stable closure.

   We have discussed perceptual forces at some length, in visual perception, the psycholinguistic laboratory, and enjambment in poetry. In music Cooper and Meyer (1960) pointed out similar perceptual forces: a steeply rising pitch sequence or intensity sequence (crescendo) has a marked forward grouping effect (it leads, so to speak, forward). The same phenomenon we find in speech, in rising intonation contours.

9.4 Perceptual forces (minute scale)

But the perceptual forces can be demonstrated at the sub-phonemic level too, in the alignment of intonation and syllable crest. At this level, the intruding event, the peak of the pitch contour, normally occurs in the middle of the syllabic crest, generating stability; in some instances, however, it occurs late in the vowel, or even on a sonorant after it; and sometimes it occurs earlier than the middle. I have found in my corpus of poetry-readings that late peaking generates an impetuous forward drive; in fact, the later the peaking, the more impetuous is the forward drive. An early peak effects backward grouping and stability. Let us observe peak delay in three recordings of line 7 from Shakespeare's second Sonnet :

9.   To say within thine ówn déep-súnken éyes

Let us listen to Marlowe Society's reading of this line. We will focus here only on certain aspects of the words "say", "within", and "own". The second syllable of "within" (being part of a function word) is perceived as unduly prominent, cued by stress, rising intonation and late peaking. Apparently, metric regularity in the first six syllables "To say within thine own" is straightforward enough, and there would appear to be no reason for such extravagant devices. But the reciter has a real problem here: the caesura occurs in the middle of a prepositional phrase. One must indicate an intruding event after "within", without disrupting the phrase.

    The over-articulation of "with*in*", coupled with an undue stress, without a pause, seems to have here one purpose: to indicate a caesura, without stopping. Listening again to the line confirms that after both words ("within" and "say") there is an impetuous drive across a discontinuity. In the case of "say" it is the contents that compels the reciter to separate the reporting phrase from the reported speech; but if he wants to preserve the line's perceptual integrity, he must preserve the first four syllables, up to the caesura, as one unit. There is no pause after "say" or after "within". In both instances, discontinuity is indicated by an exceptionally long word-final sonorant, /j/ and /n/ respectively, and a drastic change of the direction of the pitch contour. In "say" there is a late peak on the second sound of the diphthong. In the second syllable of "within" there is a double peak, one occurring at the end of /i/, the other on /n/. This late peak bestows extreme prominence on "with*in*", emphasizing the strong position, but also displays an impetuous forward push. On "own" in Position 6 there is an additional late peak: it serves the need to group the word forward with the next two words, so as to begin the string of stressed syllables in a strong position.

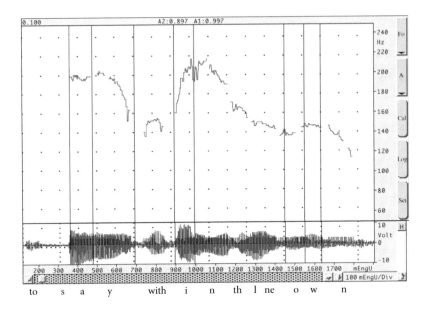

Figure 6. Wave plot and pitch extract of "to say within thine own" in the Marlowe Society's reading. The markers indicate diphthong and vowel boundaries. Notice the late peaks on *say*, *-thin* and *own*

Admittedly, the pitch movement the Marlowe Society assigns to the sequence "to say within" is exceptional: these pitch movements cannot be predicted from spoken English prosody, or from any possible metric deviation; it is, indeed, justified solely by the evasive problem of caesura and line integrity. Notwithstanding this, Callow has recourse to similar intonation contours. He seems to identify exactly the same problems in the first six syllables of the line; and offers exactly the same kind of solution. Here too there is a conspicuous late peak on the second syllable of "within", and the word-final /n/ is exceptionally long. Figure 8 reveals a rather high and exceptionally late peak on "say".

Listening to Gielgud's performance indicates a conception that is rather similar to that of the other two reciters, but with considerably different emphases. Pitch resets very high on "say", with a late peak on /j/ of the diphthong, imposing a forward impetus to the whole line. This drives across an enhanced break indicated both by a pitch discontinuity and a straightforward 100-msec pause.

In Gielgud's performance, the peak on the stressed /i/ of "with*in*" is rather moderate; but it occurs very late in the vowel, and there is an additional peak on /n/. The two syllables /(ə)in/ and /(ə)ajn/ belong to two consecutive function words. They happen to be very similar, but of different duration: the sequence /–(ə)in/ is 239 msec long, of which /n/ takes 148 msec; whereas /(ə)ajn/ is only 155 msec long, of which /n/ takes 67 msec. This relatively long duration contributes to

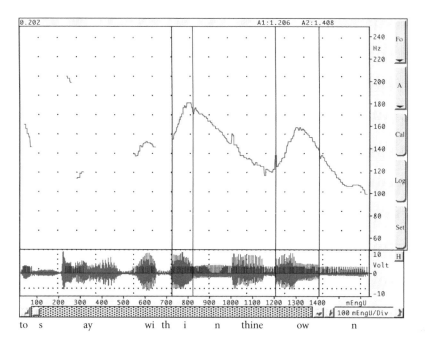

Figure 7. Wave plot and F_0 extract of "to say within thine own" in Callow's reading. The pairs of markers indicate vowel boundaries. Notice the late peak on *-thin*

the perception of great stress on "wi*thin*", also signaling conspicuous discontinuity. This combination of cues indicates a caesura after "within" and, at the same time, an impetuous drive across it. A similar story can be told of "own" in the sixth position. (19)

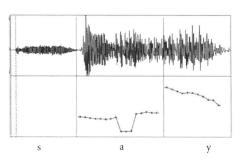

Figure 8. Wave plot and pitch extract of "say" in Callow's reading (produced on Praat)

Late peaking is a rare, relatively little-understood phenomenon. Gerry Knowles (1992) notes that in ordinary speech it usually occurs in the middle of tone groups after a pause. As to its function, Robert Ladd says: "peak delay is said to signal that the utterance is in some way very significant or non-routine" (Ladd 1996:99). The more remarkable it is that in this line three leading British actors have recourse to it several times at the same places in the line, most notably on a preposition, at places where no pauses precede them, but some forward thrust is called for, for rhythmic reasons. These actors utilize, then, a kind of vocal manipulation available in language for semantic emphasis – to cope with rhythmic complexities.

At this subphonemic level, a crucial methodological issue arises. Phonology is interested in speech categories, not in precategorial acoustic cues. There may be a variety of acoustic cues that convey a certain phonological feature, with considerable trade-off between them. Voicing of a consonant, for instance, may be conveyed by straightforward activation of the vocal folds, or by decreasing the voice-onset-time after the consonant, or by lengthening the preceding vowel. But as long as they convey voicing of the consonant, it makes little difference for the phonologist what precategorial acoustic cue performs the job. Likewise, what matters for the phonologist is that the highest peak of an intonation curve coincides with the stressed syllable of the most strongly accented word in the sentence. It makes little difference whether it "hits" the vowel in its middle or elsewhere. But, as some British phoneticians pointed out, from the expressive point of view this

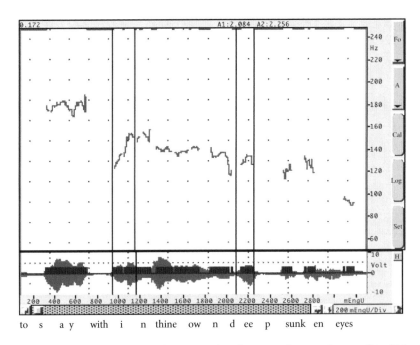

Figure 9. Wave plot and F_0 extract of "to say within thine own deep-sunken eyes" in Gielgud's reading. The pairs of markers indicate vowel boundaries. Notice the late peaks on -*thin* and *deep*

may make all the difference; and, as I have found, it may affect the rhythmic character of a verse line as well. Likewise, in Chapter 2 I suggested that in Tennyson's
"And murmuring of innumerable bees" even the [b] seems to have a fuller, richer,
more resonant body than in Ransom's rewriting "And murdering of innumerable
beeves". The voiced stop [b] is perceived in the *murdering* context as a unitary
speech sound. The *murmuring* context, by contrast, seems to separate the periodic
"voiced" feature in [b]. One may speculate that perhaps different acoustic cues for
voicing are at work here: say, in the "compact" [b] lengthening of the preceding
vowel; in the resonant [b] separation of the periodic "voiced" feature by a minute
voice onset time.

9.5   Materials and structures

I have proposed an approach to emotional qualities in poetry that closely resembles
iconicity. It does not, however, pursue an iconic relationship between form and
content. The form-and-content approach allows the critic to handle only those
instances in which the similarity between form and content exists, or else compels
him to read the similarity into them. The present approach replaces this dichotomy by the materials-and-structures dichotomy proposed by Wellek and Warren
(1956:129). It regards both the contents and the formal elements of versification
as aesthetically neutral *materials* that can be combined into aesthetic structures.
According to the Wellek and Warren model a wide range of elements (which are
independent variables) may occur in any combination, and thus the tools offered
here may serve to describe any unforeseen combination of elements in a poem.
Unforeseen combinations may display unforeseen Gestalt qualities, and Cognitive
Poetics may systematically account for them. When we say "The music is sad", we
refer to an aesthetic quality of the music. When we say "The poem is sad", we may
refer *either* to the mere contents of the poem, *or* to an aesthetic quality arising from
a configuration of divergent structure, low energy level, slow motion, sad contents.

Contents, "projected world", word meanings, phonetic structure, metaphor,
meter, rhyme, alliteration, are all materials. Structures are their various combinations. Poetic effects arise from the subtle interaction of a great variety of materials.
The sequence of stressed and unstressed syllables may converge with or diverge
from the sequence of strong and weak metric positions; syntactic units may
coincide with verse lines, or may run on from one line to another; alliteration may
work in conjunction with, or against, meter; and so forth. Briefly, they may act in
convergence reinforcing each other, yielding exceptionally strong Gestalts, sometimes with a pervasive witty quality, sometimes suggesting simplified mastery of
reality, as in nursery rhymes. Or they may act in divergence blurring each other,

so as to yield an exceptionally weak Gestalt with a pervasive emotional or subtle ironic quality. Such divergence may be reinforced by abstract nouns in a landscape defined here and now (as suggested in Chapter 5). "Hypnotic" poetry typically involves exceptionally regular meter–stress mappings, end-stopped lines but unpredictable groupings of lines, alliterations that work both in conjunction with and against meter, frequent repetition of key phrases, high energy level, the irruption of the irrational in the world stratum; and so forth.

Finally, the various configurations need not necessarily comprise homogeneous elements. Consider again "Who best bear his mild yoke, they serve him best". The strained enjambment, the relative clause preceding the main clause, the consecutive stressed syllables "mild yoke" and "best bear" with the alliteration in adjacent stressed syllables, induce a sense of fluidity and uncertainty. At the same time, the superlative "best", its symmetrical repetition at the two extremes, and the epigrammatic formulation, all inspire an atmosphere of certainty and stability. Such opposing effects need not generate a conflict between fluidity and stability or mitigate each other. On the contrary, where the powerful drift is established as dominant, the robust stabilizing elements may be perceived as vigorous intrusions at the "wrong" places, enhancing fluidity rather than stability. This divergent, fluid structure has, in Coleridge's terms, the unpredictability of life and nature, of a "feeling profound and vehement" which, at the same time, is brought "under the irremissive, though gentle and unnoticed, control of will and understanding" – effected by the closure, after the event. But notice this: we don't perceive an *analogy* between the verbal structure and emotional processes; rather, we perceive the verbal structure *as* displaying an emotional quality.

There are no rules to infer the aesthetic qualities emerging from configurations of aesthetically neutral elements. Paraphrasing Frank Sibley (1962), we decide that a piece of music is sad by listening or that a piece of poetry is dignified by reading, just as we decide that the book is blue by looking or that the tea is sweet by tasting. According to the present conception, disagreement whether a piece of convergent poetry is hypnotic, witty, playful, monotonous, cheerful or suggests simplified mastery of reality may be due to different mental organizations of the same aesthetically neutral elements.

Appendix

Observations on Larsen's criticism of the click experiment

Larsen (1971) criticized Fodor & Bever's and related experiments, pointing out that due to insufficient precision of the postulate, results obtained by the click technique seem uninterpretable at present. He pointed out two flaws in their procedure. First, two crucial categories of responses were excluded from their data analyses: responses to clicks objectively located in the major syntactic break itself; and correct subjective locations of clicks objectively located outside the major break. Second, the notion of "constituent" is rather fuzzy. Every word boundary is at the same time a constituent boundary – though at different levels in the hierarchy of constituents. The simplest prediction, therefore, on the assumption that perceptual units resist interruption would be: Noise heard during speech should tend to be located perceptually between words rather than within words. Larsen's experiment refutes this hypothesis.

I agree that the exclusions mentioned by Larsen are hard to understand. I also agree that the notion of "constituent" is rather fuzzy (I have written on this, back in 1973). But it is clear from Fodor et al.'s examples that they are not dealing with just any syntactic constituent, but with constituents delimited by major syntactic boundaries. Thus, for instance, Garret, Bever and Fodor (1966) recorded pairs of sentences such as:

(1)   As a result of their invention's *influence the company was given an award.*
                                                                        *   *

(2)   The chairman whose methods still *influence the company was given an award.*
                                                                        *   *

When subjects were asked where they hear the longest pause in the sentences, they report – as one might expect – that they hear a pause in (1) between "influence" and "the", and in (2) between "company" and "was". The perceived pause thus corresponds to the major constituent boundaries in the two sentences.

Then, the two italicized segments were interchanged. "*Subjects' perception of pause location, however, was unchanged.* The same was true of click displacement. As indicated by asterisks in the two sentences above, a click occurred either during "company" or "was". The perception of click location, however, was significantly different for the two sentences. The click in sentence (1) tended to be heard between "influence" and "the", and in (2) between "company" and "was". But remember the sentences were acoustically identical" (Slobin 1971: 25–26; italics in original). At any rate, click displacement occurs not even toward the boundary between NP and VP, but toward "major syntactic boundaries" – even when the same acoustically identical words are used.

As we have seen in Chapter 1, according to the predictions of Gestalt theory, the stronger a boundary, the greater its effect on perceptual phenomena. Thus, we shouldn't expect word boundaries and clause boundaries have the same effect on an intruding click, even though both "words" and "clauses" can be labeled "constituents".

Anyway, Larsen's criticism does not affect my argument for two reasons. First, both Fodor et al. and Larsen overlook a crucial point. Perceptual forces are expected to be caused by intrusion not anywhere inside a unit, but between the middle and the boundary of a unit. Intrusion in the middle is expected to reinforce rather than upset stability. Thus, Larsen's finding that clicks tend to be perceived in midword rather than *between* words does not necessarily jeopardize my position. Second, my main concern here is not the psychological reality of linguistic units, but two more immediate phenomena: whether perceptual forces do exist in a linguistic environment; and whether they tend to push toward the nearest boundary when dislocated from the middle. In this respect, Larsen's experiment replicated Fodor et al.'s findings. Larsen concludes that in view of his findings two alternatives and less arbitrary decisions are possible: (1) to reject the hypothesis that linguistic constituents are perceptual units; or (2) to reject the assumption that perceptual units resist interruptions. In view of the importance attributed here to the point in the middle, a third possibility is well worth experimenting too: that an intruding event reinforces perceptual units in their middle, but generate a "push" when they occur between their middle and their boundaries. Thus, for instance, one may expect that a major syntactic boundary reinforces the stability of a verse line when it falls at the caesura, but generates fluidity when it occurs between the caesura and the line boundary. This appears to apply to the alignment of intonation peak and syllabic crest as well. On one point in this respect all researchers appear to agree: that an intonation peak hitting the middle of a syllabic crest is the unmarked option, whereas late and early peaking are marked.

Moreover, I have predicted and empirically found that if you add two syllables at the end of an iambic pentameter line with a caesura after the fourth position, there is a strong tendency to move the caesura to the right, after the sixth position – if the prevailing conditions permit (and sometimes even if they don't). Consider:

3.   Invoke thy aid to my advent'rous song.

(Paradise Lost I. 13).

In this line, the caesura occurs after *aid* in Position 4. Suppose however, that we add two more syllables to the verse line, turning it into an iambic hexameter, thus:

4.   Invoke thy aid to my advent'rous song of praise.

If one continues to observe a caesura after *aid*, Excerpt 4 is liable to fall apart. Here the caesura, in harmony with the perceptual needs of the iambic hexameter, is automatically shifted to after *my* in Position 6, even though this happens in mid-phrase. Here a feeling is generated of a caesura as well as a "sense of impulsion across the [non-existent] break".

At any rate, Larsen gives no information where exactly in mid-word do the dislocated clicks occur in his experiment; and neither Larsen, nor Fodor et al.

indicate whether correct subjective locations of clicks do or do not occur at the middle of a larger syntactic constituent (e.g. clause). This problem is aggravated by another, methodological difficulty: while it is relatively easy to determine where is the boundary of a clause or the middle of a word or a verse line, we have no criteria to determine where is the perceptual middle of a clause. Thus, neither Fodor et al.'s nor Larsen's click experiments may explain why some clicks are correctly located in mid-clause and some not, nor may, perhaps, prove that syntactic constituents have psychological reality; but they strongly suggest that when clicks are subjectively displaced in mid-clause, they move in the expected direction, and seem to corroborate my assumptions. I said "seems to", because to get more compelling results one should re-devise the whole click experiment in view of the importance attributed to the middle point.

CHAPTER 10

Metaphor and figure–ground relationship

Comparisons from poetry, music, and the visual arts

There was an old joke in Soviet Russia about a guard at the factory gate who at the end of every day saw a worker walking out with a wheelbarrow full of straw. Every day he thoroughly searched the contents of the wheelbarrow, but never found anything but straw. One day he asked the worker: "What do you gain by taking home all that straw?" "The wheelbarrows". This chapter is about the straw and the wheelbarrow, about shifting attention from figure to ground or, rather, about turning into figure what is usually perceived as ground. We are used to think of the load as "figure"; the wheelbarrow is only "ground," merely an instrument. Our default interest is in the act, not in the instrument.

10.1   Basic gestalt rules of figure–ground

One of Anton Ehrenzweig's central claims in his seminal book *The Psychoanalysis of Artistic Vision and Hearing* ([1953] 1965) is that the contents of works of art is best approached in terms of psychoanalytic theory, while artistic form is best approached in terms of Gestalt theory. He has most illuminating things to say on these issues, both with reference to music and the visual arts. While I am not always convinced by his application of psychoanalysis to works of art, I find his discussions of Gestalts and what he calls "Gestalt-free" elements (discussed at the end of Section 2) most compelling and illuminating.

Further, Gestalt theory has been systematically applied to the visual arts by Rudolf Arnheim (1957), and to emotion and meaning in music by Leonard B. Meyer (1956). Cooper and Meyer (1960) applied it to the rhythmic structure of music. One of the earliest and perhaps the most important application of Gestalt theory to literature is Barbara Herrnstein-Smith's mind-expanding book *Poetic Closure* (1968).

During the past two and a half decades I myself devoted much research to poetic prosody; I have found that many of the aesthetically most interesting issues regarding poetic rhythm, rhyme patterns and stanza form can be understood only through having recourse to Gestalt theory (e.g. Tsur 1977, 1992: 111–179, 1998b, 2006: 115–141; Tsur et al. 1990, 1991). In the present chapter, I will discuss the prosodic and syntactic elements in relation to only one excerpt, by Shakespeare (Section 6); otherwise I will mostly explore figure–ground relationships in the projected, extralinguistic world.

What Gestalt theorists call "figure–ground relationship" is one of the most interesting issues in Gestalt theory, both from the perceptual and the artistic point of view. The *Fontana Dictionary of Modern Thought* provides the following definition:

> **figure–ground phenomenon** The characteristic organization of perception into a figure that "stands out" against an undifferentiated background, e.g. a printed word against a background page. What is figural at any one moment depends on patterns of sensory stimulation and on the momentary interests of the perceiver. See also GESTALT

Look, for instance, at Figures 1a and b. In Figure 1a the pattern of sensory stimulation allows to see either a goblet or two faces; the perceiver may alternate between seeing the black area as figure and the white area as ground, or vice versa. In the droodle presented in Figure 1b, obviously, the four triangular shapes with the pairs of elliptical dots in them are the shapes; the white space between them is the ground. This configuration is reinforced by the caption. However, when one shifts attention to the white space in the middle, one will discover that it has the shape of a distinct "formée" cross, which has now become the figure, and relegates the triangular shapes to the background (see also Tsur 1994).

In this respect Gestalt theorists discovered that some of the commonsense perceptual phenomena are not at all to be taken for granted as it would appear to the man in the street. They not only brought to attention a most interesting phenomenon, but also laid down rigorous rules of the perceptual organization processes that create figure–ground relationships. The better the shape, the more it tends to stand out as a figure and, less tautologically, there are rigorous principles that account for what makes a shape "better" or "worse". Indeed, we always try to experience things in "as good a Gestalt way as possible".

Let us just hint briefly at the most important Gestalt laws by which the mind organizes perception into figure and ground. Hochberg (1964: 86) names the following: (A) **Area**. The smaller a closed region, the more it tends to be seen as figure. Thus, as the area of the white cross decreases in Figure 2 from *a* to *b*, its tendency to be seen as figure increases. In Figure 1a it is easier to see a black

Figure 1a. You can either see a figure a black goblet standing in front of a white ground, or you can see two white faces, looking at each other, in front of a black ground

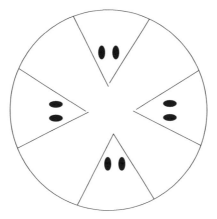

Figure 1b. Four Ku Klux Klansmen looking down a well

goblet against a continuous white ground than two faces against a black ground. (B) **Proximity**. Dots or objects that are close together tend to be grouped together into one figure. In Figure 3 the more or less evenly distributed dots constitute the ground; the figure, the enlarged print of an eye, is generated by similar dots packed more closely together. This is, also, how TV and computer screens and printers as well as photo reproductions work. (C) **Closedness**. Areas with closed contours tend to be seen as figure more than do those with open contours. (D) **Symmetry**. The more symmetrical a closed region, the more it tends to be seen as figure. I have not specifically illustrated (C) and (D), but most of our examples in this chapter illustrate them.

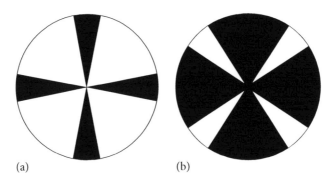

(a)   (b)

Figure 2. The 'Area' Gestalt law

Figure 3. The 'Proximity' Gestalt law

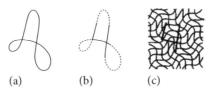

(a)   (b)   (c)

Figure 4. The 'Good continuation' Gestalt law

(E) **Good continuation.** Importantly, perceptual preference is given to the figure–ground arrangements that will make the fewest changes or interruptions in straight or smoothly curving lines or contours. All three drawings in Figure 4 contain the digit 4, but one can discern it only in (b) and (c). In (c) the ground consists of lines curving as smoothly as possible, setting off the straight lines and segregating the shape of the digit 4. In (a) and (b) the straight lines of the digit are part of the same smoothly curving contour. However, Figure (a) conceals the 4 in a larger and closed Gestalt, whose entire contour consists of a single solid continuous line, whereas (b) sets off the straight solid lines of the digit from the dotted line in the rest of the figure.

10.2 Figure and ground in the visual arts

For the study of art, one insight should be added to our basic set of rules.[1] "Shape may […] be regarded as a kind of stylistic "mean" lying between the extremes of chaotic overdifferentiation and primordial homogeneity" (Meyer 1956: 161), where "primordial homogeneity" is a sort of "nothingness," and "chaotic overdifferentia-tion" a kind of "too muchness". "Chaotic overdifferentiation" constitutes perceptual overload on the cognitive system, which alleviates this overload by dumping it into the background as an undifferentiated mass. Thus, good shapes tend to stand out as figures, whereas both "primordial homogeneity" and "chaotic overdifferentiation" tend to be relegated to ground. The minute curves with their changing directions in Figure 4c may serve as a rudimentary example of overdifferentiation.

In Figure 1b the "triangles" are well-differentiated closed shapes symmetrically distributed in the area; the pairs of dots further differentiate them. The caption reinforces our "interest" in them. The triangular areas are much smaller than the white space separating them. This space in the middle, however, yields a sufficiently symmetrical and closed shape to become figure when shifting attention to it. Once you discover this white cross, you find it difficult to suppress it. One key term for the perceptual distinction between figure and ground is, then, "relative differentia-tion". Both in music and the visual arts partially overlapping good shapes may blur each other so as to form an overdifferentiated (hence, lowly-differentiated) back-ground. Irregularly distributed lines and dots suggest chaotic overdifferentiation and make a rather poor shape; but, as we shall see soon, when they occur within the closed area of a shape, they render the shape more differentiated relative to other similar shapes and tend to shift it in the *figure* direction.

Such artists as M.C. Escher deliberately experiment with the figure–ground phenomenon in visual perception. Escher himself described the organizing prin-ciple of Figure 6 (and similar drawings) as follows:

> In each case there are three stages to be distinguished. The first stage is the reverse of the final stage – that is, a white object on a black background as against a black object on a white background. The second stage is intermediary between the two, and is the true, complete division of the plane, in which the opposing elements are equal. (Escher 1992: 164)

---

1. Other specific insights relevant for visual arts concern e.g. colour interaction in figure and ground: "The incisiveness of form, such as the comparative sharpness of its outline, or its pregnant shape, or the conflict or parallelism between superimposed or juxtaposed forms and so on, can be summed up as qualities of a "good" Gestalt. We can summarize therefore that colour interaction between figure and ground stands in inverse proportion to the good gestalt of the figure" (Ehrenzweig 1970: 172; cf. Chapter 2, above).

Three points in Escher's experiments are relevant to our problem. First, though according to Gestalt theory the better the shape the more it is likely to be perceived as figure, sometimes the same shapes may serve as figure or as ground. Thus, additional differentiating devices seem to be at work. Second, the dots and lines on some shapes seem to serve as such "differentiating devices" that may turn them into figure (some of the fish have lines on one fin, and no lines on the other, which turns them half figure, half ground, emerging, as it were, "from nowhere"). In one instance in Figure 5, one single dot within the area (indicating, as it were, the eye of the "bird") slightly shifts the shape in the direction of figure. Third, with very little conscious effort we can almost freely switch from one organization to another, sending figure shapes to the ground and vice versa. At the right end of Figure 6, for instance, the eye oscillates between seeing the white patches as schematic fish or a continuous shapeless background to the black fish; at the left end, conversely, the black patches can be seen as schematic fish or a continuous background to differentiated white fish.

Figure 5. Escher: Liberation

Figure 6. Escher: Woodcut II, strip 3

   Intimately related to figure–ground perception are Anton Ehrenzweig's (1965) terms "thing-free," "Gestalt-free," and "thing destruction", as explained in detail in Chapter 1. In poetry, as we have seen in Chapter 5, thing-free and Gestalt-free qualities are typically generated by the connotations of words, or when abstract nouns are associated with space perception, or when attributes are transformed into abstract nouns and manipulated into the referring position: "*Brightness* falls from the air," "The *gentleness* of heaven broods o'r the sea" or "This city now doth like a garment wear/The *beauty* of the morning" (cf. Chapter 5, above).

10.3   Form in other senses

Although figure–ground organization is not restricted to visual perception, its application in other domains is not always straightforward. As to the nature of the ground, for instance, there seems to be a crucial difference between the visual and the other modes of perception. Meyer writes: "It is difficult, if not impossible, even to imagine a visual figure without also imagining the more continuous, homogeneous ground against which it appears. But in "aural space," in music, there is no given ground; there is no necessary, continuous stimulation, against which all figures must be perceived" (1956: 186).

> Due to the absence of a necessary, given ground in aural experience, the mind of the listener is able to organize the data presented to it by the senses in several different ways. The musical field can be perceived as containing: (1) a single figure without any ground at all, as, for instance, in a piece for solo flute; (2) several figures without any ground, as in a polyphonic composition in which the several parts are clearly segregated and are equally, or almost equally, well shaped; (3) one or sometimes more than one figure accompanied by a ground, as in a typical homophonic texture of the eighteenth or nineteenth centuries; (4) a ground alone,

as in the introduction to a musical work – a song, for instance – where the melody or figure is obviously still to come; or (5) a superimposition of small motives which are similar but not exactly alike and which have little real independence of motion, as in so-called heterophonic textures.   (Meyer 1956: 186)[2]

In a series of brilliant experiments Al Bregman (online) demonstrated the principles of Gestalt grouping in the auditory mode. In his first example he demonstrated the principles of "Proximity" and "Area". The sequence used consists of three high and three low tones, alternating high and low tones. When the cycle is played slowly, one can clearly hear the alternation of high and low tones. When it is played fast, one experiences two streams of sound, one formed of high tones, the other of low ones, each with its own melody, as if two instruments, a high and a low one, were playing along together. When the sequence is played fast, the Law of Proximity works in two ways: the tones are "nearer" together in time than in the slow version; and the higher tones are "nearer" to each other in pitch than to the lower ones. Consequently, they organize themselves into two segregated but concurrent figures, each in its own register.

Listen online to the demo experiment:

| Al Bregman's Demo CD | Explanation of Example | Go straight to sound file 01 | Sound file 01 amplified | [20] |

In his works for unaccompanied cello and violin Bach experimented with exploiting the Gestalt rules of perception and figure–ground relationships thus generating polyphonic music on a single string instrument. When we say that two melodic lines occur *at the same time*, much depends on how long is *the same time*, that is, much depends on the duration of what we construct as the "immediate present". How does Bach fool the listener into thinking that he hears more than one line at a time? In respect of poetic prosody I have argued that the span of "the same time" is determined by the span of short-term memory. That might apply to Bach's music too.

[21]   **Music Excerpt 1**
Listen online to an excerpt from Menuet I from Bach's Unaccompanied Violin Partita No. 3 in E major.

[22]   **Music Excerpt 2**
Listen online to an excerpt from Fuga alla breve from Bach's Unaccompanied Violin Sonata No. 3 in C major.

---

2.   Meyer's use of the term "ground" refers to Gestalt theory. It should be noted that in music theory this term has a technically defined, somewhat different sense. This difference of senses may be one source of the disagreement reported below between Harai Golomb and myself.

Music Excerpt 3
Listen online to an excerpt from Menuett from Bach's Unaccompanied Cello Suite No. 2 in D minor.

㉓

To impute unity on his different melodic lines, Bach relies on the Gestalt principles of **proximity** (generating harmony and counterpoint by way of restricting each melody to its own discrete register) and **good continuation** within each register (or pitch range). He suggests simultaneity of the separate melodic lines by sounding successive fragments of each melody in alternation with the other, within the constraints of short-term memory and the Gestalt rules of grouping. In this way he generates in Excerpts 1 and 3 a melodic line plus a background texture. In Excerpt 2 he accomplishes the feat of a fugue on a single string instrument, in which the melodic line in the second voice appropriately begins in the middle of the melody in the first voice. Technically, this works as follows. The melody of the fugue sounds something like **taa–TAM–tataRAMpampam**; and so forth. The two long notes **taa–TAM–** are simple enough to be played simultaneously with a more complex, faster melody (**tataRAMpampam**) in the other register. At the same time, it is grouped into a single figure with the ensuing **tataRAMpampam** section in its own register; which, in turn, coincides–according to the rules of the fugue – with the two long notes in the other register.[3]

10.4 Figures in narrative

In narrative the figure–ground phenomenon is not at all easy to track; and sometimes, as in music, the absence of a ground implies the absence of the whole phenomenon. Nonetheless, credit is due to the sociolinguist William Labov (1972) for his ingenious attempt to put this notion to use with reference to narratives. He pointed out that certain grammatical forms tend to relegate descriptions to a static ground, while some other grammatical forms tend to "foreground" the action of the narrative, which is the perceptual figure. One of the sad results of Labov's technique – for which he certainly cannot be blamed – is that quite a

---

3. More generally, Ehrenzweig writes: "To the extent to which a musical note is fitted into a clean melodic "line" it is prevented from fusing into harmonic tone "colour"; conversely a strong chord will temporarily fuse the loose strands of polyphony into solid tone colour so that the separate melodic lines disappear altogether. I have mentioned that the ear constantly oscillates between the harmonic fusion and polyphonic separation of the melodic lines; this conflict between "form" and "colour" belongs to the very life of music. A harmonically too luscious piece will soon lose its impact if it is not poised against a tough polyphonic structure" (1970: 173).

few linguists and literary critics who ignore the Gestaltist origin of these notions "diagnose" figure and ground in a text by applying Labov's grammatical categories quite mechanically. Labov's own practice is far from "labelling"; it is, indeed, highly functional, using linguistic categories to trace the transformation of experience into story grammar showing how language can organize experience-in-time as figures and ground. Very much in harmony with common sense and intuition, he pointed out (in the stories he collected in Harlem on a "memorable fight") that certain grammatical forms tend to foreground information as figure, and some tend to relegate it into the ground.[4] But this is a relative matter, and poets may turn the distinctions backside forward. At any rate, labelling objects as "agents" or "instruments" in isolation has nothing to do with the issue. The Cognitive Linguist Ronald Langacker, by contrast, explicitly acknowledges the Gestaltist origins of the figure–ground notion. As will be seen, his conceptions are very similar to the ones expounded in the present article (Langacker 1987: 120, 1990: 75) although, again, when they were applied to poetics by others, something went astray.

I have elsewhere discussed at considerable length the figure–ground relationship in a passage by Milton resulting from an interplay between prosodic and syntactic Gestalts and Gestalt-free elements in the "world stratum" of the work, in an attempt to account for what Ants Oras (1957) described as perceptual "depth" (Tsur 1977: 180–189, 1992: 85–92). In prosodic and syntactic structures too, good Gestalts, strong shapes, tend to yield figures; where strong shapes blur each other or interact with Gestalt-free qualities, they tend to blend in a ground.

10.5 Figure and ground (?) in poetry: Emily Dickinson

In her 2000 paper, "Poetry and the scope of metaphor: Toward a cognitive theory of literature," Margaret H. Freeman discusses several poems by Emily Dickinson. In relation to one of them she discusses the nature of Time in language and poetry.

> How do we understand time? It is commonly understood in two ways, depending on figure–ground orientation. That is, we can perceive time as a figure with respect to some ground, as when we say "Time flies when we're having fun," where time is seen as passing quickly across some given funfilled space. Or

---

4. It would be worth one's effort to investigate, in a separate study, how the resulting mental images do or do not preserve the Gestalt rules for visual perception.

we can perceive time as the ground for the figure, as when we say "The train arrived on time". Both these ways of looking at time come from a very general metaphor in our thought processes: the EVENT STRUCTURE metaphor. [...]

(Freeman 2000: 266)

This is not quite accurate. While one can make out a reasonable case for detecting a figure–ground relationship in "Time flies when we're having fun," in "The train arrived on time" the arrival of the train does not occur against a ground of which "time" is a part. There is an essential discrepancy between the structure of language and the world's structure. One complex unitary event must be described by many juxtaposed words. The number of words or even the number of nouns in a clause does not reflect the number of entities referred to. If we say "The train arrived," we refer to a single event. Likewise, "The train arrived on time" refers to a single event without ground: "on time" merely specifies one aspect of the arrival. We could say, as well, "The train's arrival was marked by exact adherence to an appointed time," or "The train arrived punctually," or "The train was punctual". As we have seen in the case of the straw and the wheelbarrow, the factory guard (and the typical audience of the joke) may perceive, in certain circumstances, the instrument with which the action is performed as ground. But if we say, for instance, "He cut the tree with an axe," we are faced with a unitary event; "with an axe" merely provides more information on the one action. To such sentences, I would say, the figure–ground distinction is not applicable. But if we *must* use a figure–ground language, the appropriate notion will be: "the train's arrival on time," or "cutting the tree with an axe" is figure without ground just as, according to Leonard B. Meyer, sometimes the case may be in music too.

Freeman (2000: 267) goes on with her exposition:

> For example, a very common metaphor for time is TIME IS A HEALER. This metaphor for time depends on the EVENT STRUCTURE metaphor which entails EVENTS ARE ACTIONS, which in turn entails TIME IS AN OBJECT. The EVENT STRUCTURE metaphor is shaped by the notion of causality, in which an agent is understood to bring about an event. Thus we say "Time heals all wounds". But Dickinson rejects this metaphor:

> > They say that "Time
> > assuages" –
> > Time never did assuage –
> > An actual suffering
> > strengthens
> > As sinews do – with Age –
> >
> > Time is a Test of
> > Trouble –

> But not a Remedy –
> If such it prove, it
> prove too
> There was no Malady –
>
> Fascicle 38, H 163, 942 (J 686)

Let us confine our attention to the following aspect of Freeman's discussion of time as an "EVENT STRUCTURE metaphor": "we can perceive time as a figure with respect to some ground [...] or we can perceive time as the ground for the figure". In harmony with our foregoing observations we might add that we can also perceive time as a figure with no ground at all.

Just like jokes or Escher's drawings, poetry produces forceful aesthetic effects by figure–ground reversal. But Freeman's illustration of this process is not unproblematic. She writes: "She [=Dickinson] rejects the idea of time as an agentive figure working against the ground of suffering and replaces it by reversing figure and ground. In the second part of the poem, it is suffering or "trouble" that is perceived as the figure against the ground of time". According to the present conception, however, suffering is not ground for time as an "agentive figure," but figure (without ground) in its own right: "An actual suffering strengthens with Age". Likewise, "Time is a Test of Trouble" is not ground, but figure without ground. "Time" is not presented against a ground that is a "Test of Trouble," but it is presented as "Time-as-a-Test-of-Trouble"–the many words describe several aspects of one referent. Thus, figure–ground reversal can hardly be attributed to Dickinson's poem.[5]

Freeman founds her argument (personal communication of August 18th, 1998) upon the following assumption: "Time is a healer of wounds identifies Time as an agent; Time is a test of trouble identifies it [=time] as an instrument". According to the conception outlined above, there is no reason at all why an instrument should not be granted the status of a figure. The question is not whether Time is identified as an agent or an instrument, but what kind of attention it attracts. Consider, for instance, the following four sentences: "Time is a healer," "Time assuages," "Time is a Test of Trouble," and "Time is a Remedy". In all four cases Time is in the focus of our attention, while the various predicates attribute to it some kind (or degree) of activity.

---

5. What is the difference between "Time is a Test of Trouble" and "Time-as-a-Test-of-Trouble"? In the former case it is asserted as true that being a Test of Trouble is attributed to Time; in the latter, the unitary entity is merely presented to contemplation, not asserted as something that has actually happened. In either case, being Time and being a Test of Trouble are not attributed to separate entities, but to one unitary referent.

What is more, in this poem a distinction between agent and instrument cannot be taken for granted either. Consider "Time is a healer" and "Time is a Remedy". Both sentences attribute to Time the same kind of activity: it heals; but "healer" is said to be an agent, whereas "Remedy" is an instrument. In fact, dictionaries define "healer" as "one who or that which heals" – that is, one can hardly tell whether the word suggests an agent or an instrument. "Time heals" expresses by a straightforward verb an activity that is expressed by nouns in the other two sentences; one cannot tell, however, whether it is an agent or an instrument; that is, whether it heals as a physician or as a remedy. What is more, "Time assuages" (which is after all the phrase used in the poem), may be perceived as "comforting, soothing, lessening pain" more as an ointment than as a person. Only one thing is certain: that in all these sentences, and especially where we have their cumulative effect in the poem, "Time" stands out as a figure; and I doubt that there is a ground there at all.

One of the most fruitful insights of Christine Brooke-Rose in her *A Grammar of Metaphor* is that noun metaphors are much more effective in conveying figurative activities than verb metaphors. "Whereas the noun is a complex of attributes, an action or attribute cannot be decomposed. Its full meaning depends on the noun with which it is used, and it can only be decomposed into species of itself, according to the noun with which it is associated: an elephant runs = runs heavily, a dancer runs = runs lightly" (Brooke-Rose 1958:209). "All Genitive relationships are activity relationships," she says (149); "with *of* in other relationships, I have constantly stressed its verbal element" (Brooke-Rose 1958:155). Applying her distinction to our poem, "Time is a Test of Trouble" suggests that it *tests* troubles, *i.e.* the clause attributes a straightforward activity to Time. Brooke-Rose gives additional examples from her (huge) corpus.

As I have suggested above, in the sentences "Time is a healer," "Time assuages," "Time is a Test of Trouble," and "Time is a Remedy" the verb predicate and the various kinds of noun predicates alike attribute some straightforward activity to Time, and present it as figure in the focus of attention. We cannot know from the text in what way Time tests troubles: whether it actively puts troubles to a test, or merely turns blue in bases and red in acids as the litmus paper. Nor can we know whether troubles are static as alkaline solutions and acids to be tested by some "litmus paper," or are more active. One thing seems to be quite certain however: that the testing Time is the figure, and troubles are part of the unitary testing process. Our attention is focused on Time. In Emily Dickinson's poem, "reified" Time is perceived as a figure, whether as an agent or an instrument. Most likely, I suggested, the figure–ground distinction is irrelevant here, because such clauses are experienced as a "single Gestalt" (to use a pet phrase of Langacker's), and no labelling of isolated parts (Time as figure, Remedy as ground, or vice versa) can illuminate them in any way.

10.6   Figure and ground (?) in Shakespeare

Peter Stockwell's book on Cognitive Poetics includes a chapter "Figures and Grounds" (Stockwell 2002:13ff.). In what follows, I will reconsider one of his examples, said to be an application of Cognitive Linguistics. In order to proceed in Stockwell's own terms, I have extracted from his chapter four criteria for perceiving some part of the perceptual field as "figure":

1. A literary text uses stylistic patterns to focus attention on a particular feature, within the textual space. [...] In textual terms, [...] "newness" is the key to attention (18).
2. The most obvious correspondence of the phenomenon of figure and ground is in the literary critical notion of foregrounding. [...] Foregrounding within the text can be achieved by a variety of devices, such as repetition, unusual naming, innovative descriptions, creative syntactic ordering, puns, rhyme, alliteration, metrical emphasis, the use of creative metaphor, and so on. All of these can be seen as deviations from the expected or ordinary use of language that draw attention to an element, foregrounding it against the relief of the rest of the features of the text (14).
3. In other words, attention is paid to objects which are presented in topic position (first) in sentences, or have focus, emphasis, focalisation or viewpoint attached to them (19).
4. Locative expressions [...] are expressed with prepositions that can be understood as image schemas. [...] The image schemas underlying these prepositions all involve a dynamic movement, or at least a final resting position resulting from a movement [...]. For example, the title of Kesey's novel has a moving figure ("One") which can be pictured as moving from a position to the left of the ground ("the Cuckoo's Nest"), to a position above it, to end up at a position to the right of it. In this OVER image schema, the moving figure can be seen to follow a path above the ground. Within the image schema, though, the element that is the figure is called the trajector and the element it has a grounded relationship with is called the landmark (16).

Now consider the following passage.

> Puck: How now, spirit! whither wander you?
> Fairy: Over hill, over dale,
> Thorough bush, thorough briar,
> Over park, over pale,
> Thorough flood, thorough fire,
> I do wander everywhere
> Swifter than the moone's sphere ...
> (*A Midsummer Night's Dream*, William Shakespeare)

Figure or not, intuitively the Fairy's first four lines are exceptionally foregrounded. If we look at the first three criteria for perceiving some part of the perceptual field as figure, it will be evident why. According to the second criterion, foregrounding within the text can be achieved, among other things, by repetition, rhyme, alliteration, or metrical emphasis. Consider the anaphora in this passage. Such a repetition can certainly be seen as a deviation from the expected or ordinary use of language. It consists of the repetition of two prepositions, *over* and *thorough*, used four times each. This repetition certainly affects foregrounding. Moreover, since the pairs of prepositional phrases introduced by "over" alternate with those introduced by "thorough," one perceives a higher-level repetition pattern too. Semantically, the nouns governed by the prepositions are also perceived as repetitions, on a higher level of abstraction: all of them denote some space in nature, and suggest some opposition and difficulty to get through. In each line there are two roughly equal prepositional phrases, lending to the line a symmetrical organization. This symmetry is reinforced by another repetitive scheme, alliteration. In the first line, the two nouns end with the same speech sound: *hill–dale*. In the rest of the lines, each pair of nouns begins with the same speech sound: bush–briar; park–pale; *flood–fire*. Thanks to the nouns' place in the line, the alliterations reinforce symmetry and parallelism.

In harmony with Criterion 3, the eight adverbials of place are topicalized – they are dislocated from after the verb to the beginning of the sentence; they are brought into focus. This device is closely related to the one mentioned in Criterion 1. The question "How now, spirit! whither wander you" mentions the agent ("trajector") and the fact that she is moving in space, but the adverb *whither* focuses attention on the scene or destination of the motion, which will be the new information in the answer.

I have suggested that these four lines are perceived as exceptionally prominent, are forced on the reader's or listener's attention, and that such perception can be accounted for by the first three of those criteria. Stockwell, by contrast, quotes the first five lines of the fairy's answer as a good example of the fourth criterion, and suggests that the moving person is the figure and the places enumerated are the ground: "Trajector (I, the speaker Puck [*sic*]) takes a path flying above the landmark (hill, dale, park, pale)" (17).

In view of my foregoing discussion, this is a rather mechanical application of two notions: that scenery is typically perceived as ground; and that image schemas underlying some prepositions all involve a dynamic movement which, in turn, is perceived as figure. Suppose that instead of writing a poetic drama, Shakespeare made a silent movie. In this case, quite plausibly, the flying shape of the fairy would be perceived as figure, the hills and dales etc. as ground. But, as Stockwell writes, "a literary text uses stylistic patterns to focus attention on a particular feature, within the textual space". In the passage under discussion the stylistic patterns focus attention on the adverbials of place in the first four lines, not on the agent. Stockwell seems to have rechristened the well-worn terms "foregrounding" and "deviations from the expected or ordinary use of language" as "figure–ground relationship," to make them conform with cognitive theory. In his text analysis, however, "foregrounding" applies, while a "figure–ground relationship" is not necessarily to be found. In fact, I strongly suspect that there is no ground to be found here, even though there are differences of relative emphasis. Indeed, what Stockwell rules as "ground" happens to be the most emphatic part of the fragment under analysis.

As said, Stockwell does not mention prosodic organization, which further flaws his analysis, since the Gestalt laws of perception noticeably affect the fragment and significantly contribute to poetic effects. The first four lines have an alternating pattern of rhymes; the next two lines form a couplet. Both patterns yield strong, symmetrical Gestalts. But according to the Gestalt law of Proximity, the latter yields a stronger Gestalt than the former, capturing the reader's or listener's attention (which is a typical figure-making feature of the text). The focusing effect of the transition from quatrain to couplet ought to be reinforced by the fact that the first four lines describe landscapes (which are prone to be perceived as ground), whereas the ensuing lines describe actions (frequently perceived as figures). And when examining the transition from the quatrain to the sequence of couplets, one must notice a most unexpected experience, a transition from a more focused kind of attention to a more relaxed kind, rather than vice versa.

One reason for this is, certainly, that the stylistic devices we have discerned in the quatrain are absent from the sequence of couplets. Moreover, the devices mentioned interact with some prosodic devices. The iambic and trochaic tetrameters have a very compelling, symmetrical shape. Let me spell out this prosodic structure:

Óver hill, Ø/óver dále,
s w   s   w s w   s
Thorough búsh, Ø/thorough bríar,
  s w   s   w   s w   sw
Óver párk, Ø/óver pále,
s w   s   w s w   s
Thorough flóod, Ø/thorough fíre,
  s   w   s   w   s w   s w
I do wánder/éverywhere
s w   s   w s w   s
Swífter than the/móone's sphére …
  s w   s   w   s   w   s

In this example linguistic patterns and versification patterns are marked independently and then mapped on each other. The alternating s and w letters under the verse lines mark the regularly alternating metric strong and weak positions. The character Ø in the middle of the first four lines marks an unoccupied weak position. The accents on certain vowels mark lexical stress. In this verse instance, lexical stress occurs only in strong positions, but not in all strong positions. In the first four lines a lexical stress occurs in every third and seventh (strong) position, emphatically confirming the versification pattern. "Trochaic tetrameter" is a verse line in which an sw unit occurs four times (as in lines 2 and 4). The last w position may be dropped (as in lines 1, 3, 5–6). The trochaic tetrameter is divided into two symmetrical halves by a caesura exactly after the fourth (weak) position (marked by a slash). Caesura may be "confirmed" by a word ending or phrase ending; when it occurs in mid-word (or less critically in mid-phrase), it is "overridden," generating tension, or blurring the versification pattern. In the present instance, an unoccupied (weak) position at the caesura confirms it even more emphatically.

To let us feel the effect of the verse lines with unoccupied weak positions, I will corrupt for a moment Shakespeare's verse, so as to make it conform with the pattern from which the genuine lines deviate (occasional nonsense is inevitable):

Óver móuntain, óver dále,
s w   s   w   s w   s
Thorough bórder, thorough bríar,
  s w   s   w   s w   sw
Óver párking, óver pále,
s w   s   w   s w   s
Thorough flúid, thorough fíre,
  s w   s w   s w   s w
I do wánder éverywhere
s   w   s   w s w   s
Swífter than the móone's sphére …
  s   w   s   w   s   w   s

Returning to the genuine version, the symmetrical structure imputes an exceptionally obtrusive caesura after the fourth metrical position. The verbal structure may confirm this caesura, or may override it, generating tension or blurring the division. In the present instance, two parallel prepositional phrases occupy both sides of the caesura, reinforcing the symmetrical division. This symmetrical and well-articulated arrangement is reinforced, as we have seen, by alliteration. Both the symmetry of the segments and the articulation of the caesura are further enhanced by an unoccupied weak position, after the third position. Consequently, the line is segmented into two exceptionally well-articulated short segments. In the ensuing couplets, by contrast, no unoccupied position occurs. Syntactically, the linguistic units at the two sides of the caesura do not parallel, but complement each other, yielding a relatively long perceptual unit. What is more, in the line "Swifter than the/moone's sphere" the caesura occurs in mid-phrase, after the article "the," considerably blurring the symmetrical structure. According to the Gestalt laws of organization presented at the beginning of this article, "the smaller a closed region, the more it tends to be seen as figure," *pace* Stockwell's assertion that one of the features that will, most likely, cause some part of a visual field or textual field to be seen as the figure is that "it will be [...] larger than the rest of the field that is then the ground" (15).[6] This may explain why the continuous lines of the couplets, as opposed to the symmetrically divided lines of the quatrain, are felt to relax rather than strengthen the focus of attention.

This passage has, nevertheless, one aspect of which Stockwell could make out a very convincing case, but he does not. The emphatically enumerated places might serve as the ground against which the fairy's flight would be perceived as "swift". The less penetrable the terrain, the more wondrous is the fairy's swiftness. The shorter the phrases, the swifter is their alternation. However, he stops short of even quoting the line that indicates speed (he ends his quotation with the word "everywhere"). Apparently, his task is to label everything before OVER "trajector"; everything after it – "landmark".

One might accuse me of being unfair to Stockwell, because he did not intend to exhaust the Shakespearean passage, merely illustrate the image schema. Furthermore, there may be many additional aspects that influence our final impression from the text, but the core meaning of the image schema is appropriately illustrated by this example. In a textbook the author must be brief. However, all the examples in Stockwell's section "Figure and Ground" illustrate only this image schema; moreover, a look at the other examples of this section suggests that even those that can be discussed very briefly distort the focus of perception in a like fashion. The image schema OVER cannot be used as a diagnostic tool of figure–ground relationship.

---

6. Cf. Langacker: "Figure/ground organization is not in general automatically determined for a given scene; it is normally possible to structure the same scene with alternate choices of figure. However, various factors do contribute to the naturalness and likelihood of a particular choice. A relatively compact region that contrasts sharply with its surroundings shows a strong tendency to be selected as the figure. Therefore, given a white dot in an otherwise black field, the dot is almost invariably chosen as the figure; only with difficulty can one interpret the scene as a black figure (with a hole in it) viewed against a white background" (1987:120 and ensuing discussion).

In Stockwell's "cognitive poetic analysis" of a wide range of works figure–ground relationships boil down, eventually, to labelling expressions as "trajector" and "landmark". I said above that he applies the terms figure–ground mechanically. What moves "over" is automatically ruled "trajector," what is under the wheels – automatically "landmark". These labels are not verified against some sort of human response. The noun governed by "over" is "landmark," therefore "ground," and there's an end on it. In the following quote, however, if one may judge from the title and syntactic structure, it is the dog who is in focus.

> it gets run over by a van
>
> ("Your Dog Dies," Raymond Carver)

"The trajector (van) crushes the landmark (your dog)," says Stockwell (2002: 17). However, the fact that he became flat and motionless relative to the moving car and is under its wheels does not change the fact that the dog is in focus. Grammatically, too, it does not say "a van ran over your dog," but chooses the passive voice, which manipulates the patient (your dog) into focus.[7]

A sympathetic reader made the following critical point concerning my analysis of "it gets run over by a van":

> The discussion of Trajector–Landmark configurations apart (i.e. Stockwell's vs. Langacker's options), in functional linguistics the principle of end-weight, or end-focus, is a well-established one. As such, "by a van" receives maximal attention in terms of new information and emphasis. It (the dog/trajector) remains as given information. In the active voice ("a van ran over your dog") it is the dog which is in focus, not the van. The van remains as backgrounded, given information.

This comment forced me to refine my argument, with reference to M.A.K. Halliday's (1970: 163) following distinction:

> Given and new thus differ from theme and rheme, though both are textual functions, in that "given" means "here is a point of contact with what you know" (and thus is not tied to elements in clause structure), whereas "theme" means "here is the heading to what I am saying".

---

7.   Langacker (1990: 75) uses the terms "trajector" and "landmark" quite differently from Stockwell, much more in harmony with the conception propounded here: "The choice of trajector is not mechanically determined by a predication's content, but is rather one dimension of conventional imagery. Indeed, the asymmetry is observable even for expressions that designate a symmetrical relationship. Thus X resembles Y and Y resembles X are not semantically equivalent; in the former, Y (the landmark) is taken as a standard of reference for evaluating X (the trajector); in the latter these roles are reversed". Compare this to "A van ran over your dog" and "Your dog gets run over by a van".

Halliday calls the latter "psychological subject". In our description, then, "it (your dog)" is the "psychological subject," the "theme" (as opposed to "rheme"), the "heading to what the speaker is saying". If the figure–ground distinction is relevant at all to this line, then "figure" must be identified with the "psychological subject," the "theme," "the heading to what the speaker is saying" rather than with either the "given" or "new" information. In other words, in "it gets run over by a van" the all-important fact conveyed is that my dog is killed. The passive voice serves to highlight this all-important fact by manipulating it into the theme and relegating the instrument into the rheme. The new information, "by a van," fills in a hitherto unknown, relatively unimportant detail.

Or consider the following quote from Shelley:

> Thine azure sister of the spring shall blow
> Her clarion o'er the dreaming earth
> ("Ode to the West Wind," Percy Bysshe Shelley)

Again, "[t]rajector (from clarion blast) covers and pierces the landmark (earth)" – says Stockwell (2002). However, the spring shall blow her clarion not merely "o'er the earth" as suggested by Stockwell, but "o'er the dreaming earth". Earth is not merely the place over which the clarion will be blown, but an agent in its own right, who is to be woken up by its sound. After having rechristened figure–ground as "trajector" and "landmark," Stockwell goes on to talk about his examples in the latter terms, forgetting that he is supposed to talk about figure–ground relationship more generally. His terms, as we have seen, do not necessarily account for our perceptions of figure and ground in a poetic text. Moreover, revealing an "image schema" of dynamic movement in such prepositions as *over* is tautological in most instances. In most of the examples provided they are governed by such motion or action verbs as *wander, ran over, blow*. The dynamic movement exposed in the preposition is already expressed by the verb. This is very different from Christine Brooke-Rose's handling of the genitive link between two nouns.

To conclude, image schemata do not work wonders by themselves. One must, rather, adopt L.C. Knights' (1964: 229) position in a slightly different context: one must "admit that all the work remains to be done in each particular case". But Stockwell, in his analyses, "applies rules" rather than responds to individual poetic qualities. Thus, when Leonard B. Meyer says that, unlike in visual perception, in music one may have figure without ground, I strongly suspect that this is the case in poetry too. In other words, I suspect that figure without ground contributes to a poetic quality which is not captured by Stockwell's conceptual apparatus. Stockwell's "cognitive poetic analysis" of Ted Hughes' poem shows similar problems, but space prevents me from demonstrating this.

10.7   Figure–ground reversal in music: "Moonlight" Sonata

This section is devoted to the problematic (or flexible) relationship of figure and ground in music. In Chapter 1 I referred to Ehrenzweig, according to whom taking a close look at a good wallpaper we may see a series of similar, well-designed shapes, one beside the other. Looking at it from a distance, we will find the wallpaper Gestalt-free, ambiguous. The same applies, *mutatis mutandis*, to a series of similar, well-designed shapes, one after the other, in music. All through the opening movement of Beethoven's "Moonlight" Sonata there is a series of obsessive rising sequences of three notes, as in music Excerpt 4. In this Section I will consider one such series which in one masterpiece serves as ground, in another as figure. We will also note that the performer may manipulate the listener's perception of figure–ground relationships.

In the course of writing this Chapter I compared a wide range of performances of Beethoven's Sonata. Eventually I decided to quote here two of them, of unequal fame, by Alfred Brendel and Dubravka Tomashevich, a student of Rubinstein's, because they illustrate most clearly the contrast which I want to bring out: that the performer has considerable control over presenting the triplets as ground or as figure.

Figure 7. The first four bars of the triplets in the Moonlight Sonata

Music Excerpt 4
Listen online to Alfred Brendel's performance of Excerpt 4 (a), and Dubravka Tomashevich' performance (b).

Marcia Green drew my attention to a remarkable similarity between this passage and a passage in *Don Giovanni*: in the short trio of the three basses, Don Giovanni, Leporello and the dying Commandatore ("Ah, soccorso! son tradito!"), the orchestra plays exactly the same kind of repeated rising series of three notes. Here, however, it is deeply buried in the "ground," and even after repeated listenings I could only vaguely discern a dim um-pa-pa in the background, as in Music Excerpt 5.

Music Excerpt 5.
Listen online to the *Don Giovanni* trio in Klemperer's recording (a). Listen to the triplets at the beginning of the same when the midrange is overemphasized (b). Listen to a piano extract of the triplets alone, played by Mira Gal (c).

Andante

pp

Figure 8. The first two bars of the triplets in the *Don Giovanni* trio

Green's suggestion (with which I disagree) is that this similarity indicates a personal relationship of the oedipal kind between Beethoven and Mozart. For me the most important part of the comparison is that Beethoven took a piece of ground music, that has a typical ground texture, and placed it in the focus of the sonata movement dominating for no less than six minutes the musical space. I had a long dialogue on this issue with Harai Golomb, professor of literary theory, theatre studies and musicology, who is certainly much more competent on music theory than me, and I could not reach the ensuing conclusions without his insightful help.

We agree that Beethoven did not "imitate" the triplets from Mozart, and that this similarity does not indicate any significant relationship between them, either as composers or as persons (as Green would have us think). So, what is the point in showing the similarity besides the sheer piquancy of the comparison? The juxtaposition of the two works foregrounds the different character of the two applications of the same technique. The similarity of Beethoven's triplets to Mozart's – which in the Moonlight Sonata, in contrast to *Don Giovanni*, are in the focus of the listener's attention – foregrounds the difference between them. Golomb agrees that there is in the sonata a distinct, monotonous, repeatedly rising ta-ta-ta sequence. This sequence is exceptionally boring from the rhythmical point of view, resembling the typical "ground" texture in the *Don Giovanni* excerpt, and many other works. At the same time, the magic of the movement is due, he says, to tensions and resolutions in the harmonic structure of the whole, both in the sequence of triplets and the interplay of the various simultaneous melodic threads. There are three simultaneous threads in this movement, in, roughly speaking, the high range, the midrange and the low range. The afore-said triplets constitute the middle thread in this complex. There are the lower harmonic chords which, we both agree, generate a ground of tensions and resolutions, making a major contribution to the affective impact of the movement; and there is a higher sequence of longish notes which add up to a mildly rising and falling *melody*, which is the real figure of the movement. This melody, he says, though considerably diffuse, is more differentiated than the obstinately repeated ta-ta-ta series (as in Excerpt 6).

(29)   **Music Excerpt 6**
Listen online to Alfred Brendel's performance of Excerpt 6 (a), and Dubravka
(30)   Tomashevich's performance (b).

In my opinion, both the middle and the high threads are figure, although there is, from time to time, a "dialogue" between the highest and the lowest thread, skipping, as it were, the middle thread. Now one thing appears to be certain. That this dialogue does not turn the lowest thread into figure; it remains ground relative to the other two threads.

In harmony with my argument in the present paper, I assume here, too, that figure–ground relationships are not determined once for all in all circumstances. As we have seen, "what is figural at any one moment depends on patterns of sensory stimulation and on the momentary interests of the perceiver". My point is that in the case of a musical performance, "the momentary interests of the perceiver" can be manipulated to a considerable extent by the performer, by rather evasive cues: in different performances different threads of the "patterns of sensory stimulation" may be foregrounded, by mild shifts of attention to and fro, as e.g. in the visual arts, in Escher's drawings. My own view of the passage may have been influenced to a considerable extent by Alfred Brendel's performance on Philips 438 730–2. In this performance, the middle thread is somewhat louder relative to the other threads than in some other performances. As a result, the higher thread (as well as its dialogue with the lower thread, when perceived) is perceived as an *intrusion* into the "figure," the middle thread. This intrusion, in turn, will increase the sequence's tendency to reassert its integrity – according to the Gestalt assumption that a perceptual unit tends "to preserve its integrity by resisting interruptions". In this instance, the perception of figure–ground relationships can be further manipulated by the treatment of the longish notes of the highest thread. If their differentiation and connectedness into a melody is emphasized in the performance, they will attract attention as figure; if they are presented as more discrete notes, they will be perceived more as events intruding upon the rising sequences of three notes. My purpose here is not to offer a systematic comparative research of performances. What I want to emphasize is this: in Brendel's performance (more than in Tomashevich's), the high thread is perceived more as a series of irruptions than as a melodic line. This is due to two features of the performance. First, in 6a the second thread is louder relative to the other two threads than in 6b; and secondly, Brendel performs the higher thread in a peculiar way. Compare Excerpt 6a to 6b. In the higher thread, we hear twice a group of tam-ta-tam on the same note, followed by a slightly higher one. Owing to amplitude dynamics and Brendel's "pianists' touch," this higher note is perceived as exerting a greater effort to intrude rather than as contributing to a continuous melodic line. The result is monotonous and exceptionally dramatic at the same time.

It is illuminating to consider the amplitude dynamics of the two performances in this excerpt. Figures 9–10 show the plot of amplitude envelope of the first tam-ta-tam group in the two performances. The three notes are of equal pitch.

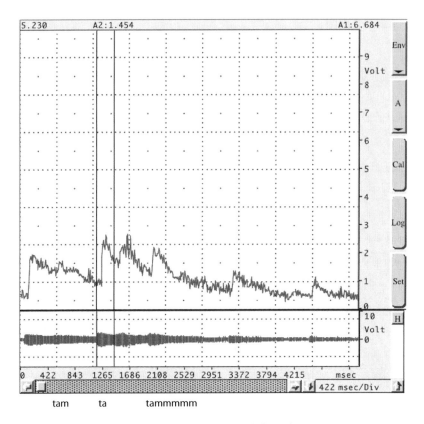

Figure 9. The envelope plot of music Excerpt 6 in Brendel's performance

But, in Brendel's performance, each one of them begins with a distinct obtrusion of the amplitude envelope. In Tomashevich's performance, by contrast, the first two notes slightly fluctuate at a low level, and are followed by a third note of disproportionately great amplitude. Add to this that though both performances are "overdotted," the duration of the middle note in Tomashevich' performance is shorter: 273 msec, as opposed to Brendel's 296 msec. As a result, in Tomashevich's performance the first two notes are subordinated to the third one; the middle note is perceived more as a "passing note," leading forward to the third note. This tends to merge the three notes into one melodic line. In Brendel's performance, by contrast, the three notes are perceived as more discrete, have relatively greater perceptual separateness. The middle note is perceived not only as a note in its own right, but also as more grouped with the preceding one. Translating Lerdahl and Jackendoff's transformational terminology (1983) into plain English, backward grouping generates tension, forward grouping – relaxation.

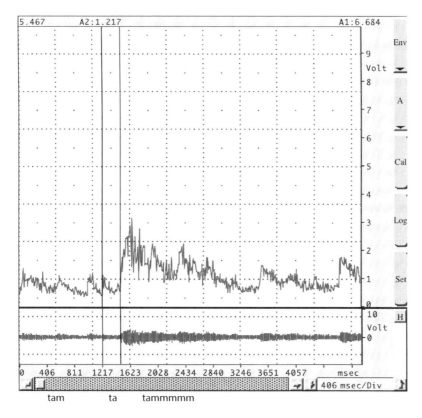

Figure 10. The envelope plot of music Excerpt 6 in Tomashevich's performance

Julian Haylock, who wrote the music notes for the sonatas on Alfred Brendel's CD, suggested, quite impressionistically, what is the perceived effect of all this: "The opening *Adagio Sostenuto* […] is quite unlike anything previously composed for the keyboard," and he speaks of "its dream-like texturing" which is in this case, certainly, the artistic purpose of promoting a typical background texture to the status of a figure or, at least, of causing it to dominate a full-length sonata movement. According to Meyer, as we have seen, "the musical field can be perceived as containing a ground alone, as in the introduction to a musical work – a song, for instance – where the melody or figure is obviously still to come" (1956: 186). It is the typical background texture pushed into the foreground throughout a full movement that is "quite unlike anything previously composed for the keyboard"; and this is also the basis for "its dream-like texturing" – reinforced by its interplay with the other two threads, as discussed above.

10.8   Literature: Figure–ground reversals of the extralinguistic

We have seen in Escher's drawings that they grant the perceiver considerable freedom to foreground certain shapes as figure or relegate them to an undifferentiated
background. Such an "aspect switching" requires only minimal mental effort. Escher
discusses at some length what kinds of shapes allow such flexibility of perception.
He does not discuss the means by which he tilts the perceiver's inclination in one
direction or the other. I have suggested that when the same closed area is repeated,
lines or dots on it tend to bestow on it differentiation and induce us to perceive it as
a figure; their absence, as ground. I have also suggested that the perceptual apparatus can easily overcome these "directive" means, by some conscious effort.

Likewise, in Beethoven's sonata the performer may manipulate the listener's
perception of figure–ground relationships by connecting the notes of the higher
thread into a perceptible melody, or leaving them as discontinuous, solitary events.
Here the listener is more at the performer's mercy, and "aspect switching" requires
greater mental effort.

In what follows, I will consider four literary texts that exploit this readiness of
human perceivers to switch back and forth between figure and ground. All four
texts achieve their effect by inducing readers to reverse figure–ground relationships
relative to their habitual modes of thought or perception. As I insisted above, my
examples, except the Shakespeare excerpt, do not concern figure–ground relationships generated by prosodic and syntactic structures (as I have done elsewhere)[8]
but perceptions of, or attitudes toward, processes in extralinguistic reality. Consider the following poem by Shelley:

> A Song
> A widow bird sate mourning for her love
> Upon a wintry bough;
> The frozen wind crept on above,
> The freezing stream below.
>
> There was no leaf upon the forest bare,
> No flower upon the ground,
> And little motion in the air
> Except the mill-wheel's sound.

---

8.   For instance: "An infringing stress obtrudes upon the integrity of the line which, in turn,
strives to establish its shape in the reader's perception. In run-on lines, deviant stresses may
exert themselves more freely, may interact with other Gestalt-free elements, blend into a
Gestalt-free ground, or even soften those features that would, otherwise, count toward strong
shape" (Tsur 1991:245).

In auditory perception, irregular noises (which constitute an overload on the cognitive system and most effectively violate the "Law of Good Continuation") are usually dumped into the background. But when Shelley ends his "Song" with these two lines, he turns into figure a percept that most commonly is dumped into the ground. And this is enormously effective here. I have elsewhere discussed this poem at some length (Tsur 2002; 2010: 3–8). Here I will reproduce only part of my discussion of the last two lines. They have a rather complex function within the whole. *Little* as a part of the sequence "There is no ... No... And little..." suggests "none at all"; in this sense, "And little motion in the air" is one more item in the list of analogous items suggesting **deprivation**. In this sense, it seems to herald an unqualified statement that generates a psychological atmosphere of great certainty. In her book *Poetic Closure*, Barbara Herrnstein-Smith indeed claims that unqualified statements generate a psychological atmosphere of certainty, of conclusiveness. Consequently, they are particularly appropriate to serve as "poetic closure," to arouse a feeling that the poem is ended, not merely ceases to be.

The subsequent preposition *except*, however, makes a substantial qualification to this statement, substituting the "a very small amount" for total exclusion; that is, there is an exclusion from the total exclusion, an exception to nothingness: a mill-wheel's sound. The relation of the mill-wheel to its sound is like the relation of a thing to a thing-free quality. In the description, attention is directed away from the stable thing itself (the mill-wheel) to the thing-free sound. This perturbation of the air becomes another item in the list of items with reduced activity; by the same token, it foregrounds the presence of the air, a thing-free entity *par excellence* pervading the scene. The shift of "little" from the meaning "none at all" to "only a small amount," i.e. this qualification of the unqualified statement, performs a "poetic sabotage" against the determined, purposeful quality of the poetic closure, replacing the psychological atmosphere of great certainty with a psychological atmosphere of *un*certainty, contributing to the emotional quality of the poem. This emotional atmosphere has been generated by the abstraction of certain qualities from parallel concrete items in the description. Both the emotional quality and the poetic sabotage of closure are reinforced by another aspect of the mill-wheel's sound, which I wish to point out through an idea borrowed from Joseph Glicksohn. The mill-wheel's sound, being continuous noise (irregular both in rhythm and pitch), displays "chaotic overdifferentiation", and is typically dumped in the auditory ground. By forcing to the reader's attention a percept that typically serves as ground, the poem increases the emotional quality of the perception, and emphasizes that *there is no* figure to be contemplated, reinforcing the quality of deprivation. Thus, the poem ends with "a ground alone, as in the introduction to a musical work [...] where the melody or figure is obviously still to come" (Meyer 1956: 186). When it occurs at the end of a work, its lack of progress does not prepare for something to come as in the introduction to a musical work, but suggests some disintegration: the poem does not *end*, it passes out of existence, fades away.

The next two examples can be regarded as displaying different degrees of one kind: reversals concerning time. Consider the following Sonnet by Sir Philip Sidney:

> Leave me, O love which reachest but to dust;
> And thou, my mind, aspire to higher things;
> Grow rich in that which never taketh rust,
> Whatever fades but fading pleasure brings.
> Draw in thy beams, and humble all thy might
> To that sweet yoke where lasting freedoms be;
> Which breaks the clouds and opens forth the light,
> That doth both shine and give us sight to see.
> O take fast hold; let that light be thy guide
> In this small course which birth draws out to death,
> And think how evil becometh him to slide,
> Who seeketh heaven, and comes of heavenly breath.
>   Then farewell, world; thy uttermost I see;
>   Eternal Love, maintain thy life in me.

I have elsewhere discussed the light imagery of this sonnet at considerable length (Tsur 1998b, 2003: 320–328). Now I will devote attention to the third quatrain.

Let us work out the internal logic of this image, in terms of mental habits and their manipulation by literary means. I will argue that the central device of this passage is a reversal of figure–ground relationship. But before discussing that, I wish to examine this passage in light of what Kenneth Burke calls "Scene-Act Ratio" and "Scene-Agent Ratio". In these Ratios "Scene" typically serves as ground to "Act" and "Agent," which are typically the figure. Burke proposed to analyse human motives and actions in terms of the "dramatic pentad": Act, Scene, Agency, Agent, Purpose.

> Using "scene" in the sense of setting, or background, and "act" in the sense of action, one could say that "the scene contains the act". And using "agents" in the sense of actors, or acters, one could say that "the scene contains the agents".
>
> And whereas comic and grotesque works may deliberately set these elements at odds with one another, audiences make allowance for such liberty, which reaffirms the same principle of consistency in its very violation. […] In any case, examining first the relation between scene and act, all we need note here is the principle whereby the scene is a fit "container" for the act, expressing in fixed properties the same quality that the action expresses in terms of development.
>   (Burke 1962: 3)

In the case of Sidney's poem, the scene and the act define the nature of the agent as well as his purpose: the Soul *comes from* heavenly breath and *goes to* (seeketh) heaven; according to Burke, this is a way to say in spatial and temporal terms that the Soul is (in the present) of a heavenly essence ("temporization of the essence"). George Lakoff and his followers would speak here of the event structure metaphor PURPOSEFUL ACTION IS A JOURNEY; the purpose of the action is expressed, very much in Burke's spirit, by the place to which the journey leads. A more specific instantiation of this metaphor is LIFE IS A JOURNEY.[9]

In this poem, the purpose of the journey is presented by two different *ends*: "Who seeketh heaven, and comes of heavenly breath," and "In this small course which birth draws out to death". These two destinations have opposite implications. One presents "Life as full of meaning"; the other presents "Life as totally meaningless". There is all the difference if "this small course" leads to the grave or to heaven.

Particular occasions of birth and death in everyday life are perceived as figures, and life only as ground, at best. But when we speak of Human Life, *Life* becomes the figure, only marked at its extremes by birth and death, which thus become ground. In Christian religious traditions Life is only a transient episode for the soul which "seeketh heaven, and comes of heavenly breath". Religious rhetoric frequently attempts to bring man to an *insight* into this truth by using paradoxical epigrammatic phrasings (such as "Whosoever will save his life shall lose it" – Mark 8.35). Religious poetry may attempt to do this by a sudden shift of attention from the habitual *figure* to its *ground*, the markers of its extremes: Sidney gently manipulates attention from "this small course" to "birth" and "death," which are only meant to mark the extremes of life.[10]

Now notice that purpose is not absent from the image; it is only translated into a different visual terminology.

> let that light be thy guide
> In this small course which birth draws out to death,

---

9. It is quite characteristic of the present critical vogue that referees of my papers frequently suggest that in some place or other I might mention Lakoff's work; but so far they have never suggested to mention Burke.

10. The changing relationship between shapes and their edges as figure–ground relationship is well brought out by the following two locutions concerning geographic configurations: with reference to the US, the phrases Western Coast and Eastern Coast foreground the dry land between them as figure, the water being part of the ground; with reference to the Middle East, the phrases Eastern Bank and Western Bank foreground the water between them as figure, the dry land being part of the ground. For political reasons, the dry land of "The Western Bank" has now become figure in its own right.

In my paper on the cognitive structure of light imagery in religious poetry I discussed this poem at great length. I pointed out a wide range of meaning potentials in the light image, many of which are exploited in this poem. *One* of them is related to Lakoff's conceptual metaphor KNOWING IS SEEING: Light gives instructions, shows the way. Another one is derived from the fact that the Light comes from an invisible and inaccessible source in the sky. Thus, these two lines do not express life's purpose by a place that serves as the destination of the journey; but this purpose is reintroduced by another conventional metaphor: light as knowing, understanding, or proper guidance.

My second illustration, a quotation from Beckett's *Waiting for Godot*, brings this same figure–ground reversal to an absurd extreme:

> Astride of a grave and a difficult birth. Down in the hole, lingeringly, the grave-digger puts on the forceps.

The tramp Vladimir sharpens Sidney's inverted image to absurdity: Man passes straight from the womb to the tomb, assisted by the gravedigger's forceps. In a world in which "God is dead," there is nothing beyond, and what is in between is meaningless and negligible. The emotional disorientation aroused by this understanding is reinforced by the grotesque image, the typical effect of the grotesque being, as pointed out by Thomson (1972), "emotional disorientation". In our everyday perception, birth is the beginning of life; death its cessation. What matters is life itself. Both in Sidney's and Beckett's image the two extremes, birth and death, or the womb and the grave become the figure; what is between them (life!) serves only to connect them. And the shorter the connection, the more meaningless life becomes.

A similar and most interesting instance of figure–ground reversal is provided by the great Hebrew poet, Nathan Alterman, in his poem "I will yet come to your threshold with extinguished lips". In this poem the speaker expresses his hope that he will yet reach his beloved, in a state of exhaustion, though. The poem ends with the only thing he can still offer her:

> The silence in the heart between two beats –
> This silence
> Is yours.

This is a variation on the age-old poetic convention "My true love has my heart and I have his," in which "heart" stands for AFFECTION, LOVE. It is also a metonymy for LIFE. Love, life, affection dwell in the heart; the heart, in turn, is enclosed in the body. Heartbeats are minute, barely perceptible events; whereas the silence between the beats is even less perceptible. We are faced with the *innermost* emotional experiences. Consider the Scene-Act ratio *innermost–intimate*. They are intimately related: the latter is derived from Latin *intimus* = innermost, superlative of (assumed) Old Latin *interus*. The Microsoft Word Thesaurus gives, among others, the following partial synonyms for *intimate*: "dear, inner, deep". Alterman's metaphor suggests something that is most minute and insignificant, but, at the same time, involves the innermost, most precious, deepest, most intimate feelings of the heart.

We are not aware that our heartbeats occur against a ground of silence; that we could not perceive beats if there were no periods of silence between them. The figure–ground reversal of Alterman's metaphor, relegating the beats to the ground, brings this to awareness. This generates conflicting emotional tendencies: a *witty* reversal foregrounding a *desperate* gesture. The reversal exposes the perceiving consciousness to an absence, a thing-free quality, instead of positive focused events to which the imagination can hold on. Typically, such lack of hold inspires the perceiver with awe and uncertainty; here this is overridden by the psychological atmosphere of certainty generated by the "ultimate" connotations characterized above as "innermost, most precious, deepest, most intimate", generating both an intense emotional quality and a powerful closure.

10.9 Summary and wider perspectives

Figure–ground relationship is an important notion of Gestalt theory. Theorists of the psychology of music and the visual arts made most significant use of it. In course of this chapter we have encountered serious problems with the application of these notions in poetry criticism. The most important attempt to import this distinction to linguistics and literary theory is William Labov's. Unfortunately, some linguists and literary critics regard Labov's work as a model for technical exercises rather than a source of insights into some significant part-whole relationship. This chapter made the point that such grammatical terms as "agent" or "instrument" are not foolproof diagnostic tools. Rather, figure–ground relationship is an important element of the way we organize reality in our awareness, including works of art. In my dealing with poetry I have focused attention on figure–ground relationships in extralinguistic reality rather than in the interaction between prosodic and syntactic structures, as I had done in my earlier work. I argued that poets may rely on our habitual figure–ground organizations in extralinguistic reality, and exploit our flexibility in shifting attention from one aspect to another so as to achieve certain poetic effects by inducing us to reverse the habitual figure–ground relationships. This flexibility has precedent in music and the visual arts. I have examined four examples from four literary masterpieces. An important concomitant of these readings was to demonstrate that in most instances one may not only identify these reversals in the text, but may also suggest their effects. In Sidney's poem and the excerpt from Beckett the resulting "message" could be paraphrased in a straightforward conceptual language. But this is quite misleading. What is important here is not so much the "message" conveyed, but the insight resulting from the shift of mental sets. In Shelley's poem, the conceptual "message" diminishes to a minimum, and the main effect of the reversal is an intense perceptual quality that can only be approximated by such descriptive terms as "uncertainty, purposelessness, dissolution, wasting away".

This may lead us to some wider stylistic perspectives. According to Ehren-zweig (1965), the irregular or endlessly-repeated "scribblings" that typically constitute ground both in visual and auditory perception are perceived sub-liminally, but render the figure fuller, more plastic. A good wallpaper in a room, he says, goes unnoticed; but it makes all the difference. Labov treats ground as a means for evaluating experience in storytelling. In the "Moonlight" Sonata it is the ground that gives the enormous dramatic accentuation to the endlessly-repeated rising triplets and the higher sequences of three notes of equal pitch. The present chapter has been devoted to instances of auditory, visual and verbal art in which the normal figure–ground relationship is defamiliarized or even reversed.

In Western art and poetry there is a "witty" as well as a "high-serious," emo-tional tradition. Figure–ground manipulation, too, may have an emotional or witty effect. The examples from Escher, Sidney and Beckett may be considered as artistic devices generating a witty quality of some degree or other. In extreme cases the witty turn may cause a shock experienced as emotional disorientation. In Romantic poetry and music, by contrast, when exposed to ground texture usurping the place of figures, readers and listeners may detect some structural resemblance between such texture and emotional processes, experiencing it as an emotional quality.[11] This is what happens, I suggest, at the end of Shelley's "Song,"

---

11.   Ehrenzweig claims that students of the great masters of painting or the violin can imitate the visual or melodic figures they produce; it is their irregular, Gestalt-free, subliminally perceived brush strokes or vibrati and glissandi "sandwiched" between the tones that they find hard to imitate. It is these irregular "scribblings," he says, that convey the unconscious con-tents of art. Ehrenzweig, however, does not tell us how these scribblings convey unconscious contents. So, I prefer to fall back on his notions of Gestalt-free and thing-free qualities in which, I suggest, viewers and listeners may detect some structural resemblance to emotions. Instances of figure–ground reversal, especially those that arouse emotional disorientation, may have an effect similar to mystic paradoxes. So, Steven T. Katz' words on mystic paradoxes may apply to some instances of figure–ground reversal too:

and more forcefully, in the first movement of Beethoven's "Moonlight" Sonata. In Alterman's poem, I suggested, both a witty and an emotional quality may be perceived; the reader may, perhaps, perceive these two aspects simultaneously, or even switch between them at will.

One of the major functions of poetry is to yield heightened awareness. It may be the heightening of the awareness of the reality perceived, or of the cognitive mechanisms that enable us to perceive reality. The self-examination of cognitive mechanisms is still an investigation of reality; the investigation has merely lost its directness (cf. Pears 1971:31). Escher's experimentation with figure and ground, for instance, yields a heightened awareness of our perceptual apparatus.

This is the conspicuous purpose of the figure–ground reversal in Sidney's poem, though considerably mitigated by its conventionality. The same device in Beckett's play is intended to shock, even shatter, the standard epistemic security of the audience so as, by contrast, to make it painfully aware of the meaninglessness of the *Condition Humaine*. In the religious poem, disorientation is followed by reorientation; in the theatre of the absurd, by contrast, the basic assumption is that "God is dead," and there is no "transcendental 'reality'".

Such linguistic ploys exist in many places throughout the world, usually connected with the conscious construction of paradoxes whose necessary violation of the laws of logic are intended to shock, even shatter, the standard epistemic security of "disciples," thereby allowing them to move to new and higher forms of insight/ knowledge. That is […], [the mystics] intend, among other things, to force the hearers of such propositions to consider who they are – to locate themselves vis-a-vis normal versus transcendental "reality".

(Katz 1992:7–8, cf. Tsur 2003:207–208)

CHAPTER 11

Size–sound symbolism revisited

11.1 Preliminary

In many of my writings I have argued that poetic images have no fixed predetermined meanings. In my 1992 book *What Makes Sound Patterns Expressive? – The Poetic Mode of Speech Perception* (originally published in 1987) I propounded the view that speech sounds do not have fixed predetermined symbolic values either. Poetic images as well as speech sounds are clusters of features, each of which may serve as ground for some combinational potential. The resulting combinations of images and speech sounds give rise to figurative meanings and sound symbolism. Unforeseen contexts may actualise unforeseen potentials of images and speech sounds. Language users may shift attention from one potential to another in the same speech sound or poetic image, and realize new figurative meanings and sound-symbolic qualities. Thus, the handling of figurative language and sound symbolism in poetry is governed by a homogeneous set of principles. The acquisition and use of language require considerable creativity. This creativity is heightened and turned to an aesthetic end in the writing and understanding of poetry. In my writings I have explored the sources of these potentials, and how human intuition handles them in generating poetic qualities.

In this way, a sophisticated interplay between sound and meaning is generated. Relevant features can be multiplied indefinitely, and one may discover unexpected phonetic or phonological features. In my 2001 paper "Onomatopoeia: Cuckoo-Language and Tick-Tacking: The Constraints of Semiotic Systems" I consider a minimal pair that can illustrate this. In Hebrew, *mətaktek* means "ticktacking"; we attend to the repeated voiceless plosives and perceive the word as onomatopoeic. *mətaktak*, by contrast, means "sweetish", derived from matok (sweet). In Hebrew, the repetition of the last syllable is lexicalized, suggesting "somewhat (sweet)". A wide range of such "moderate" adjectives can be derived in this way from "main-entry" adjectives: *ħamaṣmaṣ* (sourish) from *ħamuṣ* (sour), *adamdam* (reddish) from *adom* (red), *yərakrak* (greenish), from *yarok* (green), and so forth. Hebrew slang even derives *gəvarbar* ("somewhat man") from *gever* (man). The meaning directs our attention to this redoubling of the syllable, and we attend away from the acoustic features of the specific consonants. Benjamin Hrushovski

(1968; 1980) pointed out that the sibilants have different (even opposite) effects in "When to the sessions of sweet silent thought/I summon up remembrance of things past" and in "And the silken, sad uncertain rustling of each purple curtain". In my book I explore the different aspects of the sibilants that may generate such conflicting effects. In the former quote, meaning components related to "silent" activate one set of aspects; in the latter, meaning components related to "rustle" activate another set. This is what Wittgenstein (1967:194) called "aspect-switching".

I wish to repeat here an issue expounded in Chapters 1 and 2 above, which is crucial for an understanding of how sound symbolism works. The Haskins Laboratories researchers distinguish between a speech mode and a nonspeech mode of aural perception, which follow different paths in the neural system. In the nonspeech mode we listen to a stream of auditory information in which the shape of what is perceived is similar to the shape of the acoustic signal; in the speech mode we "attend away" *from* the acoustic signal *to* the combination of muscular acts that seem to have produced it; and *from* these elementary movements *away to* their joint purpose, the abstract phoneme sequence. In this mode, all the rich precategorial sensory information is shut out from awareness. In verbal communication it is the abstract phoneme that counts, not the precategorial sound stream or the articulatory gestures that led to the abstract category. There is, however, experimental literature that gives evidence that some of the rich precategorial sensory information *is* subliminally perceived. I have claimed that there is also a "poetic mode" of speech perception, in which emotional and perceptual qualities are generated when the precategorial auditory information is available for combination with meaning components. In the Hebrew word for "tick-tacking" the meaning directs attention to the sensory information underlying the voiceless plosives; in the Hebrew word for "sweetish" it directs attention away, to an abstract lexical model.

The present chapter was prompted by three others, by John Ohala, Eugene Morton, and Gérard Diffloth, in the mind-expanding collection of essays *Sound Symbolism* (Hinton, Nichols & Ohala eds., 1994). In the light of these essays I will recapitulate two issues from the chapter "Some Spatial and Tactile Metaphors for Sounds" of my above-mentioned book: the relation between sound frequency and the size of the body that produced it; and the relation between "high" and "low" vowels and the suggested size of their referents. The former may account for the rise of certain crucial potentials active in the latter.

11.2   Phlogiston and precategorial information

An anonymous reviewer for *Journal of Pragmatics* criticized my use of "precategorial auditory information" as follows. "The construction of an entity called 'precategorial auditory information' sounds to me like phlogiston reborn in linguistics: auditory information that is perceived without semantic understanding, yet somehow convey semantic understanding – assuming I've grasped the principle".

The phlogiston comparison is delightful, but totally unfounded. So, to avoid such misunderstanding, I restated at some length what became now one of the central tenets of this book, that is, what I mean by "precategorial auditory information". I have taken the term from Al Liberman and his colleagues (Liberman et al. 1967, 1972). Speech sounds can be uniquely identified by acoustic energy concentrations at varying frequencies, called formants. The lowest is called F1, the second lowest F2, and so on. (Intonation pitch is F0). These can be turned by a "spectrograph" into patches of light and shade (or colours) called "spectrograms". Figure 1 presents the spectrogram of the syllables /ba/, /da/ and /ga/, uttered by me.

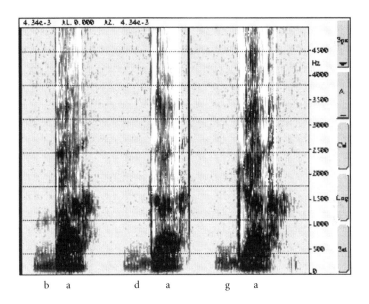

Figure 1. Spectrogram of the syllables /ba/, /da/ and /ga/, uttered by myself

From the hand painted spectrogram in Figure 2 the syllables /di/ and /du/ can be synthesized on a machine called "pattern playback". The parallel horizontal first and second formants of Figure 2 represent the vowels /i/ and /u/; the encircled portions preceding them represent rapid changes of frequency called formant transitions, in this case the second formant transitions. They give information about the vowel and the preceding consonant /d/ at the same time. This is called "parallel transmission". The syllables "ba", "da" and "ga" differ only in the second formant transition's onset frequency. There is, then, no resemblance between the shape of the perceived speech category and that of the precategorial acoustic signal that carries it. This is called "categorial perception".

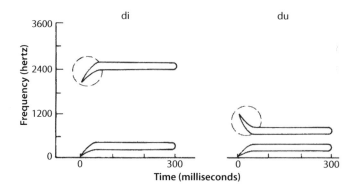

Figure 2. Simplified hand-painted spectrogram from which the syllables /di/ and /du/ can be synthesised on a pattern playback

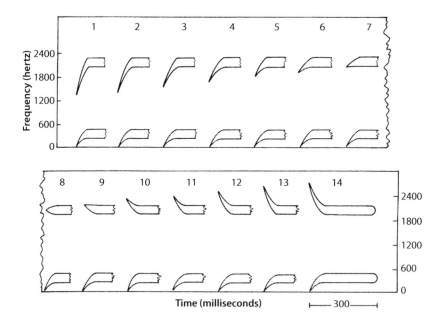

Figure 3. Hand-painted spectrograms of the syllables ba, da, ga. The ba–da–ga pitch continuum of F2 is divided into 14 steps instead of three. The two parallel regions of black indicate regions of energy concentration, F1 and F2. Notice that the onset frequency of F2 of da is higher than that of ba; and the onset frequency of F2 of ga is higher than that of da. Only stimulus 14 represents its full duration

An illuminating instance of categorial perception has been demonstrated with reference to Figure 3, where the pitch continuum between /ba/, /da/ and /ga/ has been divided into fourteen equal steps instead of three. Listeners discriminate the same difference more accurately near the category boundaries than within the categories. In the speech mode we hear only the unitary speech category, but not the sensory information represented by the spectrograms.

In certain laboratory conditions one can hear directly the precategorial auditory information. So, as a second step, the reader may listen online to the sequence of syllables represented in Figure 3, and to the sequence of isolated second formants from an unpublished demo tape by Terry Halwes. See whether you can hear a gradual change between the steps, or a sudden change from /ba/ to /da/ to /ga/. Halwes then isolates the second formant transition, that piece of sound which differs across the series, so as to make it possible to listen to just those sounds alone. Most people who listen to that series of chirps report hearing what we would expect, judging from the appearance of the formant transition: upward glides, and falling whistles displaying a gradual change from one to the next. The perception of the former series illustrates the speech mode, of the latter series – the nonspeech mode.

As a third step, I am going to quote a substantial section from my 1992 book that presents some evidence that in some "mysterious" way the "precategorial auditory information" *can* be heard while being tuned to the speech categories. One such piece of evidence is provided by Liberman et al. who describe an experiment by T. Rand:

> To one ear he presented all the first formant, including the transitions, together with the steady-state parts of the second and third formants; when presented alone, these patterns sound vaguely like /da/. To the other ear, with proper time relationships carefully preserved, were presented the 50-msec second-formant and third-formant transitions; alone, these sound like the chirps we have referred to before. But when these patterns were presented together – that is, dichotically – listeners clearly heard /ba/, /da/ or /ga/ (depending on the nature of the second-formant and third-formant transitions) in one ear and, simultaneously, non-speech chirps in the other. Thus, it appears that the same acoustic events – the second-formant or third-formant transitions – can be processed simultaneously as speech and nonspeech. We should suppose, then, that the incoming signal goes indiscriminately to speech and nonspeech processors. If the speech processors succeed in extracting phonetic features, then the signal is speech; if they fail, the signal is processed only as nonspeech.

I have arrived at the notion of the "poetic mode" on the basis of introspection and certain thought experiments, back in 1980. However, I have received massive corroboration to my speculations that nonphonetic acoustic information may be available in the speech mode too, when Repp's comprehensive survey of research on categorial perception was published in 1984. Thus, for instance, speaking of the within-categorial steps represented in Figure 3,

> Liberman et al. (1957) were able to generate a fair prediction of discrimination performance from known labeling probabilities; however, performance was somewhat better than predicted, suggesting that the subjects did have some additional stimulus information available.　　　　　　　(Repp 1984: 245)

What is more, people appear to be capable of switching modes, by using different listening strategies. Fricative stimuli seem to be especially suited for the application of different strategies, so that they may be perceived fairly categorically in one situation but continuously in another (*idem*, 287). Repp investigated the possibility that with fricatives, for instance, little training would be necessary for acoustic discrimination of within-category differences. He employed a /s/–/ʃ/ continuum, followed by a vocalic context. The success of his procedure.

> together with the introspections of the experienced listeners, suggested that the skill involved lay in perceptually segregating the noise from its vocalic context, which then made it possible to attend to its "pitch". Without this segregation, the phonetic percept was dominant. Once the auditory strategy has been acquired, it is possible to switch back and forth between auditory and phonetic modes of listening, and it seems likely [...] that both strategies could be pursued simultaneously (or in very rapid succession) without any loss of accuracy. These results provide good evidence for the existence of two alternative modes of perception, phonetic and auditory – a distinction supported by much additional evidence.　　　　　　　(Repp 1984: 307)

It is reassuring to find that my speculations concerning the nature of the "poetic mode" gain support from an increasing body of experimental evidence, and that cognitive strategies have been discovered, by which listeners may switch, at will, back and forth, between phonetic categories and auditory information.

　　As a fourth step, one could add the vast experimental literature based on the assumption that the rich precategorial auditory information in the so-called "unencoded" speech sounds facilitates performance in certain cognitive tasks relative to "encoded" speech sounds. Thus, for instance, one can discriminate by introspection that /s/ is higher than /ʃ/; but not that /da/ is higher than /ba/, and /ga/ is higher than /da/. Phoneticians call this "encodedness": the plosives /b/, /d/ an /g/ are more encoded than the sibilants /s/ and /ʃ/.

11.3　Sound symbolism and source's size

Sounds can be located along dimensions whose extremes are marked by spatial notions as LOW~HIGH, THICK~THIN or space-related notions as HEAVY~LIGHT, and the like. These dimensions seem to be correlated in certain meaningful ways. There is plenty of anecdotal as well as carefully controlled experimental evidence that intuitions concerning the "spatial" as well as the "tactile qualities" of sound are fairly consistent from observer to observer, and sometimes even from culture to culture. Some such experiments have been reported by Roger Brown in his classic of psycholinguistics (Brown 1968: 110–154). The whole chapter testifies to Brown's usually brilliant insights and subtle ways of analysis. Here, however, I am going to quote only two passages with which I disagree.

> A concept like "boulder" is referred to rocks and stone and, in comparison, judged to be "heavy", "large", "thick", and "wide". These terms are directly applicable to boulders. However, boulders have no voices. Where, then, does the concept belong on the "bass-treble" or "loud-soft" scales? We cannot doubt the answer. If Disney were to give a boulder a voice it would be "bass" and "loud" in contrast to the piping of a pebble. This could be a mediated association: a boulder must have a bass voice because creatures that do have bass voices are usually heavy and boulders are heavy. It is not necessary to assume that there is any subtle inter-sensory quality found in boulders and bass voices.

> Subjects in the study of Brown et al. felt that "thick" and "thin" simply do not apply to voices. However, "loud" and "resonant" do. Now thick people and animals and violin strings are usually loud and resonant. So, if the subject is required to guess, he will call the loud and resonant voice "thick". This need not be because the voice shares some inter-sensory quality with the visual or tactile apprehension of thickness. It could be because the voice is loud and creatures who have loud voices are usually thick, a mediated association (152–153).

The cognitive approach to Man, of which Brown is one of the most outstanding exponents, tends to regard such explanations as "mediated associations" as the last resort of the scientist, where all structural explanations fail. Now, what seems to be wrong with the "mediated associations" theory is that it reverts to a rather strong version of associationist theory, assuming that people in various cultures have been uniformly conditioned by external conditions. It seems to be all too easy to invent some mediating story that appears to be pretty convincing, until one becomes aware of not less convincing counter-examples. Thus, for instance, red colour is felt to be "warm", whereas blue is felt to be "cold"; this feeling is not culture-dependent, and thus cannot be explained by cultural conditioning. Now there is a rather widely accepted explanation, that fire is red in all cultures whereas the blue sea is relatively cold in all cultures. However, the blue sky on a tropical (or even European) summer-noon is not exactly associated with cold. The sun, on the other hand, at its hottest, would be associated with gold rather than red, whereas red would be associated with the setting rather than with the shining sun. In this case, for instance, Brown himself offers other explanations than "mediated association" for "warm" and "cold colours".

I submit that bass voices are perceived as thicker than soprano voices, not because creatures that do have bass voices are usually thick and heavy, but, precisely, because "they share some inter-sensory quality with the visual or tactile apprehension of thickness" (I happen to know quite a few thick and heavy opera singers who have tenor or even coloratura soprano voices). Whereas the relationship between thick people and bass voices appears to be quite incidental, the relationship between thick violin strings and "thick" and "low" sounds seems to have good physical reasons. Sounds are vibrations of the air or some other material medium. The thicker the string, *other things being equal*, the *slower* and *wider* the vibrations. (Not so with singers: when they get fatter or thinner, their voice range and voice quality remains essentially unchanged).

Figure 4. This is a photo of the great soprano Margaret Price from the brochure of Tristan und Isolde. And this is a photo of Samuel Ramsey, from the brochure of Mussorgsky's opera Boris Godunov, who sings Pimen's part, one of the most illustrious bass parts in the opera literature

There are, then, at least three physical dimensions of sound that are analogous and co-varying: SLOW~FAST, WIDE~NARROW, and THICK~THIN. The first two pairs of adjectives describe the vibrations, the third pair describes the strings (if there be any) that may be causally related to the first two. It should be noted, however, that whereas the SLOW~FAST and the WIDE~NARROW pairs characterize the "proximal stimulus" that actually hits the membrane of the ear and is directly experienced, the THICK~THIN pair characterizes the source of the sound, and may be attributed to the distal stimulus, the perceived sound, only as a concomitant of other measurable features of the sound wave (wavelength, overtone structure).

Michael Polányi (1967:13) argues that the meaning of the "proximal term of tacit knowledge" (and, one might add, the qualities of perception) are typically displaced, away from us, to the distal term. Phenomenologically, the relative frequency and width of sound vibrations are experienced as their relative "height" and "thickness", respectively.

As for the THICK~THIN characterization of sounds, an additional observation seems to be pertinent. The sounds we usually hear do not consist of fundamentals only, but of overtones too. Since the range of frequencies audible to the human ear is limited, and since there are no "undertones", the lower the fundamental, the greater the number of overtones that are within the hearing range of the human ear. Thus, when we strike a key near the left end of the piano keyboard, we perceive a "thick aura" of overtones (cf. Chapter 2) around the sound that is absent from the sounds produced by striking the keys near the right end (notice, by the way, that in spite of the left-to-right arrangement of the keyboard, we perceive the piano sounds as "low" or "high" rather than "left-wing" or "right-wing" as would be predicted by a mediated-association theory).

Recently I encountered a more fine-grained hypothesis which suggests a rather complex relationship between body-size, the size of articulatory organs and size of vibration, that has evolutionary implications. Even if these implications are not substantiated, the other correlations remain sound. John Ohala's paper has the telling title "The frequency code underlies the sound-symbolic use of voice pitch". Based on Eugene Morton's ethological work, Ohala explores some voice-pitch-related human responses, including responses to intonation. He claims that the frequency code underlying certain aspects of the sound-symbolic use of voice pitch is not merely an intercultural, but also a cross-species phenomenon. The reason is that this frequency code has great survival and evolutionary value both in mating and settling disputes:

> Animals in competition for some resource attempt to intimidate their opponent by, among other things, trying to appear as large as possible (because the larger individuals would have an advantage if, as a last resort, the matter had to be settled by actual combat). Size (or apparent size) is primarily conveyed by visual means, e.g. erecting the hair or feathers and other appendages (ears, tail feathers, wings), so that the signaler subtends a larger angle in the receiver's visual field. There are many familiar examples of this: threatening dogs erect the hair on their backs and raise their ears and tails, cats arch their backs, birds extend their wings and fan out their tail feathers. [...] As Morton (1977) points out, however, *the F0 of voice can also indirectly convey an impression of the size of the signaler*, since F0, other things being equal, is inversely related to the mass of the vibrating membrane (vocal cords in mammals, syrinx in birds), which, in turn, is correlated with overall body mass. Also, the more massive the vibrating

membrane, the more likely it is that secondary vibrations could arise, thus giving rise to an irregular or "rough" voice quality. To give the impression of being large and dangerous, then, an antagonist should produce a vocalization as rough and as low in F0 as possible. On the other hand, to seem small and non-threatening a vocalization which is tone-like and high in F0 is called for. […]. Morton's (1977) analysis, then, has the advantage that it provides the same motivational basis for the form of these vocalizations as had previously been given to elements of visual displays, i.e. that they convey an impression of the size of the signaler. I will henceforth call this cross-species F0-function correlation "the frequency code".
(Ohala 1994:330)

Voice frequency gives, then, information not about the mass of the body, but about the mass of the vibrating membrane which, in turn, may or may not be correlated with the mass of the body. A bass singer may be slim, it is his vocal chords that must be of a substantial size.

In another paper in the same book, Eugene Morton explores avian and mammalian sounds used in hostile or "friendly," appeasing contexts. He provides two tables in which sounds given by aggressive and appeasing birds and mammals are listed. "Aggressive animals utter low-pitched often harsh sounds, whose most general function is to increase the distance between sender and receiver. Appeasing animals use high-pitched, often tonal sounds, whose most general function is to decrease the distance or maintain close contact by reducing the fear or aggression in the receiver" (Morton 1994:350–353). Subsequently (353–356) he expounds a conception of sound–size symbolism in animals similar to the one quoted above from Ohala.

I am not claiming that I have enough data to confirm the evolutionary implications of the Morton-Ohala hypothesis. I am attempting to do two things: first, I am locating their hypothesis between Brown's and my own, comparing the three. Second, I claim that this hypothesis can account for certain sound–body relationships on the one hand, and certain intonation phenomena on the other that are difficult to account for otherwise. I compare three hypotheses by Roger Brown, John Ohala and myself regarding the relationship between the size of the sound source and the perceived quality of the sound. What I am showing is that when Ohala relates sound size to body size he does this, unlike Brown, *via* the size of the articulatory organs, corroborating (not confirming) my hypothesis. In this way he accounts also for the everyday observation that people with large body may have a thin voice, and people with a smaller body a thicker voice. Interestingly, according to Ohala and Morton, individuals in many species try to use this discrepancy between body size and voice size to fool potential partners or adversaries who act on Brown's assumptions.

Writers occasionally capitalize on a discrepancy between body size and voice register. Anton Chekhov describes Dr. Andrey Yefimitch Ragin in his "Ward No. 6" as follows:

> His exterior is heavy – coarse like a peasant's, his face, his beard, his flat hair, and his coarse, clumsy figure, suggest an overfed, intemperate, and harsh innkeeper on the highroad. His face is surly-looking and covered with blue veins, his eyes are little and his nose is red. With his height and broad shoulders he has huge hands and feet; one would think that a blow from his fist would knock the life out of anyone, but his step is soft, and his walk is cautious and insinuating; when he meets anyone in a narrow passage he is always the first to stop and make way, and to say, not in a bass, as one would expect, but in a high, soft tenor: "I beg your pardon!" [Available online: http://www.ibiblio.org/eldritch/ac/w6-05.html]

As to intonation phenomena, Ohala reports a set of experiments in one of which short samples (4 sec) of spontaneous speech were digitally processed in such a way as to remove all spectral details but to retain the original amplitude and F_0 contour, the latter of which was either linearly upshifted or downshifted by varying amounts or left unchanged. These samples of "stripped speech" were presented in pairs to listeners who were asked to judge which voice of each pair sounded more dominant or self-confident. The results indicate that, other things being equal, lower F_0 does make a voice sound more dominant. This is evident, for example, in the judgments for a pair of samples which are derived from the same speech sample but with one of them upshifted from the original by a factor of 1.25 (Figure 5). The sample with the lower F_0 was judged as sounding more dominant than the sample with the higher F_0 by 92% of the listeners. In another experiment two samples of "stripped speech" were presented to listeners. A sample which had a higher-peak F_0 but ended with a sharp terminal fall was judged as sounding more dominant (92% of all judgments) than another sample that was lower in F_0 during most of its duration (Figure 6). "The sharp F_0 terminal fall, lacking in the other sample, seemed to be the determining factor in listeners' evaluations; it suggests that the occasionally higher-peak F_0 in the voices exhibiting greater confidence is there in order to make the terminal fall seem to be even steeper, i.e. by virtue of having fallen from a greater height". The Morton–Ohala hypothesis can account for such results quite plausibly. To refute it, one must present a rival hypothesis and contrive some experiment the results of which would support one or the other.

This conception may have far-reaching implications, beyond what is conspicuously suggested by Ohala and Morton. At the end of an important theoretical statement of research done at the Haskins Laboratories, Al Liberman (1970: 321) says: "One can reasonably expect to discover whether, in developing linguistic behavior, Nature has invented new physiological devices, or simply turned old ones to new ends". I will suggest that in some cases at least old cognitive and physiological devices are turned to linguistic, even aesthetic, ends. This seems to reflect Nature's parsimony.

What is the relationship between being dangerous and having an irregular or "rough" voice quality; or between seeming non-threatening and a vocalization

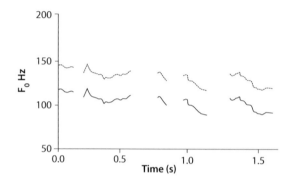

Figure 5. The F_0 contours of two samples of "stripped speech". The lower contour, depicted by the solid line, was judged "more dominant" in 92% of the judgments

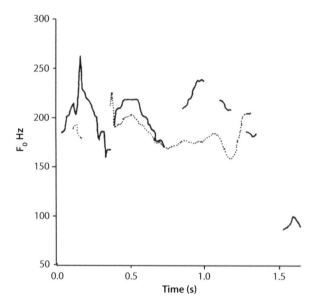

Figure 6. The F_0 contours of two samples of "stripped speech". The contour depicted by the solid line was judged "more dominant" in 92% of the judgments

which is tone-like? To answer this question, one must realize that "noises" are irregular sounds, "tones" are regular, periodic sounds. Ohala and Morton mention this merely as a corollary of "deep" and "high" voices. But this aspect of nonhuman vocalisation may throw an interesting light on certain widespread intuitions in the poetic mode of speech perception, namely, that periodic consonants (e.g. [m], [n]) are perceived as soft, mellow, and appeasing, whereas aperiodic continuants (e.g. [s], [z]) as harsh, strident, turbulent, and the like. In fact, what I wrote about the poetic effects of periodic and aperiodic speech sounds may apply, *mutatis mutandis*, to this ecological problem as well:

> Periodic sounds have been described (May & Repp 1982:145) as "the recurrence of signal portions with similar structure", whereas aperiodic stimuli as having "randomly changing waveform", that "may have more idiosyncratic features to be remembered". The recurring signal portions with similar structures may arouse in the perceiver a relatively relaxed kind of attentiveness (there will be no surprises, one may expect the same waveform to recur). Thus, periodic sounds are experienced as smoothly flowing. The randomly changing waveforms of aperiodic sounds, with their "idiosyncratic features", are experienced as disorder, as a disruption of the "relaxed kind of attentiveness".   (Tsur 1992:44)

In some circumstances unpredictability is a dangerous thing. Sound gives information about physical changes in one's environment. Randomly changing sounds give information about unpredictable changes. So they force one to be constantly on the alert. The survival purpose of such alertness is conspicuous. Even in animal communication, however, an irregular or "rough" voice quality is sometimes "symbolic"; it constitutes no danger in itself, but has a common ingredient with dangerous circumstances: unpredictability. In the poetic mode of speech perception, response to regular or randomly changing waveforms is turned to an aesthetic end: it assumes "purposiveness without purpose". I do not offer this as a fact, or a generalization, but as a hypothesis that would perhaps explain the relationship between unpredictability and being dangerous, by making a crucial recommendation to attend to certain aspects of the phenomenon.

Likewise, the foregoing conception may illuminate *the motor theory of speech perception* too from an unexpected angle. This theory assumes that in the production as well as in the perception of speech we attend *from* the acoustic signal *to* the combination of muscular movements that produce it (even in the case of hand-painted spectrograms); and from these elementary movements to their joint purpose, the phoneme. The best approximation to the invariance of phonemes seems to be, according to Liberman et al. (1967:43, and *passim*), by going back in the chain of articulatory events, beyond the shapes that underlie the locus of production, *to the commands* that produce the shapes. "There is typically a lack of correspondence between acoustic cue and perceived phoneme, and in all these cases it appears that perception mirrors articulation more closely than sound. [...] This supports the assumption that the listener uses the inconstant sound as a basis for finding his way back to the articulatory gesture that produced it and thence, as it were, to the speaker's intent" (Liberman et al. 1967:453). If Ohala and Morton are right, this mechanism underlying speech perception is a less recent invention of evolution than might be thought. The lion's roar, for instance, follows a similar course. The F_0 of voice can convey an impression of the size of the mass of the vibrating membrane and, indirectly, of the size of the signaler; in other words, the listener uses the inconstant sound as a basis for finding his way back to the articulatory organs and gestures that produced it and thence, as it were, to the roarer's intent. This does not mean that there is no qualitative leap from the lion's roar to human speech. The lion's roar can express only some general intent; not, for instance, such subtle semantic distinctions as "For fools *admire*, men of sense *approve*".

After having submitted a version of the present chapter to *Journal of Pragmatics*, I ran into Peter Ladefoged's illuminating book *Vowels and Consonants* with an accompanying CD, where one may listen to the sounds under discussion. He ends a discussion of the modes and moods suggested by intonation with a pair of examples (recorded in his own voice) in which "there are no distinguishable words, but it is obvious which was spoken in anger and which when happy. In the first of these two utterances [Figure 7] there are large changes in pitch, with the 'sentence' as a whole having a generally falling pitch. The second utterance [Figure 8] has slightly smaller peaks, but they are sharper, without the rounded tops, and the 'sentence' as a whole has an increasing pitch" (Ladefoged 2001:17). (I am responsible for the Figures 1, 7–8, 10–11).

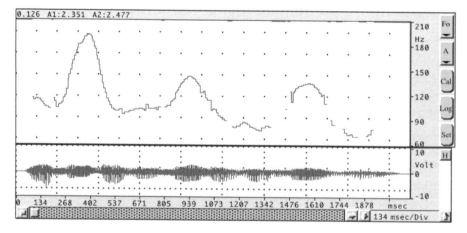

Figure 7. Wave plot and pitch extract of an utterance in which there are no words, but in which the speaker sounds contented (after Peter Ladefoged)

In light of Ohala's and Morton's papers, I wish to make two additional observations. First, the peaks of the second utterance are not just "slightly smaller"; the whole utterance is of considerably lower pitch. The pitch of the highest peak in Figure 7 is 191.739 Hz; that of the lowest peak is 135.276 Hz (my speech-analyzer application, SoundScope, specifies 80–150 as the range of typical male voice). The highest peak in Figure 8 is slightly lower than the lowest peak in Figure 7 (129.706 Hz); the lowest peak in Figure 7 is 102.083 Hz. Second, the utterance reflected in Figure 8 is uttered in a "grating" voice: its voice quality is quite "rough", considerably "harsher" than that of the one reflected in Figure 7. As Morton said, "aggressive animals utter low-pitched often harsh sounds"; and so, apparently, do aggressive humans. I would add that in Figure 7 peaks are softly rounded out, whereas in Figure 8 they constitute sharp angles; this too may affect the content or angry quality of intonation. At any rate, Ohala's and Morton's generalizations apply to Ladefoged's example of upset or angry utterance too, beyond the features pointed out by Ladefoged himself. However, my instrumental analysis of poetry readings suggests that only a small part of the poetic or conversational effects can be accounted for in terms of the "frequency code". High tone, for instance, may have a wide range of effects, depending on other elements with which it combines, besides submission (see Tsur 2006).

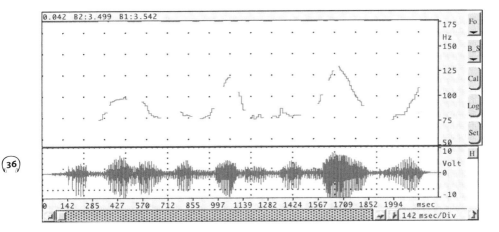

Figure 8. Wave plot and pitch extract of an utterance in which there are no words, but in which the speaker sounds upset or angry (after Peter Ladefoged)

11.3.1 Sound symbolism and referent's size

The foregoing discussion strongly suggests a causal relationship as well as structural resemblance between the frequency and perceived size of sounds on the one hand, and the physical size of their vibrating source on the other. The association of small size with high frequency and of large size with low frequency becomes a "meaning potential" of sounds, which may be actualized in sound–referent relations too. In the chapter "Some Spatial and Tactile Metaphors for Sounds" of my 1992 book I also discussed vowel symbolism for size and distance. Among others, I quoted Ultan (1978) who, by examining a total of 136 languages, tested the hypothesis that diminutive sound symbolism is associated with marked phonological features (high and/or front vowels and palatal or fronted consonants). He found that diminutive is most often symbolized by high or high front vowels, high tone, or various kinds of consonantal ablaut. Proximal distance is symbolized overwhelmingly by front or high vowels. Let me add to Ultan's sample a language not included in it, my native Hungarian, in which *itt* means "here", *ott* means "there", *ez* means "this", *az* means "that". *Így* means "in this fashion", *úgy* means "in that fashion"; *ilyen* means "of this kind", *olyan* "of that kind", and so forth. "Since high front vowels reflect proportionately higher second formant frequencies, and the higher the tone the higher the natural frequency, there appears a correspondence between a feature of high frequency (= short wavelength in physical terms) and the category of small size" (Ultan 1978: 545). Likewise, for the same reasons, the received view is that in Western languages /i/ is small and /a/ is big.[1]

In a mind-expanding paper on the word class of "expressives"[2] in Bahnar, a Mon-Khmer language of Vietnam, Gérard Diffloth claims that in this word class /i/ signifies "big", and /a/ "small". This throws my foregoing argument into an exciting perspective. At first sight the paper provides outright refutation of one of my pet beliefs; but in the final resort it lends massive support to my wider conceptions, that speech events (speech sounds and articulatory gestures) do have certain (sometimes conflicting) combinational potentials, which may be activated, *after the event*, by certain meaning components. Diffloth

---

1.   I wonder whether this system of front (high) vowels suggesting small distance and back (low) vowels suggesting great distance can be related to Morton's claim that aggressive animals utter low-pitched sounds, whose most general function is to increase the distance between sender and receiver, whereas appeasing animals use high-pitched sounds, whose most general function is to decrease the distance or maintain close contact by reducing the fear or aggression in the receiver.

2.   "I have used the term 'expressives' to refer to this basic part of speech, which is alien to Western tradition but can be defined in the additional way by its distinct morphology, syntactic properties, and semantic characteristics" (Diffloth 1994: 108).

points out the following relationships between referent size and vowel height in Bahnar:[3]

	ii	uu	i	u
"BIG"				
	ee	oo	e	o
"SMALL"	εε	øø	ε	ø

Examples ("D. red." = "Descriptive reduplication"):

1. /blooŋ-blooŋ/   "D. red. of numerous reflections caused by rays of light on a large object, elongated in shape"

    vs. /blɔɔŋ-blɔɔŋ/   "id., small object"

2. /blooŋ-blɛɛw/   "D. red. of the numerous reflections caused by a single ray of light on a big shiny object"

    vs. /blɔɔŋ-blɛɛw/   "id., small shiny object"

3. /bleel-bleel/   "D. red. of large flames appearing intermittently but remaining vivid."

    vs. /blɛɛl-blɛɛl/   "id., small flames"

4. /bliil-ɲip/   "D. red. of a large scintillating fire, of the last flashes of a large fire about to die"

    vs. /blɛɛl-ɲɛp/   "id., small fire",

and so forth. There are examples in which a three-way gradation is given, with high vowels providing a third degree: "enormous":

"ENORMOUS"	ii	uu		i	u
"BIG"	ee	oo		e	o
"SMALL"	εε	ɔɔ		ε	ɔ

In both the two-way and three-way division "the iconic values of the vowels are, roughly speaking: High = Big and Low = Small, exactly opposite to the English /i/ = Small and /a/ = Big, claimed to be universal. There is nothing peculiar about this Bahnar system, and one can easily find an iconic basis for it. In the articulation of high vowels, the tongue occupies a much larger volume in the mouth than it does for low vowels. The proprioceptive sensation due to this, reinforced by the

---

3. Let me say at once that I know nothing about Bahnar or any other Vietnamese language except what I read in Diffloth's paper. Everything I say on this language is based on what I read in that paper.

amount of contact between the sides of the tongue and the upper molars, is available to all speakers and is probably necessary to achieve a precise articulatory gesture. […] In this perspective, two different languages may easily use the same phonetic variable (vowel height) to convey the same range of sensations (size), and come up with exactly opposite solutions, both being equally iconic; all they need to do is focus upon different parts of the rich sensation package provided by articulatory gestures, in our case the volume of the tongue instead of the size of the air passage between it and the palate".

Now consider such pairs of English synonyms as *big* and *large*, or *small* and *little* one member of which contains a high vowel, the other a low one. One may account for their coexistence in one language in one of two ways: either by assuming that the relationship between sound and meaning is arbitrary, or by assuming that speakers and listeners intuitively focus upon different parts of "the rich sensation package" provided by either the articulatory gestures or the speech signal in pronouncing these words. It may well be the case that, basically, in most words the combination of the phonetic signifier with the semantic signified is arbitrary; it is only after the event that meaning directs attention to certain aspects of the vowels in *large* or *little*, but not in *big* or *small*. There is good evidence that poets in various languages exploit this flexibility of language users: they increase the relative frequency of certain speech sounds in a poem so as to generate an emotional atmosphere, directing attention by meaning to the relevant phonetic features. The relationship between the phonetic and semantic constituents of most words used may be arbitrary; but certain features of the text's meaning may direct attention to certain recurring features of the sound patterns (Fónagy 1961; Harshav, 1968, 1980). Shifting attention from one part of "the rich sensation package" to another is what Wittgenstein (1967:194 ff.) called "aspect-switching", prompted by the meanings of the words. According to Wittgenstein, one may switch between meanings attached to a single string of phonological signifiers; the present conception extends this ability to switching between different features of one string of phonological signifiers. In fact, there are good reasons to suppose that Wittgenstein did not mean specified visual or verbal aspects, but an ability (or lack of ability) to *switch* between aspects of whatever kinds.

There are two conspicuous common features in Diffloth's corpus and my foregoing examples from Hungarian. First, the sound–meaning relationship, if present, does not take the shape of a statistical tendency in a huge aggregate of isolated words; it is displayed by minimal pairs of straightforward antonyms. Second, phonetically, these pairs are opposed in only one pair of vowels; semantically, too, they are contrasted in one feature. All the rest is really equal. In other words, in such cases size–sound symbolism is formally lexicalized. This lexical feature reflects creative phonetic intuitions in the distant past which have fossilized by now; the present-day language-user may attend away from the sound symbolism of "high" and "low". So, these pairs of words are structurally different from such clusters of synonyms and antonyms as *big* and *large*, or *small* and *little*. The two systems, however, are opposed in one interesting feature. In Hungarian there is vowel harmony. Consider the pair *ilyen* (ijɛn) and *olyan* (ojɔn). The size-symbolic contrast is carried by the /i~o/ opposition; but this affects the articulatory location of the second vowel too. In Diffloth's examples from Bahnar, by contrast, the other vowels may vary independently.

I have vested theoretical interest that Diffloth's explanation should be valid. It would reinforce my conception according to which sound symbolism is part of a complex event, comprising meanings, articulatory gestures, sound waves, etc. Each one of these components has an indefinite number of features, which give rise to a multiplicity of sometimes conflicting combinational potentials. Strong intuitions concerning sound symbolism are generated by selecting a subset of available features on the semantic, acoustic, and articulatory levels. When conflicting intuitions are reported, attention is shifted from one subset to another.

When, however, I tried to pronounce the speech sounds which Diffloth designates "high", I noticed that his description suits [i] extremely well; but not [u].

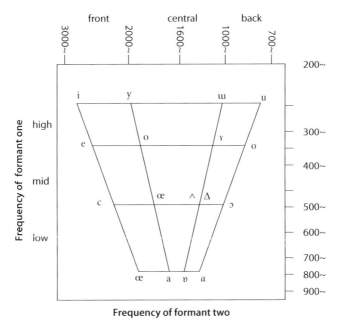

Figure 9. The acoustic and articulatory location of the synthetic vowels, plotted according to the frequency positions of the first and second formants

In view of the examples he provides, whatever explanation suits [i] should suit [u] too.[4]

When we compare Ultan's and Diffloth's explanations, we get a clue for solving the problem: they mean different things by the same words. Speaking of "high" and "low", Ultan means relative formant frequency; Diffloth means articulatory location.[5] Consider Figure 9. The words "front, central, back, high, mid, low" refer to place of articulation. The numbers refer to formant frequency. The "height" of the place of articulation of the vowel is in an inverse relation to the frequency of its first formant. The higher the place of articulation, the lower is the formant frequency. In fact, we should reformulate Diffloth's above statement as "In the articulation of *front* vowels, the tongue occupies a much larger volume in the mouth than it does for *back* vowels". This would, of course, suit the high and low vowels arranged by the frequency of the second formant, according to which /i/ is "high", /u/ is "low". But the scales of Diffloth's examples from Bahnar reflect relative frequencies of the first formant, according to which /i/ and /u/ are of equal height, /e/ and /o/ are of equal height, and so forth. So, we must assume that the conflicting sound-symbolisms of Bahnar and of Hungarian (or English) are generated not by attending to different aspects of the articulatory gesture, but by attending to different formants of the speech signal. When attending to the frequencies of the first formant, the principle of *low* is "big" and *high* is "small" is meticulously preserved in Bahnar too.

Thus, the words *high* and *low* are ambiguous in this context. If we rely on the relative height of articulation in Bahnar, *high* will be "big", *low* will be "small". If we rely on relative first-formant frequencies, high will be "small" and *low* will be "big" in Bahnar too. How can we know, then, which one is the "correct" identification? I have to admit that this is not clear at all. First, as I said, Diffloth's explanation suits [i], but not [u]. In view of the examples he provides, whatever explanation suits [i]

---

4. This does not imply that the much larger volume which the tongue occupies in the mouth and the larger surface of contact with the palate may not affect the perceived quality of speech sounds, e.g. their perceived wetness. Consider: "Les consonnes palatales ou palatalisées étaient senties comme particulièrement mouillées. Par rapport á un *l* palatisée, [...] le *l* simple passe pour *sec*" (Fónagy 1979: 19). Fónagy explains this judgment as follows: "Selon les palatographies et radiographies, les occlusives amouillées, palatales ou palatalisées, se distinguent des autres par un contact nettement plus large du dos de la langue et du palais. Ceci revient a dire que la sensation kinesthésique du contact de surfaces des deux muqueuses, donc mouillées est particulièrement nette" (Fónagy 1979: 98).

5. Characteristically, Diffloth accounts for Ultan's findings, as for his own findings, in terms of articulatory gestures, not frequencies: "in our case the volume of the tongue instead of the size of the air passage between it and the palate".

should suit [u] too. Second, my foregoing discussion apparently provides support for both possibilities, articulatory gesture and auditory information. In proposing the "Poetic Mode of Speech Perception", I relied on "rich precategorial auditory information". This would favour the "frequency code" conception. With reference to the motor theory of speech perception, however, I quoted Liberman saying "in all these cases it appears that perception mirrors articulation more closely than sound". This would favour the articulatory gesture conception.[6] I propose the following way out from this muddle. By this statement, Liberman referred to the perception of phonetic categories. Perceptual and emotional symbolism, by contrast, is founded precisely on the rich precategorial auditory information which escapes categorial perception. To be sure, articulatory gestures do have a crucial kinaesthetic effect on how speech sounds feel (see Footnote 6); but we are dealing here with an auditory phenomenon: the perceived size of speech sounds. We actually perceive high-frequency sounds as higher and thinner than low-frequency sounds even when they are played on the violin or the piano, where no articulatory gestures are involved.[7]

The notion of "consistency" too may be relevant here. Ultan accounts for his intercultural findings with reference to second-formant frequency. Ohala speaks of the "frequency code" in terms of cross-species F0-function correlation. When we apply this frequency code to first-formant frequencies in Diffloth's findings in Bahnar, they become consistent with earlier findings in other languages. "The records show that there are well-developed sound-symbolic systems where vowel quality is used with systematic results exactly opposite to those predicted" (Diffloth 1994:107) – provided that we change the rules of the game. I know, of course, nothing about the phonetic intuitions of Bahnar-speakers, or their pronunciation; nor did Diffloth make any claims about them.

Having said all this, I had some doubts about my own argument. What if the second formant is simply more salient in the stream of speech, and we have no (even subliminal) access to the first formant? If this is so, all my speculations are refuted. Indeed, as Ladefoged (2001:64) suggested (and demonstrated) in a context of speech synthesis, "the second formant by itself conveys more information than

---

6. Notice, however, that the phrase "rich precategorial auditory information", too, is derived from Liberman.

7. To avoid misunderstanding: I am not trying to explain how two different modes of perception can work to justify both Ultan and Diffloth. I am trying to explain how two different modes of perception (the speech mode and the nonspeech mode) can eliminate, within Liberman's and my conception, the contradiction I have pointed out between two opposite claims: claiming that articulatory gestures rather than precategorial auditory information determine perception and claiming its converse.

the first". But he also demonstrates (Ladefoged 2001:33) that by certain vocal manipulations in natural speech we *can* direct attention, even at will, to one formant or another. By whispering or using a low, creaky voice one may tune in to different formants: "Try whispering *heed, hid, head, had, hod, hawed* [...]; there will be a general impression of a descending pitch". The same sequence of vowels, however, may be arranged in a reverse order, and still heard as descending, if uttered in a low, creaky voice: "When saying the words *had, head, hid, heed* [in a creaky voice], this pitch goes down". The reason for this difference is that in these two conditions we are tuned to vibrations of the air in different parts of the vocal tract. "The sound that you hear when whispering is mainly that of the vibrations of the air in the front of the mouth. Conversely, the pitch changes associated with saying *had, head, hid, heed* in a creaky voice are due to the vibrations of the air in the back of the vocal tract. This resonance is the lower in pitch of the two, and is called the first formant" (listen online to Ladefoged uttering these sequences). I don't mean to suggest that Bahnar speakers resort to a creaky voice in order to attend to the first formant, just as we, in our Western culture, don't resort to whispering in order to perceive the second formant on which our size–sound symbolism is based. Perhaps there are less palpable techniques to shift attention between the front and the back of the vocal tract. But Ladefoged's exercises prove that switching attention between first and second formants *is possible* at least. There may be good reasons for attending to the second rather than the first formant. But this still does not rule out the possibility that in some culture in general, or regarding one particular "expressive" part of speech, speakers attend to the first formant. What is more, there are legitimate linguistic and paralinguistic contexts in the world's languages in which creaky voice would be natural in one way or other, and might elicit sound-symbolic intuitions.

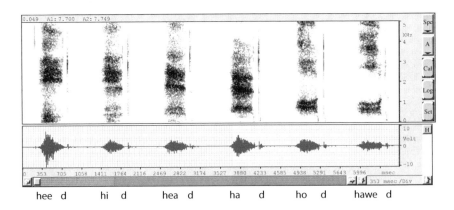

Figure 10. Wave plot and spectrogram of the words heed, hid, head, had, hod, hawed whispered

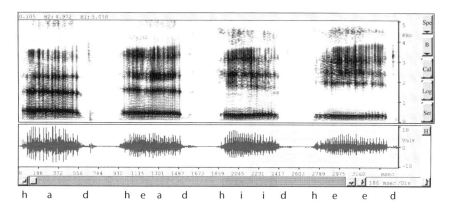

Figure 11. Wave plot and spectrogram of the words had, head, hid, heed spoken in a creaky voice

The following thought experiment would be consistent with the possibility that speakers can shift attention to the first or the second formant at will. Wittgenstein (1967: 194 ff.) says that "aspect-switching" is like understanding the request to pronounce the word "till" and mean it as a verb, or an adverb; or the word "March" and mean it once as an imperative verb, and once as the name of a month. "You can say the word "March" to yourself and mean it at one time as an imperative at another as the name of a month. And now say "March"! – and then "March *no further!*" – Does the *same* experience accompany the word both times – are you sure?" (*idem*, 215). Now suppose I strike a note near the left end of the piano keyboard, then a note near the right end. You will hear the right-end note as "higher" than the left-end note. Suppose, however, that I request you to experience them as equally high, or once the right note, once the left note as higher. You will say that you don't know what I am talking about. Now suppose I ask you to pronounce the vowels /i/ and /u/ on the same pitch and experience /i/ as higher. You will do this without any difficulty. If I ask you to experience them as equally high, you can do this too and experience the switch in a way that is similar to the switching between the meanings of "till" or "March". If, however, I ask you to experience /u/ as higher than /i/, you again will say that you don't know what I am talking about. A glance at Figure 2 may easily account for this. When you experience /i/ as higher, you attend to the second formant; when you experience the two vowels as equally high, you attend to the first formant.

When I first read Diffloth's paper, I thought that his examples were counterexamples to the widespread belief (which I too entertained), that high sounds (including high vowels) tended to suggest small referents, whereas low sounds and vowels large referents. By the same token, I thought, it supported my higher generalizations concerning human flexibility in switching between various aspects of the same speech sounds. His explanation, however, based on articulatory gestures, conflicted with the linguistic facts he adduced. The present chapter proposed an analysis that elucidated the problem and lent support to both of my former beliefs. I am most sympathetic with Diffloth in "deploring the incorrect use of the term 'universal' to mean simply 'found in a number of languages'". But, as far as the present issue is concerned, the convincing counterexamples are still to be adduced.

11.4   Descriptive reduplication in Japanese

Akita (2011) points out in Japanese similar minimal pairs of "descriptive reduplication" that differ only in the [±VOICED] feature of their initial consonant. "Overall iconic words with a voiced [initial consonant] depict large, strong, dark, and/or unpleasant referents, and those with a voiceless [initial consonant] small, weak, bright and/or pleasant referents". Thus, for instance, "*za^razara* and *sa^rasara* are minimally different from each other with respect to [...] voicedness. The former refers to a rough, coarse surface (e.g. of sandpaper), whereas the latter refers to a dry and smooth surface (e.g. of sand)" (Akita 2011:6).

As to the opposition large~small, Figure 12 shows that the spectrum of [z] is lower than that of [s], and its lowest part is particularly intense. Indeed, in harmony with the principle of "low is large", it typically designates larger referents. As to rough, coarse, and smooth surfaces, respectively, Figure 13 clearly shows that aspect of the wave form of [z] that can be interpreted as a "rough, coarse surface".

Figure 12. The spectrum of [z] is lower than that of [s]

Figure 13. Wave form of [z] and [s]. In Japanese, *za^arazara* is associated with course surfaces, *sa^rasara* with smooth surfaces

In some other languages, most notably in French, [z] is perceived in certain circumstances as expressive of tender emotions, [s] of various degrees of noises. This contradiction can easily be explained in terms of the present theory. The wave form of [z] indicates a rough surface, as compared to [s]. On the other hand, voicing (responsible for those fluctuations in the sound wave) is periodic; and periodicity in phonetics is typically perceived as expressive of tender emotions. Thus, listeners who perceive [z] as expressive of coarseness or of tenderness attend to different aspects of the same sound structure. Sound does not determine the meaning of the word; rather, meaning foregrounds one or another aspect of the sound; sound features, in turn, may foreground certain semantic features. As Akita's own experiments suggest, "iconic words do have special sound-symbolic semantics and [...] it is crucially based on their referential specificity as well as their morphophonological markedness" (*idem*, 5). In other words, whether [z] is expressive of coarseness or of tenderness depends on the interaction of the sound structure and the meaning of the text.

11.5   Methodological comments

Some of my arguments here are not exactly of the kind linguists would expect and can, therefore, easily be misunderstood. So, in order to avoid misunderstandings and to elucidate my point, I propose to make a few methodological comments. On my discussion of Bahnar, for instance, the referee quoted above on phlogiston said that I was relying on one very obscure language and a single case study of certain aspects of it. "The conclusions from this thin material are stretched too thin for the universal validity that Tsur wants to find". This arouses an intriguing methodological problem. The validity of my argument depends here, to a considerable extent, on the purpose of my discussion. Had I tried to find some universal validity, that criticism would have certainly been fatal to my argument. But I was engaged in a very different kind of activity: I was trying to expose a hidden inconsistency in Diffloth's argument. I was not universalizing, I was refuting an alleged counter-example to a received view by comparing the rules of the game followed by two scholars, as well as the outcomes of their inquiries. Pointing out that two scholars obtain different results by following different games and that one obtains similar results if one follows the rules of the same game with reference to the two corpora in question does not need a huge database. It requires just these two arguments to compare.

When I realized that my anonymous reviewer had misconstrued the status of my theoretical activities and speech acts, I was forced to ask the fundamental question: If I am not "generalizing" or "universalizing" from my data, what kind of theoretical activities and speech acts I am performing, anyway? In elucidating this issue, I will rely on three classical papers, one in aesthetics (Weitz 1962); one in the philosophy of science (Smart, 1966) and one in the history of science (Kuhn 1977). The latter two derive their test cases from physics. In what follows, I will elucidate the kinds of statements I am making, and the kinds of activities I am involved in. First, in critical discourse sentences of the indicative form may suggest several degrees of adherence to facts. Accordingly, my statements are of three different kinds, at least: indicative, representing the denoted act or state as an objective fact; hypothetical, suggesting an attitude toward the merely possible; and "crucial recommendations as to what to look for and how to look at it" in sound symbolism in particular, and poetic language in general (Weitz 1962). Second, in many instances I am not "generalizing" or "universalizing", but am engaging in two other kinds of intellectual activity: theory construction and thought experiments. Neither requires a huge data base like "generalizing" or "universalizing", but rather certain kinds of manipulations of a limited amount of data on various levels of organization.

We are dealing with a complex event: there are strings and sound waves that have certain measurable co-varying physical properties; there is a psychological assumption that the ear membrane and outer skin, which perceive the sound waves, subliminally perceive some of those properties as well; this assumption, in turn, may account for the perception of such aesthetic qualities of the sounds as "thickness". All this can be described, at various levels, in physical, psychological, and aesthetic terms. Theory construction has to do with the integration of various levels into a coherent whole, and moving from one level to another. The sentences describing each level by itself are typically indicative; the sentences that suggest moving from one level to another are typically hypothetical; the sentences that concern the relative emphasis of elements in the complex event are typically crucial recommendations. Such is the fuzziness of human natural language. When we say "I'll come tomorrow", we rely on our interlocutor's communicative competence to decide what speech act we are performing: a statement or a promise. If a student introduces a question with "I want to ask a question" and I answer "do ask", students laugh because they know that I have deliberately misconstrued the speech act as asking for permission. Likewise, when all my statements are treated as simply indicative, some of them are misconstrued.

A thought experiment has to do with the manipulation of an act or state of affairs, given in reality or contrived by the experimenter, so as to clarify one's system of concepts and, simultaneously, yield new understanding of the act or state of affairs by exposing and eliminating hidden conflicts in one's system of concepts. When I compared Ultan's and Diffloth's arguments, I was exposing a hidden conflict in the latter's system. In performing thought experiments one does not treat the denoted act or state as an objective fact, but assumes, again, an attitude toward the merely possible.

Now consider the following issue. In this chapter I disagree with Brown's hypothesis as to the relationship between *Sound Symbolism* and *Source's Size*. Let me recapitulate step by step the data upon which my position rests. Physicists have unambiguously established that the size of strings co-varies with their speed of vibration, and that speed of vibration co-varies with wavelength (that is, with the size of the wave). This is certainly quite rigorous. From the direction of psychology, there is an ubiquitous perception that when one strikes a note near the left end of the piano keyboard (where strings are thicker) it sounds deeper and thicker than a note at the right end. At this point a leap becomes inevitable. When I speak of the causal relationship between the measurable thickness of a string and the perceived thickness of the sound produced by it, I am committing an unavoidable leap. I must *assume* that the perception of thickness is mediated by the measurable length of the sound waves produced and the measurable amount of overtones in the perceptible range that strike the perceiver's ear membrane and outer skin. More precisely, I must assume that these features of the wave are perceived as "thickness", offering this as a *plausible hypothesis* to account for the similarity of the perceived sound and its source. I am not presuming that there is hundred percent certainty that this is so, only that this hypothesis is more *plausible* than Brown's.

These correlations between string size, speed of vibration and wavelength are well-known enough, and the intuitions discussed here, though unprovable, are general enough to meet Thomas Kuhn's restriction in characterizing thought experiments: "if we have to do with a real thought experiment, the empirical data upon which it rests must have been both well-known and generally accepted before the experiment was even conceived" (Kuhn 1977: 241). As to the intuitions that boulders have low and thick voices whereas pebbles have high and thin voices, their force can be demonstrated by imagining a reverse situation. Suppose Disney gave a low thick voice to the pebble, and a high thin voice to the boulder; it would certainly be felt anomalous or ironical. There arises, therefore, the inevitable question posed by Kuhn: "How, then, relying exclusively upon familiar data, can a thought experiment lead to new knowledge or to new understanding of nature?", that is, "What sort of new knowledge or understanding can be so produced?" (*ibid*). Kuhn argues that from thought experiments most people learn about their concepts and the world together. Adapting his argument to the issue in hand, in learning about strings, vibrations and wavelength, readers also learn how intuitions concerning size–sound symbolism work (*idem*, 253). Adapting further Kuhn's discussion of Galileo's thought experiment with the concept of speed, one may try to better understand what is wrong with Brown's concept of "mediated association". In Kuhn's words, its defects lay "in its failure to fit the full fine structure of the world to which it was expected to apply. That is why learning to recognize its defects was necessarily learning about the world as well as about the concept" (*idem*, 258). A slight shift of focus could considerably improve the internal logic of Brown's position on Walt Disney's "problem". One may, for instance, apply to it Aristotle's notion of analogy on which "proportional metaphors" are based: pebbles are to boulders like children to grown-ups. Consequently, the voice of pebbles must be to the voice of boulders like the voice of children to the voice of grown-ups. The voice of children is relatively thin and high; the voice of grown-ups is relatively low and thick. It should, however, be clear what is it that we have explained by this Aristotelian analogy. We have NOT explained why we hear low-frequency sounds as thick and high-frequency sounds as thin. We have only explained why the attribution of low-frequency sounds to boulders and high-frequency sounds to pebbles is perceived as more natural than the other way around.

In such a formulation the principle of mediated association would work exceptionally well, with reference to the voices of pebbles and boulders. However, in Brown's formulation it fails "to fit the full fine structure of the world to which it is expected to apply". Consider: "Thick people and animals and violin strings are usually loud and resonant. So, if the subject is required to guess, he will call the loud and resonant voice 'thick'. This need not be because the voice shares some inter-sensory quality with the visual or tactile apprehension of thickness". There is, however, much commonsense indication that the voice quality and body size of humans and animals are independent variables. First of all, thick people may have soprano voices and thin people may have a resonant bass voice (see the photos of opera singers in Figure 4 above, and hear online their voices). Secondly, in the present context, "thick people and animals and violin strings" are not to be treated as one kind. "Thick sounds" and thick strings strictly co-vary, whereas the assertion about "thick people and animals" has only anecdotal, not even statistical, validity. Third, the voice does share "some inter-sensory quality with the visual or tactile apprehension of thickness", irrespective of the external shape of its source: the size of vibration waves, or the amount of overtones in the audible range. And fourth but not least, as I have insisted time and again, our intuition is that we directly perceive a note struck near the left end of the piano keyboard as thicker than a note near the right end, and not by relating the sounds to some extraneous circumstances.

One could further improve upon Brown's argument by referring to string instruments: the double bass, for instance, has not only thicker strings, but also larger overall body than the cello or the violin. This would point up an interesting difference between string instruments and people. String instruments have a hollow body full of air, so built as to amplify the sound by reverberating the vibration of the strings. Inside the human body, by contrast, there is no such hollow reverberating space. Vibrating air, unlike vibrating flesh, may generate a resounding sound. Likewise, we do not think of the inside of boulders as of some hollow space full of air. Again, it is the volume of the vibrating medium, not the visible size of a body that determines the perceived thickness of the sound.

No amount of measurement can prove or disprove a causal relationship between the measurable thickness of a string and the perceived thickness of the sound produced by it. In such leaps, in J.J.C. Smart's (1966) words in a context of theory construction in physics, "expressions like 'make more plausible', 'lead us to expect that', or 'strongly suggest' apply, but where the logical relations of implication and contradiction do not strictly apply" (239). Smart points out that "'rigour', in the sense in which it is pursued in pure mathematics is not an ideal in applied mathematics (or physics). The conception of 'rigour' involved in physics is that whereby it makes sense to say 'rigorous enough'" (*idem*, 237). It would not be too far-fetched to claim that in literary theory, speech perception and other human disciplines less rigour is 'enough' for leaps even than in physics. But, in any case, if you want to do measurements, you must start out with a hypothesis, which I provide. The experimentalist will have to contrive an experiment to decide whether the perceived thickness of sound is correlated with the mass of one's body or with that of one's vibrating membrane.

CHAPTER 12

Issues in literary synaesthesia

A brief glance

12.1 Synaesthesia as a neuropsychological and a literary phenomenon

The term *synaesthesia* suggests the joining of sensations derived from different sensory domains. One must distinguish between the combination of *impressions*, and the joining of *terms* derived from the *vocabularies* of the various sensory domains. The former concerns synaesthesia as a neuropsychological phenomenon, consisting in anomalous sensory perception: a stimulus in one sensory modality triggers an automatic, instantaneous, consistent response in another (e.g. sound evokes colour) or in a different aspect of the same modality (e.g. black text evokes colour). The latter is known as *verbal synaesthesia*, which, when exploited for specific literary effects, is called literary synaesthesia. I will discuss its *emotional and witty effects* shortly.

One conspicuous contrast between "genuine" and literary synaesthesia is that the former involves rigidly predictable combinations of sensory modes, whereas the latter requires exceptionally great flexibility in generating and understanding unforeseen combinations, and, by the same token, abandoning established combinations. Literary synaesthesia is typically concerned with verbal constructs and not with "dual perceptions". When we use a synaesthetic metaphor, it is its *terms* that are derived from two sensory domains; the reality referred to may be elusive, undifferentiated, or "ineffable", even "supersensuous", but it need not necessarily belong to two different sensory domains. Neurological mechanisms underlying "genuine" synaesthesia may contribute to certain literary effects; but in *some* instances, as we shall see, they fail to account for them.

In Romantic poetry and in 19th century French Symbolism, Literary Synaesthesia typically contributes to some undifferentiated emotional quality characteristic of certain altered states of consciousness: "vague, dreamy, or uncanny hallucinatory moods" (Stanford 1942), or a strange, magical experience or heightened mystery. In some varieties of Mannerist poetry, as in some modernist and 17th century Metaphysical poetry, by contrast, synaesthesia typically makes for a witty quality. How can we account for this contrast? According to Coleridge, imagination involves "the balance and reconciliation of opposite or discordant qualities" (*Biographia Literaria*, Chapter IV). I submit that when the "opposite or discordant qualities" are more emphasized in a poem, the effect is witty; when their "reconciliation", the effect is emotional. The poet may manipulate attention, by rhetorical means, to the discordant qualities or their reconciliation. Synaesthesia (as well as the oxymoron) violently yoke together opposite or discordant qualities, inducing tension. So, they may contribute to a witty context, metaphysical or modernist. There may be, however, elements in a context that mitigate the perceived clash of opposites, one of them being heightened emotional energy; another, imagined spatial orientation (see Chapter 5). In such instances, synaesthesia and oxymoron strengthen rather than disrupt emotional qualities in poetry.[1]

Sometimes the two figures occur together, reinforcing each other's effect, as in.

1.   Heard melodies are sweet, but those unheard
     Are sweeter; therefore, ye soft pipes, play on;
     Not to the sensual ear, but, more endeared,
     Pipe to the spirit ditties of no tone...   (Keats, *Ode on a Grecian Urn*)

Here the two figures are meant to convey or evoke an intense, supersensuous, thing-free quality perceived in the silent drawings on the Urn.

12.2   Four kinds of explanation

To avoid confusion, one must be aware of what it is that one is explaining when discussing synaesthetic metaphors. I distinguished four possibilities. The first one is **genetic explanation**. In "*Voyelles*", for instance, what is it that made Rimbaud think of precisely these associations, e.g. the spelling book theory (that is, the vowel–colour associations in the poem reflect the letter–colour associations in his spelling book), and some versions of the alchemy theory (that is, these associations are derived from alchemy).

I call the second kind **rhetorical explanation**: What is it that makes the reader accept these associations. Rimbaud's specific spelling book, if it existed at all, may

---

1.   This is in perfect harmony, but with a twist, with Longinus' claim: "Wherefore a figure is at its best when the very fact that it is a figure escapes attention" (Longinus, XVII). "For just as all dim lights are extinguished in the blaze of the sun, so do the artifices of rhetoric fade from view when bathed in the pervading splendour of sublimity" (*ibid.*). Longinus' assertions apply exceptionally well to Classicism or Romanticism. However, what is bad Classicism or Romanticism may be excellent Mannerism or Modernism.

be unknown to the general reader. I would include here, for instance, Genette's Structuralist explanation of this sonnet, which suggests that human beings are inclined to accept the colour-system and the vowel-system as somehow analogous. According to Genette (1966: 151–152), "There is a spectrum of vowels as there is a spectrum of colours, the two systems evoke and attract each other, and the global homology creates the illusion of a term-by-term analogy". The particular colours attributed to particular vowels in Rimbaud's poem are not the ones associated in "genuine" synaesthesia; it is the global homology that creates the illusion of a term-by-term analogy. Ramachandran and Hubbard's (2001) explanation based on brain structure would belong to both kinds.

The third kind I would call **semantic interaction explanation**: What specific meanings arise from the attribution of certain colours to certain vowels, and to the imagery associated with them. Words and speech sounds are bundles of (semantic or phonetic) features. When such visual images as "Gulfs of shadow" are attached in an arbitrary manner to [a] or "candours of vapours and of tents" to [ə], the two terms of the figure may activate certain features in each other. In this way unforeseen dormant features and connotations can be activated in the speech sounds and the visual image.

The fourth kind is concerned with poetic effects, e.g. witty, emotional, lowly-differentiated, etc. (see below). By these distinctions I want to make one sometimes overlooked point. Offering a genetic explanation *cannot* account for the literary appeal of a poem.

I will give here only one example of activating dormant features and connotations in vowels and colours by synaesthetic attribution. There is a very sharp contrast between the high /i/ and the low /a/. There is an equally sharp contrast between black and white. In Rimbaud's sonnet, however, *black* is attributed to /a/, whereas *white* is not attributed to its opposite, but to French e, which is a rather colourless, pale (i.e. intermediate) vowel: it is pronounced with the tongue in an intermediate position, neither low as /a/, nor high as /i/ or /u/; it also clearly avoids the contrast of grave and acute (è and é), or of rounded and unrounded. White, in turn, is an ambiguous colour, as Rudolf Arnheim pointed out:

> White is completeness and nothingness. Like the shape of the circle, it serves as a symbol of integration without presenting to the eye the variety of vital forces that it integrates, and thus is as complete and empty as a circle. Not so the complementary colours. They show completeness as the balance of opposites.
> (Arnheim 1967: 352)

In our everyday awareness "black~white" is the archetypal contrast. Arnheim's analysis of white draws attention to different kinds of contrast: the opposition and balance between the complementary colours; which, in turn, are opposed to the colour white where the complementary colours are neutralized, not balanced. Likewise, in phonology there are the /i/~/u/ and the /i/~/a/ oppositions. These are, again, not balanced but neutralized in the vowel [ə]. Thus, the vowel [ə] and the colour white activate in each other the dormant feature "neutralized oppositions".

12.3   Panchronistic tendencies in synaesthesia

As to literary synaesthesia, *aesthetic* considerations are most important for it: what aesthetic effects are generated by synaesthetic transfers? Important stylistic considerations may be derived from Ullmann's Panchronistic Tendencies (1957). If upward transfers are intuitively more natural than downward ones, then "soft colours" or "warm sounds" (which are upward) would be appropriate to suggest some "genuine" experience in a poem. However, we should not be surprised that Mannerist poets like John Donne or Oscar Wilde have occasionally recourse to such downward transfers as "a loud perfume" or "mauve Hungarian music" and "the scarlet music of Dvořák", for witty effects. I will briefly explore two stylistic considerations, one based on Ullmann's Panchronistic Tendencies, another on Gestalt qualities. We may find, however, quite frequently that in Impressionist and Symbolist poetry even downward transfers may occasionally be perceived as "smooth", suggesting some "genuine mood". This may happen when its differentiating effect becomes part of some fluid reality intensified by "chaotic overdifferentiation" (and reinforced, more often than not, by the activity of the orientation mechanism, in a concrete situation defined "here and now"). Ullmann (1957:276) claims that his statistical investigations "will give no information concerning any single transfer, but may say something about the general movement and dynamics of the processes". I shall claim, however, that knowing "something about the general movement and dynamics of the processes" may give us valuable insights into stylistic intuitions concerning single transfers as well. In other words, "the general movement and dynamics of the processes" is the unmarked option, whereas transfers that go counter such movement is the marked option, resulting in less natural qualities.

Just to remind ourselves. Ullmann found that in Romantic poetry "transfers tend to mount from the lower to the higher reaches of the sensorium, from the less differentiated sensations to the more differentiated ones" (touch → taste → smell → sound → sight) (*idem*, 280). Out of some 2000 transfers, only a little more than one sixth go downward (*idem*, 282). "It is in strict conformity with the first tendency that the touch, the lowest level of the sensorium, should be the main purveyor of transfers" (*ibid.*). The predominant destination, however, turned out to be surprising. It was not the sense of sight, but that of sound, the second highest in the hierarchy. Ullmann interprets this as follows: "Visual terminology is incomparably richer than its auditional counterpart, and has also far more similes and images at its command. Of the two sensory domains at the top end of the scale, sound stands more in need of external support than light, form or colour" (*idem*, 283). This explanation is not very convincing. Poverty of terminology is not the only (or even the main) reason for using metaphors in poetry. On the contrary rather, a principle of the Biblical "pauper's sheep" seems to be at work here. The richer the sensory domain, the more it "borrows", the poorer the domain, the more it "lends". As for the relative scarcity of the visual domain in Ullmann's findings, I shall argue that there may be certain elements that hinder intersense transfer. When those elements are circumvented, the visual sense does become the pre-dominant destination in synaesthesia.

According to Ullmann's own data, it is precisely touch, the lowest level of sensorium (with the poorest vocabulary) that is the main purveyor of transfers. For this, the reason seems to be that speaking of the more differentiated sensory domain in terms of a less differentiated one is a powerful means of dedifferentia-tion. As I have been arguing throughout the present book, language being a highly categorized conceptual system, it would appear impossible to talk about undiffer-entiated, pre-categorical sensory or emotional information. If this were true, such phrases as "verbal art", or "mystic poetry" would have been a contradiction in terms. We know that this is not the case. One of my major assumptions in Cogni-tive Poetics is that poetry in general, and figurative language in particular, consist of a permanent pursuit after finding ways to overcome the tyranny of highly dif-ferentiated linguistic categories. Talking about sounds and colours in terms of the tactile or thermal vocabularies may convey just such an impression of their undif-ferentiated, pre-categorical sensory aspects. In downward transfers, by contrast, the discordant qualities are usually felt to be less reconciled than in upward transfers. As we shall see, this generalization is very frequently born out by the perceived quality of individual transfers. When we use such phrases as "soft colours" or "warm voice", the adjectives refer to certain undifferentiated perceptual aspects that elude conceptual language.

12.4   Aesthetic qualities: Witty and emotional

What is, then, the explanation for the relative paucity of synaesthetic metaphors involving the visual domain? Intersense transfer is, as I have observed, more apt to generate discordant qualities than ordinary metaphor. To evoke an emotional rather than witty response requires a smooth fusion of sensations. As we have seen in Chapters 1, 2 and 7 in great detail, in the visual and auditory mode colour induction, illusory contours and overtone interaction are inhibited across well-defined boundaries; the weaker the boundaries, the stronger the colour and over-tone interaction across them. It would appear that in the semantic dimension too things that have stable characteristic visual shapes tend to resist such fusion, whereas thing-free qualities are particularly suitable to it. It is this that may account for the relative scarcity of synaesthetic metaphors involving the sense of seeing as compared with the less-differentiated sense of hearing in Romantic poetry. Notice this: only the visual sense presents us with stable shapes that do not change while we go away and come back. Music may display, as Leonard B. Meyer's work (1956) demonstrates, both exceptionally strong or poor Gestalts; but even the strongest shapes are transient.

Now consider the following four excerpts from Keats and Donne.

2. And taste the music of that vision pale.   (Keats, *Isabella*: XLIX)

3. The same bright face I tasted in my sleep   (Keats, *Endymion*, I: 895)

4. [...] lost in pleasure at her feet he sinks,
   Touching with *dazzled lips her starlight hands*.   (*Endymion*, IV. 418–19)

5. A loud perfume, which at my entrance cryed,
   Ev'n at thy father's nose.   Donne, Elegy IV (*The Perfume*)

I propose to illustrate *via* Excerpt 2 my above notion of **semantic interaction**. It contains a double intersense transfer, both in the expected direction: both are **upward** transfers, that is, the line speaks of **vision** in terms of **music**; and of **music**, in turn, in terms of **taste**. A closer scrutiny of the interaction of semantic features in these transfers may account for the impassioned, uncanny atmosphere perceived by many readers in this line. The word "vision" denotes an abstraction that has no stable visual shape. In distinction from "sight", it suggests not only the thing seen, but also an impassioned state of mind with supernatural connota-tions. The paleness of the vision may be associated with the that of the dead, or of Isabella, or of the moonlit sight, but none of them is explicitly mentioned, nor can they usurp each other's place. So, we only have a vague, indistinct, diffuse quality of paleness. The interaction of the two terms of the genitive phrase deletes the feature [+AUDITORY] in "music" which, in turn, implicitly turns Gestalt-free "vision" into a perceptual object that is a pleasant fusion of something, full of energy and expanding toward the perceiving self. In the sensory domain of taste no shapes are possible at all. The interaction of "taste" with "music" deletes the feature [+GUSTATORY], foregrounding such meaning components as "directly perceiving reality, or undergoing experience, or perceiving some fine texture or elusive quality". The upward transfer from the less differentiated sense **taste** enhances the indistinctness of the fused sensations. The powerful fusion of the discordant senses heightens the discharge of emotions, deleting the contradictory sensuous ingredients, leaving the reader with the **feel** of a supersensuous, uncanny atmosphere. Excerpt 2 does not refer to three different referents in the gustatory, auditory and visual domains, but to one referent in the visual domain. "Taste" transfers certain transfer features to "music" which, in turn, transfers certain transfer features to "vision". The same holds true, *mutatis mutandis* in relation to Excerpts 3–5.

Excerpt 3 too applies the verb "taste" to an object derived from a higher sense ("The same bright face I tasted in my sleep"). Yet it makes a very different impression. Ullmann finds that it is a strange phrase (1957: 287), but cannot account for this strangeness. I have suggested above that intersense transfer is more capable of splitting the focus than ordinary metaphor. Inducing an emotional rather than witty quality requires fusion into a soft focus. Stable characteristic visual shapes tend to resist such fusion, whereas thing-free qualities facilitate it. In these two examples, "The same bright face I tasted" and "And taste the music of that vision pale" there is an "upward" transfer, from tasting to seeing, and as such, both ought to be perceived as "smooth" and "natural". The stable characteristic visual shape of *face*, however, appears to resist *tasting*. Suppose Keats wrote "The same brightness I tasted in my dream" – this would sound at once less strange.

Ramachandran and Hubbard (2001: 28) hypothesized that if there is crosswiring between adjoining brain regions, "between primary gustatory cortex and adjoining hand and face regions of primary somatosensory cortex, the result might be a person who 'tastes shapes' ". What can we learn from this about Excerpt 3? Not very much. Suppose we became convinced that Ramachandran and Hubbard's hypothesis applied to Keats's brain. We would account by it for the genesis of the figure, not its literary effect. It would not change Ullmann's impression that "it is a strange phrase", that is, that tasting an object with a stable characteristic visual shape yields a marked synaesthetic metaphor, with all the stylistic implications of this. Genetic explanations are guided by principles that are different from those guiding aesthetic explanations.

With this problem in mind, I had a look at Cytowic's (2003) book *The Man Who Tasted Shapes*. To Cytowic's surprise, the phenomenon had nothing to do with visual shapes. "'This a mental image you see?' I asked. 'No, no,' he stressed 'I don't see anything. I don't imagine anything. I *feel* it in my hands as if it were in front of me' " (65). Later Cytowic summed up: "His sensations were elementary things, like hard and soft; a smooth, rough, or squashy texture; warm or cool surfaces" (67). Moreover, in the passage "Oh, dear," he said, slurping a spoonful, "there aren't enough points on the chicken" (3), Cytowic's informant doesn't speak of shapes in terms of taste (as "tasting shapes" would imply), but of tastes in terms of the sense of touch. This, then, turned out to be a touch → taste association, in perfect compliance with Ullmann's Panchronistic Tendencies, as well as with my claim that stable visual shapes resist smooth synaesthesia. So, tasting a face would not comply with the synaesthetic perceptions of Cytowic's informant either.

Richard H. Fogle discusses Excerpt 4 at length in his paper "Synaesthetic Imagery in Keats": "lost in pleasure at her feet he sinks,/Touching with *dazzled lips her starlight hands*". He remarks on it that "There is a trace of 'wit' of conscious ingenuity which lends to the image a certain flavor of modernity" (Fogle 1964: 43). But Fogle is at pains to point out the source of this impression. He devotes sixteen lines and a footnote to the explication of this metaphor, restating that "the image in question is on the surface a witty conceit" (43–44), without saying anything that might account for its "wit" and "flavor of modernity".

The two principles discussed here can account for this impression. First, we have here a sight → touch transfer, a transfer that runs contrary to the Panchronistic Tendencies; second, the synaesthetic transfer involves here two solid "objects", *lips* and *hands*. A third principle, characteristic of the metaphysical conceit, may be at work here too. A conceit, says John Crowe Ransom (1951: 786), "is but a metaphor if the metaphor is meant; that is, if it is developed so baldly that nothing else can be meant". In the present instance, "dazzled" is a figurative expression for something like "overpowered, deeply affected". The phrase "starlight hands" reinforces the metaphoric vehicle, so that the literal meaning "losing clear vision especially from looking at bright light" *must* be meant too. The dead metaphor has been revived. The case is similar in Excerpt 4: "A loud perfume, which at my entrance cryed,/ Ev'n at thy father's nose". It is a metaphysical conceit proper not only owing to the downward transfer from sound to scent, but also owing to the literal development of the vehicle. *Loud* means here something like "obtrusive and/or offensive"; the feature [+AUDITORY] is deleted by *perfume*. The verb *cryed*, however, reactivates this feature and, at the same time, reinforces the meanings "obtrusive and/or offensive". Indeed, W.B. Stanford (1942) says it suggests not an experience, but the concoction of an experience – again, without supporting his judgment by reasons.

When Shakespeare parodies synaesthetic metaphor, he violates exactly the two principles discussed here in order to achieve a ludicrous effect:

6.   Pyr. I see a voice; now will I to the chink,
      To spy an I can hear my Thisby's face.

"I see a voice" is a downward transfer; and the upward transfer "hear my Thisby's face" involves a stable characteristic visual shape. The ludicrous effect is reinforced by the mechanical interchange of the verbs "see" and "hear" – something mechanical encrusted on the living.

My second principle is corroborated by Erzsébet Dombi's (1974) findings. Ullmann (1957:285) remarks that "it would have been unwise to examine synaesthesia in the highly artificial form which it has assumed in some Symbolist and post-Symbolist poets". Dombi, however, provides good evidence to the contrary. In her paper "Synaesthesia and Poetry" she investigated Hungarian Impressionist poetry, and compared her findings to Ullmann's. She concludes that her "statistical data confirm unanimously the validity of the panchronistic rules as revealed by Ullmann" (*idem*, 32). I would say that Hungarian Impressionism conforms even better with the Panchronistic Tendencies than Romantic poetry: here, the most frequent recipient of transfer is the visual domain. I have argued at some variance with Ullmann that stable visual shapes are hostile to the fusion of senses, and that the presence of solid objects and stable visual shapes resists the smooth fusion of sense-impressions. Dombi's explanation (*idem*, 33) for her findings is in essential harmony with my speculations: "The most frequent solicitation of the sight as a dominant sensation may be considered a characteristic feature of Hungarian impressionistic style [...]. This phenomenon may be explained by the inclination of impressionists for colours and light. The effects of light and colour conceived *independently from the concrete objects* [my italics, RT] may get easily into connection with sensations from different other domains of perception". In other words, it is thing-free qualities rather than objects endowed with stable visual shapes that dominate the visual domain of synaesthesia in Hungarian Impressionist poetry, just as predicted by the present theory. Apparently, the same holds true in Chinese, as suggested in a series of more recent articles by Ning Yu (e.g. 2003).

12.5 Overriding downward transfers

In the following excerpt, I am going to consider an instance of downward transfer in synaesthetic metaphor in which two sensory dimensions are in a metonymic relationship to an underlying situation, providing a **genetic explanation**, as well as a **rhetorical explanation**: What is it that makes the reader accept these associations? At the same time, however, **semantic interaction** arises between the two terms derived from the different sensory domains. As I indicated above, in certain conditions "downward" synaesthetic transfers too may be perceived as

indicating "genuine" experience. Consider the excerpt from a Hebrew poem by
Lea Goldberg:

בְּשׁוּק הַדָּגִים

צְחָנָה קוֹלָנִית וּמֶשֶׁק סְנַפִּירִים,

גֵּיהִנֹּם מְפַרְפֵּר בִּדְלָיַיִם.

לֹא הוּשַׁר מִזְמוֹרֵךְ, לֹא הוּשַׁר בָּשִׁירִים,

הַמּוֹשֶׁלֶת בִּדְגֵי הַמַּיִם!

> 7.   At the Fish-Market
>   Vociferous stench, and flapping of fins,
>   Gehenna wriggling in buckets…
>   Your song of praise has not yet been sung,
>   Mistress and ruler of the fish.

The first two lines arouse an intense impression of one who suddenly finds himself in the tumult of a fish-market. Confounded spatial orientation processes are
at work. The poem begins with a series of intense sense-impressions detached
from their sources, presented as Gestalt-free and thing-free qualities. The most
convenient construal of these phrases is metonymic. The stench and clamour
both are violent and inarticulate attributes of the fish-market, attacking the perceiver, who in the tumult cannot discern their precise sources. As realistic motivation this might suffice. The poem begins with three elliptic sentences in rapid
succession, which reinforce this impression. The typical structural meaning of
elliptic sentences is to point to some immediate presence or immediate sensations. In addition they may indicate some sense of urgency. But there is more
to it. "Stench" in the referring position suggests a thing-free and Gestalt-free
object of perception. "Vociferous" and "stench" are abstracted from their concrete objects or situations, and attributed to each other, generating metaphoric
interplay. When "vociferous" is attributed to "stench", there arises a contradiction between the conflicting features [±AUDITORY]. [+AUDITORY], being irrelevant to the noun "stench", is cancelled in the epithet "vociferous", in which,
thus, such features as [+INTENSE +OFFENSIVE +VULGAR] are foregrounded,
and transferred to "stench" in which, in turn, similar features are amplified.
But since "vociferous" is a metonymy in its own right, it is only grammatically
subordinated to "stench". As far as the reality described is concerned, it could
be the other way around, and the feature [+OLFACTORY] would be cancelled in
stench, foregrounding the remaining features, such as [+INTENSE +OFFENSIVE
+VULGAR], and transferring them to "clamour", "noise", or the like. The confounded orientation process diffuses the percepts suggested by the metaphor,

inducing a perception of "vociferous stench" as a "genuine" experience, in spite of the downward transfer.

Now notice this: Had the poem said "flapping fins", it would have suggested a visible and audible object; the actual genitive phrase "flapping **of** fins" indicates that only the audible action of a barely discernible agent has been perceived. Semantically, the epithet (or predicate) "flapping" is nominalized and manipulated into the referring position, reinforcing the thing-free quality of the first phrase. Such transformation I call "topicalized attribute".[2] The third phrase amplifies this to an enormous degree. Here again we have something like a "topicalized attribute". The facts described could be put thus: "the fish flutter with infernal pain" or simply "the fish flutter like hell", or the like. By nominalizing *infernal* as *Gehenna* (which, in the New Testament and Rabbinical Literature means "hell"), and by turning it into the main notion of the phrase, the poem emphasizes a thing-free quality, a sense of terrible pressure, condensing the invisible and infinite within the trivial and small. Buckets are stable objects with characteristic visual shapes; here, however, attention is focussed upon the Gestalt-free turmoil in the internal space rather than upon their solid shape. Transferring attention from "fish" to an abstract noun, the impact of agitation, of very quick motion, is reinforced: one may see that *it* is "wrigggglng", but so violently, that one cannot discern *what*. The "downward" transfer in "Vociferous stench" becomes acceptable as "genuine" owing to the interplay of five factors. The two terms of the transfer are metonymic abstractions from the same situation; they are thing-free abstractions; the tension generated by the clashing terms is absorbed in the violent energy connoted by the extra-linguistic reality described; the extra-linguistic reality described is characterized by chaotic overdifferentiation of auditory and olfactory impressions; and the activation and disruption of spatial orientation suggested by the immediate situation amplifies the non-conceptual, diffuse nature of the thing-free qualities.

12.6   Synaesthesia and ecstatic quality: Two French sonnets

Synaesthesia is associated with a wide range of altered states of consciousness. We should not be surprised, therefore, that it is frequently associated with ecstatic poetry too. In what follows, I will briefly discuss two notoriously synaesthetic poems which happen to have ecstatic elements too.

---

2. See Chapter 5 above. As will be seen, such constructions are relatively abundant in Rimbaud's "*Voyelles*" too as, e.g., "candours of vapours and of tents".

8.   *Correspondances*
     La Nature est un temple où de vivants piliers
     Laissent parfois sortir de confuses paroles;
     L'homme y passe à travers des forêts de symboles
     Qui l'observent avec des regards familiers.

     Comme de longs échos qui de loin se confondent
     Dans une ténébreuse et profonde unité,
     Vaste comme la nuit et comme la clarté,
     Les parfums, les couleurs et les sons se répondent.

     Il est des parfums frais comme des chairs d'enfants,
     Doux comme les hautbois, verts comme les prairies,
     – Et d'autres, corrompus, riches et triomphants,

     Ayant l'expansion des choses infinies,
     Comme l'ambre, le musc, le benjoin et l'encens,
     Qui chantent les transports de l'esprit et des sens.

     Correspondences
     Nature is a temple, where living pillars
     Emit sometimes indistinct speech;
     Man passes there through forests of symbols
     That observe him with familiar gazes.

     Like long echoes that mingle in the distance
     In a dark and profound unity,
     Vast as the night and as the light,
     The perfumes, the colors, and the sounds respond to one another.

     There are perfumes, fresh as the flesh of children,
     Sweet as oboes, green as meadows,
     And others, corrupt, rich, and triumphant,

     Having the expansion of infinite things,
     Like amber, musk, benzoin, and incense,
     Which sing the raptures of the spirit and the senses.

I have elsewhere devoted a full-length chapter to the analysis of this sonnet (Tsur 1992a: 455–470 [2008[2]: 495–510]). Here I only want to recapitulate certain aspects of the interaction between thing-free qualities and synaesthesia in generating an ecstatic quality in the poem.

Let us recall that synaesthesia, in general, is deemed to be a regression to a less differentiated mode of perception (i.e. to a stage when the mind does not differentiate between the stimuli registered by the various senses). This is of special significance in a sonnet such as the present one, the "essence" of which is said to lie in indistinct, "mystical" intuitions. Further, it should be recalled that when a higher, more differentiated sensory domain is treated in terms of a lower, less differentiated one, extremely intense emotional effects may be achieved. These effects are considerably enhanced when they occur in a context of thing-free and Gestalt-free qualities, where no stable, characteristic visual shapes are involved. By contrast, when a lower, less differentiated sensory domain is treated in terms of a higher, more differentiated one, some witty effect is typically achieved. This effect, however, may be overridden in an exceptionally fluid context that can be described as "chaotic overdifferentiation": here, there arises some kind of "perceptual overload", which the cognitive system handles by fusing the "overwhelming" amount of information into some continuous, lowly-differentiated mass, very much in the way that in painting and music all the information that exceeds the system's capacity is "dumped" into the background. Impressionist and Symbolist poetry not infrequently resort to such 'downward' transfers in a context that generates precisely this chaos and overdifferentiation. In line 8, "*Les parfums, les couleurs et les sons se répondent*", we are faced with a "chaotic" state of fusion, in which it is quite insignificant whether the less differentiated senses draw upon the more differentiated ones, or *vice versa*. The immense "intuitive" effect of this description is reinforced by the fact that the sensations or percepts are mentioned here apart from the objects or events of which they are attributes. In lines 9–10 we have a series of mainly downward transfers, "*Il est des parfums frais* [...], *Doux comme les hautbois, verts comme les prairies*": "sweet perfumes" involves an insignificant downward transfer, between two related senses; "sweet sounds of oboe" involves an upward transfer, whereas the perfumes described in terms of the sounds of the oboe and in terms of the greenness of the prairies are downward transfers of the most prominent kind. Nevertheless, owing to the thing-free and Gestalt-free vision in the vast dimensions of an infinite setting, and owing to the intense fusion of the senses, we have here an overdifferentiated, chaotic universe that cannot be disturbed, only corroborated, by these downward transfers, so that the mystic-ecstatic effect also is reinforced, rather than disrupted.

Newberg et al. (2001:89) provide information on ritual that may illuminate an ecstatic poem in which the appeal to the olfactory sense combines with other typical poetic devices.

> These feelings of awe can be further augmented by the sense of smell, which might account for the customary use of incense and other fragrances in religious rites. The middle part of the amygdala receives nerve impulses from the olfactory system, so strong smells could stimulate the watchdog to generate alertness or a mild fear response. [...] When rituals combine fragrances with marked actions and repetitive sounds [...] the resulting stimulation to the amygdala might result in an intensification of the sense of religious awe.

Skipping the details, we may sum up the process of perceiving this sonnet as follows. In the first quatrain there is a fairly consistent central image, through which one can "intuit" some suprasensuous presence, by perceiving some less articulate secondary meanings (e.g. "Emit sometimes indistinct speech"). In the following stanzas, the process of thing-destruction becomes increasingly dominant, thing-free perceptions are gradually intensified, culminating in a rapture of the senses, an overwhelming ecstasy. In the second stanza there are no things, only thing-free and Gestalt-free qualities mingling and responding to each other – presented in a complex syntactic structure. In the sestet, by contrast, the syntactic structure is outrageously simplistic. It begins with a formal subject and predicate "*Il est des...*" (there exist), followed by a casual list of phrases denoting fragrances "that exist", with no contextual constraints at all. I used to perceive this sudden change of style as an anticlimax. But later I realized that this was part of a significant structure.

As I have suggested in many of my writings, the second stage of the death-and-rebirth archetype consists in an expansion or outburst of vital forces; it is also this emotional pattern that organizes the texture of divergent elements in ecstatic experience. In other Romantic and Symbolist poems, e.g. by Blake, Rimbaud, Wordsworth, Coleridge, and Keats, a similar process is found, which I have called "emotive crescendo". On reaching the culminating point of ecstasy, the reader "retro-relates" it (William James's term, quoted by Ehrenzweig 1965) with the preceding scattered sense perceptions, so that he may perform what Ehrenzweig would call a "secondary elaboration", or a "superimposition", of an all-pervasive pattern.

Baudelaire has excessively frequent recourse to olfactory imagery; and he uses them to suggest the amplification of sensations. Perfumes are prototypical instances of thing-free and Gestalt-free percepts, and provide "direct gratification". Here, too, this is one of their conspicuous functions. For Baudelaire the olfactory sense is a lowly-differentiated sense; indulgence in it leads to regression from the more rational modes of experiencing the world. In other words, indulgence in odours and perfumes constitutes a regression from rational consciousness in two respects: there is a regression from well-organized Gestalts to Gestalt-free and thing-free qualities; and from the more differentiated senses (like sight and sound) to a less differentiated one. These sensations are evasive, diffuse, yet exceptionally intense. The perfumes "*l'ambre, le musc, le benjoin et l'encens*", act by cumulation of thing-free, sensory stimuli, as a preparation for the final metaphor.[3] Only when we arrive at the last line it becomes clear that this feast of diffuse sensations throughout the sonnet did have a well-conceived end: a rapture of ecstasy. This is what "*les transports de l'esprit et des sens*" suggests quite clearly, also, perhaps, emphasizing some exalted features of *chantent*. The latter verb, however, continuing "*se*

---

3. This use of olfactory imagery must be distinguished from such verse lines as Shakespeare's "Lilies that fester smell far worse than weeds", where the olfactory images are not indulged in for the sake of their sensory qualities, but as "exemplary, strikingly representative" of certain moral abstractions.

répondent", has some harmonizing effects as well. Add to this the verb "singing", with its combination of spiritual and sensuous aspects from which, in a context of excessive olfactory sensations, some sense like "bring forth" or "express" may be abstracted. The last line seems to have, then, retroactively, some organizing effect. While reading the sonnet, we have gradually passed from "thing-like" to "thing-free" perceptions, finding these perceptions constantly increasing in strength. The disorder that was apparent before we became aware of the underlying pattern has its own intensifying and "thing-destroying" effect. Retroactively, all of these factors take on a new significance (i.e. order): they become part of the "transport of spirit and senses".

9.   *Voyelles*
     A noir, E blanc, I rouge, U vert, O bleu: voyelles,
     Je dirais quelque jour vos naissances latentes:
     A, noir corset velu des mouches éclatantes
     Qui bombinent autour des puanteurs cruelles,

     Golfes d'ombres; E, candeurs des vapeurs et des tentes,
     Lances des glaciers fiers, rois blancs, frissons d'ombelles;
     I, pourpres, sang craché, rires des lèvres belles
     Dans la colère ou les ivresses pénitentes;

     U, cycles, vibrements divins des mers virides,
     Paix des pâtis semés d'animaux, paix de rides
     Que l'alchimie imprime aux grands fronts studieux;

     O, suprême Clairon plein des strideurs étranges,
     Silence traversés des Mondes et des Anges:
     – O l'Oméga, rayon violet de Ses Yeux!

     Vowels
     A black, E white, I red, U green, O blue: vowels,
     I shall tell some day your latent [mysterious] births:
     A, black velvety corset of brilliant [exploding] flies
     Who bombard [assail] around cruel stenches,

     Gulfs of shadow; E, candours of vapours and of tents,
     Lances of proud glaciers, white kings, shivers of cow-parsley;
     I, purples, vomited [spat] blood, laughter of beautiful lips
     In anger or penitent intoxications;

     U, cycles, divine shudderings of bluish-green seas,
     The peace of pastures sown with animals, the peace of wrinkles
     Which alchemy prints on broad studious foreheads;

     O, supreme Clarion full with strange stridours,
     Silences crisscrossed by Worlds and by Angels:
     – O the Omega, violet ray from His [Her] Eyes!

In this sonnet colours are attributed to the vowels; and these coloured vowels are identified with a wide range of visual images. I will mainly discuss the latter (I have elsewhere discussed this sonnet at great length: Tsur 1992b: 111–135). In this respect, I will not discuss here how Rimbaud treats the objects that have stable characteristic visual shapes. I shall only point out that this poem too is dominated by "thing destruction", and "thing-free" and "Gestalt-free" entities. In such expressions as "exploding flies/ Who bombard around cruel stenches" the flies lose their characteristic visual shape, and fuse into a larger, shape-free entity, centered around a typical Gestalt-free and thing-free but energetic quality: "cruel stenches". The phrase "purples, vomited blood" too denotes Gestalt-free entities. Some of the objects with stable visual shapes occur in the prepositional phrases of genitive constructions, in which the attribute has been "topicalized", as in "candours of vapours and of tents", "shivers of cow-parsley", "laughter of beautiful lips", "divine shudderings of bluish-green seas", "the peace of pastures sown with animals", "the peace of wrinkles", etc. In some of these constructions the prepositional phrase too contains a Gestalt-free quality. In all these constructions an attribute of an object has been turned into an abstract noun and manipulated into the referring position (such structures have been discussed at great length in Chapter 5). I will resist the temptation to analyse the exceptionally complex Gestalt-free and thing-free entities "supreme Clarion full with strange stridours" and "Silences crisscrossed by Worlds and by Angels". I will merely point out that the thing-free quality "supreme Clarion" and the negative entity (absence of sounds) "Silences" are turned into undifferentiated but dense presences by the energy-loaded attributes attributed to them.

Briefly, the coloured hearing of vowels is embedded here in a thick texture of thing-free and Gestalt-free qualities. But one of the most decisive contributions to the overwhelming thing-free vision of the sonnet is to be ascribed to the series of vowels modified by the colour adjectives. A, or E, or I, or U, or O have a certain systematic ambiguity. They may refer to an abstract phonetic category, or to certain streams of acoustic energy spread over bands of specified frequencies. Some critics of this poem would add a third possibility: the graphemes signifying the abstract phonetic categories. This difference of construal may be decisive in our frame of reference. Graphemes have stable characteristic visual shapes, whereas streams of acoustic energy lack them. It should be also noted that colours too are Gestalt-free streams of (visual) energy. In the case of graphemes fusion is obstructed by stable visual shapes; in the case of streams of acoustic and visual energy it is not.

As I have argued throughout the present book, speech categories are transmitted through streams of acoustic energy which are then recoded into a string of discrete phonetic units. Only the abstract category enters awareness; the rich precategorial auditory information that transmitted it is excluded. This is called "categorial perception". One cannot tell from introspection that, for instance, the nonsense syllables [ba], [da], and [ga] differ only in that the onset frequency of a small portion of the acoustic stream is higher in each later item than in the preceding ones. Some speech sounds, however, are less thoroughly recoded than others. Thus, for instance, we can tell that the vowel [i] is "somehow" higher than [u]. Stop consonants are more "encoded" than vowels or fricatives, for instance. In a series of carefully-controlled experiments Rakerd (1984) found that vowels are more linguistically perceived (that is, are more thoroughly recoded) in consonantal context than in isolation; and conversely, perceptual features are more readily perceived in isolated vowels than in consonantal context. One possible explanation is that in consonantal context "the talker often coarticulates the neighboring segments of an utterance (that is, overlaps their productions) such that the acoustic signal is jointly influenced by those segments" (Rakerd 1984: 123). Likewise, Repp (1984: 307) found that when speakers isolate the fricatives [s] and [ʃ] from their vocalic context, they can tell that the former is acoustically higher than the latter. One of Rakerd's major findings strongly suggests that the difference between the two modes is not based on what the perceiver *knows* must be the case but on perceiving something out, there, in the stimulus.

Rimbaud's *"Voyelles"* is one of the very few poems in the Western languages in which isolated vowels are systematically presented to the reader's perception. In Chapter 2 I also mentioned the symbolist poem *"Ilona"* by the Hungarian poet Kosztolányi, inspired by his wife's name. When isolated vowels are qualified by colour adjectives, there may be a tendency to perceive the vowels as thing-free streams of (acoustic) energy, the impact of which may be enhanced by some thing-free stream of (visual) energy – at least in certain conditions, when the directly perceived acoustic information and the semantic information referring to the visual domain are perceived as if somehow they were interacting. My conception of this poem is founded, then, both on the coupling of specific vowels with specific colours and the verbal devices that may evoke, jointly, an overall "thing-free vision" and on the kind of performance in which this may occur.

There are good reasons to suppose that in some performances, at least, as in *"Correspondances"*, a crescendo pattern is superimposed on the stream of thing-free and Gestalt-free qualities, culminating in an ecstatic vision. J. P. Houston (1963: 63–64) pointed out a crescendo pattern in this poem, though he is more interested in the contents than in structure.

> *"Voyelles"* is arranged as a kind of apocalyptic crescendo in which evil yields to good. It has the pattern of a Great Chain of Being [...]. The lower life of the flies gives place to that of men, [...] with their tents and kings and then presented as violently emotional beings. [...] Finally knowledge ushers in a vision of divinity, which is at the top of the hierarchy of creation. (Houston 1963: 63–64)

It might be interesting to compare this process where "evil yields to good" to Baudelaire's poem, where the peak experience occurs when the scents of purity give way to corrupted smells.

Such an ecstatic reading of "*Voyelles*" is possible only in an interpretation which takes the hint from the capitalised "*Ses Yeux*" and from the "ultimate" connotations of "*Oméga*", and construes "*Ses Yeux*" as the eyes of the Supreme Being; it is obviously impossible in interpretations that construe "*Ses Yeux*" as the eyes of Rimbaud's mother.

12.6.1 To sum up

This paper distinguishes between synaesthesia as a neuropsychological and a literary phenomenon. Both kinds consist in the joining of different sensory domains. In the former the sensations themselves are derived from two sensory domains, in the latter the terms that refer to them. While in the former sense associations are involuntary and rigidly predictable, the latter leaves room for great flexibility and creativity. I was concerned with literary synaesthesia only. I insisted that when explaining a synaesthetic image, one must be aware of what it is that one has explained, e.g. its genesis, its emergent meaning or aesthetic effect. Much confusion may result when this distinction is not clear. From the stylistic point of view, synaesthetic images are "double-edged": they may generate witty or strongly emotional effects. Coleridge defined imagination as the balance or reconcilement of opposite or discordant qualities. If in the reconciliation of opposite or discordant qualities the opposition or discordance are emphasized in the text, the effect is witty; if the reconcilement, it is emotional. I have explored three devices in the service of these opposing strategies. First, upward transfer typically generates emotional effects, downward transfer – witty effects. Secondly, stable characteristic visual shapes tend to resist fusion and increase the incongruence of the terms derived from the different sensory domains; thing-free and Gestalt-free qualities tend to facilitate fusion. Third, chaotic overdifferentiation may override the witty effect of downward transfer. In certain circumstances it may constitute "perceptual overload", which the cognitive system handles by dumping into some continuous, lowly-differentiated mass. Finally, I consider very briefly two French Symbolist sonnets notorious for their synaesthetic imagery. I have elsewhere explicated in great detail the particular synaesthetic transfers in these poems (Tsur 1992a: 455–470 [2008[2]: 495–510]; 1992b: 111–135). Here I mainly concentrate on the verbal strategies by which the poems generate thing-free and Gestalt-free qualities which lead to the indication of an ecstatic state in the last line. On reaching the culminating point of ecstasy, the reader "retro-relates" it with the preceding scattered sense perceptions, so as to superimpose an all-pervasive pattern of emotive *crescendo* leading to ecstasy. In this way, "telling" about an ecstatic state becomes "showing".

CHAPTER 13

The place of nonconceptual information in university education

13.1 Logic of *What*?

In one of his Minnesota Seminars on the philosophy of science thirty-something years ago, Walter Weimer made the following remark: The title of Sir Karl Popper's book *The Logic of Scientific Discovery* is a misnomer; it should be called *The Logic of the Completed Scientific Report*. Scientific discovery is governed by a different kind of logic, and it makes ample use of what Polányi (1972) calls "tacit knowledge". Wolfgang Köhler (1972: 163) refers to the *three B*s, "the Bus, the Bath, and the Bed", where some of the greatest scientific discoveries have been made (remember Archimedes and Kékulé!). As for the various insights reached in this way,

> they all agree on one point. After periods during which one has actively tried to solve a problem, but has not succeeded, the sudden right organization of the situation, and with it the solution, tend to occur at moments of extreme mental passivity (*idem*, 160).

Universities usually teach techniques and conceptual systems required for scientific research, but have no courses in achieving moments of extreme mental passivity, that is, taking a hot bath or dozing on a rocking bus. However, not only insights cannot be taught without having recourse to nonconceptual means, but the very application of the conceptual apparatus depends, to a considerable extent, on tacit, not explicit, knowledge. The academy provides clear-cut definitions of the concepts in the conceptual apparatus of a discipline. There is an illusion that one can correctly apply definitions if one learns the necessary and sufficient conditions for their application. It is only rarely realized that their correct application crucially depends on the refinement of the explicit conditions by the user's tacit knowledge. Such tacit knowledge is transmitted in nonconceptual ways.

In Borges' short story "Averroes's search" (cf. Chapter 8) the protagonist tries to understand the meaning of the terms "tragedy" and "comedy". At the end of his quest, in his commentary on Aristotle, Averroes arrives at the following conclusion: "Aristu (Aristotle) gives the name of tragedy to panegyrics and that of comedy to satires and anathemas. Admirable tragedies and comedies abound in the pages of the Koran...". Then the *real author* steps in: "In the foregoing story, I tried to narrate the process of a defeat. [...] I remembered Averroes who, closed within the orb of Islam, could never know the meaning of the terms tragedy and comedy". Aristotle's definitions are quite clear: tragedy presents its personae as better than the ordinary man; comedy as worse. When contextualized to the genres known to Averroes, they turn out to be "panegyrics" and "satires and anathemas", respectively. "Averroes, want[ed] to imagine what a drama is without ever having suspected what a theatre is". The explicit conditions for the correct application of definitions are refined by intuitions based on tacit knowledge abstracted from meaningful contexts.

During their academic education, students acquire not only knowledge of their subject matters and methodologies, but also certain mental sets, both in the exact sciences and the humanities.

> [Science textbooks] exhibit concrete problem solutions that the profession has come to accept as paradigms, and they then ask the student, either with a pencil and paper or in the laboratory, to solve for himself problems very closely related in both method and substance to those through which the textbook or the accompanying lecture has led him. Nothing could be better calculated to produce "mental sets" or *Einstellungen*. Only in their most elementary courses do other academic fields offer as much as a partial parallel". (Kuhn 1977: 229)

On this level of abstraction, the need to share certain mental sets is common to interpretive communities in the exact sciences and the humanities. Only in the humanities these mental sets are infinitely more varied. What is more, even in the most exact sciences the need to acquire the mental set through practicing on shared examples gives rise to a certain degree of "pluralism". "Many scientific communities share, for example, the Schrödinger equation, and their members encounter that formula correspondingly early in their scientific education. But, as that training continues, say toward solid state physics on the one hand and field theory on the other, the exemplars they encounter diverge. Thereafter it is only the uninterpreted, not the interpreted Schrödinger equation that can unequivocally be said to share" (Kuhn 1977: 307n). Only the application of the conceptual apparatus is infinitely less uniform in the humanities. What they share is that both in the humanities and the natural sciences the "lack of uniformity" arises from the variety of tacit knowledge underlying the application of the conceptual apparatus.

In literary education, each individual in every interpretive community must acquire a plurality of mental sets and intuitions, by being exposed to a wide range of literary works and genres, as well as the ability to switch from one mental set to another, according to the circumstances. But both in the humanities and the exact sciences, the explicit rules will be insufficient for an accurate application of the conceptual apparatus. A shift of relative emphasis will be noticed here. Kuhn points out a contrast between the sophistication of mental sets acquired in the exact sciences and the humanities; I have pointed out some similarity in the acquisition and application of mental sets *in spite of* the differences in their sophistication.

Sometimes it is the critical terms acquired by the students that determine the mental sets deployed. The tutor's task is to make the students familiar with the meanings and applications of those terms; but also to equip them with the appropriate tools to transcend them, so as to handle kinds of situations to which they were not exposed before. Thus, the conceptual apparatus of criticism may serve as a lever to induce intuitions required for the handling of literature – up to a certain point; beyond that point, it may bar the intuitions. The psychologist Maslow once said that a person whose only tool is a hammer will treat everything as a nail. A student of literature whose only tool is "connotations" will look in every text for positive and negative connotations. The tutor's task is, among other things, to enrich the students' toolbox and, by the same token, widen their range of intuitions while still applying the tools with considerable rigour.

13.2 Rapid and delayed categorization

Another factor that may determine people's intuitions regarding texts is their respective cognitive strategies. I have adopted from psychologists of perception-and-personality the pair of terms "rapid and delayed closure",[1] and adapted them to academic activities as "rapid and delayed categorization". These cognitive strategies are usually deployed in all life situations, and people tend to display some consistency across situations. Thus, persons who tend to deploy a certain kind of decision style in life situations, will also tend to deploy it in scientific research or reading literature. Although, as Else Frenkel-Brunswik says, "rigidity in one respect may go with flexibility in another", she also adds: "There is some indication

---

1. "Closure" is the achievement of perceptual (or, more generally, cognitive) constancy, that is, the point when uncertainty disappears. "Tendency toward closure" refers to the way in which perceiving, remembering, or thinking strive toward patterned wholes that are as coherent and stable as circumstances will allow. Rapid closure involves simplification of those circumstances.

that in the case of distinct intolerance of emotional ambivalence one may as a rule be able to locate at least some aspect of intolerance of cognitive ambiguity although these may often be apparent on a higher level than that of perception proper" (Frenkel-Brunswik 1968: 139–140).

Inclination toward rapid or delayed closure (or categorization) is determined, to a considerable extent, by a person's personality or cognitive style. But in academic activities it may also be influenced by the conceptual apparatus and mental sets acquired at a particular academic institution or through a particular disciplinary school. Strategies of delayed categorization may be threatening for some rigid people who, in extreme instances, may resist acquiring them.

This brings us to one of the crucial issues in scientific thinking and critical activities alike. Our thinking crucially depends on the relative speed of the recoding of the rich precategorial information into compact concepts. Too much delay may flood our cognitive system and render our thinking ineffective; too little delay, however, may impair the adaptive value of our thinking. We keep in touch with the flux of reality by virtue of our ability to handle rich precategorial sensory information. Our academic education encourages the handling of the categories, but ignores the precategorial information.

Creative insights (like those associated with the three Bs mentioned above) consist in the release of precategorial information from the control of established categories and in their reorganization into new categories. The "moments of extreme mental passivity" mentioned by Köhler relax the rigorous control of hard and fast categories over the stream of (precategorial) information. Persons intolerant of delayed categorization are incapable of such creative insights; in extreme cases they may think and talk in clichés.

Different categorization strategies may generate different poetic qualities. Different poetic texts may require different categorization strategies. In the instances considered shortly, the particular poetic characteristics of poetic passages is missed, if treated by way of rapid categorization; we have found, by contrast, that the poetic potential of Omar Khayyam's Rubáiyáths may not be fully realized by readers who are too tolerant of delayed categorization (cf. Tsur et al. 1990, 1991; see now also Tsur 2006: 115–141).

It is a commonplace that poetry is intimately associated with sensuous information. However, personality styles associated with the intolerance of delayed categorization may be more at ease with attending to the conceptual than to the sensuous aspects of the information on which interpretation relies. At this point I wish to repeat here a passage quoted in Chapter 2, concerning two opposing personality styles:

> The leveler is more anxious to categorize sensations and less willing to give up a category once he has established it. Red is red, and there's an end on't. He levels (suppresses) differences and emphasizes similarities in the interest of perceptual stability. For him the unique, unclassifiable sensation is particularly offensive, while the sharpener at least tolerates such anomalies, and may actually seek out ambiguity and variability of classification.
>
> (Ohmann 1970:231)

This may crucially influence the kind of interpretation they are likely to offer (cf. Tsur 2006:11–77; 115–141).

The main question explored by the present chapter is: how can one *teach* delayed categorization and convey perceptions based on it? How can I explain with words the nature of my sensations? Furthermore, how can I make my students *feel* these sensations, not merely take my word for it? To be sure, some students will reject all in all any attempt to expose them to delayed categorization. Some others, by contrast, will display a natural inclination toward it. The majority of students will be in between these two extremes. I assume that they may be induced to delay categorization, and eventually exposed to some new kinds of intuitions. Once they discover that such response strategies are possible, they may have recourse to them also when they encounter unexpected kinds of texts.

For this end, I have developed the following teaching strategy. I tell my students: "Say about this stanza [or line] anything you feel relevant". I ask no guiding questions. Since it is sometimes difficult to suppress some response of assent, I add "Whenever I say yes, it means that I have understood you, not necessarily that I agree". At some point students begin to produce responses that indicate increased attention to perceptual aspects of the situation (cf. Chapters 4–5). Most students, even the more flexible ones, frequently find this procedure disturbing, or even painful. In the majority of courses they feel they are expected to produce certain specific answers; and they usually receive feedback as to whether the answer produced was the expected (or "correct") one. Here they are exposed to an extended period of uncertainty. Uncertainty is a painful experience, and some persons tolerate it more, some less.

It is interesting to observe this process. At the beginning students are prone to produce responses for which there are names in the conceptual apparatus they have acquired at the university. But when they get no feedback from the tutor only an uneasy silence indicating that more could be said, they begin to produce answers which they would have never ventured in a normal class situation. Eventually, a whole range of evasive impressions may crop up, which in a normal class discussion would have been blocked by an all-too-readily available critical term.[2] Members of a seminar group become encouraged when they see that their peers too do produce such responses, and the tutor does not show signs of disapproval. In my opinion, the tutor should not stop at this point. Students should not get the impression that it is a feast of aimless free associations. At a certain point, the tutor should attempt to analyze and integrate those responses, and introduce a conceptual apparatus to account for the emerging effect.

Or, consider the following issue. According to Jespersen (1960: 19), every speech activity involves three aspects: **expression, sup**pression and **im**pression. *Expression* is what the speaker actually says. *Suppression* is what he might have said, but did not say. *Impression* is what affects the hearer: meaning, or the perceived quality emerging from the interaction of expression and suppression. According to the semantic definition of literature, "a literary work is a discourse in which an important part of the meaning is implicit" (Beardsley 1958: 126). In certain circumstances, such suppressed meanings may give rise to the perception of vague, elusive, but quite intense perceptual qualities (as, for instance, in the TOT state, see Chapter 3). In extreme cases, some romantic and symbolist poems are characterized by such vague, elusive, but intense perceptual qualities (see, e.g. Chapters 5–6). One of the crucial issues of critical communication in the classroom is to draw the students' attention to the very existence of such elusive, nameless qualities, and to point out their relationship to the verbal structures (that is, the interaction of the expressed and suppressed meanings and/or diffuse prosodic structure). A person who has never experienced, or is not aware of having experienced such a quality will never understand a verbal description of it. How can the tutor ascertain that students understand what he is talking about? One way I have found is to ask them whether they have ever experienced being unable to recall a word they have on the tip of their tongue; then to ask them to describe the feeling. Usually they are eager to do so, though they find the task not easy at all. Quite frequently they speak of being engulfed by some undifferentiated, darkish, ethereal but dense mass. Some even report a faint tactual sensation on the outer surface of their body. Familiarity with such a sensation could be drawn upon, for instance, in a discussion of Excerpt 1 below.

---

2. This DOES NOT mean that I object to the use of a critical metalanguage. On the contrary, in my various writings I insist that without a proper metalanguage no critical communication or efficient teaching is possible. In my book (Tsur, 1992: Chapter 21 = 2008: Chapter 22) I discuss at length the proper use of metalanguage (see also Tsur 2006: 212). I also make a distinction between two conceptions of style: Style-as-diagnosis and Style-as-hypothesis (Tsur, 1992: Chapter 12 / 2008: Chapter 13). In the former, critical terms serve to block insight; in the latter – to advance it.

In the ensuing examples, I will argue for a double approach: a bottom-up process from the students' intuitions (e.g. feelings during the tip-of-the-tongue experience) and a top-down process from the conceptual apparatus of the discipline (e.g. Jespersen's and Beardsley's generalizations).[3] During a substantial part of the process, criticism should be put "on hold", reserving it for a later "critical stage". Owing to the exigencies of "the completed scientific report", I will dwell less upon the stream of responses, more on the "critical stage", the sorting out of the arising problems, and the theoretical framework that emerges from the previous stages.

I wish, in fact, to emphasize three crucial points: that the sensuous element in poetry should receive a more elaborate theoretical apparatus than it usually does; that in the classroom the elaboration of such an apparatus should be preceded by a process of inducing openness to delay closure; and that exposure to unevaluated sensations may be a painful experience that arouses resistance. In what follows I will report both how I attempted to induce such attitudes, and how I elaborated such a theoretical apparatus,

In several of my publications I report such seminar discussions. In some of them (e.g. Chapters 3–4; Tsur 2003) elements of my own intuitions cropped up during this procedure, without my intervention. In what follows I will reproduce (from Tsur 2002) reports of two discussions in which the process was less smooth: in one, students showed distinct signs of resistance; in the other, part of the group produced "conceptual" interpretations, part of the group – interpretations based on sensuous elements. I suppose that these less smooth instances are more illuminating of the process than the smoother ones.

FIRST CASE STUDY In an undergraduate seminar on Alterman's poetry, I isolated the following line from its context, and asked the students to make any comments that seemed relevant to them, without asking them any specific questions.

מִן הַכְּפָר הַטוֹבֵעַ בִּנְהִי הַפָּרִים

   min hakfar hatove'a binhi haparim

1. From the village drowning in the moan of the oxen

The first responses received from the students represented the view that one may not refer to an isolated line, without relating it to its context. This is an academically approved, well-proven strategy to shift attention to the context, so as to avoid the need to experience elusive, "perceptual", poetic qualities, that cannot be subsumed under some clearly-defined, conceptual category. When I promised

---

3. Usually I also mention here Roger Brown's (1970) tip-of-the-tongue experiment, to account for the generation of those vague, elusive but intense perceptual qualities (quoted at length in Chapter 3).

them that after discussing the peculiar qualities of the isolated verse line we shall examine it in its wider context, students began making such remarks as that the words *drowning* and *moan* have sinister connotations. This too is a well-proven strategy, with full academic backing, to avoid the direct experiencing of unevaluated and unclassified stimuli. So I asked the students "Does the image really evoke unpleasant, or sinister feelings?" This can be construed, as was by Jean-Jacques Weber (2004), as a "loaded question", tipping off the students what response they are expected to produce, irrespective of what they feel. I admit that the question *is* "loaded". But, in view of the foregoing theoretical framework, I suggest, it has a very different purpose. "Closed within the orb" of a conceptual apparatus acquired at the university, students were not aware of possibilities which the conceptual apparatus doesn't cater for. Nor are they usually encouraged to "introspect" to reflect on their own feelings. In this respect, the tutor's task is to draw the students' attention to hitherto ignored possibilities.

The students were surprised to discover that the image was experienced as quite pleasant, but had trouble in answering my question, how can we explain that a verse line in which two of the key terms have sinister connotations arouses pleasurable feelings. So I began a second round of disconcerting questions: "What do we feel when taking a warm bath?" Here it is more difficult to find academic legitimization for avoiding immediate sensations. The first answer I received was "purification". This is an excellent example of shifting the focus of discussion from immediate, unevaluated – possibly nameless – sensations to some stable concept with a venerable spiritual history. The next answer was "wetness", which is tautological, and quite uninformative. Both answers are perfectly true, but involve a kind of "breaking the rules", reserved for cases in which it is difficult to find some respectable academic justification for evading the need to face elusive, nameless sensory experiences.

The response "wetness" is an excellent example for one of my earlier claims. It satisfies both the necessary and sufficient conditions for applying the term "sensations when taking a warm bath". Some (or perhaps most) students, however, have a tacit knowledge that this might be an absolutely correct, but improper answer to the question, though nobody has ever told them that. I strongly suspect that even those students who gave this answer do have this tacit knowledge, suggesting rather a sarcastic attitude: "I am not going to fall into your trap (to talk of unique, unclassifiable sensations)".

Eventually, the following account began to emerge: There is an undifferentiated, diffuse sensation all over the outer surface of the skin, with an heightened feeling of unity of the various parts of the body, and a kind of harmony between the body and its immediate environment, even an abolition of the separateness of the body from its environment. This account was found acceptable by most seminar members. Fast achievement of perceptual or conceptual constancy would have blocked the perception of such elusive sensations. It will be noticed that this verbal description has some conspicuous affinities with the above description of the tip-of-the-tongue experience.

Returning now to Alterman's metaphor, the village is perceived as if immersed in some Gestalt-free and thing-free entity, wrapping as it were the whole village or person, enhancing the unity of the parts of the village (or of the person), or transcending the split between the person and his environment. There is here a kind of regression of the perceiving consciousness from a state of cognitive stability that discriminates between the physical objects themselves, as well as between ego and the physical objects perceived. Hence the pleasant relaxation experienced through the metaphor, in spite of the sinister connotations of several key terms in it.

Consider now the noun *moan*. *The Random House College Dictionary* defines it as follows: "prolonged, low, inarticulate sound uttered from or as from physical or mental suffering". This definition has two parts; one part gives a description of the sensory information of "moan", the other suggests its human significance and evaluation. Rapid categorization will concentrate only on its second part; delayed categorization will linger on its first, sensuous, part for as long as possible, turning it into a lowly-differentiated spatial entity. Only later, if at all, it will proceed to its latter part. In Alterman's verse line, there is a logical contradiction between the prepositional phrase "in the moan of the oxen", and the verb suggesting immersion in water. *Drown* and related verbs transfer the transfer feature ⟨+LIQUID⟩ to their abstract indirect objects (see Chapter 4, above). Sounds are perceived as thing-free entities, that have no material mass. Consequently, they cancel the material ingredient in the transfer feature ⟨+LIQUID⟩, and retain such ingredients as "slight touch, diffuse and undifferentiated, all over the outer surface of the body; suspension of the boundaries of the body". At the same time, the immersion of a solid body in a thing-free entity arouses a feeling of condensation of that wrapping entity (cf. Chapter 4, above). At this point, not earlier, the process may be related to the Freudian notion "oceanic dedifferentiation", applied to the arts by Ehrenzweig.

The relative merits of this procedure will be foregrounded if we compare it to a thoroughly top-down (perfectly legitimate, and more logical) procedure: the tutor explains the Freudian notion of "oceanic dedifferentiation"; he notes that this notion has been fruitfully applied to the arts by Ehrenzweig, and that it could be fruitfully applied to poetry too; finally, he quotes and analyzes Alterman's verse line.

In a symposium on Cognitive Poetics (Tel Aviv University, 30.3.1993), I told the audience the story of this seminar session. One of the questions in the ensuing discussion concerned the "death" ingredient of *drown*. My answer referred to the feature-cancellation theory of metaphor: metaphoric contradiction deletes those features of the metaphoric term that are irrelevant to the frame, and foreground the relevant ones. *Moan* in Alterman's verse line foregrounds the peculiar sensuous quality of the oxen's lowing, and has nothing to do with "physical or mental suffering". *Drowning* suggests here immersion of the village in this peculiar sensuous quality, as perceived by the observer. The village gradually disappears in the darkness; the thing-free qualities in the visual and aural modes "darkness" and "prolonged, low, inarticulate sound" are perceived as somehow indistinguishable: prolonged low sounds are perceived as "darker" than rapidly-changing high sounds; and both darkness and inarticulate sounds impede the distinction of shapes. The outlines of the village gradually disappear in this "audio-visual" inarticulate mass, and the death ingredient is irrelevant here. Such an analysis, however, ignores any possible differences between "the village *drowning* in the moan of the oxen", and "the village *immersed* in the moan of the oxen". A graduate student, member of the Cognitive Poetics workshop, suggested that the death ingredient may suggest here a state wherein individuality seems "to dissolve and fade away into boundless being" – to use Tennyson's phrase quoted by William James; and, I think, this is the better answer. Methodologically, this would be a further Freudian step from "oceanic dedifferentiation" to mystic experiences.

13.3   Sensuous metaphors and the grotesque

SECOND CASE STUDY I claimed above that persons intolerant of delayed categorization may be reluctant to attend to the sensuous aspects of the information underlying their interpretation, preferring to attend to the conceptual aspects; whereas persons tolerant of delayed categorization would be tuned to the sensuous aspects as well. "The moan of the oxen" as a spatial entity in which the village may drown is a thing-free and Gestalt-free entity; "village" is a collective entity, with indistinct outlines. In the present section I am going to report a seminar meeting that applied the same procedure to a very different kind of image, involving objects with stable, characteristic visual shape. I have no independent information about my students' cognitive styles; but, interestingly, two distinctly different interpretations emerged from the discussion, a sensuous and a conceptual one. At that meeting we discussed two lines by the Hebrew poet Abraham Shlonsky:

יָרֵחַ מֵת תָּלוּי עַל בְּלִי־מָה,

כְּשַׁד לָבָן זוֹלֵף אֶת חֲלָבוֹ.

        yareaḥ met taluy ʿal bli-ma,
        kəʃad lavan zolef ʾɛt ḥalavo

2.   A dead moon is hanging on nothingness
       Like a white breast shedding its milk.

Let me begin, again, by reporting intuitions that some of my students had about these lines. Some of the students tended to interpret the "breast shedding its milk" as the embodiment of the principle of **giving**, of the life principle, having a contradictory relationship to the moon as "hung" and "dead" in the preceding line. The moon is associated here, paradoxically, with the principles of both life and death, with the principles both of passivity and of "giving". Running into difficulties, one of the students changed his interpretation and said that "shedding its milk" implies waste rather than feeding. All these interpretations, however, were incompatible with the intuitions of other participants in the seminar. Before going into a possible other interpretation, it should be noted that the above kind of interpretation is far from illegitimate. It relies on one of the most important principles of **literary competence**, formulated thus: "The primary convention is what might be called the rule of significance: read the poem as expressing a significant attitude to some problem concerning man and/or his relation to the universe" (Culler 1975: 115). The interpretation is further corroborated by one of the fundamental aesthetic principles going back through Cleanth Brooks to Coleridge, viz., that good poetry is paradoxical, that is, it consists in the fusion of incompatible or discordant qualities. The "rule of significance", peculiar as it may seem from a literary point of view, is an operating instruction realizing, in the literary domain, a principle that has much wider cultural applications. This principle is formulated by D'Andrade (1980) as follows: "In fusing fact and evaluational reactions, cultural schemata come to have a powerful directive impact as implicit values". In fact, applying the "rule of significance" is the default mode of interpretation. As we shall see, however, suspension of the rule of significance may yield in this case exceptionally significant results.

The above interpretation of Shlonsky's lines also relies on "the convention of metaphorical coherence – that one should attempt through semantic transformations to produce coherence on both levels of tenor and vehicle" (Culler 1975: 115). There is an attempt to produce coherence on the level of the tenor, associating the moon with the principles of life and death, through the appropriate semantic transformations. The level of the vehicle, however, is "incoherent": there is a "mixed metaphor" here. The moon as hung and dead (like the head of a hanged man?) is visually conflicting with the moon as a white breast. This line of thought may lead us to an alternative way to handle such metaphors. The first step in this direction goes *via* Christine Brooke-Rose's work. "Very broadly speaking, metaphors can be divided, from the point of view of idea-content, into functional metaphors (A is called B by virtue of what it does), and sensuous metaphors (A is called B by virtue of what it looks like, or more rarely, sounds like, smells like, feels like, tastes like)" (Brooke-Rose 1958: 155).

Now, let us use Brooke-Rose's categories here to apply explicit structural descriptions to the conflicting intuitions. It is clear that the former interpretation of Shlonsky's image treated it as a functional metaphor, whereas in the latter, "the moon [...] like a white breast shedding its milk" is treated as a conspicuous sensuous metaphor. Hence the conflicting intuitions. The moon is called "a white breast shedding its milk", not by virtue of its life-giving activity, but by virtue of what it looks like: the moon is a round object, near which a white mass, "the Milky Way" is seen (pouring forth from it, as it were). Now, why should a poet bother to provide such rich imagery, if it were not to obtain some human significance? For the precision of description, some critics say. But the precision-explanation breaks down when one considers the incompatible details that the various images lump together. By contrast, one of the major assumptions of Cognitive Poetics is able to explain the conflict. Such sensuous metaphors as Shlonsky's interfere with the normal process of orientation; the conflict delays the appraisal of the human significance of the image. In this respect, it forces delayed categorization, as it were.

I have elsewhere claimed that a psychoanalytic discussion of puns and caricatures may illuminate certain aspects of figurative language (Tsur 1987b: 19–32).[4] On first approximation, it seems obvious that the image in Excerpt 2 fuses two visual images into one, while preserving their warring identity. The visual conflict on the one hand, and the saving of mental energy resulting from the fusion on the other hand, generate the particular witty effect typically associated with caricature. On a closer look, however, such an explanation cannot account for the intuitive difference between a "functional" and a "sensuous" construal of the images involved. At most, we may say that the saving of mental energy intensifies the reader's involvement in whatever quality is generated by the metaphor, whether construed as "functional" or "sensuous".

More generally speaking, the urgency to evaluate the significance of a stimulus appears to be a deeply rooted biological response.

> Most emotions involve an intuitive appraisal of a stimulus as good (beneficial) or bad (harmful). [...] It is very unlikely that organisms can unequivocally evaluate all stimuli with which they make contact. Some period, extended or brief, is necessary before tissue damage occurs, or internal injury develops, or pleasurable sensations occur. During this critical period of direct contact with an unevaluated object, a pattern of behavior apparently develops which, at the human level, is usually called surprise.   (Plutchik, 1968: 72)

---

4. In this I am relying on Kris and Gombrich's (1965) classical paper "The Principles of Caricature".

Sensuous metaphor may, then, be regarded as another literary device to delay the smooth cognitive process consisting in the contact with some unevaluated image; the device's function is thus to prolong a state of disorientation and so generate an aesthetic quality of surprise, startlement, perplexity, astounding, or the like. Thus, Shlonsky's simile generates, under the pretense of precise description, a perceived effect of startling, or even emotional disorientation. But the two lines contain additional devices of emotional disorientation, which will be discussed in the following. The "sensuous" reader lingers at the visual images, without appraising their significance. These images, in spite of their common elements, are visually incompatible. The moon, the female breast, and the head of a dead person may be similar in their round shapes, but they are different in many details. The reader can join them visually only by the essentially comic technique of caricature, thereby demonstrating that the intolerable, inextricable mixture of incompatibles is a fact of life, perhaps the most crucial one. No wonder that such a reader perceives the image as grotesque, in an essentially divided response, which conveys the notion of something that is simultaneously laughable and horrifying or disgusting. Both laughter and horror or disgust are defense mechanisms in the presence of threat, the latter allowing the danger its authority, the former denying it (cf. Burke 1957: 51–56). The grotesque is *the experiencing of emotional disorientation* when both defense mechanisms are suddenly suspended (cf. Thomson 1972: 58). Shlonsky's image contains additional components of the grotesque. Some writers on the grotesque claim that "the grotesque is essentially physical, referring always to the body and bodily excesses and celebrating these in an uninhibited, outrageous but essentially joyous fashion" (Thomson 1972: 56). "Our laughter at some kinds of the grotesque and the opposite response – disgust, horror, etc. – mixed with it, are both reactions to the physically cruel, abnormal or obscene" (*idem*, 8). There is in the grotesque a kind of "delight in seeing taboos flouted". The white breast of cosmic dimension represents such an obscenity, or bodily excess.

The excerpt from Shlonsky presents us with yet another device of emotional disorientation, the 'realization of the idiom' "Milky Way" that is, the unexpected use of the idiomatic expression in its literal sense (the syntactic structure is, in fact, ambiguous here: insofar as the moon sheds its milk(y way), the expression is figurative; insofar as the white breast is shedding its milk, it is literal). Such sudden shifts of meaning may produce in the reader "a strange sensation – making one suddenly doubt one's comfortable relationship with language – not unlike the sense of disorientation and confusion associated with the grotesque" (Thomson 1972: 65).

The grotesque, then, makes use of poetic devices that produce an emotional disorientation which is experienced as a shock, perplexity, surprise, or the like.

It is, indeed, this quality that enables the various devices in these lines to combine and be integrated into a whole.

If one looks for an aesthetic justification of the above process, a sufficient answer will be: emotional disorientation is an intensive human quality perceived by the reader. One may justify one's positive evaluation of an aesthetic object with reference to three general canons: unity, complexity, and some intensive human quality (cf. Beardsley 1958: 465–469). It is obvious from the above analysis that Shlonsky's two lines are quite complex from the viewpoint of figurative language. Insofar as this complexity is achieved by means of what Neo-Classic critics would call "mixed metaphors", these lines appear to be deficient from the point of view of unity. Notice, however, this: the various kinds of poetic devices, each in its own way, are aimed at giving a shock and arousing a sense of emotional disorientation. This generates an intense human quality of perplexity and emotional disorientation. This quality, in turn, bestows perceptual unity upon the diverse images. In this respect, the role of Cognitive Poetics is to describe the mechanisms of defense and orientation, the disturbance of which has generated the intense human quality. It also helps to define the nature of this quality and to relate it, systematically, to the poetic structures.

Members of the seminar group proposed two quite different interpretations of Shlonsky's two lines, a sensuous and a conceptual one. I, as their tutor, helped them to further elaborate them, so as to make aesthetic sense of them. I am not aware of a method to refute any one of them. The only way to justify the preference of one of them is to work out both interpretations, and then point out that one of them yields more satisfactory results and, perhaps, is more in conformity with Shlonsky's imagistic poetics than the other.

The foregoing discussions of two excerpts were exercises in rapid and delayed categorization. The purpose of the exercise was to make students aware of their own categorization strategies; to expose them to the experiencing of sensuous information frequently blocked by rapid application of the critical apparatus; to make them aware that sensuous and conceptual construal of poetic images may give rise to different kinds of interpretation; and, finally, to provide them with a critical apparatus that allows them to handle sensuous information and to integrate it in an aesthetic whole.

Western academic education gives conspicuous priority to conceptual instruction and neglects, to a considerable extent, sensuous information, intuitions and tacit knowledge. It becomes, however, more and more obvious that both in the natural sciences and the humanities significant achievements can be achieved only if research is governed by intuitions, and even the application of definitions according to necessary and sufficient conditions crucially involves tacit knowledge. What was thought to be the logic of scientific discovery turns out, in fact, the logic of the completed scientific report.[5]

13.4   Summary and conclusions

This chapter investigated the place of nonconceptual information in university education, with special focus on the teaching of literature. It argued for a "double vision": a bottom-up process from the students' intuitions and tacit knowledge, and a top-down process from the conceptual apparatus of the discipline. The present approach advocates in teaching rigorous application of the conceptual apparatus, and, at the same time, procedures to elicit the students' intuitions. I have tried to show how the conceptual apparatus may be used to apply explicit structural descriptions to conflicting intuitions.

I pointed out three stages in categorization: precategorial sensory information; the grouping of precategorial information into categories; and the application of a name to the category. I have distinguished between rapid and delayed categorization. The perception of precategorial information demands delayed categorization, and is the basis of creative thinking, and of emotional processes. Rapid categorization does not linger on precategorial information, but skips right to the organized category. When a person skips the first two stages right to the category name, we say he is thinking and talking in clichés.

---

5.   Two anonymous referees of this paper made comments to the same effect: "I miss an explicit distinction between delayed categorization and defamiliarization. The processes seem to me to be very close to each other". This point is very well-taken. In a recent paper "Defamiliarization Revisited" (included here as Chapter 8) I observe: "Defamiliarization ('making it strange') is an effective stylistic device resulting from a disturbance of, or delay in, the process of categorization". Then I quote Shklovsky: "Art exists that one may recover the sensation of life; it exists to make one feel things, to make the stone *stony*". Briefly, the two notions are deceptively similar, but by no means coextensive. The difference is this: "Defamiliarization" is a stylistic device deployed by the poet, "to make one feel things". "Delayed categorization" is a cognitive strategy deployed by the perceiver, whatever the techniques deployed by the poet. Devices of defamiliarization can be discerned in the structure of a text, irrespective of the perceiver's perception strategies; delayed categorization is a cognitive strategy to handle all life situations as well as poetic qualities, including effects regularly perceived as defamiliarization, but also, e.g. elusive atmospheres generated by other techniques. One of those referees also comments: "Why is the author unpacking delayed categorization solely in relation to sensations? What about other forms of delayed categorization that have nothing to do with the sensual? Are there such forms?" Certainly, there are. All creative thinking, for instance, presupposes delayed categorization. I am merely insisting on an extreme case that is central to poetry, so as to enforce a fundamental change of attitudes.

I noted above that most students of literature find the process of commenting on a poetic excerpt without feedback disturbing or painful. But some of them find the rigorous application of the conceptual system too exceptionally frustrating or annoying. Toward the end of the term of the seminar in which we discussed Alterman's excerpt, a student asked me whether I was willing to accept criticism of my teaching. "By all means", I said. She said I was turning poetry into exact science. Though I have my reservations from this way of putting things, I didn't deny it. Instead, I pointed out that I spent quite a lot of time to force the students to use their senses and reflect on their feelings when reading poetry. "Don't think that all your efforts were wasted on me", she said. "The other day I dropped a coin from my purse, and tried to decide what coin it was from its sound, without looking. And then I thought of you".

In the teaching game, there is a tutor who wants to generate a complex process, in which the students bring to surface their own attitudes toward the text; the tutor, too, shamelessly expresses his own attitudes (at a late stage, to be sure, in order not to preempt the students' spontaneous responses). The tutor and the students analyze together what elements in the text and what general theoretical considerations support each response. In the foregoing discussion of the Shlonsky excerpt, for instance, I pointed out several theoretical considerations that support the interpretation which I don't endorse. Finally, the tutor may provide a theoretical apparatus (with which the students may not be familiar) systematizing the principles behind the students' responses. At this point, the tutor may even shamelessly explain why he thinks one interpretation is preferable to the other.

One purpose of the exercise is to make the students' tacit attitudes and responses explicit; a second purpose is to verify those attitudes and responses against the text and wider theoretical generalizations. A third purpose is to make students aware of aspects of the text and of possible emotional responses of which they were not aware before.

There is a danger that the foregoing exercise may be misconstrued as encouraging students to indulge in their own "adolescent half-baked intuitions", or "real" and "authentic" feelings. I am not pursuing their "authentic" feelings. The question is, how do you obtain crucial information about perceptual qualities. You can't follow rules to find out whether the book is red or the tea is sweet. You know that the book is red by looking, and that the tea is sweet by tasting it. Similarly, you can access certain aesthetic qualities only by being exposed to them (cf. Sibley 1962), and then examine your own thoughts and feelings.

Now, consider the comment that *drowning* and *moan* have sinister connotations, and my question: "Does the image really evoke unpleasant, or sinister feelings?". Trained in their discipline, students were looking for the connotations of isolated words, and paid little attention to how the image feels. The question was intended to draw attention to a possible discrepancy between the connotations of isolated words and the feel of the whole. It is easier to make a "good/bad" judgment regarding the connotations of isolated words than respond to a "unique, unclassifiable sensation" which, as Ohmann pointed out, "is particularly offensive" to some persons. By shifting attention from the connotations of isolated words to the feel of the image, there is a good chance that students would notice something they haven't noticed before. Some students earnestly welcome such a discovery – not merely to please their tutors – and feel that they became better equipped to respond to poetry. But, as expected, some would find it particularly offensive. At any rate, the tutor's task is to point out that the possibility of such a "unique, unclassifiable sensation" exists;[6] at the same time try to make sure that the students do not "take their tutor's word for it" but genuinely discover it for themselves, and then offer a theoretical apparatus that may relate the sensation to the structure of the text and integrate it in an aesthetic whole.

To put it differently: The point is not to manipulate students into "intuitively" hitting upon the tutor's interpretation, nor to convince them after the event that the tutor's interpretation is the "correct" one, but to make them aware that the possibility of certain perceptions and emotional responses exists; briefly, to increase the number of their perceptual and emotional hypotheses. I have quoted Maslow saying that a person whose only tool is a hammer will treat everything as a nail. As the psychologists of perception-and-personality have taught us, "The smaller the number of alternative hypotheses held by the person concerning his environment at a given moment, the greater their strength will be. [...] The closer to monopoly a hypothesis is, the less information will be required to confirm it and the more tenaciously will it be retained in the face of stimulus contradiction" (Bruner 1973: 94). The question: "Does the image really evoke unpleasant, or sinister feelings?" was intended to break the monopoly, to induce readiness to perceive such "stimulus contradiction".

When I was a secondary school teacher, I had a student who, when asked a question, would be looking at my face and reading my reactions. When I put on a poker-face, she would stop talking in the middle of the sentence. This student had a decisive contribution to the development of the procedure outlined above. When students are required to make comments without getting any feedback, they

---

6. A colleague, a former graduate student and supervisee of mine, read this paper and asked me to add the following. It's not only the discovery that certain (sensuous, or intuitive) responses exist, but also the experience of the "liberating shock" that such responses are *permissible*, legitimate. When I first asked her class to say about an excerpt whatever they thought relevant, she asked whether this could be impressions of the atmosphere. She vividly recalls her pleasant surprise when she received a positive answer.

undergo a prolonged experience of uncertainty, not unlike the period of uncertainty of delayed closure, but in an amplified version. By way of this, they may discover that the possibility of delayed closure exists, and that it allows access to certain kinds of information.

The same act in the teaching game has been construed above as an attempt to make students aware of hitherto unnoticed possibilities, or as tipping them off regarding the responses they are expected to produce. The two alternatives will stay with us for long. The tutor must constantly be on guard lest the attempt to make students aware of unnoticed possibilities pass into tipping-off. There is little more we can do. The alternative would be a more or less straightforward, foolproof exposition of the conceptual apparatus of literary criticism, its illustration by examples, followed by some practicing. Such an alternative is not too bad; but not good enough either.

CHAPTER 14

Points and counterpoints

14.1 Persinger's findings and poetry criticism

In this chapter I discuss theoretical and practical issues that arose in the course of this book. I do not discuss them in the abstract, but focus on concrete examples. Cognitive poetics is an interdisciplinary approach to poetry. The foregoing book claims that such an approach may be very useful in accounting for elusive poetic effects. But, as I have argued in many of my writings, it may also obstruct fruitful application. In Chapter 2, for instance, I write:

> In such a hierarchic structure there always lurks the danger of reductionism. The critic is prone to merely restate in acoustics-language (or brain-language) what could be said in phonetics-language. Cognitive Poetics is particularly susceptible to this danger.

In this section, I propose to present my approach to this problem by suggesting what it is not. The application of neuropsychological research to poetry is not a unitary endeavour. Much depends on the implied or explicit purpose of the study. I will elucidate my application of Persinger's findings to religious experiences and poetry by comparing it to another application of the same, by Carole Brooks Platt, in her illuminating paper, "Presence, Poetry and the Collaborative Right Hemisphere" (2007). Platt and myself are asking different questions and give different answers. The two attempts are sufficiently similar to be compared: we both purport to account for what is usually perceived as some felt presence in a poem; and we both invoke Persinger's findings in the neuropsychology of God beliefs.

In Chapter 6 I quote Persinger's (1987) claim that God experiences (as well as some pathological conditions) are associated with temporal lobe transients, which are electrical perturbations of the temporal lobe in the human brain. A characteristic of such states "is an alteration in the description of the self". In his words, "Depersonalization is typical" (Persinger 1987: 18). He points out that some of the great religious innovators seem to have had temporal-lobe epilepsy. In this same chapter I also discuss Keats's Elgin-marbles sonnet at considerable length. This is one of the exquisite instances in which Keats claims to have achieved one of his "many havens of intensity", a claim quoted by many critics with approval. This suggests a kind of "peak experience", similar to ecstasy; and it is, definitely, a prominent kind of "altered state of consciousness". In Chapter 7 I apply the same battery to Hopkins' "The "Windhover".

Here I will reproduce some of my discussion of Keats's line

So do these wonders a most dizzy pain,

I describe the preceding two lines as displaying a conspicuous high-intensity state of depersonalization, said to be typical of such peak experiences. Keats does not say "Such dim-conceivèd glories of *my* brain/ Bring round *my* heart an indescribable feud", but "*the* brain" and "*the* heart". This line too speaks of "*a* most dizzy pain"; it doesn't say *whose* dizzy pain. This stream of images, dissociated from the self as thinking, feeling, and willing, and distinguishing itself from other selves and from objects of its thought, leads to a state of consciousness designated as "a most dizzy pain". "Pain" merely names an acute but undifferentiated feeling. While not diminishing the intensity of pain, "dizzy" blurs its contours. "Dizzy" refers to a whirling state of uneasy feeling, sometimes extremely intense, blurring one's perception of the external world. Thus, the very presence of "dizzy" contributes to the structural resemblance of Keats's poem to an altered state of consciousness. As Persinger says in his study of the neuropsychological bases of God beliefs, "Few people appear to acknowledge the role of vestibular sensations in the God Experience. However, in light of the temporal lobe's role in the sensation of balance and movement, these experiences are expected. [...] Literature concerned with the God Experiences is full of metaphors describing essential vestibular inputs. Sensations of 'being lifted', 'feeling light', or even 'spinning, like being intoxicated', are common" (Persinger 1987: 26). Thus, even such opposite descriptions as 'feeling light' and 'spinning like being intoxicated' may contribute to the perception of a God experience in a poem. This may account for the contribution of "a most dizzy pain" to a perception of an altered state of consciousness in this specific poem. I elsewhere appealed to this observation in accounting for the conspicuous occurrence of "floating" in two additional poems usually deemed as ecstatic: Wordsworth's "I wondered lonely as a cloud", and Coleridge's "Kubla Khan". Thus, Keats's lines evoke, by verbal means, two nonverbal features of God-experiences: depersonalization and vestibular sensations.

I submit that such an application of neuropsychological studies of God experiences to poetry has several advantages. On the one hand, it relates religious experiences to brain processes in a publicly verifiable manner that may, by the same token, account for certain poetic effects as well. On the other hand, it provides terms that have sufficient descriptive contents to make subtle distinctions in the verbal texture of a given poem and point out specific verbal devices that contribute to such effects in it. When, for instance, Persinger writes that in a certain state of consciousness "depersonalization is typical", it can be translated into grammatical terms that point out depersonalizing strategies in a text. In this way it may convey not merely the general principle, but may also suggest some of the elusive, undifferentiated features of the experience. It is such elusive features that enable to detect some structural resemblance between the poetic text and the emotional experience.

While my concern is, explicitly, with poetic effects, Platt deliberately addresses nonliterary issues, in which texts are merely evidence for certain psychological arguments (regarding neuroscience and the creative process). She explicitly states that she uses the words of famous male religious figures and poets to show how destabilization of the self through maternal deprivation plays a major role in the creation of divine presences, and addresses the reasons for a more pronounced sense of presence in women, using the examples of famous poets, writers and mystics. But she does not point out, e.g. what kinds of verbal construct can indicate "destabilization of the self" or "the creation of divine presences" in a text. Platt too appeals to the same findings of Persinger's research, but with somewhat different emphases. Then she applies these findings to a sense of merged presence in two poetic passages, by the Arab poet Rumi, and by Rainer Maria Rilke:

> Shams disappears and Rumi's quest to find him ends in a sense of merged presence: 'Why should I seek? I am the same as/he. His essence speaks through me./I have been looking for myself!' (quoted in Barks, 'On Rumi'). Rainer Maria Rilke, while standing on a bridge in Toledo, Spain, described how a star fell from boundless outer space into his equally boundless inner space. He termed this sensed merger a 'divine visitation'. Later, Rilke was 'given' the initial line of the Duino Elegies by the voice of an angel, the sound of a violent storm converted into poetic speech: 'Who, if I cried out, would hear me among the Angel's orders?' He had been contemplating 'an important letter he had to write', according to a biographer, when this 'inspirational conversion' took place (Freedman, 1996, p. 323). The next line of 'The First Elegy' [1922] speaks in terms gleaned from his spiritual and poetic predecessors: 'Even if one of them suddenly held me to his heart, I'd vanish in his overwhelming presence'.

Platt doesn't seem to be interested in some structural resemblance between the text and the spiritual experience described. She is merely interested in the fact that "a sense of merged presence" is *mentioned* in the text. The texts are treated as "strikingly representative examples" of a principle, to use Riffaterre's formulation out of context, that is, as illustrations to certain claims about brain structure and religious experience.

Platt presents a wholesale relation between brain structures and brain processes on the one hand and, on the other, such spiritual experiences as "a sense of merged presence", without going into the niceties of the correspondences. Such poetic expressions as "His essence speaks through me" or "I'd vanish in his overwhelming presence" are more or less direct expression of the merger, and are quoted as evidence for a generalization, not for some poetic effect. In this sense, poetry is used not for the sake of its aesthetic effect, but as one of several kinds of evidence for the activities of the temporal lobe. This is, of course, perfectly legitimate; my business here is merely to bring out the contrast between the two approaches. To put the difference more bluntly: Platt uses the contents of poetic texts to illustrate certain neuropsychological generalizations by Persinger. I am using Persinger's generalizations to make stylistic distinctions in poetic texts.

To further elucidate what I am missing here, I will consider two descriptions from Chapter 5 above, of a spiritual experience by Tennyson, and of a brain mechanism by Newberg et al. (2001).

Ehrenzeig speaks of the "suspension of boundaries between self and not self" (see above, Chapter 4). William James quotes an illuminating description of such an experience from a letter by Tennyson (see Chapter 5, p. 67). James chooses here a description where "the consciousness of individuality" is a delimited, compact concept in which, in turn, the boundaries of individuality gradually vanish – ending up in a state of "boundless being". The process is indicated by the metaphors "dissolve and fade away", suggesting a gradual physical change from solid to fluid, and from existence to nonexistence (or, rather, from perceptibility to imperceptibility), respectively. Paradoxically, the dissolution of individuality is initiated by "the *intensity* of the consciousness of individuality", suggesting some peak experience (note the double genitive phrase, manipulating an attribute of an attribute into the referring position). There seems to be a structural resemblance between the physical features of the gradual blurring of boundaries, dissolution of solids into fluids and "fading away" on the one hand, and the fusion of individual being with God or infinity in mystic experience. Tennyson's last paradoxical phrase "the loss of personality (if so it were) seeming no extinction, but the only true life" is disconcerting. Such baffling descriptions are usually handled by subsuming them in some established category, e.g. "Well, such states are characteristic of mystic experiences". What can this mean, apart from pointing at an observational fact? We lead a trivial, petty life, what T.S. Eliot's choir in *Murder in the Cathedral* describes as "living and partly living".

Release from such "partly living" may go in two diagonally opposite directions: death, annihilation, or attaining an intense, full life. Kenneth Burke's discussion of "The Principle of Oxymoron" (1962: 848–852) presents the paradox of their co-occurrence in a more fine-grained texture. "Identification achieves its ultimate expression in mysticism, the identification of the infinitesimally frail with the infinitely powerful" (p. 850). This explains how the loss of personality may be experienced as "the only true life" – by becoming one with the infinitely powerful.

Can we point out some brain processes to account for such Oceanic experiences, that would be more specific than a general notion of "temporal lobe instability" said to be responsible for most God experiences? Newberg et al. relate such experiences to what they call "the orientation association area" of the brain. They point out that there are two orientation areas, situated at the posterior section of the parietal lobe, one in each hemisphere of the brain. The left orientation area is responsible for creating the mental sensation of a limited, physically defined body, while the right orientation area is associated with generating the sense of spatial coordinates that provides the matrix in which the body can be oriented.

Newberg et al. provide a SPECT camera image of the two orientation areas, of the brain at rest and during meditation, showing that the activity of the left orientation area is markedly decreased compared to the right side. According to their foregoing description, this would suggest that during meditation the sensation of boundaries between one's limited, physically defined body and surrounding space should be gradually suspended (see Chapter 5, p. 67).

Now consider this. Stable visual shapes with solid boundaries separate objects from one another and from the perceiving self, and resist fusion. Fluids, by contrast, merge easily. Tennyson uses such abstractions in his description as "consciousness. individuality … boundless being", that have no stable visual shapes, nor solid boundaries. However, such nouns as "consciousness" and "individuality" are perceived, by default, as delimited conceptual entities, unless manipulated in certain ways. The verbs "dissolve and fade away" suggest the gradual weakening and disappearance of those conceptual limits. Thus, the structural resemblance between Tennyson's description and the mystic experience, as well as the functional correspondence between the experience and the brain mechanism become conspicuous.

We have, then, two different conceptions of "felt presence", or "merged presence" in poetry. According to one conception, the presence and the merger are indicated in the poem by direct telling. According to the other, the presence and the merger need not be explicitly mentioned, but generated as a perceptual quality by certain verbal structures, irrespective of their explicit contents. Such metaphoric constructs as IMMERSION in an ABSTRACTION, e.g. Shakespeare's "Steeped me in poverty to the very lips", or Keats's "Till Love and Fame to nothingness do sink", do not suggest merely the dissolution of the self into a boundless being, but also somehow turn the abstraction, or even absence, into a supersensuous, dense mass, an invisible presence. Likewise, metaphors of the ABSTRACT of the CONCRETE structure, such as Wordsworth's "The gentleness of Heav'n broods o'er the sea" generate a sense of invisible intense presence; and so do constructs consisting of an abstraction and some deictic expression. In Alterman's "The estrangement of these walls" we have the combination of two devices: the ABSTRACT of the CONCRETE structure, where the ABSTRACT member of the phrase serves in the ABSTRACTION plus DEIXIS construct as well. In his "From the village drowning in the moan of the oxen" we have again the ABSTRACT of the CONCRETE structure, where the ABSTRACT member of the phrase serves as the abstraction in which the immersion takes place. Thus, in both verse lines two devices are merged, reinforcing each other's effect.

The upshot of the foregoing comparison is this. Platt and myself are asking different questions and give different answers. Platt deliberately addresses non-literary issues, in which texts are merely evidence for certain psychological arguments. Platt's work goes mainly topdown, from experimental results to examples; mine goes mainly bottom up. I had the good luck that, long before I had any notion of brain research, I encountered an insufficiently-explained stylistic problem for which I tried to find an explanation, and after decades came up with an explanation based on brain structure and brain function. The comparison shows that Persinger's notion of temporal lobe transients may be invoked to account for *any* religious experience, but in certain circumstances can be used to make significant distinctions within a poetic text (e.g. personal or impersonal formulations in Keats's sonnet). His discussion of "vestibular sensations" may account for, e.g. the conspicuous occurrence of certain "innocent-looking" expressions in notorious "ecstatic" poems (e.g. "floats on high" or "dizzy pain" or "Windhover"). Likewise, Newberg et al.'s findings regarding the Orientation Association Area during meditation may account, specifically, for the perception of lowly-differentiated presences, and experiences related to the dissolution of the self into those presences, as well as for certain verbal structures that typically evoke such perceptions and experiences in poetry. Explicit statements in poetry *can* be used to illustrate certain generalizations about brain structures and brain functioning. But what we need in Cognitive Poetics is a system that may account for subtle poetic effects as well. To accomplish this, it must offer critical terms that have sufficient descriptive contents to make significant distinctions between them.

14.2   "Dover Beach" – two cognitive readings

Another way to point up my particular approach would be through a brief application of the present book's distinctions to Margaret Freeman's reading of Matthew
Arnold's "Dover Beach". In fact, the differences between our approaches are
smaller than will emerge from the ensuing comparison, owing to different focuses
of our endeavours. In this paper she was rather focusing on the broader question
of how one can understand Arnold's poem from a Vician perspective rather than,
e.g. exploring the characteristics of the prosody *per se*. Historically, she says, the
poem has been universally interpreted as a statement of alienation arising from
the secularization of the scientific age. Her reading "differs from these earlier ones,
because it focuses on the poem's aesthetic patterns that lead us to experience its
iconic semblance of felt life" (Freeman 2011:735). This sounds very much like the
conception put forward in the present work. Where, however, our works are most
similar, there one may also point out subtle differences.

Before going into the comparison of our critical approaches, I wish to
compare some aspects of this poem to Wordsworth's Calais-Beach sonnet. In
Chapter 5 I discuss verbal devices which poets typically use to generate diffuse
percepts, most notably a combination of deixis with an abstraction and the
ABSTRACT-of-the-CONCRETE metaphor. The effects of both devices can be amplified by what Aristotle calls *energeia* (vividness), that is, the application of a physical
or mental process predicate to an abstract or concrete noun to which a predicate
of state would be more appropriate. Abstract nouns typically denote clear-cut categories, just as concrete nouns typically denote clear-cut objects. In certain circumstances, the ABSTRACT-of-the-CONCRETE metaphor isolates an attribute of the
concrete object and manipulates it into the referring position, focusing attention
on a thing-free quality. At this point I made a further distinction. If the attribute
(e.g. a sound) can be perceived without perceiving simultaneously the object
whose attribute it is, it tends to be perceived as a category in its own right rather
than a thing-free quality; it tends to be perceived as a thing-free quality if it is perceived simultaneously with the object whose quality it is. Consider again the line.

> The gentleness of heaven broods o'er the Sea

Wordsworth resorts here to the aforesaid poetic device. If you construe "heaven"
as "firmament", the "gentleness of heaven" is perceived simultaneously with the
heaven, and "broods" is a predicate of mental or perhaps physical process, applied
to a noun to which a predicate of state (e.g. "hovers") would be more appropriate.
This invests the abstraction with energy and, as I said, is a conspicuous device
to direct attention *away from* the objects and concepts *to* their felt qualities and

render them more vivd.[1] Now compare this construction to the following lines from Arnold's poem:

9. Listen! you hear the grating roar
10. Of pebbles which the waves draw back, and fling,
11. At their return, up the high strand,
12. Begin, and cease, and then again begin,
13. With tremulous cadence slow, and bring
14. The eternal note of sadness in.

"The grating roar/Of pebbles" is a conspicuous instance of the ABSTRACT-of-the-CONCRETE construction. However, it does not have the elusive quality of "the gentleness of heaven" – and not only because its semantic ingredients are more compelling, but also because it is perceived as a thing in its own right out there. Indeed, the grating roar *can* be perceived without the pebbles and the rest. It would appear that Arnold has here a different poetic conception. Instead, unlike Wordsworth, he elaborates at great length, in lines 10–12, what Wimsatt would call "the irrelevant texture" of the metaphor, the physical setting.

The really interesting twist, however, comes now. In line 13, we have "tremulous cadence slow", which *cannot* be perceived without perceiving simultaneously "the grating roar", whose cadence it is; this may generate, precisely, the kind of quality I missed in the genitive phrase. Here a question arises to which I don't know the answer. Do readers perceive this relationship between "grating roar" and "tremulous cadence slow" after all that intervening physical description? The discussions of Freeman and Kövecses don't suggest a positive answer. It took me, too, several readings to realize it; but once I did, I cannot ignore it.

> When Zoltán Kövecses (2010:671) says of lines 13–14 in Arnold's poem "of course we know that waves cannot actually bring in sadness or notes of sadness – they can only be metaphorically responsible for our sad mood when we hear the tremulous cadence slow," then he, like Ruskin, is representing metaphor as indicating the false impression given by the pathetic fallacy. However, I suggest that the causality implied by Kövecses's phrase "metaphorically responsible" in fact reflects domain crossing among the physical sound, its musical "cadence," and its emotional effect on the listener. (Freeman, 2011:739)

---

1. See also in Chapter 5 my discussion of the lines "Listen! the mighty Being is awake,/ And doth with his eternal motion make/A sound like thunder – everlastingly", which are conspicuously comparable to these lines of Arnold – but with a difference.

Here, perhaps, Morris Weitz's assertion would be opportune: the role of theory in aesthetics is to make crucial recommendations what to look for in art, and how to look at it. If we treat Freeman's and Kövecses's statements as such crucial recommendations, I propose to make a different one. The metaphor does not necessarily suggest "our sad mood when we hear the tremulous cadence slow". In view of Persinger's observation in the preceding section, the "sadness" in question is depersonalized: it does not say whose sadness it is. We may, rather, *perceive* the "tremulous notes of sadness" out there, as an attribute of the "grating roar". In terms expounded in Chapter 9, I can be perfectly consistent when saying "those tremulous notes of sadness evoked a serene mood in me". I would rather go into some detail to explain how that "domain crossing among the physical sound, its musical 'cadence' and its emotional effect" works, namely, that the listener perceives some structural resemblance between the "tremulous cadence slow" of the waves' sound, the "tremulous cadence slow" of the music, and sadness (a mood typically characterized by slowness).

This conception gains support from Freeman's brilliant analysis of Arnold's manuscript changes, culminating in the observation:

> The question is why Arnold chose to substitute "tremulous" for "mournful." The adjective "mournful" in this context indicates that the sound of the pebbles' roar is in itself mournful, an example of Ruskin's pathetic fallacy, whereas the adjective "tremulous" can apply to both the turbulent action of the waves and the physical trembling of an emotional response. (*idem*, 740)

In terms of the view expounded here, "tremulous" provides an additional structural detail of the physical process that may render the structural resemblance detected between it and sadness more fine-grained. In this way, "The eternal note of sadness" becomes a *perceived* thing-free quality out there in the world. This quality would be more pronounced if we didn't construe the tremulousness of "sadness" as "the physical trembling of an emotional response", but rather as the fine fluctuations of the emotional process itself.

Actually, this conception is already implicit in Ruskin's paragraph quoted by Freeman: "the word 'Blue' does not mean the sensation caused by a gentian on the human eye; but it means the power of producing that sensation; and this power is always there, in the thing, whether we are there to experience it or not, and would remain there though there were not left a man on the face of the earth" (*idem*, 741). There is, however, a substantial difference between the phenomenon mentioned by Ruskin and the one discussed here. Blueness is a quality of the gentian, "grown together" with other qualities in a physical object that has a characteristic stable visual shape. The "tremulous cadence slow", by contrast, is a thing-free and Gestalt-free quality "abstracted" and isolated to some extent from its object (which, in this case, happens to have no stable visual shape either).

Regarding the last stanza of the poem, another subtle difference between Freeman's and my position may be detected:

29. Ah, love, let us be true
30. To one another! for the world, which seems
31. To lie before us like a land of dreams,
32. So various, so beautiful, so new,
33. Hath really neither joy, nor love, nor light,
34. Nor certitude, nor peace, nor help for pain;
35. And we are here as on a darkling plain
36. Swept with confused alarms of struggle and flight,
37. Where ignorant armies clash by night

The immediate situation addressing the beloved fades here into sermonizing on the *condition humaine*, at a very high level of generalization, pointing out the opposition between appearances and the true nature of the world. How do the last three lines relate to this sermon? Freeman comments: "we are left, like Sophocles's victims who cannot escape their doom, with Sophocles's "taste of pain" that accompanies us 'here' on Thucydides's 'darkling plain' of the world" (*idem*, 744). Freeman's last phrase, "of the world", shifts Thucydides's "darkling plain" to the highly generalized level of the preceding discourse.[2] But the image has a very powerful effect even if one misses the allusion to Thucydides – and, perhaps, a somewhat different one.

I don't dispute that interpretation, but would add my own different emphasis. I would conceive of this stanza in terms of Platonic philosophy. According to Plato, friendship (*filia*) and love are half way between the absolute good and the absolute bad. The ideal world would be all harmony, constancy and wisdom, grasping the true nature of things; the real world is full of disharmony and ignorance, mutability, being exposed to the illusion of appearances. Love and friendship are islands of harmony, wisdom and constancy in a stormy sea of uncertainty. In light of this, I would construe differently such expressions as "confused alarms"

---

2. In a personal communication she adds: "The whole point of Thucydides' description of the battle of Epipolae is that the Athenians were routed because they were fighting at night and, therefore, not being able to see their fellow soldiers, they were shouting out their secret password to each other. The Spartans, of course, hearing the word, promptly started using it themselves, thereby creating the chaos and confusion that caused the rout. Apparently Arnold's father was very fond of the passage and quoted it frequently in his classes as (presumably) a moral lesson for his students." Such moral lesson reinforces, of course, the generalized view of the image.

and "ignorant armies clash by night". The soldiers are ignorant of the purpose of the war, and are suffering and dying they don't know for what. To make things worse, clashing by night arouses a feeling of confusion, uncertainty and chaos. This, of course, too can be understood as a general summary of the *condition humaine*, lending it a closural quality (reinforced by a closing couplet pointed out by Freeman). But it can also be construed as a sudden shift to an immediate experience, an image in which the immediate sensations of confusion, disorientation, chaos, meaninglessness are efficiently coded – a sense of uncertainty sabotaging closure. In this case, the couplet form would bear all the burden of closure, played up against the thematic *lack* of closure. The New Critics were particularly interested in the subtle qualifications which the various elements in a context receive from the context (Wellek 1963: 329; Brooks 1968: 171). The above sudden shift is just such a subtle qualification. Thucydides told the story of the armies fighting on a darkling plain as a historical fact; Thomas Arnold found a moral lesson in it; in Matthew Arnold's poem it may suggest some immediate experience. Briefly, in lines 33–34, Arnold's speaker gives a highly general and abstract description of all the wrongs of the world; lines 35–37 do not merely complete the foregoing exposition of all our misery on this earth, but suggest a shift to an immediate experiencing of it.

Consider: "why his armies in the final line of the poem are ignorant. He could have chosen "hostile" or "warring" or some other two-syllable adjective that would have described more typically the nature and function of armies. [...] We are led to ask what it is that they don't know, to begin to realize that perhaps their not knowing is the cause of their hostilities." (*idem*, 745). In my construal, ignorance suggests a more immediate sensation, as I said, the confusion of the soldiers who don't know whether they are killing friends or foes, and perhaps are also ignorant of the reasons of the fighting (rather than *causing* the hostilities). To be sure, the two construals are compatible; but mine emphasizes the immediate experiencing of the situation.

Unlike many other critics, Freeman also devotes considerable attention to the poem's rhythmic texture. She carefully avoids the widespread practice to regard certain relationships as an iconic relationship between form and content. In agreement with this position of hers, I will further specify her argument, in the spirit of Chapter 9 above, at a level of greater delicacy. I will refer here only to one issue. I find her following observation intriguing: "As readers, we respond to the aesthetic pattern created by the rhythmic sounds of the two lines that mimic the "tremulousness" of syncopation, lines in which an anapestic rhythm occurs in two syllables occupying one metrical position" (*idem*, 740). I would sharpen this observation. Arnold does not substitute here anapestic for iambic metre, but generates a kind of deviance-in-regularity. The regular iambic alternation of weak and strong positions is preserved, and the verse instances strictly conform with the stronger version of conditions for disyllabic occupancy of metrical positions as laid down by generative metrists a century later, namely, where the syllables consist of two adjoining vowels, or where they are separated by a liquid or nasal (Halle & Keyser 1966: 209; Donald C. Freeman 1969: 197–198).[3]

> With tremulous cadence slow, and bring
> The eternal note of sadness in

I would add that there seems to be a third instance of the same principle in this stanza:

> Glimmering and vast out in the tranquil bay

"Glimmering" means "to give off a subdued unsteady reflection". Two of three syllables are assigned to one metrical position, whether the first and second, separated by a nasal ([m]), or the second and third, separated by a liquid ([r]). Thus, the same kind of deviance-in-regularity may generate the same kind of interaction between the vibrating light and metre. As I pointed out at some length in Chapter 9, this is not an *iconic relationship* between form and content, but rather *interaction* between metre and contents. Disyllabic occupancy is a fairly widespread feature of English metered verse, and poets have recourse to it irrespective of contents. Consider, for instance, the lines:

> Swept with confused alarms of struggle and flight
> Where ignorant armies clash by night

They have nothing to do with vibration or unsteady reflections. Regarding "ignorant", as we have seen, Freeman herself raises the question, why did Arnold not choose "some other *two-syllable* adjective". In fact, "ignorant" is a trisyllabic word, with its last two syllables (separated by a liquid) assigned to one metrical position. In "struggle and", a syllable with a liquid ([l]) as crest is followed by a syllable beginning with a vowel. Perhaps the principle is this: disyllabic occupancy of a metrical position is neutral with regard to contents, but may have a wide range

---

3.   I don't think that "syncopation" is the right word here. It seems to me that the term would better suit another kind of deviation from regularity, as in

> Upon the stairs; on the French coast the light

or

> Lay like the folds of a bright gridle furled

In both lines, a sequence of four alternating weak and strong positions is occupied by a sequence of two unstressed and two stressed syllables (what I have elsewhere called a "strass grade" (Tsur 2012). As to the vocal performance of such stress grades, see Tsur 2012: 137–188; 414–423.

of general dormant combination features. When a dormant feature of disyllabic occupancy (e.g. unsteadiness) encounters a similar feature in the contents, they activate each other, and the general potential of the metric figure is individuated. It is such "aesthetic patterns [of the poem] that lead us to experience its iconic semblance of felt life".

14.3   Speculative vs. empirical

As I said in the Introduction, my work is basically theoretical and speculative, but has elements of empirical interest. On the one hand, it heavily draws upon empirical work by others in non-aesthetic contexts; on the other hand, it offers some empirical work by myself. Moreover, some outstanding empiricists found my theoretical work of considerable empirical interest. The "hardest science" I have done so far is, of course, my computer analysis of recorded readings. However, in the introduction to my book *Poetic Rhythm – Structure and Performance* I insist at considerable length that the computer's output is meaningless unless interpreted within the framework of an adequate theory and verified against one's intuition. The same principle with the necessary changes will be demonstrated in the next section of this chapter.

Or take Jackson's think-aloud experiment quoted in the Introduction. This paper heavily relies on my theoretical work, and provides findings that may strongly support my theoretical expectations. At the same time, this paper sharpened my awareness that I am engaged in a very different kind of enquiry. I am more interested in the question what arguments can be given to support a certain kind of poetic intuition than to assess how many people do actually have that intuition. This, as the present example would suggest, may be, nevertheless, conducive to empirical experiments by others.

Let me give a further example from the present book. In Chapter 13 I report a seminar session in which we discussed two verse lines by the great Hebrew imagist poet Abraham Shlonsky. In the course of discussion, two diametrically opposed responses emerged. I was not interested in the question how many students embraced one or the other response, but what alternative structural descriptions can be given to the intuitions underlying those incompatible responses.

14.4   "The Sound of Meaning"

Chapters 2 and 11 amplify and further develop the conception of sound symbolism put forward in my 1992 book *What Makes Sound Patterns Expressive? – The Poetic Mode of Speech Perception* (Duke UP, the Roman Jakobson Series; first published in 1987). More recently, Michael Wiseman and Willie van Peer (2002) published a paper on the same topic, "The Sound of Meaning: An Empirical Study". I find it very rigorous, but based on a rather insufficient conception of sound symbolism. Its conclusion that "literary critics' intuitions about sound symbolism are based on a real phenomenon, i.e. the fact that some sounds are better suited to express particular emotions than others" (*idem*, 382) isn't as informative as could be. Much more is known about sound symbolism, and much more sophisticated things, some of them from empirical studies, though not necessarily with Bonferroni-connected *p*-values.

The specific finding of this article, that "nasals and back vowels seem to be preferred to express grief, while joy is better expressed by plosives and front vowels" (*idem*, 382) is well-known for long, and is only a small part of the story. Suppose Wiseman and van Peer asked their informants about nasals versus plosives whether they express tender or aggressive emotions, they would have got the answer that nasals are tender and plosives aggressive. Now, it is easy to see why nasals can express both grief and tender moods, because grief is a tender emotion. It is more difficult to see how plosives can express both joy and anger. This you can explain only by analyzing the phonetic structure of the speech sounds and the structure of the emotions. In Chapter 9 I claim that when you say, e.g. "This music is joyful [or aggressive]", you report that you have detected some structural resemblance between the music and an emotion. We may assume that in "aggressive" music low-frequency sounds will be more conspicuous than in "joyful" music, as well as low brass instruments with irregular, "rough" sounds – both in harmony with Ohala's analysis in Chapter 11. In poetry, by contrast, it is mainly the semantic element that will have to make the difference between aggressive and joyful plosives (though there may be significant rhythmic differences too, cf. Chapter 9).

As I report in Chapter 2, Iván Fónagy took six especially tender and six especially aggressive poems by French, German and Hungarian poets, and compared the relative frequency of the various speech sounds, controlling for deviation from their frequency in standard language, and came up with significant correlations, though without Bonferroni-connected *p*-values. Thus, for instance, in six especially tender and six especially aggressive poems by the Hungarian poet Sándor Petőfi

> the majority of sounds occur with the same relative frequency in both groups. All the more striking is the fact that the frequency of certain sounds show a significant difference in both groups. The phonemes /l/, /m/, and /n/ are definitely more frequent in tender-toned poems, whereas /k/, /t/, and /r/ predominate in those with aggressive tone. For some reason, precisely these sounds seem to be the most significantly correlated with aggression, either positively, or negatively.
>
> (Fónagy, 1961:195)

The voiceless stops /k/ and /t/ are significantly less frequent in tender poems by Petőfi, Verlaine, Hugo, and Rückert (Hungarian, French, and German poets). To account for Fónagy's findings I had recourse to the structural description of speech sounds in standard phonetics. Plosives are abrupt, nasals are continuous and periodic. "Periodic" means that the same sound shape is repeated indefinitely. Nasals are perceived as softer, smoother, more relaxed, because their structure is predictable. Now suppose you ask your informants to make a forced choice and attribute to the pairs of nouns "grief" and "joy", or "tenderness" and "aggressiveness" the pairs of adjectives "predictable" and "unpredictable", or "assertive" and "unassertive", or "fuzzy-ended" and "clearly-articulated", or "smooth" and "jerky" (that is, characterized by abrupt stops), you will find that grief and tender emotions are smooth, fuzzy-ended, unassertive and predictable, whereas joy and aggressive emotions are jerky, assertive, unpredictable and clearly-articulated. More generally, periodic sounds are perceived as smooth, soft, tender, whereas a-periodic, abrupt sounds are perceived as hard, aggressive, clearly-articulated. As I point out in Chapter 2, voiced stops are ambiguous: they consist of an abrupt stop plus voicing, that is periodic.

This analysis can explain one of Fónagy's most intriguing findings regarding the relative frequency of /g/ and /d/ in Victor Hugo's and Paul Verlaine's poems. /g/ occurs over one and a half times more frequently in Verlaine's tender poems than in his angry ones (1.63: 1.07), whereas we find almost the reverse proportion in Hugo's poems: 0.96% in his tender poems, and 1.35% in his angry ones. As to /d/, again, the same sound has opposite emotional tendencies for the two poets, but with reverse effects. For Verlaine it has a basically aggressive quality (10.11: 7.93), whereas for Hugo it has a basically tender quality (7.09: 5.76) – again, in almost the same reverse proportion. The reason seems to be similar to the one I have offered for the shift of perceived qualities of [b] in the murmuring and murdering contexts: "aspect-switching". If you attend to the [g] or [d] as a unitary abrupt stop consonant, it may have a strong aggressive potential; if you attend to the periodic voiced ingredient, it may contribute to a tender quality. Obviously, Hugo and Verlaine applied the same cognitive mechanism to these voiced stops, but with a reverse focus.

Or, consider the consonant [r]: it is continuous, periodic, and multiply interrupted. It is frequently used in poetry to imitate rough, frightening sounds, as in.

> Blow, winds, and crack your cheeks! rage! blow!
> You cataracts and hurricanoes, spout
> Till you have drench'd our steeples, drown'd the cocks!
> *King Lear*, III.2.

The [r], [k], [t] and [d] sounds abound in this passage, by which Lear not only addresses, but also creates the storm.[4] [r], however, frequently appears in tender poems too, in an environment of periodic consonants, such as [l], [m], and [n]. Here I will mention only the name "Lili Marleen" in which the [r] is perceived as soft and pleasant, even when pronounced in the German way. In the former context its multiply interrupted structure is perceived as its most prominent feature; in the latter, the surrounding periodic consonants foreground its periodicity.

We may agree, then, that "some sounds are better suited to express particular emotions than others" (Wiseman & van Peer 2002: 382); but this does not do justice to the complexity of the issue. Speech sounds may have a wide range of "meaning potentials" that may be realized by specific meanings of a text. Changing contexts "switch" from one potential to another. Or, in the terms of Chapter 9, phonetic features of speech sounds and sound configurations may suggest some generalized psychological atmosphere characterized as, e.g. energetic, assertive, unpredictable, outward-turning and abrupt, which the specific contents may individuate as "joy" or "anger". As I argued in the preceding section, it is important to assess how many people do actually entertain a certain kind of poetic intuition; but there is no escape from the question what arguments can be given in its support. With reference to speech sounds we must also ask in what contexts those intuitions arise.

14.5 Coding strategy and storage time

In Chapter 1 (Introduction) I quote Helen Keller, who acquired the basic skills of communication as late as at the age of six. Before that, she says, she was driven "hither and thither *at the dictates of my sensations*"; when she acquired a vocabulary, these sensations "vanished forever". I quoted George Miller on recoding information so as to save mental processing space; one way to do this is "to group the input events, apply a new name to the group, and then remember the new name rather than the original input events". I suggested that this may apply to Helen Keller's case too, where the new name, the word, replaced the rich sensations.

A sympathetic reader (professor of psychology) criticized this suggestion as follows: "in the illustration of Helen Keller you refer to Miller's (1970) work and explain how Keller's mental economy is similar to the process Miller describes. I don't think it is. In fact, Miller's point focuses on short-term memory very much

---

4. "This is no mere description of a storm, but in music and imaginative suggestion a dramatic creating of the storm itself" (Granville Barker 1993: 37).

in line with a mind-as-computer metaphor". It would appear that the "mind-as-computer metaphor" is not limited to short-term memory. In the target article of a special issue of *Pragmatics and Cognition* dealing with neuroscience [issue 18(3), 2010], on the emergence of consciousness, Christopher Frith says: "My basic assumption is that the brain is an information processing device" (p. 498).

True, Miller presents this view on coding in the context of short-term memory, but he does not say, at least, that it does not apply to long-term memory. I could not help feeling that this coding strategy is not limited to one kind of memory, and that Miller's proposal is relevant to Helen Keller's case, and both *are* illuminating of my subject. The issue at stake is whether short-term and long-term memory may use the same kind of coding. Having consulted the relevant research literature, it would appear that *some* leading researchers in the field might lend support to my proposition. Robert G. Crowder, whose work on other topics I quote throughout this book, addresses precisely this issue: "The distinction between long and short-term memory is, of course, completely neutral about coding. But, once different codes are assigned to the two memory mechanisms, we have a fundamental confounding: Which is the more important, the distinction in storage times or the distinction in codes?" (Crowder 1993: 144). Crowder suggests, by contrast, "that the proper metaphor for short-term memory [is] with the microscope: Ordinary things look strange when placed under a high-powered microscope, but they are not, in fact, different objects. They just look different because the detailed structure of an object is apparent under a microscope in a way it is not to the naked eye" (*ibid*.). The computer and the microscope metaphors are by no means mutually exclusive: they illuminate different aspects of the same phenomenon. One of them refers to the mode of handling information; the other to different conditions in which the same process appears to consciousness (or to the researcher?). Crowder's position seems to me psychologically more parsimonious, because it does not assume a change of coding strategies when information passes from short-term memory to long-term memory and back.

One conspicuous example of shifting information from long-term memory back to short-term memory would be Halle and Keyser's theoretical construct "stress maximum" in metric research. This is a lexically stressed syllable between two unstressed ones, within the same verse line and the same syntactic unit. "A gárden" contains a stress maximum, "a róck gárden" does not. According to Halle and Keyser (1971), all deviations from metric regularity are acceptable, except a stress maximum in a weak metrical position, which renders a verse line "unmetrical". The stress-maximum theory has stimulated numberless new insights in prosodic research all over the world, in spite of the fact that it merely coded all the conditions for the acceptance of stressed syllables in weak positions (which had been well known to prosodists for centuries) into one well-articulated, easily manipulable concept. This is a clear-cut case of "grouping the input events, applying a new name to the group, and then remembering the new name rather than the original input events". The term "stress maximum" and its definition are stored in long-term memory; but when the term gets into working memory, it is, as I said, easily manipulable, and retrieves, with great speed, only the relevant input events from long-term memory, thus requiring relatively little mental space. When confronted with different instances of metric deviation, it retrieves different conditions – thus involving rapid "aspect-switching". That is why it is so conducive to insights.

14.6   On interpretation

A reviewer commented on this book: "Chapter 6 relies perhaps too much on close reading, which can sometimes be disputable. For instance, readers could take issue with some interpretations, as seeing irony in '*le Regret souriant*' (smiling Repentance) and bitterness rather than something gentle". I see nothing wrong in taking issue with an interpretation. As to the comment on "*Le Regret souriant*", the ironic construal is interesting and plausible. But in the present context it seems to have a different character. The title "*Recueillement*" (Contemplation), the first line "*Sois sage, ô ma Douleur, et tiens-toi plus tranquille*" (Be wise, my Dolor, and keep yourself more quiet), the line "*Ma Douleur, donne-moi la main; viens par ici*" (My Sorrow, give me your hand and come with me) and other parts of the sonnet evoke an intimate affectionate atmosphere. And "*Regret*" appears to be opposed here to its near-synonym "*remords*" (remorses). True, the sonnet gives a twist to the values of Mediaeval and Renaissance allegory, which certainly yields irony in Cleanth Brooks's sense, structural irony, that is almost synonymous with paradox, and lacks most of the elements of an ironic attitude, which the reviewer seems to attribute to the phrase. In Spenserian allegory, "Dolor" and "Night" would certainly belong to the negative pole of the emotional scale. In the last line, by contrast, Baudelaire addresses the former as "*ma chère*" (my dear), to the latter he refers by the phrase "*la douce Nuit*" (the sweet Night). In such a context, I can't see how "*le Regret souriant*" can be construed as ironical, though in principle I don't rule out such a possibility. This, of course, does not preclude a bitter ironic construal of, e.g. "*Et nous alimentons nos **aimables remords**,/ Comme les mendiants nourrissent leur vermine*" (and we nourish our **lovable remorses**/ as baggers feed their vermin) in Baudelaire's "*Au Lecteur*" (my emphasis).

In a wider perspective, as Joseph Margolis (1962) argues in his "Logic of Interpretation", there are no right or wrong interpretations, only more or less plausible ones. And what is plausible, its opposite is plausible too. Some recent empirical researchers tend to regard such a solution as "unscientific", and look for more solid evidence. Interpretation serves to resolve discrepancies and contradictions in a work of art and render it coherent. The interpretation of a work of art is like a scientific hypothesis, says Margolis, but they differ in that in scientific hypotheses new evidence may be discovered that would settle the uncertainties. In a work of art, all information is given from the beginning, and no new evidence may come to light (though hitherto unnoticed aspects can be foregrounded). The more plausible hypothesis would be the one that accounts for more data in the text, and imputes greater unity on it, by adding less outside information. Thus, in an important sense, interpretation is constrained by what is explicitly said, as well as the discrepancies and contradictions to be resolved. Margolis speaks of coherent schemata or "myths" as such unifying patterns. Such a "myth" must be one in terms of which substantial parts of reality can be viewed.

My discussion above of the last stanza of Arnold's "Dover Beach" may conveniently illustrate this conception. An odd causal relationship is suggested in this stanza: "Ah, love, let us be true/To one another! *for* the world [...]/Hath really neither joy, nor love, nor light,/Nor certitude, nor peace, nor help for pain", etc. I could envisage several much better reasons for lovers to be true to each other. I applied to this, as a plausible hypothesis, Plato's theory of love and friendship (which certainly is a system in whose terms substantial parts of reality can be viewed) to account for this causal relationship and thus impute unity on the text: Love and friendship are an island of harmony, constancy and truthfulness in a "sea of troubles". Only when I was writing up this explanation I noticed that there was an additional detail which significantly reinforced the Platonic hypothesis. Lines 30–32 ("which *seems*/To lie before us like a land of dreams,/So various, so beautiful, so new") present appearances as opposed to the true nature of the world described in the rest of the stanza. This opposition between appearances and the truth is a central issue in Platonic philosophy and theory of love.

I have another paper on this Baudelaire sonnet, where I detect in it a pervasive emotional pattern of the Death-and-Rebirth Archetype (Tsur, online). I don't argue for a Jungian interpretation, but I point out that such a pattern would account for the sonnet's figurative language and emotional oppositions, reinforced by its syntactic and prosodic structure. If one embraces Jungian theory, it may lend additional force to this interpretation. Such a reading does not exclude other readings, incompatible with it. My construal of "*Le Regret souriant*" is highly compatible with this interpretation of the sonnet, but this does not mean that the ironic construal would not be consistent with some other plausible interpretation. In principle, we can even imagine an ironic reading of this line in the middle of a passage opposed to "*Va cueillir des remords dans la fête servile*", but then we need a plausible hypothesis compatible with our overall interpretation to justify its occurrence there.

For me, this is an essential feature of aesthetic objects in general, and poems in particular, and it cannot be settled empirically. If you submit Baudelaire's poem to subjects, even if none of them come up with the archetypal interpretation, it will not prove that this is not a plausible interpretation. If you present such an interpretation to your subjects, you may convince some or the majority of them; but then you predetermine the results of any further experiment. The easiest way out of this dilemma is to decide that interpretation is not a legitimate object for literary research. We have recently seen such approaches; but then you throw out the baby with the dirty water. Briefly, I am more interested in the question what arguments can be brought in support of a reading than whether responses elicited from a group of undergraduates (or laymen, or professors of literature) would substantiate it. According to Margolis, then, statements in interpretation are not factual, but hypothetical. In Chapter 11 I quote Morris Weitz (1962) suggesting that statements in aesthetic theory are not necessarily factual statements, but "crucial recommendations as to what to look for in art and how to look at it".

14.7   On major/minor keys

In Chapter 9 I suggested that the adjective "sad" has different meanings in the sentences "My sister is sad", and "The music is sad". In the former it refers to the mental processes of a flesh-and-blood person. In the latter it reports that the listener has detected some structural resemblance between the music and an emotion, such as low energy level, slow movement, and a withdrawn, unassertive attitude suggested by the minor key. One of my basic commitments throughout my research in general and in the present book in particular is not to take "common knowledge" for granted as evidence for the perceived effects of, e.g., those of the two musical keys. Perceived effects are regional qualities of complex structures. Impressionist criticism indulges in subjective responses to the perceived effects. Structuralist criticism focuses on the analysis of structures. Cognitive poetics, as I understand it, attempts to account for the perceived effects, by systematically relating them to the complex structures. In this case, I do not take for granted the assertive nature of one key and the withdrawn nature of the other, but try to explain what structural properties are responsible for them.

I am not so much interested to find out how many people do indeed experience the major key as more assertive than the minor key, but rather by what arguments can one account for such a prevalent perception. Accounting for the perceived qualities of the major and minor keys constitutes continuous embarrassment in music theory. In what follows I will present three would-be explanations. It would be, of course, most illuminating to contrive an experiment that might establish one of the three as more plausible than the others. The present discussion may offer alternative hypotheses for such an empirical investigation.

In a footnote in Chapter 9 I briefly refer to Norman D. Cook's attempt to account for this character of the minor key, in an ecological–evolutionary framework. In Chapter 11 I discuss at length the Morton–Ohala hypothesis regarding the apparently cross-species "frequency code", along with Ohala's experiments with the intonation contours of samples of "stripped speech", the results of which indicate that, other things being equal, lower F0 contour does make a voice sound more dominant and self-confident. Cook invokes the "frequency code" in an attempt to account for the assertive, outgoing character of the major key and the withdrawn, unassertive affective character of the minor key in music. In this context, Cook and Hayashi (2008: 311) quote Jean-Philippe Rameau, the French composer and author of an influential book on harmony, who wrote in 1722: "'The major mode is suitable for songs of mirth and rejoicing,' sometimes 'tempests and furies,' [...] as well as 'grandeur and magnificence.' The minor mode, on the other hand, is suitable for 'sweetness or tenderness, plaints, and mournful songs." This relationship between pitch phenomena in diatonic music and emotion, says Cook (2002), requires an explanation; the sound-symbolism hypothesis advocated by Ohala may provide such an explanation on an evolutionary basis.

> [I]f three pitches intoned within the psychological "now" produce two intervals of the same magnitude, unresolved harmonic "tension" is perceived. From such a state of tension, a decrease in pitch resolves toward a major mode, and an increase in pitch resolves toward a minor mode. Probably for evolutionary reasons related to animal calls, most people hear major mode harmonies as having positive affect, whereas minor mode has negative affect.

According to this view, then, the decisive factor in determining the emotive character of the major and the minor scales is not a straightforward lower or higher sound register as one might expect from what we seem to know about animal calls (both major and minor scales may include low or high notes), but by the direction of resolving harmonic tension: whether it involves the upward or downward movement of a note. What this may mean I try to explain online, with sound illustrations, at http://www.tau.ac.il/~tsurxx/CreakyFolder/Creaky7.html. If it involves a downward step, it sounds more dominant, more self-confident; if an upward step, it sounds more withdrawn, softer, more appeasing, less assertive, in harmony with Ohala's experiment. It should be noted, however, that mostly we do not hear an augmented or diminished chord which is then resolved in one or the other direction, but the "resolved" sequences and chords. We hear the emotive difference even where no augmented or diminished chords precede them.

I am quite ambivalent as to relying on the frequency code for such an explanation. I have very strong intuitions about this opposition. Even as a child, when I thrummed a major and a minor scale on the piano, I heard the minor "plaintive" as opposed to the major. Every now and then I am trying to find out whether my intuitions concern the direction of the resolving step in the chord (as Cook suggests), or the intervals between the notes. My latest insights tilt the pendulum in the latter direction.

Suppose we propose a rather wild hypothesis (that is, for which we don't know how to produce evidence), that the major key has a stronger Gestalt than the minor key. And then quote Leonard B. Meyer, who accounts for the association of weak and strong Gestalts with emotional and intellectual qualities respectively, as follows. "Because good shape is intelligible in this sense, it creates a psychological atmosphere of certainty, security, and patent purpose, in which the listener feels a sense of control and power as well as a sense of specific tendency and definite direction" (Meyer 1956: 160). Poor shapes generate an opposite atmosphere. We still don't know how to argue that the major key has a better Gestalt than the minor key. But, intuitively, the major key *is* characterized by "a psychological atmosphere of certainty, security, and patent purpose, in which the listener feels a sense of control and power"; the minor key by an opposite psychological atmosphere.

So, what arguments can we give to support the claim that the structure of one of the two keys is more "predictable", more "intelligible" than the other? One obvious criterion is the number, size, and relative placement of structural changes.[5] Under the Law of Good Continuation, sequences of whole intervals would be regarded

---

5.   It is the number of structural features of a figure that determines whether its Gestalt is stronger or weaker. Consider the following series of geometrical figures:

Each later design has a weaker Gestalt than the preceding one. Figure *a* has the strongest Gestalt of the four: it has only one structural feature, the radius (that is, each point on its circumference is at an equal distance from the center point). Figure *b* has two structural features: it has four sides of equal length, and four equal angles. Figure *c* has three structural features: two pairs of sides of equal length each, and four equal angles. Figure *d* has four structural features: two pairs of sides of equal length each, and two pairs of equal angles each; and so forth. Note that in Figures b, c, and d, each pair of opposite sides are parallel, that is, each point on them is of equal distance from its opposite, unlike the trapezoid, that has only two sides parallel.

as "Good Continuation", and the single half intervals as "deviations".[6] Both keys
have the same number of "whole" and "half" intervals (5+2), but differently distributed. When I was a schoolboy, I learnt that the formula of the major key is
"two wholes and one half; three wholes and one half", whereas that of the minor
key is "one whole and one half; two wholes and one half; two wholes". Thus, the
sequence of whole intervals in the major key is divided by the semitone intervals
into two parts; in the minor key into three parts. Indeed, even as a child, I used to
perceive the sound sequence in a minor scale as if it were "mollified" (in both the
musical and affective sense) precisely on the second of two adjacent white keys of
the keyboard (that is, on the third and sixth note). In the "natural minor scale" it
is precisely the third and sixth note (that is, the ones after the semitone intervals)
that sound relatively more plaintive than the rest; and the ensuing (whole-tone)
intervals sound relatively less plaintive, displaying a psychological atmosphere of
relative certainty. Now listen online to the "harmonic minor scale". To my intuition at least, its seventh note sounds exceptionally plaintive, more than the third
and sixth notes that follow semitone intervals. A look at the accompanying table
(online) shows that it is exceptionally deviant: having raised the seventh note by
a semitone, an interval of three semitones has been created. In this case, then,
a "plaintive", unassertive quality is generated after a "deviant" interval, whether
smaller or greater than a whole interval. In the "melodic minor scale", by contrast,
regularity is enhanced by a sequence of four full-tone intervals, and the plaintive
quality at that point disappears too.

What is more, the two semitones occur in the major key at the end of the
sequence and at a point that divides the sequence into what is nearest to symmetrical, equal parts. I said "nearest", because a sequence of seven intervals cannot
be divided into two equal parts (it must be either 3 + 4, or 4 + 3). Where there are
two entities of equal importance but unequal length, the well-ordered structure is
that the longest segment comes last. There are good cognitive reasons for this. This
is, then, the more natural, "unmarked", order of things. Thus, the first semitone
divides the whole sequence into what is the most natural quasi-symmetrical division, whereas the second semitone ends the sequence. (This part of my argument
replicates, with the necessary changes, my argument concerning the placement of
caesura in the iambic pentameter).

---

6. The reader may discern here an apparent inconsistency. Earlier I associated the predictability of periodic speech sounds with certain withdrawn emotional qualities; here I associate
predictability with the actively organizing mind. But there is a difference. In [m], [n] or [l],
the same wave shape is repeated *indefinitely*, without differentiation; in strong shapes predictability occurs *in spite of* differentiation, and the major scale also displays a self-generated end:
the intruding leading note is followed by the tonic, restoring stability.

Furthermore, deviation in the middle of a sequence enhances symmetry and balance; near the end it upsets balance and generates a sense of incompleteness. The nearer to the end, the stronger is the sense of incompleteness, the stronger the requiredness of the missing part, and the greater the satisfaction when the missing part is supplied (cf. Chapter 9). Thus, the last semitone interval in a major scale both intrudes upon the sequence, and exerts a greater demand for the last note than a full-tone interval would. As a result, the last note gives an exceptionally strong sense of reassurance. That is why the seventh note in the major key is called the "leading note". Significantly, the two semitones are followed in the major key by the fourth and eighth notes, clearly articulating the middle and the end of the sequence.

Traditional musicians and theorists have long recognized this effect of the last semitone interval; this led to the raising of the seventh note by a semitone in the "harmonic" minor scale, and of the sixth and seventh note in the "melodic" minor. But, in the former case, the effect of requiredness and satisfaction has been achieved by enhancing the deviant structure of the scale: by increasing the number of semitones, and by generating a three-semitone interval.

I can already see one vulnerable point in this argument. When we listen to a symphony or a piano concerto, or even a single chord, we don't hear the sequence of the whole scale, note after note, but a quite different combination of intervals constrained, not determined, by the intervals available in the key. The question is how those combinations are directly perceived as something governed by the dynamics outlined above. Perhaps the key is in the notion of "tonality". "Tonality means simply that quality in music which presents one particular tone as the principal one – called the tonic – while all the other tones are dependent on it" (Bernstein 2004: 195). The tonic is the first and eighth note of the scale. The scale is not an arbitrary sequence of notes, but a system determined by certain physical properties of the sounds; and, at the same time, determines the character of its parts. An octave above C, for instance, would be C'. The frequency of the higher C' will be exactly twice that of the lower C. The third and fifth chord of a scale are not arbitrary either: they are determined by the overtone structure of the tonic. But the major and the minor keys bestow different characters on their respective chords.

I have confronted Norman Cook's evolutionary explanation and my own Gestaltist counterproposal of the contrasting emotive characters of the major and minor scales. Just before sending this book to the printer I ran on the net into a discussion by Canadian musicologist Robert Fink that explains in purely physical terms the typical perceptual qualities regularly attributed to the major and minor scales in music. I will supplement his discussion with observations from Parncutt's (2001) "Critical Comparison of Acoustical and Perceptual Theories of the Origin of Musical Scales". Fink starts with spelling out at great length a conception that goes back to Helnholtz (1863), and which I briefly quoted from Leonard Bernstein in Chapter 2 (I have also alluded to it in the preceding paragraph). It is both evolutional and compatible with Gestalt theory, but in a different way. At any rate, it squares exceptionally well with the central thesis of this book in three respects.

First, as we have seen in Chapter 2, overtones are normally grown together in a solid note perceived as a thing out there; when artificially released from the fundamental, they may reverberate as thing-free qualities. When, however, isolated one by one from the complex fundamental, they turn into things out there. In Chapter 5 I suggest an analogy of this double nature of overtones with the thing-free qualities related to the ABSTRACT of the CONCRETE construction in poetic language, where attributes isolated from the concrete objects may become thing-free qualities or things in their own right.

Fundamental frequencies (pitches, melodies) are perceived as "things out there"; overtones generate their felt qualities. Overtones are higher tones produced *simultaneously* with the fundamental, with which they are "grown together" into a complex, unitary musical note. If, however, we isolate one overtone from the complex and play it alone, it becomes the fundamental. Fink points out that this is, precisely, how major chords and major scales are generated from the overtone structure of the tonic. "The most audible overtones of any one note *add up to its major chord*, when played out loud rather than as overtones: Tonic, Fifth & Third". Likewise, "if you write out the overtones of these three notes and string out the three most audible ones of each within the span of an octave, *you will get the major scale*". Thus, the major chords and scale have solid physical basis, and are generated through what in terms of the present work may be described as separating precategorial features from compact notes and turning them into notes in their own right.

Secondly, Fink distinguishes between simple and complex frequency ratios between overtones. "Historically, the ear has preferred simple ratios as harmonious, and complex ratios have been avoided or considered noisy or dissonant (to be used only as an artistic contrast to harmoniousness [...]). For example, two notes on the piano right next to each other have a complex ratio". The most audible overtones of a tonic or keynote, by contrast, "all have simple ratios, like 2:1 (octave), or 3:2 (fifth note of scale), and the 4th note of the scale, whose first different overtone is the given tonic, has a ratio of 4:3. In fact these three notes are present in *virtually every musical scale known on earth*".[7]

---

7. Parncutt (2001) agrees regarding these ratios, but observes: "Western musical intervals are perceived *linearly* and *categorically*, and intervals are defined by the center and boundaries of the category – not by ratios such as 5:4 or 81:64".

Where simple ratios are concerned, the notes reinforce each others' overtones, yielding relatively well-organized, compact entities. In complex ratios, by contrast, coincidence of overtones is less perfect, resulting in less compact, more diffuse textures.

Why, then, is the minor key "sad" – or more accurately – why it evokes a richer or wider range of emotions than the "bright" major key? I cannot follow here Fink's step-by-step demonstration. But the bottom line is this: "The major 3rd is less sad (or the minor 3rd is more sad) simply because the major 3rd is more harmonious than the minor third, which has a more complex ratio of vibrations. In other words (plain English), the minor is more on the edge of discord than is the major". In this, Parncutt concurs: "Major triads are more prevalent than minor, because their roots (and hence their tonal function) are clearer" (*ibid*). In terms of the present book, this affects not only their relative prevalence, but also their Gestalt qualities.

Thirdly, put differently, what is perceived as harmonious or dissonant is not determined by arbitrary cultural traditions, but by certain measurable features of the sound stimulus. The key-term is, then, "clearer tonal function". Consequently, in harmony with the Gestaltist conception expounded here, the major scale (as well as strong Gestalts) creates a psychological atmosphere of certainty, security, and patent purpose, in which the listener feels a sense of control and power as well as a sense of specific tendency and definite direction, whereas the minor scale (as well as weak Gestalts) displays a richer or wider range of emotions, because the overtone structure of the major scale and chord has a better organization than that of the minor scale. Briefly, we are up against the relative structuring of precategorial information.

I firmly believe that the major and minor scales and related issues are not arbitrary inventions of cultural history but, rather, that a wide variety of musical traditions evolved within certain cognitive and physical constraints. Fink adopts a similar but more radical position. At any rate, he elaborates on the physical constraints within which the cultural processes take place. Again, I cannot reproduce here the wide range of historical, developmental and evolutional evidence he offers. But I wish to mention one piece of intriguing EVIDENCE OF the NATURAL FOUNDATION TO DIATONIC SCALE he offers: the NEANDERTHAL FLUTE (discovered in 1995), the Oldest known Musical Instrument, whose "4 Notes Match 4 of the Do, Re, Mi [fa] Scale".[8]

(48)

---

8.   For the debate "Who made the Neanderthal Flute? Humans or carnivores?" see http://www.greenwych.ca/divje-b.htm

Farncutt (2001) seems to allude to the Neanderthal Flute when saying: "*Categorical pitch perception*. Music separates from speech as the pitch continuum is divided, in production

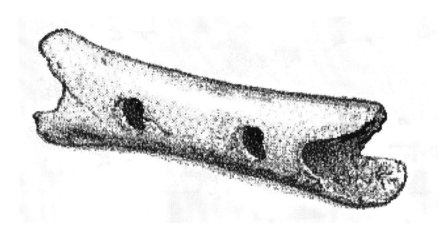

Figure 1. The Neanderthal bone flute (age: between 40,000 and 45,000 radiocarbon years). http://www.greenwych.ca/fl-compl.htm

Finally, I would venture cautiously to integrate my Gestaltist view with Fink's and Parncutt's physical explanation. As Fink observes, notes separated by one semitone have a mildly dissonant effect. The majority of intervals in both scales are of two semitones. Thus, the semitone intervals both weaken the consonance of the sequence and interfere with its Good Continuation. Now the crucial question is, where in the sequence this combination of dissonance and interference occurs. If it occurs between the seventh and eighth notes (that is, at the "leading note"), the disturbance is the greatest. But then the tonic follows suit, achieving closure and stability. The greater the disturbance, the more gratifying are the closure and balance achieved. Musicians have long discovered that, far from being an unsatisfying feature, the final semitone interval is perceived as a musical asset. As a matter of fact, I proposed the bottom line of such an integration long before I ran into Fink's and Parncutt's work, which have filled the *lacunae* in my understanding. In the paragraph preceding my discussion of their explanation I write: The scale is

---

(singing) and perception, into musically meaningful categories or *scale steps*. The archeological record (bone pipes) suggests that this occurred more than 40,000 years ago". Incidentally, "categorical perception" was long thought to be an exclusive feature of speech perception.

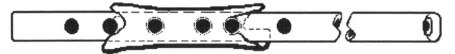

Listen online to music played on a replica of the Neanderthal Bone Flute, by Beethoven, Verdi, Ravel etc. http://www.youtube.com/watch?v=sHy9FOblt7Y

not an arbitrary sequence of notes, but a system determined by certain physical properties of the sounds; and, at the same time, it determines the character of its parts.

14.8   The split brain and poetic qualities

"Split-brain" is a term to describe the result when the *corpus callosum* connecting the two hemispheres of the brain is severed to some degree. The surgical operation to produce this condition is usually used as a last resort to treat otherwise intractable epilepsy.

Michael Gazzaniga and other neuropsychologists found that split-brain patients were an inexhaustible source of information about how the human brain works. Consider the following experiment:

> We showed a split-brain patient two pictures: A chicken claw was shown to his right visual field, so the left hemisphere only saw the claw picture, and a snow scene was shown to the left visual field, so the right hemisphere only saw that. He was then asked to choose a picture from an array of pictures placed in full view in front of him, which both hemispheres could see. The left hand pointed to a shovel (which was the most appropriate answer for the snow scene) and the right hand pointed to a chicken (the most appropriate answer for the chicken claw). Then we asked why he chose those items. His left-hemisphere speech center replied, "Oh, that's simple. The chicken claw goes with the chicken," easily explaining what it knew. [...]. Then, looking down at his left hand pointing to the shovel, without missing a beat, he said, "And you need a shovel to clean out the chicken shed." Immediately, the left brain, observing the left hand's response without the knowledge of why it had picked that item, put it into a context that would explain it. It interpreted the response in a context consistent with what it knew, and all it knew was: chicken claw. It knew nothing about the snow scene, but it had to explain the shovel in his left hand. [...] It confabulated, taking cues from what it knew and putting them together in an answer that made sense. We called this left-hemisphere process *the interpreter*.   (Gazzaniga, 2011: 82–83)

All this is fascinating, and the "Interpreter" may illuminate a variety of literary processes. The most obvious one is, of course, interpretation. "It is the left hemisphere that engages in the human tendency to find order in chaos, that tries to fit everything into a story and put it into a context" (85). A literary text is, typically, characterized by greater chaos than non-literary texts; it involves more and greater gaps and/or discrepancies. Consequently, the Interpreter's task is more strenuous. But this would be mere restating in brain language what we already know from literary theory and thus liable to be criticized as "Reductionism", of which I expressed disapproval in the first section.

This process can be fine-tuned and rendered more informative by further observations:

> If after observing a green ball on a screen move toward a red ball, stop when it contacts it, and then the red ball immediately moves away, most people report that the green ball caused the red ball to move. This is perceptual causality: It is the direct perception, in this case by observation, that some action occurred as a result of physical contact. If, however, a time gap takes place between when the balls contact each other and when the red ball moves off, or if the balls don't actually touch and the red ball moves off, most report that there is no causal relationship. It is the right hemisphere that can see this difference. The left hemisphere is unaffected by the time or space gap when it reported causality and reports that the green ball caused the red one to move in all three cases. (*idem*, 99)

Furthermore, "the right parietal lobe has a system that [Ramachandran] calls an anomaly detector, which squawks when the discrepancies get too large. The literal right brain chimes in" (p. 98).

Now suppose you are reading a literary text, that is, one that involves more and greater gaps and discrepancies than a non-literary text. If you let the left hemisphere have its way, which is the normal course of things, it will tend to ignore those gaps and discrepancies, and read the text as continuous, uninterrupted prose, adding the minimum information needed to render the text coherent. If, however, the right hemisphere's activity is boosted in some way, several things will happen. The gaps and incompatibilities will more readily be noticed; the left-hemisphere Interpreter will have to work harder to mobilize information to fill in the gaps and settle incompatibilities; the right hemisphere will keep that additional information more fluid, more diffuse, more emotion-like.

Fascinating as such an insight may be, it is not exempt from the charge of stating what is already known from literary theory. Much of the foregoing process too has been realized by literary theory without the help of brain research. As we have seen in the section on interpretation, analytic philosophers and structuralist critics have pointed out that literary texts are riddled with gaps and inconsistencies, and that the mind, searching for coherence, fills out those gaps (Perry & Sternberg 1968), or confabulates a "story" (a "myth") imputing unity. In the foregoing experiment, the "story" is taken from real life, constrained only by the co-presence of a chicken claw and a spade, whereas in aesthetic interpretations additional constraints must be observed (Margolis 1962). Phenomenologist critics went one step further, and pointed out that areas of indeterminacy compel the reader to play an active role in perceiving a text's meaning; this is what generates a text's arousing potential (Iser 1989). Cognitive Poetics goes still one step further. While Iser focuses on "meanings and judgments", Cognitive Poetics is interested in the *perceived qualities* of those meanings. While Iser speaks of more than one possible meanings, according to Cognitive Poetics they may blur or sharpen each other into emotional or witty qualities. It assumes that in certain circumstances those meanings can be kept in a more fluid, diffuse, emotion-like state. In Chapters 5–6 we saw some of those stylistic circumstances. As we have seen in Chapter 5 and the first section of this chapter, it even has some assumptions as to how the space-perception mechanism (located in the right hemisphere) may accomplish this. In this respect, the present discussion gave us additional knowledge about the neural correlates of this process.

To foreground the merits of such an approach, I propose to compare the fore-going application of Gazzaniga's findings with Ramachandran and Hubbard's work reported in Chapter 12. These researchers (2001: 28) hypothesized that if there is cross-wiring between adjoining brain regions, "between primary gustatory cortex and adjoining hand and face regions of primary somatosensory cortex, the result might be a person who 'tastes shapes'". This is a "what if" suggestion: the authors do not claim that they have actually encountered such cross-wiring in any person, nor point out any literary instance which could be accounted for by such a hypothesis. They offer it as a hypothetical instance of a more general hypothesis, that synaesthesia may result from cross-wiring between two or more adjacent brain regions. I offered a taylor-made example from Keats, a verse line that may *illustrate* this hypothesis ("The same bright face I tasted in my dream"); but the hypothesis *cannot illuminate* the stylistic problems related to this metaphor. As to Cytowic's (2003) book *The Man Who Tasted Shapes*, the hypothesis turned out to be relevant only to the title, not the case reported.

The findings quoted from Gazzaniga, by contrast, do not refer to some local (hypothetical) cross-wiring, but attacks the very essence of consciousness. It proposes a richly-documented answer to the mystery: "Even though we know that the organization of the brain is made up of a gazillion decision centers, that neural activities going on at one level of organization are inexplicable at another level, and that as with the Internet, there seems to be no boss, the puzzle for humans remains. The lingering conviction that we humans have a 'self' making all the decisions about our actions is not dampened. It is a powerful and overwhelming illusion that is almost impossible to shake" (Gazzaniga 2011: 75). This is due to the Interpreter's activity integrating the output of gazillions of brain circuits into one coherent "story". That is why we feel *unified*.

What is more, this complex, well-documented interaction between the left and right hemisphere brain circuits seems thoroughly to correspond to – nay, underlie – the process of literary interpretation as expounded by structuralist critics and analytic philosophers without relying on brain research. Here we have a fairly detailed and comprehensive neurological model of brain functioning significantly corresponding to a detailed comprehensive structuralist-analytic model of aesthetic interpretation. Beyond that, Cognitive Poetics observed an association of certain emotional qualities in poetry with verbal structures suggesting orientation and space perception; this can be accounted for only by referring to the structure and functioning of the brain. At this point, at least, the charge of "Reductionism" does not apply.

So, what is the use of applying the aforesaid brain mechanisms to what analytic philosophers and structuralist critics have realized long before? Is it not mere restating in brain language what we have already said in aesthetics-language? I suggest that Gazzaniga's discussion has the merit of *defamiliarizing*, showing the automatic working of the brain in slow motion, thus yielding insight into the claim that the realization of an aesthetic object is governed by a special use of the most commonplace, everyday activities of the human brain, a claim that many people find difficult to accept.

In Chapter 13 I quote Walter Weimer claiming that Popper's "logic of scientific discovery" is, in fact, the logic of the completed scientific report. The actual process of the discovery follows a completely different kind of logic. A theoretically expounded methodology is judged by its results: it need not reflect the workings of the brain or the cognitive system; but sometimes it does. An analogy with computer science may illuminate the issue. Computers can be programmed to play chess, taking most efficient advantage of the computer's specific capabilities, irrespective of how the human mind works. An artificial intelligence program, by contrast, would imitate the way flesh-and-blood chess players make decisions, even if this would not secure the best results in a game. The comprehensive correspondence proffered above may indicate that the structuralist-analytic theoretical model of interpretation may have substantial psychological reality in the reader's actual experience.

We have encountered another, more elusive phenomenon in the perceptual domain, which could perhaps be better understood if it could be shown that Gazzaniga's notion of "hijacking the Interpreter" is relevant to it. In Chapter 9 I raise the question: "How do systems of music-sounds and verbal signs assume perceptual qualities endemic to other systems, such as human emotions or animal calls?" Briefly, they display some structural resemblance. Here the "lower sciences" can become useful by analyzing the structures of speech sounds, emotions and animal calls that display those resemblances. The source phenomena have an indefinite number of features, of which only a relatively small number can be found in the target systems. The cues available in the target system constrain the nature of the perceptual qualities acquired. The cuckoo's call, for instance, is imitated in language and in music by utilizing different subsets of features. The best one can do, then, is to choose the nearest options available in the target system (e.g. the abrupt onset of the cuckoo's call is indicated in Western languages by the voiceless plosive [k]; in Chinese: "pu-ku").

In poetic rhythm, as we have seen in Chapter 9, similar deviations from metric regularity are perceived in different contexts as having a dignified character or indicating dullness. I argue that certain features of those deviations generate a vague emotional atmosphere of, e.g. slowness, that is individuated by the context as dignified or dull quality. I assume that the brain is somehow quick to seize upon a small number of relevant features which it construes as the said feelings. This process would be better understood if it could be accounted for by invoking the "hijacking" of the Interpreter. In fact, we have here two aspects of one string of words: meaning, and a perceptual quality generated by the interplay of semantic, syntactic and sound information. How does the Interpreter handle such perceptual qualities?

Gazzaniga's discussion of how the sensory inputs from the visual and auditory systems affect our judgment may give us, again, a clue. "I jumped out of the way of many a rattlesnake, but that is not all. I also jumped out of the way of grass that rustled in the wind. I jumped, that is, before I was consciously aware that it was the wind that rustled the grass, rather than a rattler" (*idem*, 76).

> If you were to have asked me why I had jumped, I would have replied that I thought I'd seen a snake. That answer certainly makes sense, but the truth is I jumped before I was conscious of the snake: I had seen it, but I didn't know I had seen it. My explanation is from post hoc information I have in my conscious system: The facts are that I jumped and that I saw a snake. The reality, however, is that I jumped way before (in the world of milliseconds) I was conscious of the snake. (*idem*, 77)

Gazzaniga discusses at some length how the Interpreter can be "hijacked" (*idem*, 94–98) in the psychological laboratory by feeding false sensory information into it, forcing persons to respond to the false cues, in spite of what they *know* is the case. In the natural example of the grass rustling in the wind, the mind seizes upon the sensory input generating an emotional response *before* an appraisal of the true situation. I speculate that a similar mechanism underlies the verbal or musical imitations of emotions and animal calls. In speech perception, for instance, the mind seizes upon a subset of the perceptual features of [k], followed by a situation appraisal whether it refers to the abrupt onset of the cuckoo's call, or the metallic click of the clock, eliminating the irrelevant features. Similarly, it seizes upon the perceptual quality "slowness" displayed by a string of stressed syllables in an iambic verse line; this is followed by an appraisal whether this perceptual quality is individuated as "dignity" or "dullness", according to the con-tents. In all these instances, a partial identity between the perceptual features of the "signifier" and the "signified" (falsely) evokes an emotional or perceptual response appropriate to the signified. Since in consciousness this chronological order is scrambled, the sensory information and the situation appraisal are expe-rienced as simultaneous.

All this, however, still does not indicate how much information is required to "fool the Interpreter" in the case of, e.g., verbal structures. Nor does it explain (from the neurological point of view) the crucial *difference* between perceiving the rustling of the grass in the wind as a snake, and perceiving the slowness sug-gested by a string of stressed syllables in an iambic line as "dignified". Cognitive poetics has a non-neurological answer to that: in the response to poetry, adapta-tion devices are turned to an aesthetic end; that is, attention is shifted from the practical implications of the situation to its perceived quality as an end in itself. When you perceive a partial identity between the grass rustling in the wind and a snake moving around, you treat the perceived quality as a cue for the action to be taken; when you perceive a partial identity between a string of stressed syllables and dignified behaviour, you don't treat the perceptual quality as a cue for any-thing but merely focus your attention on it. (Don Quixote destroyed the puppet show to rescue the heroine: the play aroused his noble emotions, which in turn instigated him to act. A more mature spectator would intently attend to the emo-tional quality itself, and do nothing).

14.9   To conclude

Some of the foregoing sections converge in this last one. The first section dis-cusses the limitations and advantages of applying brain science in literary criti-cism. The section on aesthetic interpretation elaborates on procedures that correspond to the logic governing the brain mechanisms that generate our sense of having a unified, conscious self. "The Sound of Meaning" explores the perceptual qualities of speech sounds, foregrounding a process for which we have tried to account here by Gazzaniga's notion of "hijacking the Interpreter". The "Dover Beach" section explores the logic of interpretation, as well as the structural resemblance of nature descriptions and rhythmic configurations to emotions and perceptual phenomena. Finally, "On Major/Minor Keys" explores three hypotheses regarding the structural resemblance of these keys to emo-tional qualities. The present section, in turn, explores the brain mechanisms that seem to process interpretation and structural resemblances in real life and aesthetic objects.

Finally, ordinary consciousness, one of human beings' greatest achievements, organizes a pandemonium of information into manageable, relatively stable categories. This it does at the expense of losing direct contact with reality. What poetry does, then, is to make precategorial information available to awareness and thus it achieves its unique effects. Paraphrasing the Russian Formalists, Cognitive Poetics assumes that the response to poetry is organized violence against cognitive processes. This book has explored verbal devices by which poetic language delays or disrupts categorization in order to make precategorial information – semantic and phonetic – available for aesthetic purposes.

References

Akita, K. 2011. Toward a phonosemantic definition of iconic words. In *Semblance and Signification* [Iconicity in Language and Literature 10], P. Michelucci, O. Fischer & C. Ljungberg (eds), 3–18. Amsterdam: John Benjamins.

Alcock, T. 1963. *The Rorschach in Practice*. London: Tavistock Publications.

Alterman, N. 1953. *The Stars Outside: Poems*. Tel Aviv: Makhbarot Lesifrut.

Arnheim, R. l967. *Art and Visual Perception*. London: Faber.

Austin, J.H. 2000. Consciousness evolves when self dissolves. In *Cognitive Models and Spiritual Maps*, J. Andresen & R.K.C. Forman (eds), 209–230. Thorverton: Imprint Academic.

Baudelaire, C. 1972. Correspondances. In *Les Fleurs du Mal*, 38. Paris: Gallimard.

Beardsley, M.C. 1958 *Aesthetics: Problems in the Philosophy of Criticism*. New York NY: Harcourt, Brace & World.

Bernstein, L. 2004. *The Joy of Music*. Pompton Plain NJ: Amadeus Press.

Bierwisch, M. 1970. Poetics and linguistics. In *Linguistics and Literary Style*, D.C. Freeman (ed), 97–115. New York NY: Holt, Rinehart & Winston.

Bierwisch, M. 1970. Semantics. In *New Horizons in Linguistics*, J. Lyons (ed). Harmondsworth: Pelican.

Bodkin, M. 1963 [1934[1]]. *Archetypal Patterns in Poetry*. London: OUP.

Brady, S. Shankweiler, D. & Mann, V. 1983. Speech perception and memory coding in relation to reading ability. *Journal of Experimental Child Psychology* 35: 345–367.

Bregman, A. 1996. Audio demonstrations of auditory scene analysis (Stream segregation in a cycle of six tones). ⟨http://webpages.mcgill.ca/staff/Group2/abregm1/web/downloadstoc.htm#01⟩

Brooke-Rose, C. 1958. *A Grammar of Metaphor*. London: Secker & Warburg.

Brooks, C. 1968. *The Well-Wrought Urn*. London: Methuen.

Brooks P.C. 2007. Presence poetry and the collaborative right hemisphere. *Journal of Consciousness Studies* 14(3): 36–53.

Brown, R. 1968. *Words and Things*. New York NY: The Free Press.

Brown, R. 1970. The 'tip of the tongue' phenomenon. In *Psycholinguistics: Selected Papers*, 274–303. New York NY: The Free Press.

Bruner, J.S. 1973. *Beyond the Information Given – Studies in the Psychology of Knowing*. New York NY: W.W. Norton.

Bullough, E. 1913. Psychical distance as a factor in art and as an aesthetic principle. *British Journal of Psychology* 5(2): 87–118.

Burke, K. 1957. *The Philosophy of Literary Form*. New York NY: Vintage.

Burke, K. 1962. *A Grammar of Motives* and *A Rhetoric of Motives* (in one volume). Cleveland NY: Meridian Books.

Coleridge, S.T. 1951. Biographia literaria. In *Selected Poetry and Prose*, D.A. Stauffer (ed), 109–428. New York NY: The Modern Library.

Cook, N.D. 2002. *Tone of Voice and Mind. The Connections between Intonation, Emotion, Cognition and Consciousness* [Advances in Consciousness Research 47]. Amsterdam: John Benjamins.

Cook, N.D. & Fujisawa, T.X. 2006. The psychophysics of harmony perception: Harmony is a three-tone phenomenon. *Empirical Musicology Review* 1(2): 1–21.

Cook, N.D. & Hayashi, T. 2008. The psychoacoustics of harmony perception. *American Scientist* 96: 311–319.

Cooper, G.W. & Meyer, L.B. 1960. *The Rhythmic Structure of Music.* Chicago IL: Chicago University Press.

Crowder, R.G. & Wagner, R.K. 1992. *The Psychology of Reading.* New York NY: OUP.

Crowder, R.G. 1982a. A common basis for auditory sensory storage in perception and immediate memory. *Perception & Psychophysics* 31: 477–483.

Crowder, R.G. 1982b. Disinhibition of masking in auditory sensory memory. *Memory & Cognition* 10: 424–433.

Crowder, R.G. 1983. The purity of auditory memory. *Phil. Trans. R. Soc. Lond. B* 302: 251–265.

Crowder, R.G. 1993. Short-term memory: Where do we stand? *Memory & Cognition* 21: 142–145.

Culler, J. 1975. *Structuralist Poetics.* London: Routledge & Kegan Paul.

Cytowic, R.E. 2003. *The Man Who Tasted Shapes.* Cambridge MA: The MIT Press.

D'Andrade, R.G. 1980. The cultural part of cognition. Address given to the 2nd Annual Cognitive Science Conference, New Haven CT.

Dahl, H. 1965. Observations on a 'natural experiment': Helen Keller. *JAPA* 13: 533–550.

Darwin, C.J. & Donovan, A. 1979. Perceptual studies of speech: Isochrony and intonation. Paper presented at the Conference on Language Generation and Understanding, Bonas (Gers).

Delattre, P. Liberman, A.M., Cooper, F.S. & Gerstman, L. 1952. An experimental study of the acoustic determinants of vowel color. *Word* 8: 195–210.

Diffloth, G. 1994. i: *big*, a: *small.* In *Sound Symbolism*, L. Hinton, J. Nichols & J.J. Ohala (eds), 107–114. Cambridge: CUP.

Dombi, E. 1974. Synaesthesia and poetry. *Poetics* 11: 23–44.

Donovan, A. & Darwin, C.J. 1979. The perceived rhythm of speech. Paper presented at the IXth International Congress of Phonetic Sciences, Copenhagen.

Duffy, E. 1968[1941[1]]. An explanation of emotional phenomena without the use of the concept emotion. In *The Nature of Emotion*, M.B. Arnold (ed), 129–140. Harmondsworth: Penguin.

Ehrenzweig, A. 1965. *The Psychoanalysis of Artistic Vision and Hearing.* New York NY: Braziller.

Ehrenzweig, A. 1969. A new psychoanalytical approach to aesthetics. In *Psychology and the Visual Arts*, J. Hogg (ed), 109–128. Harmondsworth: Penguin.

Ehrenzweig, A. 1970. *The Hidden Order of Art.* London: Paladin.

Empson, W. 1955. *7 Types of Ambiguity.* New York NY: Meridian Books.

Escher, M.C. 1992. The regular division of the plain. In *M.C. Escher – His Life and Complete Graphic Work*, J.L. Locher (ed), 155–172. New York NY: Harry N. Abrams.

Fink, R. 2004. The natural forces bringing the 'do, re, mi, scale' into existence in the Origin of Music. ⟨http://www.greenwych.ca/natbasis.htm⟩

Fodor, J.A. & Bever, T.G. 1965. The psychological reality of linguistic segments. *Journal of Verbal Learning and Verbal Behaviour* 4: 414–420.

Fodor, J.A. 1979. *The Language of Thought.* Cambridge MA: Harvard University Press.

Fogle, R.H. 1964. Synaesthetic imagery in Keats. In *Keats*, W.J. Bate (ed.), 41–50. Englewood Cliffs NJ: Prentice-Hall.

Fónagy, I. 1961. Communication in poetry. *Word* 17: 194–218.

Fónagy, I. 1979. *La métaphore en phonétique.* Ottava: Didier.

Fowler, R. 1974. *Understanding Language.* London: Routledge and Kegan Paul.

Freeman, D.C. 1969. Metrical position constituency and generative metrics. *Language and Style* 2: 195–206.

Freeman, M.H. 2000. Poetry and the scope of metaphor: Toward a cognitive theory of literature. In *Metaphor & Metonymy at the Crossroads*, A. Barcelona (ed.). Berlin: Mouton de Gruyter.

Freeman, M.H. 2011. The aesthetics of human experience: Minding, metaphor, and icon in poetic expression. *Poetics Today* 32(4): 717–751.

Frenkel-Brunswik, E. 1968[1948[1]]. Intolerance of ambiguity as an emotional and perceptual variable. In *Perception and Personality*, J.S. Bruner & D. Kretch (eds), New York NY: Greenwood Press.

Freud, S. 1952. *Psychopathology of Everyday Life*. New York NY: Mentor.

Frith, C. 2010. What is consciousness for? *Pragmatics & Cognition* 18(3): 497–551.

Fromkin, V.A. 1973. Slips of the tongue. *Scientific American* 229(6): 110–17.

Garrett, M.F., Bever, T.G. & Fodor, J.A. 1966. The active use of grammar in speech perception. *Perception and Psychophysics* 1: 30–32.

Gazzaniga, M.S. 2011. *Who's in Charge? Free Will and the Science of the Brain*. New York NY: Ecco, HarperCollins (Kindle ebook edn).

Genette, G. 1966. *Figures*. Paris: Du Seuil (Tel Quel).

Glicksohn, J., Tsur, R. & Goodblatt, C. 1991. Absorption and trance-inducing poetry. *Empirical Studies of the Arts* 9(2): 115–122.

Goldberg, L. 1956. The fish-market. In *Early and Late*, 60–61. Merkhavya: Sifriyat Poalim (in Hebrew).

Gombrich, E.H. 1963. *Meditations on a Hobby Horse – And Other Essays on the Theory of Art*. London: Phaidon.

Goodblatt, C. 1990. Whitman's catalogs as literary gestalts: Illustrative and meditative functions. *Style* 24: 45–58.

Goodblatt, C. & Glicksohn, J. 1986. Cognitive psychology and Whitman's 'Song of myself'. *Mosaic* 14: 83–90.

Granville-Barker, H. 1993[1927[1]]. *Preface to King Lear*. London: Nick Hern Books and the Royal National Theatre.

Guilford, J.P. 1970[1959[1]]. Traits of creativity. In *Creativity*, P.E. Vernon (ed), 167–188. Harmondsworth: Penguin.

Halle, M. & Keyser, S.J. 1966. Chaucer and the study of prosody. *College English* 28: 187–219.

Halle, M. & Keyser, S.J. 1971. *English Stress: Its Growth and Its Role in Verse*. New York NY: Harper and Row.

Halliday, M.A.K. 1970. Language structure and language function. In *New Horizons in Linguistics*, J. Lyons (ed), 140–165. Harmondsworth: Penguin Books.

Harvey, O.J. 1970. Conceptual systems and attitude change. In *Thought and Personality*, P.B. Warr (ed), 315–333. Harmondsworth: Penguin.

Harshav (Hrushovski), B. 1980. The meaning of sound patterns in poetry: An interaction view. *Poetics Today* 2: 39–56.

Herrnstein-Smith, B. 1968. *Poetic Closure*. Chicago IL: Chicago University Press.

Hochberg, J.E. 1964. *Perception*. Englewood Cliffs NJ: Prentice-Hall.

Houston, J.P. 1963. *The Design of Rimbaud's Poetry*. New Haven CT: Yale Universtiy Press.

Hrushovski, B. 1968. Do sounds have meaning? The problem of expressiveness of sound-patterns in poetry. *Hasifrut* 1: 410–420 (in Hebrew). English summary: 444.

Jackson, S. 2009. Does 'Ash Wednesday' enable a reader to perceive an altered state of consciousness? ⟨www.pala.ac.uk/resources/proceedings/2009/jackson2009.pdf⟩

Jakobson, R. & Waugh, L.R. 1979. *The Sound Shape of Language*. Bloomington IN: Indiana University Press.

Jakobson, R. 1980. *Brain and Language*. Columbus OH: Slavica.

James, W. 1902. *The Varieties Of Religious Experience. A Study in Human Nature*. New York NY: Longmans, Green and Co.

Jespersen, O. 1960. *Essentials of English Grammar*. London: Allan & Unwin.

Kane, J. 2004. Poetry as right-hemispheric language. *Journal of Consciousness Studies. Controversies in Science & the Humanities* 11(5–6): 21–59. Special feature on consciousness and literature edited by Roberta Tucker. Reproduced in PSYART, 2007. ⟨http://www.clas.ufl.edu/ipsa/journal/2007_kane01.shtml#kane01⟩

Katz, S.T. 1992. Mystical speech and mystical meaning. In Mysticism and Language, S.T. Katz (ed), 3–41. Oxford: OUP.

Keats, J. 1951. *The Complete Poetry and Seleccted Prose*. Harold E. Brigg (ed). New York NY: Modern Library.

Kinsbourne, M. 1982 Hemispheric specialization and the growth of human understanding. *American Psychologist* 37: 411–420.

Knight, W. 1964. Time and eternity. In *Discussions of Shakespeare's Sonnets*, B. Herrnstein (ed). Boston MA: Heath & Co.

Knights, L.C. 1964[1928[1]]. Notes on comedy. In *The Importance of Scrutiny*, E. Bentley (ed), 227–237. New York NY: New York University Press.

Knowles, G. 1992. Pitch contours and tones in the Lancaster/IBM spoken English corpus. In *New Directions in English Language Corpora. Methodology, Results, Software Developments*, G. Leitner (ed.), 289–299. Berlin: Mouton de Gruyter.

Köhler, W. 1972. *The Task of Gestalt Psychology*. Princeton NJ: Princeton University Press.

Kris, E. & Kaplan, A. 1965. Aesthetic ambiguity. In *Psychoanalytic Explorations in Art*, E. Kris. New York NY: Schocken.

Kris, E. & Gombrich, E.H. 1965. The principles of caricature. In *Psychoanalytic Explorations in Art*, Ernst Kris. New York NY: Schocken.

Krueger, F. 1968[1928[1]]. The essence of feeling. In *The Nature of Emotion*, Magda B. Arnold (ed.), 97–108. Harmondsworth: Penguin.

Kuhn, T.S. 1977. A function for thought experiments. In *The Essential Tension: Selected Studies in Scientific Tradition and Change*, 240–265. Chicago IL: The University of Chicago Press.

Labov, W. 1972. *Language in the Inner City: Studies in the Black English Vernacular*. Philadelphia PA: University of Pennsylvania Press.

Ladd, R.D. 1996. *Intonational Phonology*. Cambridge: CUP.

Ladefoged, P. 2001. *Vowels and Consonants. An Introduction to the Sounds of Languages*. Oxford: Blackwell.

Lakoff, G. 1993. The contemporary theory of metaphor. In *Thought and Metaphor*, A. Ortony (ed), 202–251. Cambridge: CUP.

Landow, G.P. 1918[1877]. A reading of Gerard Manley Hopkins's "The windhover". ⟨http://victorianweb.org/authors/hopkins/hopkins10.html⟩

Langacker, R.W. 1987. *Foundations of Cognitive Grammar*. Stanford CA: Stanford University Press.

Langacker, R.W. 1990. *Concept, Image and Symbol*. Berlin: Mouton de Gruyter.

Larsen, S.F. 1971. The psychological reality of linguistic segments reconsidered. *S.1. Psychol.* 12:113–118.

Legouis, É. & Cazamian, L. 1935. *A History of English Literature*. New York NY: Macmillan.

Lerdahl, F. & Jackendoff, R. 1983. *A Generative Theory of Tonal Music*. Cambridge MA: The MIT Press.

Lewis, C.S. 1936. *The Allegory of Love*. London: OUP.

Liberman, A.M. 1970. The grammars of speech and language. *Cognitive Psychology* 1:301–323.

Liberman, A.M., Cooper, F.S., Shankweiler, D.P. & Studdert-Kennedy, M. 1967. Perception of the speech code. *Psychological Review* 74:431–461.

Liberman, A.M., Mattingly, I.G. & Turvey, M.T. 1972. Language codes and memory codes. In *Coding Processes in Human Memory*, A.W. Melton & E. Martin (eds), New York NY: Winston.

Liberman, I.Y. & Mann, V.A. 1981. Should reading instruction and remediation vary with the sex of the child? *Status Report on Speech Research* SR-65. New Haven CT: Haskins Laboratories.

Lloyd, B.B. 1972. *Perception and Cognition*. Harmondsworth: Penguin.

Longinus. 1951. *On the Sublime*, W.R. Roberts (transl.). In *The Great Critics*, J.H. Smith & Edd W. Parks (eds), 65–111. New York NY: W.W. Norton. ⟨http://classicpersuasion.org/pw/longinus/index.htm⟩

Mann, V.A. l984. Reading skill and language skill. *Developmental Review* 4:1–15.

Margolis, J. 1962. The logic of interpretation. In *Philosophy Looks at the Arts: Contemporary Readings in Aesthetics*, J. Margolis (ed), 108–118. New York NY: Charles Scribner's Sons.

May, J. & Repp, B.H. 1982. Periodicity and auditory memory. *Status Report on Speech Research* SR-69:145–149. New Haven CT: Haskins Laboratories.

Meyer, L.B. 1956. *Emotion and Meaning in Music*. Chicago IL: Chicago University Press.

Miall, D.S. 2011a. Enacting the other: Towards an aesthetics of feeling in literary reading. In *The Aesthetic Mind: Philosophy and Psychology*, P. Goldie & E. Schellekens (eds), 285–298. Oxford: OUP.

Miall, D.S. 2011b. Wordsworth's first-born affinities: Intimations of embodied cognition. *Poetics Today* 32(4): 693–715.

Miller, G.A. 1970. The magical number seven, plus or minus two: Some limits on our capacity for processing information. In *The Psychology of Communication*. Harmondsworth: Pelican.

Mizener, A. 1964. The structure of figurative language in Shakespeare's sonnets. In *Discussions of Shakespeare's Sonnets*, B. Herrnstein (ed), 137–151. Boston MA: D.C. Heath and Company.

Morton, E.S. 1994. Sound symbolism and its role in non-human vertebrate communication. In *Sound Symbolism*, L. Hinton, J. Nichols & J.J. Ohala (eds), 348–365. Cambridge: CUP.

Nadeau, Stephen E. 2012. *The Neural Architecture of Grammar*. Cambridge Mass., and London: the MIT Press. (Kindle eBook edn).

Newberg, A., D'Aquili, E. & Rause, V. 2001. *Why God Won't Go Away: Brain Science and the Biology of Belief*. New York NY: Ballantine Books.

Ohala, J.J. 1994. The frequency code underlies the sound-symbolic use of voice pitch. In *Sound Symbolism*, L. Hinton, J. Nichols & J.J. Ohala (eds), 325–347. Cambridge: CUP.

Ohmann, R. 1970. Modes of order. In *Linguistics and Literary Style*, D.C. Freeman (ed), 209–242. New York NY: Holt, Rinehart & Winston.

Oras, A. 1957. Spenser and Milton: Some parallels and contrasts in the handling of sound. In *Sound and Poetry*, N. Frye (ed), 109–133. New York NY: English Institute Essays.

Ornstein, R.E. 1975. *The Psychology of Consciousness*. Harmondsworth: Penguin.

Otto, R. 1959. *The Idea of the Holy*, J.W. Harvey (transl.). Harmondsworth: Penguin.

Parncutt, R. 2001. Critical comparison of acoustical and perceptual theories of the origin of musical scales. In *Proceedings of the International Symposium of Musical Acoustics (Perugia, Italy)*, D. Bonsi, D. Gonzalez & S. Domenico (eds), Venice: Fondazione Scuola di San Giorgio. ⟨http://www.uni-graz.at/richard.parncutt/publications/Pa01_Scales.pdf⟩

Pears, D. 1971. *Wittgenstein*. London: Fontana.

Perry, M. & Sternberg, M. 1968. The king through ironic eyes: The narrator's devices in the biblical story of David and BathSheba and two excursuses on the theory of the narrative text. *HaSifrut* 1(2): 263–293 (in Hebrew, with extended English abstract: 449–452).

Persinger, M.A. 1987. *Neuropsychological Bases of God Beliefs*. New York NY: Praeger.

Polányi, M. 1967. *The Tacit Dimension*. Garden City NY: Anchor Books.

Posner, M.I. 1973. *Cognition: An Introduction*. Glenview IL: Scott, Foreman & Co.

Rakerd, B. 1984. Vowels in consonantal context are more linguistically perceived than isolated vowels: Evidence from an individual differences scaling study. *Perception & Psychophysics* 35: 123–136.

Ramachandran, V.S. & Hubbard, E.M. 2001. Synaesthesia. A window into perception, thought and language. *Journal of Consciousness Studies* 3–34. ⟨http://psy.ucsd.edu/chip/pdf/Synaesthesia%20-%20JCS.pdf⟩

Ransom, J.C. 1951. Poetry: A note in ontology. In *The Great Critics*, J.H. Smith & E.W Parks (eds), 769–787. New York NY: Norton.

Reinhart, T. 1976. On understanding poetic metaphor. *Poetics* 5: 383–402.

Repp, B.H. 1984. Categorical perception: Issues, methods, findings. In *Speech and Language: Advances in Basic Research and Practice*, Vol. 10, N.J. Lass (ed), 243–335. New York NY: Academic Press.

Reuven Tsur 2001. *The Death-and-Rebirth Archetype in Poetry—An Homage to Maud Bodkin*. Proceedings of the 16th International Conference on Literature and Psychoanalysis. 221–228.

Richards, I.A. 1929. *Practical Criticism*. New York NY: Harcourt, Brace and Company.

Riffaterre, M. 1978. *Semiotics of Poetry*. Bloomington IN: Indiana University Press.

Rimbaud, J.A. 1962. Voyelles. In *Collected Poems*, O. Bernard (ed), 171–172. Harmondsworth: Penguin Books.

Rorschach, H. 1951. *Psychodiagnostics*. Bern: Huber.

Shklovsky, V. 1965. Art as technique. In *Russian Formalist Criticism*, L.T. Lemon & M.J. Reis (eds), 3–24. Lincoln NB: Nebraska University Press.

Shusterman, R. 2008. *Body Consciousness: A Philosophy, of Mindfulness and Somaesthetics*. Cambridge: CUP.

Sibley, F. 1962. Aesthetic qualities. In *Philosophy Looks at the Arts: Contemporary Readings in Aesthetics*, J. Margolis (ed.), 63–88. New York NY: Scribner.

Slobin, D. I. 1971. *Psycholinguistics*. Glenview IL: Scott, Foreman & Co.

Smart, J.J.C. 1966. Theory construction. In *Logic and Language*, A.G.N. Flew (ed), 222–242. Oxford: Blackwell.

Snyder, E.D. 1930. *Hypnotic Poetry: A Study of Trance-inducing Techniques in Certain Poems and its Literary Significance*. Philadelphia PA: University of Pennsylvania Press.

Spitzer, L. 1962. *Essays on English and American Literature*. Princeton NJ: Princeton UP.

Stanford, W.B. 1942. Synaesthetic metaphor. *Comparative Literature Studies* VI–VII: 26–30.

Stockwell, P. 2002 *Cognitive Poetics. An Introduction*. London: Routledge.

Strawson, P.F. 1967. Singular terms and predication. In *Philosophical Logic*, P.F.Strawson (ed). Oxford: OUP.

Thomson, P. 1972. *The Grotesque*. London: Methuen.

Todd, H.J., quoted by Youmans, G. 1989. Milton's metre. In *Phonetics and Phonology*, Vol. 1: *Rhythm and Meter*, 341–379. New York NY: Academic Press.

Tsur, R. 1977. *A Perception-Oriented Theory of Metre*. Tel Aviv: The Porter Institute for Poetics and Semiotics.

Tsur, R. 1972. Articulateness and requiredness in iambic verse. *Style* 6: 123–148.

Tsur, R. 1987. *On Metaphoring*. Jerusalem: Israel Science Publishers.

Tsur, R. 1988. 'Oceanic' dedifferentiation and poetic metaphor. *Journal of Pragmatics* 12: 711–724.

Tsur, R. 1992a. *Toward a Theory of Cognitive Poetics*. Amsterdam: Elsevier.

Tsur, R. 1992b. *What Makes Sound Patterns Expressive: The Poetic Mode of Speech-Perception* [The Roman Jakobson Series]. Durham NC: Duke University Press.

Tsur, R. 1994. Droodles and cognitive poetics. Contribution to an aesthetics of disorientation. *Humor* 7: 55–70.

Tsur, R. 1998a. *Poetic Rhythm: Structure and Performance. An Empirical Study in Cognitive Poetics*. Bern: Peter Lang.

Tsur, R. 1998b. Light, fire, prison: A cognitive analysis of religious imagery in poetry. *PSYART: A Hyperlink Journal for the Psychological Study of the Arts*, article 980715. ⟨http//www.clas. ufl.edu/ipsa/journal/articles/tsur02.htm⟩

Tsur, R. 1998c. Archetypal pattern in Baudelaire's Recueillement. ⟨http://www.tau.ac.il/~tsurxx/ Recueillement.html⟩

Tsur, R. 2001. Onomatopoeia: Cuckoo-language and tick-tocking. The constraints of semiotic systems. *Iconicity In Language*. ⟨http://www.trismegistos.com/IconicityInLanguage/ Articles/Tsur/default.html http://www.tau.ac.il/~tsurxx/Cuckoo_onomatopoeia.html⟩

Tsur, R. 2002. Aspects of cognitive poetics. In *Cognitive Stylistics – Language and Cognition in Text Analysis* [Linguistic Approaches to Literature 1], E. Semino & J. Culpeper (eds), 279–318. Amsterdam: John Benjamins.

Tsur, R. 2003. Deixis and abstractions: Adventures in space and time. In *Cognitive Poetics in Practice*, J. Gavins & G. Steen (eds), 41–54. London: Routledge.

Tsur, R. 2003. *On The Shore of Nothingness: Space, Rhythm, and Semantic Structure in Religious Poetry and its Mystic-Secular Counterpart. A Study in Cognitive Poetics*. Exeter: Imprint Academic.

Tsur, R. 2004. Some mannerist ingenuities in mystic poetry. *Journal of Consciousness Studies. Controversies in Science & the Humanities* 11(5–6): 60–78. Special feature on 'consiousness and literature', edited by Roberta Tucker.

Tsur, R. 2006. Archetypen, Szenerie und Metaphorik in Goethes Faust I. Ein kognitiver Ansatz. *Der Deutschunterricht*, R. Müller & E.Z. (Hrsg.) *Metapher*, 61–69.

Tsur, R. 2006. *Kubla Khan. Poetic Structure, Hypnotic Quality and Cognitive Style: A Study in Mental, Vocal, and Critical Performance* [Human Cognitive Processing 16]. Amsterdam: John Benjamins.

Tsur, R. 2007. The structure and delivery style of Milton's Verse: An electronic exercise in vocal performance. *ESC:English Studies in Canada* 33: 149–168. (appeared in 2009).

Tsur, R. 2008.[2] *Toward a Theory of Cognitive Poetics*, 2nd, expanded and updated edn. Brighton: Sussex Academic Press.

Tsur, R. 2012.[2] *Poetic Rhythm: Structure and Performance. An Empirical Study in Cognitive Poetics*, 2nd, expanded edn. Brighton: Sussex Academic Press.

Tsur, R. & Benari, M. 2001. 'Composition of place', experiential set, and the meditative poem. A cognitive-pragmatic approach. *Pragmatics and Cognition* 9(2): 203–237.

Tsur, R., Glicksohn, J. & Goodblatt, C. 1990. Perceptual organization, absorption and aesthetic qualities of poetry. In *Proceedings of the 11th International Congress on Empirical Aesthetics*, L. Halász (ed), 301–304. Budapest: Institute for Psychology of the Hungarian Academy of Sciences.

Tsur, R., Glicksohn, J. & Goodblatt, C. 1991. Gestalt qualities in poetry and the reader's absorption style. *Journal of Pragmatics* 16(5): 487–504.

Ullmann, S. 1957. *The Principles of Semantics*. Oxford: Blackwell.

Ultan, R. 1978. Size-sound symbolism, J.H. Greenberg (ed.), *Universals of Human Language*, Vol. 2: *Phonology*. Stanford CA: Stanford University Press.

Weber, J. 2004. A new paradigm for literary studies, or: The teething troubles of cognitive poetics. *Style* 38(4): 515–523.

Weitz, M. 1962. The role of theory in aesthetics. In *Philosophy Looks at the Arts*, J. Margolis (ed), 48–59. New York NY: Scribner.

Wellek, R. 1963. *Concepts of Criticism*. New Haven CT: Yale University Press.

Wellek, R. & Warren, A. 1956. *Theory of Literature*. New York NY: Harcourt, Brace & Co.

Werner, H. 1978. A psychological analysis of expressive language. In *Developmental Processes: Heinz Werner's Selected Writings*, Vol. 2, S.S. Barten & M. Franklin (eds), 421–428. New York NY: International Universities Press.

Whaler, J. 1956. *Counterpoint and Symbol: An Inquiry into the Rhythm of Milton's Epic Style* [Anglistica 6]. Copenhagen: Rosenkilde.

Wimsatt, W.K. 1954. *The Verbal Icon*. New York NY: Noonday.

Wittgenstein, L. 1967. *Philosophical Investigations*, G.E.M Anscombe (transl.). Oxford: Blackwell.

Youmans, G. 1989. Milton's metre. In *Phonetics and Phonology*, Vol. 1: Rhythm and Meter, 341–379. New York NY: Academic Press.

Yu, N. 2003. Synesthetic metaphor: A cognitive perspective. *Journal of Literary Semantics* 32(1): 19–34

Zeki, S. 2004. The neurology of ambiguity. *Consciousness and Cognition* 13: 173–196.

Recorded Readings

Callow, S. reading *Shakespeare's Sonnets*. Hodder Headline AudioBooks HH 185.

Gielgud, J. reading *Sonnets of William Shakespeare*. Caedmon SRS 241 C-D.

The Marlowe Society and Professional Players reading *Shakespeare: The Sonnets*. Argo ZPR 254.

Richard A. Reads the Poetry of Gerard Manley Hopkins ⟨http://victorianweb.org/authors/hopkins/windhover3.html⟩

Audio processors

SoundScope 16/3.0 (ppd)
Praat 5.0.43
Audacity 1.3.23 – beta

Index

Plate 1 Chevreuil's demonstration of colour induction replicated: A gray square on a green ground gradually turns pink. The small square on the green ground is exactly the same as the one on the top of the figure.

Plate 2 When covered with a semitransparent tissue paper, colour induction is increased rather than decreased. Here the tissue-paper effect was simulated by the Opacity function of Adobe Illustrator. The more and less opaque versions side by side. In the lower field, the pink of the small square is more pronounced.